# ORTHODOX JEWS IN AMERICA

THE MODERN JEWISH EXPERIENCE

PAULA HYMAN AND DEBORAH DASH MOORE, EDITORS

# ORTHODOX
# JEWS
# IN
# AMERICA

Jeffrey S. Gurock

Indiana University Press
Bloomington & Indianapolis

This book is a publication of

Indiana University Press
601 North Morton Street
Bloomington, IN 47404-3797 USA

http://iupress.indiana.edu

Telephone orders  800-842-6796
Fax orders  812-855-7931
Orders by e-mail  iuporder@indiana.edu

The paper used in this publication meets the minimum requirements of
American National Standard for Information Sciences — Permanence
of Paper for Printed Library Materials, ANSI Z39.48-1984.

Manufactured in the United States of America

Library of Congress Cataloging-in-Publication Data

Gurock, Jeffrey S., date-
Orthodox Jews in America / Jeffrey S. Gurock.
p. cm. — (The modern jewish experience)
Includes bibliographical references and index.
ISBN 978-0-253-35291-0 (cloth : alk. paper)
ISBN 978-0-253-22060-8 (pbk. : alk. paper)
1. Orthodox Judaism — United States — History.
2. Jews — United States — History. 3. Jews — United States —
Social life and customs. I. Title.
BM205.G885 2009
296.8'320973 — dc22
2008041921

1 2 3 4 5   14 13 12 11 10 09

In memory of Jack, Kelly, and Julie and in honor of


the
"whiz kids" of the Young Israel of Parkchester

# CONTENTS

# ACKNOWLEDGMENTS

It is a pleasure to thank the many people and institutions that have assisted me intellectually and emotionally in writing this book. A quarter-century ago, after the publication of my first major study, I decided to explore in greater detail what was perhaps the more salient finding of my initial research: the difficulty of categorizing the diverse nature of Jewish — and especially Orthodox — religious experiences in America. Defining and delineating the nuances of individual and Jewish organizational attitudes toward the faith and its practices became the hallmarks of the many monographs that followed. All of the labors informed this present synthetic work. Along the way, I have been fortunate to have had several colleagues take time from their own important investigations to improve the quality of my publications. These friends include Professors Benjamin R. Gampel, Marc Lee Raphael, Dale Rosengarten, William B. Helmreich, Lloyd P. Gartner, and Jack Wertheimer, not to mention innumerable anonymous readers who have evaluated my contributions. As this present work took shape, I turned for assistance to, among others, Professors Ephraim Kanarfogel, Kimmy Caplan, Steven Zipperstein, and Tobias Brinkmann. I also gained much from the insightful comments on my book prospectus from three additional anonymous readers whose suggestions I took deeply to heart. However, my greatest thanks for helping me to improve the quality of my conceptualization and writing go to Professor Deborah Dash Moore, who coedits the series wherein this book appears. Professor Dash Moore pushed me with a gentle but assertive touch to make my ideas meaningful to what I hope will be a wide readership that has yet to be exposed to the diversity of Orthodox life in America. Needless to say, any and all interpretations and errors of fact or judgment are mine alone. I am also grateful to Janet Rabinowitch and her staff at Indiana University Press for managing and bringing their professional care and expertise to this project.

Several friends and associates at my home institution, Yeshiva University, deserve special recognition. Foremost among them is its distinguished chancellor Dr. Norman Lamm with whom I have been privileged to have had a very special personal and professional relationship for close to twenty-five years. Our president Richard M. Joel has encouraged me — and all others in the university family — to dream and realize our academic dreams. Yeshiva's provost, Dr. Morton Lowengrub, has been my "rabbi" this past decade and has supported my research in so many ways. I am grateful to Yeshiva's extraordinarily dedicated library staff, especially Zalman Alpert, Zvi Erenyi, John Moryl, and the indefatigable Mary Ann Linahan. I am also pleased to note the excellent and caring professional assistance of Norman Goldberg and Peter Robertson of our photography department.

I am blessed with a wonderful and growing family who provide me with constant love and emotional support. Since my last book appeared, Dan has joined our family. Sheri and Eli are the proud parents of another precious child, Zev Jacob. I hope that Audrey — who has begun to read — and Mira will like this book and will someday read it from cover to cover. I expect nothing less from Sheri, Eli, Dan, Rosie, and Michael. As always, I am most thankful to Pamela who has the mixed blessing of living with a compulsive husband who is obsessed both about his academics and athletics.

This book is dedicated to the memory of Jack, Kelly, and Julie and in honor of the "whiz kids" of the Young Israel of Parkchester with whom I have an unending kinship.

Riverdale, New York
September 2008

# ORTHODOX JEWS IN AMERICA

# PROLOGUE: WITHIN THE WIDE TENT OF A BRONX ORTHODOX CONGREGATION, CIRCA 1960

Growing up some fifty years ago within an Orthodox congregation in a working- and lower middle-class neighborhood in the East Bronx, I was deeply impressed with the sincere piety of a Jew who sat three rows away from me in the men's section of the synagogue, two seats over from my father. On Sabbath mornings, he would arrive with his son at the very start of prayers — well before the Gurock men made their appearance — and would follow the liturgy carefully, often reciting his favorite lines out loud from the psalms that began the services. He paid close attention to the portion of the Torah that was read weekly and observed the enforced protocol in that congregation. No talking or other noises were permitted. To make clear to all the seriousness of that stricture, a sign outside the sanctuary read: "If you must whisper, whisper a prayer." His only break with synagogue etiquette was that he habitually fell asleep, with his mouth wide open, as soon as the rabbi ascended the pulpit to deliver a sermon. But then again, that entire row of gentlemen — tired from their week's labors — all caught forty winks during the fifteen-minute homily.

Occasionally, I would follow him home. I was friendly with his son who was a couple of years older than I was. As the day wore on, I was always struck by how dark their four-room apartment became. In keeping with Sabbath traditions, no lights could be turned on during the holy day. The only artificial light came from a few bulbs that had been switched on before the Sabbath had started the prior evening, and these did not effectively illuminate the dwelling. The family did not have a "Sabbath Clock" — a timer that could automatically turn on the electricity at a set time — an accommodation that most Orthodox rabbis countenanced when the device was introduced in the late 1950s. Of course, the cold snack that they always offered me — the devout also do not cook on the Sabbath — was kosher. He and his no-less-pious wife were likewise scrupulous that foods brought into their home bore a kosher certification symbol. Failing that, they would examine the list of ingredients to determine that no forbidden elements, such as gelatin, a pork derivative, might be found in a bread or cake. One of the early disappointments in my own life occurred when I learned that Hostess Twinkies, that sugary snack, contained that forbidden foodstuff and was thus out of bounds. My friend's parent's punctilious lifestyle also mandated that they were extremely careful about what they ate outside their home. Since there were no unquestionably kosher restaurants in our Bronx neighborhood — the local Jewish delicatessen that was open on Saturday, a red flag hinting that its religious reliability was not up to snuff — they generally dined at home or at the residences of friends, like my parents, who also kept a kosher kitchen.

During the work week, this Jew regularly attended the synagogue. As always, early to arrive at his seat, he donned his prayer shawl and phylacteries with love and devotion, careful always to return them properly to their respective *talis* and *tefillin* bags, ready for use the next day. He also returned to *shul* [synagogue] at least once every week to study Talmudic texts or other sacred Jewish sources with the rabbi and other interested laymen. Proud of what he learned at these gatherings as an adult, his only regret was that as a youth he had not been privileged to receive the type of extensive Jewish education some others around the table had. So disposed, this sincere role model and his wife conveyed this love of learning to their children. A Sunday morning men's club meeting that provided him with a chance to pray, eat, socialize, and study again with these Jews was his most anticipated leisure time activity.

His love for Jews and all things Jewish transcended his affinity for the faith's ritual routines and his affection for friends in the congregation. An extraordinarily philanthropic person, defined here as one who gave abundantly, often beyond his means, he was always among the first to raise his hand when the synagogue conducted an appeal on behalf of poor Jews in the community or the oppressed elsewhere in the world. His special concern for Israel's needs reflected its primacy in his prayers and consciousness. Such charitableness only added to his sterling reputation among all those who knew and respected him as one outstanding pious Jew who performed the *mitzvoth* [commandments], as the *halacha* [Orthodox understanding of Jewish law] prescribes with verve and scrupulousness.

There was, however, one aspect of his lifestyle that departed fundamentally from the Orthodox traditions to which he reverently subscribed. Occasionally, on Saturdays during the busy season in the garment industry where he worked, or when the Jewish calendar linked together two days of a holiday — as when the first or last days of Passover occur on Thursday and Friday — before the onset of the Sabbath, which, in total, call for a seventy-two hour cessation from mundane activities, he disappeared from synagogue life. He went to work early in the morning of the holy day to support his family. He may have mitigated his deviance somewhat when he stopped off at the Garment Center Synagogue in mid-Manhattan and sat among similarly conflicted Jews who wanted to say their holiday or Sabbath prayers that spoke explicitly about the biblical prohibition against labor on those days. Chagrined but not ashamed of what he did, he once inquired, in all candor, of our rabbi, whether he should don his tefillin at that service for workers — according to the rules that ritual object is not worn on Sabbath and holidays — since he was effectively treating those days as regular weekdays. The rabbi could not accommodate his request — the halacha could not be clearer on the question — but he was duly impressed both with his congregant's honesty and with his quest to affirm the tradition despite his deeply regretted actions. Our sometimes Sabbath and holiday worker returned to his seat in our synagogue for afternoon services after his labors were done, and strictly observed the rest of the day[s] of rest in his home.

What are we to make of this man's religious values? From a traditional Jewish point of view — one that Orthodoxy believes began some three millennia ago with the giving of the Torah to the Jewish people, the theophany on Mount Sinai — he unquestionably broke a cardinal principle of the faith. He worked on Saturday, thus shattering the most explicit of the prohibitions for keeping the Sabbath day holy as dictated in the Ten Commandments. Even though the sages and rabbis, throughout the ages, debated what sorts of human acts precisely constitute "work" on the Sabbath, laboring for wages at one's job, profession, or craft is definitely a clear violation of the letter of Jewish law. Talmudic law identified some thirty-nine categories of forbidden works on that day, and later rabbinic authorities, interpreters, and codifiers down to the present day applied these rubrics to many endeavors never dreamt of in prior centuries. Such Torah scholars might debate whether turning on lights through a pre-set timer — that aforementioned "Sabbath Clock" — constitutes starting a fire, another explicit biblical prohibition. But there would be no doubt in their minds that a man who is profiting from labors on Saturday has transgressed Jewish law.

In pre-modern times, particularly during the medieval age, such a person would have been tarred as an offender of communal norms. By not living up to prescribed religious standards, he would have been outside the fundamental pale of acceptable Jewish behavior. To bring him back toward conformity, the rabbis with their power to control all aspects of a Jew's existence would rain down whatever penalties they had in their arsenal to force him into line. Such were the powers or threats that pressured deviants of all varieties — with a Sabbath desecrator high up on the list of miscreants — to mend their ways. Perhaps the only question that the Jewish judges of that past civilization had to consider in assessing his guilt, was whether the wrongdoer broke the ordinances under duress, voluntarily, or worse, smashed the regulations out of spite.[1]

However, by the 1960s, roughly three to four centuries had passed since all Jews everywhere could suffer halachic sanctions. From the dawn of modernity, and at least among European Jews, wherever Jews moved toward and ultimately gained their emancipation, established communities surrendered their powers in return for civic freedom and opportunities. Blessed with the chance to act as they saw fit, independent spirits emerged in incipient ways as early as the seventeenth century. Residual social pressure kept some Jews, who ordinarily would have bolted from the pack, close to the traditions. But the power to put offenders in their places and to force conformity was eventually lost everywhere. Once largely on their own, answering to their consciences, by the nineteenth century in places such as Germany and France, the Jewish law breakers became the majority as only a few stalwarts persisted in opting voluntarily to follow ancestral ways. A decline in religious observance — with all sorts of bold and even spiteful breaking of halachic precepts — also obtained among elements within East European society where freedom, through most of modern Jewish history, was a goal rarely reached.

Then there is the saga of Jews in America where a legally powerful Jewish community never has existed and where so many who have disdained much of the basics of ancestral faith have always run free, fettered only by the most distant memories of parental pieties. If anything, this country has been the place, more than anywhere else in the modern Jewish world, where the demands and attractions of the welcoming society often have undermined the commitments of even those once intent on remaining true to their religious pasts. Thus, in this libertine universe and wilderness, where so many Jews have transgressed the traditions — if not angrily then at least with carefree relish — it would be both unwise and unfair to simply judge that East Bronxite as just another miscreant, a violator of the halacha. Such an unnuanced designation, focused narrowly on his noteworthy lapse, fails to countenance, first, how he chose to affirm, within a free and uncontrolled environment, so many Orthodox values and teachings. It also ignores how, through his pious religious acts, he stood above most of his contemporaries who observed far fewer of the precepts even as he harbored an intense desire to be counted among those who practiced Jewish law more punctiliously.

Finally, calling him an offender, as medieval authorities would have done, says nothing about his own total disinterest in identifying with Conservative or Reform Judaism, the alternative, popular Jewish religious movements of his era and locale. By his time, for more than a century and a half, first in Central Europe and then in the United States, Orthodox Judaism was not the only option available for those who wished to associate themselves religiously with their people. Indeed, the very nomenclature *Orthodoxy* initially entered into the Jewish lexicon in that same era in Germany as an unflattering, provocative designation that religiously liberal Jews coined for what they deemed as an outdated faith tradition, a system of practice and behavior, fossilized and unresponsive to modern conditions.[2]

Concomitantly, in Eastern Europe — from where my friend's family hailed — as early as the midpoint of the prior century there was already on the Jewish street a variety of freethinking and antireligious forms of Jewish identity that saw nothing wrong with Saturday work. Although the Reform, Conservative, and Reconstructionist Judaism of his era would certainly not have given him a pass on his Sabbath-work transgression even if their theological understandings of why his action was wrong differed from Orthodoxy's, these alternative Jewish religious expressions would not have held him to so many of the halachic strictures that he let govern his life. For example, if he had been a Conservative Jew of the 1960s, just a decade earlier his rabbis — given their own definition of the demands of Jewish tradition — had determined that it was permissible for him to drive to services on the Sabbath if his home was situated beyond walking distance of the synagogue. However, this Orthodox Jew was not interested in any such official accommodation.

The proper way of gauging this man's religious values is rather to situate them within the spectra of Jewish behaviors that those who identified with Orthodox Judaism displayed within his own time and place. According to this calculus, this loyalist, who believed in and followed the halacha exactingly except when economic exigencies took their toll, occupied a honored position among all of his fellow Jews who positioned themselves, as will presently see, within what was our community's wide Orthodox tent.

Two rows up from him, one step away from the readers' desk, sat one of his closest friends whose piety was unquestionably acknowledged in our community. Otherwise, this man would not have been given the holy privilege and obligation of reading the Torah every week—from his decades of experience, he knew the entire Five Books of Moses by heart—and of conducting the High Holiday services as chief cantor. Such a role was reserved, said the tradition, to the fully punctilious alone. He qualified because, along with his wife who fully agreed with his religious choices, he was scrupulous in his observance of the Sabbath and the keeping of the kosher laws; those fundamental Orthodox signposts. He was unflinchingly willing to suffer financially from fidelity to the faith. A cutter by trade, he too worked in the garment industry downtown, where in his spare time, he would fabricate matching socks, ties, and yarmulkes that he wore with pride to shul. Of course, he always stayed within the precincts of home and synagogue on the holy days.

Apart from his family, the synagogue was his life. Like his friend, he regularly attended daily services and frequented the rabbi's study groups. But beyond that, he was often on the congregational premises to assure, for example, that the Torah scrolls were in perfect shape—any smudge of the parchment lettering was a serious matter—or that certain ritual items—such as the Four Species necessary for the observance in autumn of *Succoth* [The Festival of Tabernacles]—were available both for his family and all other congregants who desired to perform that seasonal commandment. In a classier congregation, he would have carried the title of sexton. To us, he was simply the most committed of laymen we could ever have imagined.

Even more significantly, he was deeply dedicated to raising a generation of youngsters who would share his religious values. He was particularly concerned that the future would find our synagogue—or any other shul to which we might belong—blessed with skilled men who could lead the services and read the Torah. The art of reading from these ancient scrolls, written as they are without vowels, is perhaps Judaism's most difficult performance skill. That commitment to excellence transcended training his own son, who became an Orthodox rabbi, and was extended to other boys whom he also schooled. Even those with less than the best of voices, like my brother and myself, came under his tutelage, although only the most melodious were taught how to officiate at the prime-time High Holidays services. The high point for us was when, biannually, we actually conducted the services from start to finish on "Youth Shabbes." Then we chanted the Torah portion of the week, served as cantors, and even offered "learned" summaries of the Torah reading, Prophetic section [*Haftarah*] and the sermon; these were often prepared with the rabbi's help as a ghost writer. When we were not on display we also sat quietly in shul. With our parents' ready assent, our lay leader par excellence taught us how to behave properly. In our specially designated youth section, we were monitored closely. No talking was allowed among us during the important sections of the services. A withering dirty look from the tough-love mentor, who routinely frightened the dickens out of us, was enough to melt any youngster who stepped out of line.

Given the pre-feminist times and the Orthodox place of my youth, those who were scared straight when they were not being touted as Judaism's future sat on only one side of the sanctuary. Neither the devout lay leader nor anyone else thought of equipping girls with comparable synagogue service skills. The chief cantor did conceivably have at least three distaff acolytes at hand. His trio of daughters was quite melodious, far better singers than the off-tuned Gurock duo. They performed publicly in a Jewish camp choir that would eventually gain international renown, bringing to the fore harmonious talents that they honed weekly as they sang *zemirot* [religious songs] at their parents' Sabbath table. However, they never pushed within or without their home for an active role in the shul. The closest our synagogue ever came to according young women opportunities of this sort was the one time a female friend was designated to give a summary of the Torah portion on a "Youth Shabbes." I do not recall any hubbub when she opened the door to the *mechitza* [the physical partition that separates the genders during Orthodox prayers] and strode to the pulpit. Neither she nor we saw her performance as tradition-shattering or statement-making. We did, however, remark favorably on the high quality of her erudite presentation.

However, for all of our mentor's and his wife's pious conformities, once a year they broke with a more subtle Orthodox regulation. Then they abridged a social convention and did so, interestingly enough, in a very different realm of religious gender relations. The couple participated in a public act that would have raised some eyebrows in other communities in the 1960s and certainly would cause concern in many Orthodox locales today.

The halacha prescribes a strict code of conduct for intimate and private relations between husbands and wives. According to the rules, a man and woman may not touch one other — let alone engage in sexual relationships — during certain times in the female's menstrual cycle. Normal contact can be resumed only after she immerses herself in the ritual bath [*mikveh*]. Pubescent Jewish singles, the tradition mandates, really should never touch — even such an innocuous American social act as shaking hands is forbidden — since the woman involved is always assumed to be ritually unclean. That means, of importance for this particular story, that social dancing is out of bounds even if the married woman has been to the mikveh at the appropriate time. In that case, the more subtle question of modesty as a Jewish legal concept comes into play. The most devout would not dance in public — and we are talking about waltzing, not any forms of "dirty dancing" — because it would indicate to those who might watch them where the couple is in the monthly cycle of engagement and disengagement, which is no one's business.

It was also no one's business, including mine, to know how scrupulously this couple honored the marital laws, although the assumption is that they followed its teachings as rigorously as they did all other major halachic dictates. However, they fissured the rules slightly once a year, ironically at the synagogue's annual dinner, when they comfortably and expertly moved up and down the dance floor. How may we judge their demure deviation at an Orthodox-run social event? Here too, like the Sabbath-worker, the actions of this couple requires consideration not so much against halachic absolutes, especially in an environment where such subtle strictures were widely honored in the abuse. Instead, they must be calibrated in comparison to the religious values of those around them. What they unself-consciously evidenced, as they joined their fellow congregants on the lacquered party floor, was that while their uncommon high reverence for the halacha reserved for them a central, revered space in the community's Orthodox tent, they just were not as devout as were their rabbi and his wife. Not only did the spiritual leader and his *rebbitzin* [wife of a rabbi] refrain from dancing together at the banquet — he did, of course, lead the men in conga line-style Jewish dancing that was also part of the festivities — but when introduced at the reception that preceded the dinner, they walked down the aisle to the dais, perambulating next to one other, but not arm in arm.

How did the respected Torah reader and his self-effacing wife learn their delicate steps? Decades earlier, they had frequented, as singles, Saturday night "socials" which an Orthodox synagogue movement sponsored to attract their generation of young people away from Christian and socialist-run dances. I will devote more time later on to the realities that produced and maintained these secular practices that so many Orthodox congregations once maintained within their precincts, and today generally do not. But suffice it to say now that their son — the Orthodox rabbi — and their daughters, including one who would become a rebbitzin, would today not consider such activity in public places.

Where did my parents, who also loved social dancing and readily joined the synagogue lay leader and his wife as the band struck up a waltz, fit within this spectrum of Orthodox behavior? On the one hand, my parents did not work on the Sabbath and holidays. Fortunately, with his front office job in the Division of Fire Prevention of the New York City Fire Department, and later as a clerk in a private trade organization, my father was obliged to work only a five-day week. At least by the time my brother and I came around, he was doing well enough that he did not have to "moonlight" as he once did in a bowling alley on Friday nights. As far as the Jewish holidays were concerned, when he worked in the city department, he could trade days with sympathetic gentiles who wanted special times off for some of their religious observances.

My father's boss in the fire department was unusually sensitive to Jewish tradition and acted accordingly when antisemites would protest to him about those alleged fire hazards cause by Jews who built temporary huts for Succoth. The chief would send the "offending" citizens an official city "fifteen-day show-cause order," demanding the removal of the questionable structure by that time, knowing that the Jewish holiday lasted but nine days. My mother, who worked as a bookkeeper at a five-day-a-week firm, had a boss who also understood her wanting to be home with the children on Jewish holidays. He was a good Jew.

But, in some other major respects, they were far from pious in their religious protocols and behaved much like the majority of the congregation's membership, as did most American Jews of their time who regularly ignored the halacha. At home, we did our share of Sabbath and holiday violations. In our private domains, we were not nearly as observant as our friend who worked on the Sabbath in the garment center. Saturday and holiday afternoons found our apartment better lit as we routinely turned the electricity on and off. The radio or small screen television was generally on. Our complicated religious compromises also prescribed that our family car usually rested on Saturday unless we traveled on occasion to be part of a relative's Bar or Bat-Mitzvah celebration in a suburban locale. When we attended these Conservative or Reform services, my father was sure to assert his loyalty to Orthodox Judaism through uncharitable comments about the ritual goings-on. In his view, who ever heard of a cantor leading the prayers with the help of a guitar on the Sabbath? Millennia earlier, instrumental music had been part of the Temple cult in Jerusalem, but the halacha had long forbade such accompaniments to the liturgy on holy days as constituting "work," a rabbinic subset of one of those thirty-nine categories. As he saw Judaism, it was nothing less than a reprehensible offense for a Jew to be in God's house without his head covered. By the Middle Ages, the custom of the yarmulke had taken on the power of Jewish law.

Sabbath automobile violations sometimes also took place when my parents left home "early" in the spring and summer months before the stars were visible in the sky — the traditional sign that the holy day was over — to join their far-less-observant Jewish friends for dinner or a movie. Still, when they ate out, they dined on flounder, salmon, and sole and had no interest in tasting the shellfish delicacies, pork, or other meat dishes that their compatriots relished. Although they never spoke — nor do I believe ever thought — in these terms, they ended up subscribing to the Torah's proscriptions against eating certain fish and animals while not adhering to rabbinic regulations that prescribed how these food products had to be prepared. Rather, their decisions on what they would eat beyond their visceral abhorrence of pig products — for many Jews of their generation as well as many that pre-

9

ceded them consuming ham or bacon was almost a violation of an ancient tribal taboo — were solely derived from inherited family traditions, which, for them, my mother's older brother, a Hebrew school principal in Brooklyn, personified. To offer a sense of how his religious values influenced our lives, out of respect for him whenever he visited our home, we boys were dressed up in our best clothes to greet this honored guest. He, too, was among the most pious Jews we knew. In further deference to him, the boys and the man in our house always wore our yarmulkes in his presence.

Given that background of reverence for the traditions, it is no surprise that I also have no memory of my parents ever taking us out to an unkosher meat restaurant. It was kosher delis for us, unless we went off to the less-than-luxurious kosher cafeteria of the Albert Einstein College of Medicine of Yeshiva University in the Morris Park section of the borough. However, unlike their more scrupulous synagogue friends, my folks gave no thought as to whether the delis that we more generally frequented were open on Saturday. Nor did they ever peek into the back room to see if there was a *mashgiach* [kosher supervisor] on the premises. The Hebrew words *basar kasher* [kosher meat] that appeared on the eatery's window and the Hebrew National brand on the menu were sign points enough of an establishment's religious reliability.

For all of their ambivalences about strict religious practice, where my parents differed most substantially from most members of that modest two-hundred-and-fifty family congregation was in their uncommon commitment to providing their sons with an Orthodox day school education. From first grade through high school, they scraped together sufficient money to send us, with the help of scholarships, to an elite Jewish school, a forty-five minute ride from the East Bronx into the silk-stocking district of Manhattan. As youngsters of the late 1950s–1960s, we were part of that first generation of students that did not hail from strictly observant families who would attend such institutions dedicated to educating Orthodoxy's future leaders. To understand how my parents' school choice, emblematic of elevated religious dedication, earned them their own well-respected place within our locality's Orthodox tent, that decision too has to be set in the context of its time and place.

Initially, when an American yeshiva movement began on the Lower East Side in the 1880s, its mission was to produce a cadre of young boys who would grow to stand apart from American society and help their parents transplant the religious culture of Eastern Europe to these shores. Slowly and unsurely, the all-day Jewish school mission changed as it began, in the late 1910s–1920s, to bespeak the possibility of training and socializing boys — and eventually girls — to live harmoniously as observant Orthodox Jews within a secular American society. But the small pre–World War II cohorts that were exposed to that form of still-separatist education — all other American Jews continued to have great faith in this country's public schools — came largely from families that were more dedicated to following Orthodoxy's core teachings than were my parents. We, and the modern Jewish "academy" that we attended, were different. By the time we were ready to attend that school, it had already earned a reputation for admitting youngsters from families with religious values like the Gurocks.

Still, when we returned to our home borough, we were known in the neighborhood as very Orthodox children, unlike so many other congregational youngsters. Our parents had disdained for us the combined public school–Talmud Torah education that our own congregation proffered and which was still the common fare both where we lived and within most Orthodox communities nationally. Although it was not trumpeted then, we were on the cusp of the future efflorescence of day school education that would become Orthodoxy's late twentieth-century calling card. So situated, the Gurock boys, along with the children of the garment cutter, the son of the community's highly respected Sabbath worker, and just a handful of scions from likeminded families, were known as the "day-school whiz kids," with a special spot set aside for us in our broadly based religious assemblage. It also needs to be said that most of our neighborhood's precocious, educationally privileged, pupils were boys. As late as my youth, all too often committed families of limited means perceived financial sacrifice for their sons' high-level Jewish training as a necessity; not so their daughters. In retrospect, I should also say that we who were granted this chance lived under considerable pressure to be local success stories in the classroom and to be the synagogue's future on the weekends.

From what I recall of the religious practices of our congregation's larger cohort of families who affiliated largely when their children attended the Talmud Torah, they were less observant than we were, although none of them spitefully so. The parents were irregular synagogue attendees, although they were sure to purchase and occupy seats in the sanctuary on the High Holidays. Their children, more often than not, drifted away from synagogue life after their Bar Mitzvahs. When they were seen on Rosh ha-Shanah and Yom Kippur it was only for a few minutes in shul or for hours outside of the building. They stood on the fringes of that neighborhood Orthodox canvas within which their parents had placed themselves, at least while their children attended the Hebrew school. Ironically, I think what frightened these youngsters most, when they fidgeted in the sanctuary, was that someone might call on them to read in Hebrew and thus discover how little they had learned in those congregational classes.

As a child, I really did not know these "other" kids well. At most, I would meet up with them in the neighborhood playgrounds on the weekends.

Otherwise, I was to them one of the "Orthodox boys" who disappeared Monday–Friday while I spent that long Jewish school day in Manhattan. As a young adult, I developed somewhat of a bond with these boys' younger brothers because I ran a post–Bar Mitzvah youth group called the "Minyanaires" that offered Sunday morning services, breakfasts, and a sports period in the hope of holding on to those teenagers after that Jewish rite of passage. I also connected with these teens because of the special relationship I had with another lay leader of the congregation whom I affectionately referred to as my "uncle." Unlike the elitist cutter who focused his attention upon the whiz kids, this equally observant layman paid special attention to the best of the Talmud Torah's products. When he identified a youngster in the afternoon school with aptitude and interest in learning how to be a youth cantor, he would make a deal with the Bar-Mitzvah boy. He would train him gratis to officiate on the special day. In return, the soon-to-be teenager had to promise to attend Sabbath services for at least a year after his Bar Mitzvah. No such deal was ever tendered to any of the outstanding girl students in the co-ed classes. As just noted, at that time Orthodoxy had no avenue for a young female to demonstrate her abilities publicly. Indeed, one of the known points of difference between us and the local Conservative synagogue just a few blocks away was that we did not have Bat Mitzvahs.

This gentleman toiled long and hard in his avocation with the boys and most of those who signed on followed through on their obligations. One of them was destined to use the skills that he acquired in that informal learning session to good use, some years later, in an unanticipated environment. Drafted into the army during the Vietnam War and stationed at some God-forsaken southern base, he became the Jewish chaplain's assistant and used his uncommon skill to lead his fellow Jewish servicemen in prayers.

Finally, within this small Orthodox congregation's very wide tent, there were individuals who appeared at services but once a year and for only one hour. They were the people who showed up around noon on Yom Kippur for the "overflow" *Yizkor* [Memorial] recitation. I remember once seeing a poor local Jewish tailor who entered the sanctuary with the safety pins that he was using that day in his shop, open on the holiest Jewish day of the year, affixed to the breast pocket of his work shirt. Other people of significant means, who possessed the economic wherewithal to purchase Rosh ha-Shanah tickets but who had no use for the extended High Holidays prayers, joined him for that abbreviated service. Although those to whom we gladly surrendered our seats for that hour were surely egregious transgressors in the eyes of Jewish law, they too had a place within the Orthodoxy of our time and place. They belonged in the encampment because, to their minds and hearts, if and when they went to God's house, it had to be an Orthodox abode. The neighborhood's Conservative synagogue would also have welcomed these worshippers. Certainly those who wore their silk suits or fancy dresses to our shul could have afforded that other synagogue's membership fees, which were just a bit higher than ours. However, its more modern service was not for them at that special filiopietistic moment when, and where, they would offer prayers for, and recall fond memories of, their dear departed. Such was the enduring embrace that the ancestral faith and tradition held even over them.

Still, while all of us worshipped at the same Orthodox synagogue, we "whiz kids" and our parents lived fundamentally different Jewish lives from all other Jews in the neighborhood. Though occasionally we gathered together, we sat under different flaps of our Orthodox tent. Within our group, we were extremely tolerant of one another's failings. The two garment center district employees — the one who observed the Sabbath completely and the one who sometimes worked on the sacred day — were the best of friends, as were their sons. The boys traveled together as elementary day-school youngsters to the same classy school that I attended. Only after his Bar Mitzvah did the future rabbi go off to a more Talmud-centric yeshiva. These inseparable youngsters and elders ate in each others homes as they trusted each others' standards of kashruth.

The rabbi and the families who were more observant than us Gurocks appreciated and respected our willingness to help them fulfill their religious needs. Our sterling qualities were apparent whenever the rabbi admonished the congregation about poor attendance at the morning minyan. Without a quorum of ten post–Bar Mitzvah males, public prayers could not proceed. Often, to make his point and to punctuate the problem, he would stand in his Saturday pulpit, toward the close of the services, and wait out the worshippers until three volunteers raised their hands for each day of the Monday–Friday workweek. Quick to respond affirmatively, my father regularly and resolutely "volunteered" us. Along with him, the troika of Gurock men fulfilled our communal obligations, even though at home he and I did not ordinarily recite the daily morning prayers as the tradition prescribes for males. In the wintertime, I was often "rewarded" for my attendance by being handed a snow shovel and directed to clean off the synagogue's walkway while a few of the real old-timers in shul imbibed a shot or two of "schnapps" to prepare their bodies for the cold outside. A more tangible sign of how well we got along was that my father, his Sabbath-working seatmate, and, for that matter, all regular attendees, routinely received synagogue honors despite their imperfect record of Orthodox deportment. Under a strict construction of the sanctions of Jewish law, a known or public Sabbath desecrator could be denied, for example, the very significant privilege of being "called to the Torah." The honoree is given the opportunity of standing at the side of the reader as that expert chants a section of that week's weekly portion of the Law. A formulaic blessing is subsequently bestowed upon him and his family. In many shuls — but not in ours — the man called up responds with a contribution to congregational coffers. In any event, restrictions on designees based on lack of piety were never enforced within our community. Each of us had a card with our name on it, kept in a green metal box next to the Torah reader's seat. We waited our turn as the honors were rotated among habitual worshippers. It was certainly a big deal for a Bar-Mitzvah boy when he could find his name within that special list. It was another male rite of passage as he was again counted as a man in this Orthodox community's circle.

While we, the deeply involved members, lived together and coped each in our own particular ways with the demands of our distinctive religious lifestyles, few of the Talmud Torah families knew either of the coveted green box or of the problems with the daily minyan, nor about the floating guilt that some harbored about their periodical breaks with the tradition. Their religious existences were really untied to ours. Only the rabbi who headed up the Hebrew school and officiated at all congregants' life-cycle events, and the gentleman who went out of his way to train the best of those kids, maintained anything approaching an enduring relationship with those who represented the majority of the Orthodox Jews on the congregation's membership roll.

As a historian, I have come to recognize that the diverse Orthodox environment that enveloped me as a youth, though special in some distinctive ways, was far from unparalleled in this country's Jewish experience. For more than three-and-a-half centuries, America has been home to Jews who have possessed a vast range of commitments to halachic traditions and practices. This mix includes those who began their lives with only the most minimal ties to such teachings and then aspired to be inexorably bound and those who did precisely the opposite. In fact, over the course of this country's Jewish experience, the diverse sagas of these Jews has been nothing less than the story of the challenges, dilemmas, and opportunities that the majority of men and women who looked to lead religious lives faced as they made their ways in America.

What has changed over time are only the numbers within each of these strains of observance and — as just indicated — their proportion among the total American Jewish population. Across the sweep of American Jewish history, up to the years of my youth (I was born in 1949), the minimally connected, periodic, or only seasonal Orthodox Jews not only outnumbered their deeply devoted brethren, but this aggregation of occasional affiliates constituted the largest segment of Jews who chose to link up with synagogues and otherwise associate with religious forms of Judaism in this country. Only over the last quarter–half century have the figures been reversed, as Orthodoxy remained home to far more devotees than deviants and still fewer Jews who are comparable to our family's friend. And while this expression of Judaism has declined in popularity, most of those who persisted within its fold have become more punctilious than any prior group in American Jewish history.

I have likewise become aware through my work that the challenges to daily ritual observance that American conditions posed within my East Bronx neighborhood has its own 350-year history. The dilemmas that this country wrought were twofold. First, there was the issue of the devout often not having at hand the essential requisites to live their religious lives. In the seventeenth–eighteenth centuries, the absence in this country's frontier environs of an established communal infrastructure and of skilled functionaries made, for example, the keeping of kashruth requirements extremely difficult. Similar problems surely upset those who were determined to uphold the laws of family purity. Probably in most locales, before a mikveh was built, resolute women and some men — if they too had the need — might have "use[d] . . . a natural spring . . . for those ritual purposes."[3] This is what the ladies of Congregation Shearith Israel, New York's and America's first synagogue, reportedly did in "its earliest days." Daunting circumstances like these as well as the absence of the schools, cemeteries, and even the minyans necessary for organized prayers kept those committed to staunch observance of the ancient rules to a bare minimum.

In time, that is by the middle of the eighteenth century, this situation improved significantly due to the efforts of the few pious Jews who, notwithstanding these weighty problems, ventured to America and succeeded in establishing enduring religious presences in the early eastern seaboard communities. Their institutions were certainly up and running when larger-scale Jewish migration from Central Europe began in the 1820s. In other words, as of that time period, newcomers who cared could settle in New York, Philadelphia, Baltimore, and other cities and be reasonably certain that they could have their halachic wherewithal. Their presence, in turn, expanded the critical mass necessary to effectively sustain a religious community's way of life. Starting in 1840s, these Jews also could look to the guidance of Orthodox rabbis to help them navigate their way as Jews in America. However, in mid nineteenth-century America, the most dynamic action took place out west as this country expanded its continent-wide reach. For those devout Jews who contemplated taking part in this country's manifest destiny adventure, there was the recurrent problem of how to avail themselves of the commodities necessary to regularly perform the commandments. It took yeoman efforts to live a halachic life in what was again an American frontier.

The pious among the millions of East European Jews who arrived from the 1880s to World War I and who settled — as most did — in the urban economic frontiers of New York and other east coast and midwestern hubs did not face such large-scale problems. Even if back in the lands of oppression, sage rabbis admonished the faithful not to come to the *treif* [lit: unkosher] land of America, the warnings were not due to the unavailability of kosher foods nor of mikvehs nor of any perquisites necessary to observe the commandments. If anything, with so many wanting these commodities — and at certain seasons during the year it was far more than the devout who wanted items such as matzahs and kosher wines — entrepreneurs, Jewish and gentile, alike recognized and accommodated Jews of so many religious stripes as valued consumers. In succeeding decades, Orthodox consumerism became big business with robust competition making it increasingly easy to live a devout Jewish life in America. To cite, for now, but one example of how these realities play out today: if the son of the Sabbath worker from my youth and his closest childhood friend, the Orthodox rabbi, want an evening out to reminisce about East Bronx days, they and their wives have their choice of scores of up-scale and neighborhood strictly kosher restaurants in the metropolitan area where they both still reside. Fifty years ago, finding an appropriate place was still an issue. There were few such eating establishments in town and none, it will be recalled, in their neighborhood. Dining choices are not nearly as extensive outside of Orthodoxy's largest hub; still, many cities have kosher restaurants anxious to serve the observant.

But even as the problem of providing requisites for the devout in this country has been largely solved, the second problem with American freedom has persisted to date; and at least many of its ramifications are still felt. It has always taken quite a resolute Jew to ignore a largely accepting society's challenge to advance himself or herself socially and economically since the price of success or full acceptance has usually resulted in transgression of the halacha. For example, when it came to observance of the Sabbath — the most trying of dilemmas — to honor that day meant, in the economic sphere, that such Jews had to resign themselves to work less than those around them, since in so many places and for centuries in American history, government restrictions precluded the opening of shops and businesses on Sunday, the Christian Sabbath, the civic day of rest. Through such Sabbath absenteeism, the devout also risked losing chances at promotions or even their very job opportunities. In social realms, those who kept the Sabbath traditions effectively sequestered themselves on that holy day from both other Jews and Americans with whom they might regularly interact at all sorts of cultural and recreational venues. Certainly, for some of the most pious, that sort of separatism was precisely what they wanted. Thus it was not a challenge for them to avoid integration with those who did not share their utmost values. But for many others who desired to be very much like all

other Americans, finding ways to be both faithful and friendly was a significant issue.

In the years following my youth, namely in the mid-1960s and beyond,
many of the legal barriers that undermined pious practices fell away as a
more tolerant America abolished most of its so-called Blue Laws. Orthodox
activists played no small role in sensitizing government officials to the patent
unfairness of past discriminatory practices even as they used the power of
the properly placed "Orthodox vote" to clinch their argument. As important, the increased affluence of devout Jews also eased mightily the crises of
economic choices. In other words, the children of Sabbath-workers whose
parents were otherwise devout did not have to work on holy days. However,
social dilemmas remained, and continue to this day, for those who wish to
take part in American activities that do not countenance Jewish tradition's
clock and calendar. Difficult decisions still haunt some of those who wish to
be fully part of these secularizing pursuits.

Not every major aspect of Orthodox Jews' lives in America was exempli-
fied through my personal experience growing up in the East Bronx. But
these dimensions, too, warrant close consideration. For example, as much
as this country's unbridled religious world allowed both its strong adherents
and its mere affiliates to live diverse and parallel religious existences, their
stories are also ones of strains between groups who often found themselves
at loggerheads with one another. Where I came from, the religious lives of
the committed minority ran largely apart from those of all others; the more
devout the family, the less they had to do with the synagogue's rank and file.
Only the rabbi and the gentleman who trained a select group of Bar-Mitzvah
boys had much to do with them. But there was little conflict in the congregation. Such peaceful coexistence among Orthodox groups, though also evident elsewhere has, however, not always been the norm throughout this
country's Jewish history.

Indeed, a narrative of palpable tension dates back to the earliest periods
of Jewish life in America—roughly from the mid-seventeenth to the early
nineteenth century—when in their first encounters, some among the pious
minority tried aggressively to affect the lifestyles of their coreligionists. For
the former, it was a halachic obligation not only to lead their own devout
Jewish existences, but also to ensure that all Jews acted likewise. When they
felt that they had the power to do so, they tried, through excoriations, fines,
and even expulsions to engender conformity to fundamental Jewish practices in their midst. They succeeded in their efforts only to a lesser degree.
More often than not, all that they accomplished was to limit the number of
those who would sit comfortably in their community's first, narrow tent.
Then, for more than half a century, such remonstrations largely were held
in abeyance born of the recognition that religious control of others' obser-

vances in America was well-nigh impossible, especially when other Jewish denominations beckoned. At that juncture, Orthodox's defensive lines were extended out against religious competitors who tendered to both its devout and deviant followers attractive visions of how Judaism should be understood and practiced. This nineteenth-century Orthodox struggle for institutional survival during an age of Jewish religious reform in this country would be replicated almost a hundred years later as battles royale broke out in post–World War II among American synagogue groups.

In the era of large-scale East European migration, although the rigorously observant minority was rarely silent about the crisis of disinterest among so many fellow Jews, it spoke with several voices about what to do. The debate centered on whether it was better to focus energies on maintaining an elite cadre of the committed or to work among the increasingly disinterested majority. To some degree that particular dilemma resonated still in our Bronx congregation two generations later.

Meanwhile, for most of American Jewish history, it was not so much that the less devout tried to change the way the more scrupulously Orthodox Jews behaved, but rather that they sometimes looked askance at their counterparts' hidebound traditionalism. By the midpoint of the last century, while still part of a large and wide Orthodox canvas, the groups and their innumerable subsets, as we have already suggested, lived largely separate Jewish lives. Today, however — meaning the last quarter-century or so — in keeping with a religious quest to spread their understanding of the Torah's teachings to all Jews, some of the most punctilious have renewed efforts to turn around those Orthodox Jews who do not share most of their religious values. They have prosecuted their positions on a grand scale. For them, it is but part of a confident, triumphalist or even eschatological agenda to spread their vision of Judaism to all Jews. Usually through soft-touch suasion, but also occasionally with polemics, they have sought to "reach out" — to use contemporary parlance — with a strong sense of righteousness. Sometimes, their ministrations extend even to those who are dedicated to the same basic truths as they are but who do not always see eye to eye on all Orthodox outlooks. When these encounters take place, they exacerbate yet another type of long-standing Orthodox tension: there are disagreements among the committed about the depth of the challenges that modern Jewish and general movements and influences pose to their own continuity of faith.

For more than a century, first in Europe and then here, debates ensued among the devout, for example, over the extent to which the precepts of Jewish nationalism could coexist with Orthodoxy's view of the Jews' ultimate destiny. With this issue still unresolved, disagreements over Zionism and the fate of Israel still separate the most dedicated Orthodox Jews. Similarly, for almost the same amount of time, profound differences of opinion over how much of modern culture can be countenanced within a truly pious life has splintered many of those same groups. Today, the debate rages on, and it does more vociferously than ever. Those who resist the incursion of many American values — while tacitly admitting others — are generally on the attack against those who actively and avowedly seek to integrate such values within what they define as the limits of the halacha. To touch upon but one very sore point that is perhaps the most intriguing contemporary intra-Orthodox struggle: attitudes toward so vital a present-day force as feminism — or even more generally stated — toward gender roles, has engendered much controversy among those who share so many of the most traditional Jewish values.

Finally, there is one other, very different calculus of religious concerns that always has roiled the Orthodox community that demands unflinching examination. It is a phenomenon that either did not obtain where I grew up or I did not notice it as a youth. But my research, coupled with personal observations of contemporary Jewish life — where some manifestations of this problem recently have received high-profile publicity — has sensitized me to the following inescapable reality. Throughout American Jewish history there have been those who ostensibly have committed themselves to devout observance of the Torah's teachings. But in actuality, they have been egregious violators of the halacha. These reprehensible offenders have strictly upheld day-to-day halachic requirements. In ritual regards, they have been among the most punctilious and, not incidentally, by virtue of those performances have frequently positioned themselves within the center of many an Orthodox tent. But, in committing acts of unethical and even illegal turpitude, these transgressors have denigrated Orthodox Judaism's most fundamental teaching. The faith sees itself as both a divinely ordained system of laws and customs and as a community rooted in an exacting set of moral principles. That tradition abjures the Jew unqualifiedly to observe both the laws governing humankind's relationship with God and those between men and women to one another with equal sincerity and diligence. Though only a distinct minority within each generation, these moral miscreants have included, for example, those who have substituted unkosher for kosher meat to maximize their profits, those rabbis in name only, who, during Prohibition, sold bootleg kosher wines in violation of the intent of the Volstead Act, and those male offenders who, in our more contemporary times, have used their refusal to grant their estranged wives a writ of religious divorce [a *get*] to torture and extort monies from female Orthodox unfortunates. Without that document, an observant woman cannot remarry religiously and is "chained" to a sorry future life. If there were such religious family abusers in our East Bronx community neither I nor my family or friends were aware of this social pathology. Nor did we suspect our butcher's honesty or know of Orthodox civil law-breakers. Such forms of behavior were certainly not addressed — let alone pilloried — from the pulpit nor even whispered about in the pews. Perhaps, we were all just naïve.

However, my ability now to take into account ethical malefactors of all stripes adds yet another dimension to this history of America's Orthodox Jews. Accordingly, what follows is a complex narrative exploring how such men and women lived diverse religious lives in this country for three-and-a-half centuries within and without Jewish law — and sometimes outside of government statutes — often conflicted with one another while some staunchly defended their faith against other Jewish expressions and others cared less, all against the backdrop of a free society's changing challenges.

# 1

## ALL ALONE AND OUT OF CONTROL

In the middle of the seventeenth century, there were few Jews in the world quite like Asser Levy. At a time when almost all of his co-religionists did not even dream of being treated as equals within their hostile gentile worlds, Levy strode purposefully through the streets of New Amsterdam demanding that he be judged on the same footing as all other local inhabitants. He was not satisfied merely with the right to settle, as had occurred in the case of Jewish refugees from Brazil who were granted asylum by the Dutch West India Company—the owners of the outpost—in 1655, over Peter Stuyvesant's protest. The recalcitrant governor had not wanted these indigents, who, in his prejudiced view, were "blasphemers of the name of Christ" to "infect and trouble the new colony" and had requested that they be told "in a friendly way" to "depart." Not daunted in the least, Levy—who apparently came to New Netherlands as a fortune-seeker a month earlier than the refugees with a Company passport securely in his pocket—felt entitled to more than just the vague right that his poor fellow Jews had garnered to "travel and trade to and in New Netherland and live and remain there." He wanted instead to be defined as a respected member of the host society. Thus Levy protested to the

Amsterdam mercantile conglomerate when the ever-antagonistic Stuyvesant denied him the manly and community-defining right of joining the colonial militia during a conflagration with the Swedes in Delaware. The governor had made it known that his military men had "aversion and disaffection . . . to be fellow soldiers . . . and to mount the same guardhouse" with Jews. Levy had been directed to pay a humiliating tax ostensibly to support others doing the fighting.[1]

Levy possessed a remarkable sense of entitlement somehow born of his own personal fortitude. The only precedent for Jews serving in a modern army was, ironically enough, the experience of those who, just a few years earlier, had helped the Dutch put down a colonial rebellion in Brazil. By contrast, back in the Netherlands, where unlike in Recife the Dutch did not strongly feel the need to have all loyal, able-bodied men, regardless of their religion, at the frontier outposts' barricades, Jews were not counted in that home country's militia.[2]

When he ultimately prevailed over his enemies — the Jew had been told during this dispute that if he did not like Stuyvesant's policy he and another petitioner could also "depart whenever and wither it please them" — Levy continued to assert boldly his status in town, fighting for the right to be recognized as a burgher. Once he won that subsequent battle, Levy, the pugnacious petitioner, then possessed a wider range of emancipation rights than even the Jewish patrons — those supporters of the Dutch West India Company whose own courageous letters had both helped the Brazilian refugees secure their stay and improved Levy's status in New Amsterdam. The so-called "father of American Jewish history" had all of the Dutch Jews' economic privileges and was also allowed to fight. Some years later, after 1664 when the British gained control of the colony, the litigious Levy made it clear to another opponent that he was not one to be trifled with. In 1673, he took a minor city official, a weigher named Dietloffson, to court for "affronts" — most likely an antisemitic remark — and the plaintiff had to be very pleased when the magistrate affirmed his position.[3]

The independent Levy was also highly unique for his time as a Jew who — along with his wife Miriam — lived alone in this new world without the support of other Jews or an incipient infrastructure of a Jewish community around him. There were few Jews around the world who held Asser Levy religious values and faced his dilemmas. Here was someone who knew of, wanted to, and could practice the dictates of his faith without fear or harassment. But at the same time, he and his wife were separated for close to a decade by geography from other Jews.

Early on in their lives in America the Levys did have some company, as the original New Amsterdam Jewish group had shown some signs of settling down as a religious entity. Notwithstanding Stuyvesant's presence and predilections, other New Netherlands officials were actually respectful of the Jewish faith. In July 1655, Levy and his friends were granted some plots outside the city for a cemetery. Jewish tradition instructs that that is the inaugural institution that Jews must build in any new area of residence. Although the minority group had yet to receive the formal right to conduct public prayers, they had permission to pray as a minyan in a private home. They used a Torah scroll that the leaders of the Amsterdam community gave them. Meanwhile, two legal decisions in 1658 may have further heartened those who wished to practice Judaism as they pleased. Twice in June of that year, Jacob Barsimson was excused from a default judgment for failure to appear in court because "he was summoned on his Sabbath." Still, by 1664, some ten years after Stuyvesant had stood four square against the Jews' very presence in his "weak and newly developing place," the Dutchman almost got his wish. All the Jews of New Amsterdam, with the exception of Asser and Miriam Levy, departed in a friendly way from the fledgling colony. The Torah scroll was returned to Amsterdam in 1663.[4]

The out-migration seemingly had all to do with the problems of making a living within this economically unstable colony. New Amsterdam was not blessed with great natural resources. It lacked the cash crops of sugar or tobacco, and trade in furs was its most profitable commodity. Local commercial enterprise was under the control of four Amsterdam-based merchant combines. While Jews in Holland had some financial control over the governing company, they had no say or sway over these independent financial operatives that were not particularly disposed toward Jews or toward anyone else who was not part of its family-based network. Certainly, in the mid-seventeenth century the Caribbean, for one, promised far greater economic opportunities than did New Netherlands.[5]

But the Levys stayed in town through the end of Dutch rule in 1664 and for a full generation under the British. Asser would die in 1682, Miriam some six years later. Their persistence perhaps had much to do with his choice of livelihood, as he maintained steady work as a skilled butcher and did well at his trade. An inventory of his possessions upon his death was valued at 550 £, making him one of the more affluent members of New York society. His belongings included a black velvet jacket, a silver-banded sword, a black hat, and shoes with silver buckles. He was quite the seventeenth-century colonial dandy.[6]

How did Levy survive as a Jew? The sources, as such, simply are not there to tell a full story of his religious life, particularly about how he lived bereft of a community of co-religionists. Still, there is evidence to ascertain the following: this Vilna-born Jew — who grew up in an environment where the traditional practices of Judaism were certainly robust — undeniably knew and cared about the demands of Jewish law and attempted to follow them.

His travels from his childhood community to Amsterdam and on to the New World did not involve fleeing from his ancestral traditions. Otherwise, the self-assertive Levy would not have petitioned for the right to be exempted from killing hogs. Rabbinic ordinances proscribe a Jew from slaughtering that patently unclean animal. The English authorities acceded to this request. His trade and occupation also may have helped him observe a central Jewish practice in this frontier setting. That is, if he knew the ins and outs of kosher slaughtering procedures, perhaps the "parcel of old books" in his possession may have included some sort of guide to this skill.[7]

Those personal inventories also hint that Asser and Miriam did their level best to observe kashruth within their home. A relevant scenario might testify to their religious sensibilities: they possessed two items of everything in their kitchen from chopping knives, to pans, to skimmers, to basins, and an inordinate number of plates. In other words, in accordance again with rabbinic ordinances, they seemed to have kept meat separate from milk. Alternatively, of course, these multiple implements and dishes may simply be signs of the rich butcher and his wife's conspicuous consumption. They may have needed many plates when they invited guests into their home. While day-by-day it was just the two of them at the table — they were not blessed with children — occasionally they may have been gracious hosts. What they did about the dietary laws on the road or when they visited with gentile friends like the prominent Cornelia Steenwyck or Stephan Van Cordlandt is not known.[8]

It is also conceivable that Asser and Miriam Levy observed the Sabbath, at least to some extent. They owned a "Sabbath lamb [*sic*]" and wine cups that could have been used for Kiddush, the blessing over wine that sanctifies the holy day, as well as a spice box that might have been designated for the Havdalah ceremony that concludes the day of rest. However, we absolutely do not know if they were punctilious beyond their possible performance of these basic Sabbath rituals. We can only wonder whether they were a strict, unyielding religious couple who habitually absented themselves on Saturday both from the work-a-day world and the social life of their remote outpost. But, whatever the Levys' precise level of observance of these fundamental mitzvoth was — we know nothing about if and how they maintained family purity regulations bereft of a mikveh in town — the essential and remarkable point is again here that they did so without the support and fellowship of other Jews. As such, their religious lives, marked by loneliness, were almost unparalleled within the Jewish world of that time.[9]

In the seventeenth century, almost all Jews, whether resident in pre-Emancipation Europe or in Islamic lands, lived either comfortably or in tension within organized Jewish communities. These legal entities provided them with all their religious necessities even as these corporate entities controlled and monitored daily existences. Of course, starting some three centuries earlier, first in Spain and ultimately in Portugal too, there were some co-religionists — crypto-Jews — who perforce practiced what they could in a subterranean manner without a recognized community or interaction with other Jews. But by the time the Levys came on the scene, those who had succeeded in getting out of Iberia and their descendants were either long along the way toward becoming reintegrated with fellow Jews into Western European religious establishments or they were nonconformists who chafed at rabbinic teachings or regulations. Most notably, in seventeenth-century Netherlands some were fighting dissidents whose works and statements challenged the most basic assumptions that undergirded Jewish tradition. Uriel da Costa, who twice recanted his heresies, and the unrepentant Baruch Spinoza, who never backed off attacking his people's religious beliefs, were among the most renowned critics of that time and place. Then there were others who just did not follow the rules rigorously, like men who were punished by communal officials for honoring religious obligations in their abuse when they "journeyed (usually for business) to 'lands of idolatry.' " However, no one lived voluntarily separate and apart from the community. Outsiders were those whom communal authorities placed there, in limbo, through excommunication or less stinging bans and punishments until they fell into line. The Levys, on the other hand and on the other side of the Atlantic, were neither dissenters nor miscreants. Their uncommon isolation resulted solely from their residence on Manhattan Island, hundreds if not thousands of miles removed from those who shared their ancestral past.[10]

The closest analogue to this contemporary condition in New Amsterdam was the condition of the inaugural Jewish settlers in the Caribbean. On their islands, the first arrivals, whether refugees from Brazil, migrants from Europe, or peripatetic Jews who had left Recife, returned to Holland to catch their collective breaths and accumulate possessions before trekking back to the New World, were likewise faced with the daunting task of building Jewish lives for themselves and their children. That is if they chose to practice their faith. Here too, in another remote part of the early modern Jewish world — away from communal authority — there would be those who would avail themselves of the opportunity to abandon their ancestral ties. But if Jews in a frontier setting decided to stay — a few of their outposts, including Essequibo and Cayenne, came and went — and wanted to make the effort to preserve their religious life, they always had similarly minded fellows around them. Once established, these aggregations, albeit admittedly small, persisted and in short order could speak of minyans or more of practicing Jews. In flourishing Curaçao, "the more than seventy souls, adults as well as children," who came in 1659 from Holland to stay, with a Torah in their possession, would have continued use of that holy scroll. In the succeeding decade, Congregation Mikve Israel would be a reality. No Jew was left alone.[11]

How comfortable could Asser and Miriam Levy have been, totally bereft of even a semblance of a Jewish community? It is an unanswerable question, except to say that evidently they persisted in this new land and may have made the best of the situation. Projecting a bit, may we suggest that their not needing to be concerned with the future of those who literally would follow in their footsteps made this challenging Jewish life decision somewhat easier. The father and mother of American Jewish history had no offspring of their own and thus did not have to be concerned about education and a welter of life-cycle events from circumcisions to finding marriage mates for youngsters. Is it just ironic or is it highly symbolic that Levy's inventories do not list a *milah* [circumcision] kit, that would include the scalpel and clamps that a *mohel* [performer of circumcisions] needs? But one thing is certain, or to put it another way: Dutch Jewish merchant Solomon Pieterson, who seems to have arrived in town just before Levy set foot in New Amsterdam, had it very much easier in America. He married a Christian woman and their daughter was baptized at birth. He was not worried about Judaism sustaining a foothold in this frontier world.[12]

In the very last years of the Levys' lives, they finally gained some permanent Jewish company. Under the British, New York began to flourish economically and attracted both fortune seekers and just plain future solid citizens of the colony, among them some Jews. We really know nothing definitive about the range of these Jewish newcomers' personal religious values. How many, for example, were like the Levys, who seemingly strove to find ways of surmounting the kashruth problem or were interested in keeping the Sabbath, as opposed to the number who emulated Solomon Pieterson and quickly abandoned their Jewish connections? What we can say is that in 1682, Joseph Bueno de Mesquita acquired a cemetery plot for the group. By the early 1680s, enough of his fellows had gravitated together to reestablish the New York minyan. And in 1685, twenty families petitioned the authorities for the right to worship their God in public. The British, in keeping still with established Dutch policy toward that minority — dating back to Stuyvesant's days — turned down the request. But despite this rebuff, some resolute Jews may have gone right ahead anyway and built an edifice that was remembered around town as the "Jewes Synagogue." At least that's how the structure was referred to in 1695 on a map of the colony that a Protestant minister named John Miller drew.[13]

This New York Jews' move, which appears more audacious than it really was, had absolutely no impact upon British authorities, if they noticed it at all. Since the readmission of Jews to England in 1655, the Crown and Parliament back home were still developing their attitudes to Jews. There too laws were on the books prohibiting non-Anglican religious services. These restrictions were often honored in their abuse, and when offenders were apprehended or nasty enemies made much of their transgressions, Jews were rarely punished. So disposed, the independent-minded religious actions of Jewish colonialists were at most an afterthought.[14]

In any event, sometime in the next decade — certainly by 1704 — a recognized congregation stood, on rented space, among the houses of worship in New York on Mill Street due south of Wall Street, on what is today South William Street in Lower Manhattan. There in 1730 Shearith Israel, practicing its public Judaism according to the Sephardic rite, constructed its inaugural enduring synagogue home.[15]

Concomitant with this moment of rebirth for New York's Jewish religious presence, several other colonial seaboard proprietary centers permitted the establishment of enduring Jewish settlements. Until the Revolutionary era, the minority group was kept out of southern colonies like Maryland and Virginia and those in New England where staunch Christian religious teachings held sway. Where Jews were admitted, over the course of succeeding decades — most dramatically from the late 1720s through the 1760s — these aggregations experienced patterns of slow, early development comparable to that of their older, sister community of New York. Always, there were those who upon arrival in America blithely walked away from their religious past. More generally, Jews made efforts to buy and consecrate cemetery lands and create places for private devotions and finally synagogues for public prayer. When they reached this concrete level of communal maturity, the congregations that they consecrated — such as the mother Congregation Shearith Israel — all practiced the faith in their pews in line with the Sephardic rite, even if more members were Ashkenazim, hailing primarily from Central and Eastern Europe.

Such was the case in Newport, Rhode Island, which had a cemetery as early as 1677, but due to the ebb and flow of its Jewish population in this mobile, fluid mercantile world did not house a lasting congregation until the early 1750s. By that time, Charleston had its own cemetery and congregation and had plans to build a synagogue — with assistance from New York Jewry — when the revolution intervened. Philadelphia Jews were renting space for public prayers in the 1760s. The construction of its first synagogue would wait for the war years when the City of Brotherly Love would benefit from the migration there of Jewish Whig brethren, many of them from British-occupied New York. The renowned cantor cum minister, patriot Gershom Mendes Seixas, Torah in hand, led the refugees from Crown control southbound and would contribute to the maturation of Philadelphia Jewry. Seixas, who was known in general societal circles as a "rabbi," or as that "handsome young Priest in a black gown," returned to New York after the war. There he subsequently was honored as the Jewish religious representative at the inauguration of President George Washington. Seixas, quite the good-looking fellow, as a miniature painting of him complete with his clerical collar attests, did not stand out among the dozen Christian minister colleagues as each blessed the new government and its tolerant elected leader. Savannah Jews were initially quick to plan to build a synagogue after their acceptance in Georgia in the 1730s. But the first example of internecine Jewish rivalries within an all-too-small community chilled those inaugural plans. The move within that southernmost American Jewish colonial outpost would not gain momentum until the 1790s.[16]

During that same era, smaller pockets of Jewish life came into being in the Pennsylvania outpost towns away from the coast of York, Lancaster, Easton, and Reading. Typically, as early as 1747, two Lancastrian Jews purchased a cemetery plot for their "Society of Jews." During the next forty-seven years, only five co-religionists would be laid to rest there. While that town would not have a formal synagogue until the nineteenth century, from the 1760s on, Lancaster Jews had what its historian has called an "almost congregation," groups of co-religionists having a minyan, especially during the High Holidays. In the 1770s the first Jews of Easton congregated for services in private homes. But with the comings and goings of Jews within and without this frontier town, no cemetery area was purchased until 1800. For years thereafter, it was essentially the private "[Michael] Hart family burial ground." Easton Jewry's first synagogue would not be established until the 1830s.[17]

Among those many Jews who wanted that all-important communal cemetery and were pleased also that their city established a synagogue, were those who desired to have much more Judaism in their lives. Notwithstanding the endemic difficulties of establishing and maintaining their faith in America, in the late seventeenth and eighteenth centuries, a coterie of very committed Jews sought these shores, wagering that they and their families could secure their traditions here even as they availed themselves of all the bounties of a new world.

Aaron Lopez began his American merchant career in Newport, Rhode Island, and migrated with some other Jews to Leicester, Massachusetts, during the Revolutionary War. In both venues, they earned for themselves a reputation as pious Jews. They were known to have "brought with them and scrupulously maintained while here their peculiar forms of faith and worship . . . and rigidly observed the rites and requirements of their own laws, keeping Saturday as holy time." So disposed, Lopez himself was keenly aware of Judaism's clock and calendar and was sure to shut down his office before sundown on Friday. Likewise sensitive to the demands of the Christian Sabbath, he did not reopen until Monday morning. This entrepreneur also made certain that none of the ships that he owned left port on the Sabbath day. German-born commercial agent Jonas Phillips, who lived in Charleston and New York and moved to Philadelphia during the Revolutionary War — he fought for the patriotic cause — harbored similar religious values. We know, for example, from a contemporary's account of the ritual how punctilious he was in making sure his sons were circumcised properly, the most basic rite for entering males into the Abrahamic covenant. As he was the father of twenty-one children, that religious operation was more than just an occasional event. There is also some evidence that at least one of his children followed in his and his wife, Rebecca's, footsteps. Rachel Phillips and her bridegroom fasted the day before their wedding. This custom punctuates the religious seriousness of the impending nuptials, projecting a wedding day as solemn as Yom Kippur. Rebecca Phillips reported with pride on this indicative mark of sensitivity, if not fidelity, to traditional strictures.[18]

Easton's Michael Hart did not have such good fortune with at least one of his children who clearly did not share his religious values. While the elder Hart was scrupulous in his observance of the Sabbath and kashruth — local traditions have it that "as a good Jew, he abhorred pork" — his son loved that forbidden food. Angered by a son's actions that gave him no familial satisfaction, the hot-tempered Hart once meted out summary parental judgment on his son. He choked the youngster until the miscreant threw up the offensive matter; Hart then reportedly declared: "Now, the devil is out of him." Meanwhile, the Phillips' and Hart's contemporary Manuel Josephson was not only highly observant but also extraordinarily learned in the ways of the Jewish tradition. A sutler and merchant who made his mark upon both Philadelphia and New York Jewry, he was not only able to articulate religious questions on behalf of the faithful that were addressed to rabbinic authorities in England, but occasionally, Josephson, a scholar but not an ordained official, rendered his own halachic decisions on this side of the Atlantic. We will presently see that he did so with a very strict hand.[19]

The piety of such Jews did not remain unnoticed among gentile business associates who sometimes were less than pleased when Jewish strictures inconvenienced them. "As the Devil will have it," complained Philadelphian Michael Murray in 1774, about his business associate Michael Gratz taking off time because of Shavuoth [The two-day Festival of Weeks commemorating the giving of the Torah on Mount Sinai]. "That Moses was upon a top of a mountain in the month of May," Murray wondered facetiously, "consequently his followers must for a certain number of day cease to provide for their families?"[20] Two years earlier and not so far away in Lancaster, another Christian businessman was less than impressed when his Jewish colleague used a halachically permissible stratagem to seal a deal without violating the Sabbath. When David McClure showed up at Joseph Simon's home on the holy day to collect payment on an account, the observant Jewish merchant initially would "not do business," requesting that he "call tomorrow." Realizing the inconvenience he had caused to his associate, Simon enlisted the help of a neighbor to serve as a "*Shabbes Goy.*" Jewish law permits the enlisting of a gentile to perform certain acts on behalf of a Jew on the holy day that are otherwise impermissible. The most common assistance at that time was in the lighting of lamps or the tending to a fire or stove in a Jewish home so that the devout might have light and warmth as they celebrated the Sabbath. Simon, frankly, stretched the rules when he engaged a Christian associate in an entrepreneurial function. The designee dutifully "counted out the money and gave a receipt" while Simon, reportedly, "sat looking on, to see that all was rightly transacted, but said nothing and thus quieted his conscience against the rebuke of a violation of the Sabbath." To McClure's way of thinking, this was not a way of living within the Jewish legal system but a hypocritical act.[21]

What McClure missed in his criticism was the real-life reality that Simon confronted here. To survive religiously as he sought to make his way in America — engaging as he did in commercial relations with those whose Sabbath was different from his — required that Jews like Simon possess some dexterity to find some play within the flexible lines of the halacha. Beyond such constant dilemmas, there was the often-daunting challenge of having available all the pertinences for maintaining traditional observances in this still-frontier society. Significantly, within this segment that kept the commandments rigorously in the eighteenth century, there were individuals blessed with religious skills and talents essential for their group's survival and growth.

Mordecai Sheftall was one of the first Jews in Georgia and came to that colony with both his circumcision scalpel and animal-slaughtering knives in hand. He entered his own sons into the covenant, undoubtedly performed this most basic mitzvah for others, and was a resource for kosher food for those who desired it. Beginning in the 1750s, Lancaster storekeeper Bernard Isaac Jacobs rode the circuit among the five cities and towns where Jews lived in Pennsylvania and kept a record of the thirty-three boys whom Jacobs circumcised from 1757–1790. He averaged but one a year. Merchant Michael Hart, that unhappy parent, did the slaughtering for his very small Jewish group in Easton. New York's Benjamin Gomez, likewise a merchant, made his services as a mohel available both in his home community and in sister cities. When he could not be there himself, he offered his brother Daniel as a substitute.[22]

The entrepreneurial Michael Gratz did not know the many details of proper kosher slaughtering. Even if he did, probably like most affluent Jewish merchants of his time this gentleman was not about to get his hands filthy in an abattoir. To insure that he, his family, and his friends had a ready supply of kosher meat, he hired a *shochet* [ritual slaughterer] to do the dirty work. He also laid out his own money to engage a *shamash* [beadle] to gather the Jews in town for their minyan. Soon thereafter, subsequent to a trip to the West Indies, in 1765, he realized the profitability of the business of kashruth. Philadelphia businessmen were already supplying these Caribbean islands with treif meats and fats. Why not do the same for kosher eaters? Therefore, in 1768 he negotiated a deal with those in Curaçao, became the purveyor, and connected with Abraham I. Abraham, Shearith Israel of New York's jack-of-all-religious-trades, to obtain certification for his products. Some years later, Gratz hired Philadelphia's own multitasked employee, Ezekiel Levy, for the "Jewish Society held here," and charged him with the responsibilities of serving as "a Jewish killer, reader in the synagogue and to teach six children the art of reading the Hebrew tongue."[23]

When there were enough Jews around to begin formal congregational life, people like these — the observant merchants, the professional functionaries, and the economically modest businessmen like Jonas Phillips — who worked as a slaughterer to supplement his incomes — formed the core of synagogue leadership. Wherever they ensconced themselves, they set as a high priority making certain that their communities had properly prepared and supervised kosher meats, that the women and men had a mikveh available for ritual purification rites, and that there was a teacher engaged to instruct their youngsters in the rudiments of the faith. Manuel Josephson was an emphatic advocate for Philadelphia's first congregation, Mikveh Israel, to build a fitting ritualarium both for those who already followed the laws of separation during the menstrual cycle and those would might be "induce[d] . . . to a strict compliance with that duty so incumbent on them."[24]

New York's committed Jews were so well organized, that as early as the late 1720s, they had in place a paid cantor, shochet, beadle, and teacher with each occupation's responsibilities fully defined. The school master, for example, was obliged, in one instance, to "open a school at his own house everyday of the week" except weekday holidays and fast days and to teach "Hebrew, Spanish, English, writing and Arithmetic . . . in the summer from 9 to 12 in the forenoon and from 2–5 in the afternoon and in the winter from 10–12 in the forenoon and from 2 to 4 in the afternoon." Sometimes, one man did more than one job, and at other times men actually competed for these posts. For candidates like a Phillips or an Abrahams, as suggested above, such employments were more than a way, privilege, or honor of performing an essential commandment; they were a means of supplementing their own modest incomes.[25]

The trustees of the congregation who did the hiring were not only careful about whom they brought on but also monitored their performances quite scrupulously. Even as publicly renowned a figure as Gershom Mendes Seixas was not beyond the reach of the board that controlled his purse strings. One teacher-cantor, who served the synagogue before Seixas came aboard, had to put up with monthly visits to examine the "children and judge if the

Scholars under the *Hazan*'s [cantor's] care advance in their learning." When it came to kashruth, the oversight was more than just punctilious; it was downright suspicious. Occasionally, the shochet was called in on the carpet and risked suspension if he failed "to clear himself of accusations," that he had, for example, "mixed at one time *Terefa* [unkosher] and *Kasher* [kosher] tongues" or, in another instance, that he made "*Kasher* the haslet of a calf which [was] allege[d] to be *Trepha.*" With no rabbis around, trustee committees conducted the inquests themselves, going so far as to actually examine the meat in question to determine if the slaughtering was done right. Clearly, at least some within this coterie of committed Jews knew their way around or within the rubrics of this complicated part of Jewish law.[26]

In keeping with tradition, those concerned with kashruth also had to make certain that the butchers who handled slaughtered meat did more than simply custom-cut the carcasses to the satisfaction of the consumers; proper Jewish standards had to be followed. A problem was that some of the butchers were untrained Jews, others were Christians, and, worst of all, some were corrupt and would place kosher seals on products that were treif. On occasion, the municipal government assisted Shearith Israel's leaders by stepping in and punishing those who engaged in patently fraudulent activities.[27]

This elite cadre of trustees also demanded that the congregational rank and file act as rigorously as they themselves ostensibly did. As subscribers to the dictates of the halacha, the leaders were obliged not only to follow its strictures, but to see to it that other Jews behaved likewise. Having said this, it must be noted that we have few sources that ascertain for certain that those setting the rules in these communities always followed the straight and narrow in their own personal habits. Certainly, any merchant who traveled away from his home was challenged over dietary choices. What we do know is that those in charge were on the record as hard-nosed toward their fellow Jews' delinquent practices. While these policies, when enforced, effectively limited severely the number of Jews with whom the devout associated — such narrowness was a threat to communal continuity — still they persevered to uphold religious standards.

When it came to domestic kashruth, for example, Shearith Israel's officials once ordered a housewife to "properly cleanse all her spoons, plates and all other utensils used in the house, otherwise to be looked upon as a *Treffa* [*sic*] house." They warned that if she failed to comply, the punctilious members of the community, with whom she seemingly wished to associate, would not dine in her home. In another draconian case, a member who was a candidate for hazan was placed on congregational "trial" for being observed eating in a "trepha house." Fortunately for the defendant he was able to convince his judges that "whenever he ate at [that otherwise unkosher home], everything was prepared for him as it ought to be."[28]

On the question of Sabbath observance, synagogues in America had strict regulations for threatening or punishing public miscreants. In the strongest-worded statement, Shearith Israel, in 1757, admonished members whom they called "Sinners of Israel" that "brethren [who] . . . do dayly [sic] violate the principles of our holy religion, such as Trading on the Sabath [sic], Eating of forbidden Meats and other heinous crimes . . . will not be deemed a member of our congregation, have none of the Mitzote [mitzvoth] of the Sinagoge Confered [sic] on him and when Dead will not be buried according to the manner of our brethren." In its first synagogue constitution, Mikveh Israel made it clear that "if it is known that a person has desecrated the Sabbath, that person has no right to receive a religious courtesy in the synagogue." Some sort of "sentence" would be imposed on him. Charleston's Beth Elohim's regulations prescribed that "any person or persons publicly violating the Sabbath, or other sacred days, shall be deprived of every privilege of the Synagogue and the services of its officers." "Fines and penalties" for these misdeeds would be assessed. Savannah's Mickva Israel's regulations rules were almost identical. There it was written that anyone "who shall violate the Sabbath or holydays . . . shall be deprived of every honor in the synagogue until he . . . make such concessions as may appear satisfactory." Reportedly, in that Georgian community, those accused of religious wrongdoings were hard pressed to prove their innocence.[29]

For example, in 1792, Isaac Polack felt the long, heavy hands of synagogue strictures when, based on "information . . . that contrary to the law of God and the rules of the congregation" he kept his "store open on the Sabbath," Polack was summarily summoned to appear before the Mickva Israel board "to show cause, if any you have, why the 12th rule of this congregation" — regarding punishment for Sabbath desecration — "should not be put in force against you." It was not uncommon for rumors or allegations of Sabbath violations to be reported to synagogue leaders. Anxious to stay within the good graces of these officials, Polack appeared for his hearing and explained that while his store was indeed open on Saturday, a gentile manned his business establishment; another example of a Shabbes Goy in early America. The employee was on site to receive goods that had been sent initially "to his [Polack's] home without his knowledge." Happily for Polack, his method of living within the Jewish system without injuring his commercial enterprise was ultimately adjudged satisfactory.[30]

These stiff rules, of course, had absolutely no impact upon those resolute transgressors who did not feel any calls — however attenuated — of Jewish tradition. For example, these Jews may not have cared about whether the punctilious felt comfortable eating in their homes. They certainly would never have submitted to a committee in their kitchen. But very few early American Jews failed to experience some tugs toward all that the synagogue and their Jewish pasts stood for, especially at meaningful life-cycle moments or at special times during the Jewish year. Often the more devout did not notice or countenance their Jewish co-religionists' episodes of reverence toward ancestral traditions. Rebecca Samuel, for one, who lived during the early 1790s in Petersburg, Virginia, did not appreciate the residual observances — albeit minimal and seasonal — of her Jewish neighbors. In her town, she believed "Jewishness is pushed aside [by the] . . . ten or twelve Jews [who are] . . . not worthy to be called Jews." They do not know, she complained, "what the Sabbath and holidays are. On the Sabbath all the Jewish shops are open as they do during the whole week." But in her dissatisfaction, she missed the power the High Holidays held over them. By her own account, "on Rosh ha-Shanah and on Yom Kippur the people *worshipped*," even if, to her great consternation, they did so without a Torah scroll — they probably read the portion of the Law from a printed Bible — and "not one of them wore a *tallit*, except her husband, Hyman and one other man." For the rest, praying in precisely the appropriate way was not nearly as important as observing the holidays together. Samuel's answer to what she understood as religious deprivation was to get out of town and to migrate to Charleston where she could live among like-minded folks. In any event, it is reasonable to assume that the Jews she left behind would not have liked to be deemed unworthy of being counted as Jews at those times when they felt close to the synagogue.[31]

Other Jews who did more than their level best to follow the rules when at home, but faced dilemmas when traveling for business, probably chafed more strongly when lay religious authorities ostensibly counted them out. In 1748, nine years before Shearith Israel came down hard on their "Sinners of Israel" who ate "forbidden meats," Peter Kalm, a Swedish visitor to New York, described a situation that may have eventually provoked the trustees to move against transgressors. Kalm was reportedly told "by several men of credit, that many of them (especially among the young Jews) when traveling, did not make the least difficulty about eating this or any other meat that was put before them." Perhaps, some of these eighteenth-century traveling salesmen drew the line for themselves when it came to pork products even as they relished other treif delicacies. We do know that one Jewish fur trader out of Lancaster, Pennsylvania, reportedly abstained from bacon but was so enamored of barbecued turtle that he divined — incorrectly — that such a dish must be kosher.

However, the Kalm account also suggested that when back in New York, these same types of Jews were scrupulous in following the laws of the Sabbath and kashruth. Incidentally, the Lancaster turtle-epicurean displayed similar strict religious values when he was home. He seems to have even once allowed that "for a family to be remote from . . . [Jewish] society is shocking." In any event, those who "never boiled any meat in Saturday" and who "commonly ate no pork" could not have been content to be judged as outsiders for their malfeasances away from home.[32]

Episodic connectedness to synagogue life was also not totally lost even upon some Jews who married non-Jews. Congregational regulations came down hardest on them. To synagogue leaders, these people were the most grievous of miscreants, worse offenders of the halacha than even Sabbath workers and treif eaters. They not only transgressed cardinal Jewish laws but through their exogamous choices endangered the very continuity of the community; there was such a small marriage pool to begin with. Yet within that group of deviants, there were those who occasionally wanted to avail themselves of what the synagogue had to offer. For example, in the small town of Norwalk, Connecticut, the merchant Michael Judah wedded Martha Raymond, a Christian, but still felt attached enough to the Shearith Israel community that he left some money in his estate "to the Sinagouge in Newyork." Perhaps he was grateful that its mohel, Abraham I. Abrahams, had circumcised his son. At least through this essential act, Judah still defined himself and, prospectively, his son, as within the Jewish fold. Or perhaps Judah felt indebted to the congregation for its largesse in lending him some money when he had been just starting out.[33]

David Franks felt similar soft spots in his heart for organized Jewish life — in his case, Philadelphia's Mikveh Israel — even if he too had married out. Franks was the scion of one of the most famous and articulate early American Jewish families. His father, Jacob, was a wealthy New York merchant who sat high up within Shearith Israel's leadership. Franks's mother, Abigail, was deeply committed to maintaining traditional Jewish practices as she and Jacob moved comfortably within the elite echelons of local general society. Abigail was sure to instruct her children both to recite their daily prayers and to scrupulously avoid eating "anything . . . unless it be bread & butter . . . where there is the least doubt of things not done after our strict Judicall [sic] Method." However, to their great chagrin and embarrassment, some of their children departed sharply from their parents' religious paths. Two of them intermarried, and the other seven never married at all, which also could not have gladdened the hearts of the parents. In the most celebrated scandal of its time, their daughter, Phila, wed New York notable Oliver Delancey and subsequently dissociated herself from the Jewish community.[34]

David, too, found a Christian life partner, Margaret Evans. However, upon relocation to the City of Brotherly Love, he not only maintained a close business relationship with a relative, Nathan Levy — a leader of Mikveh Israel — but as Levy's executor, made sure to direct monies to the synagogue. In a subsequent communal dispute over the ownership of the cemetery, he testified in support of the congregation's claims. Franks also maintained an intriguing, supportive relationship with his parents' home congregation. In 1769, it was recorded that "he wou'd pay the Sedaka [charity], five Pounds Annually, exclusive of the offering he may make in the Synagogue." That report does suggest that although as an intermarried Jew he was denied the right to be called to the Torah, he wanted to contribute at the time when the Law was read. Though adjudged an outsider, David Franks nonetheless showed through his philanthropy that he wished to be part of congregational life.

Franks's connectedness may have had much to do with his gentile wife's attitudes toward her husband's faith. She was both knowledgeable of, and respectful toward, Jewish tradition. When her daughter Rebecca was born, she recorded the blessed event in her family Bible as having taken place on Good Friday and Purim. So disposed, we can surmise that she did not object to David's continued fraternal relationships with more committed Jews. Here, very likely, was a classic case of an intermarried Jew who was not so much running away from his ancestral faith as running into the arms of a beloved Christian.[35]

Given these undeniable proclivities — so many Jews who transgressed the halacha to lesser or greater extents still sought the synagogue and certainly saw themselves as Jews — ultimately only the most doctrinal of congregational officials could consistently oppose some accommodations to communal realities. All others seemingly reasoned that unless the pegs of the communal tent were loosened somewhat, it would not long continue to stand. By the 1790s, for example, Shearith Israel determined that it was enough of a punishment to deny Torah honors or "or any other Mitzva or be eligible to any office to those . . . breaking the Sabbath or any other sacred day." Denial of the most fundamental rite of burial in Jewish hallowed ground was deemed too extreme. But countenancing communal standing to intermarrieds was a far more complex and delicate matter.[36]

Early on in his adult life, Moses Nathans probably would not have agreed with any sort of lenient approach. At that point, he was aggressively antagonistic toward Sabbath desecrators, going so far as to inform upon an acquaintance whom he publicly accused of smoking in a coffeehouse on a Saturday. There, in very strictly defining the halachic obligation to see to it that those around him acted properly, he perhaps risked making an enemy of an erstwhile associate. Subsequently, he was part of a congregational committee at Philadelphia's Mikveh Israel that ruled against granting full religious burial rights in a special case involving an intermarried Jew. In this complicated matter, a year before his death the transgressor, Benjamin Moses Clava, had publicly confessed — reciting the formulaic *viddui* in anticipation of his passing — even as he continued to live with his Christian wife until his demise. However, in later years, Nathans's hard-line attitude changed dramatically when he himself consorted with a Christian woman who bore him a son. Nathans then asked that the cantor of Philadelphia's Mikveh Israel to circumcise the child. When, in 1790, Nathans petitioned for this accommodation, notwithstanding his evident transgression, this former synagogue leader found that at least one of his erstwhile colleagues, Manuel Josephson, stood strongly against him. Josephson also was undeniably none too pleased with another consequence of the shifting trends in Nathan's lifestyle. Three years later, in 1793, Nathan's petitioned the synagogue to approve the conversion and sanctify his subsequent marriage to his mistress.[37]

If Josephson stood his religious grounds — and there is every indication that he would do just that — he would have continued to stridently opposed Nathan's requests. Josephson had come to Philadelphia from New York during the Revolutionary War possessed of a synagogue tradition that he helped foster as a *parnass* [member of the presidium] at Shearith Israel that forbade admission of, and marriage to, proselytes. While the terse synagogue minutes do not elaborate on why Josephson and his fellows would not be inclusive — the minutes only indicate that applicants were turned down — it is reasonable to project that two interrelated problems provoked their opposition. There was no established rabbinical court in America to ascertain the sincerity of the petitioner's intentions. Determining what constitutes a conversion of conviction is particularly complicated when a marriage is in the foreground. Questions have to be asked as to whether the proselyte is truly dedicated to the Jewish faith or is only enamored of a potential Jewish spouse. Strict constructionists of the halacha have, thus, been reticent to countenance most conversions in a marriage encounter. The closest American Jews then had to a recognized *beth-din*, constituted to make these difficult calls, were ad hoc congregational committees of the most learned and observant Jews around. Josephson was invariably included in these decision-making entities. Moreover, Shearith Israel's leaders also had to have wondered what sort of message "letting down the bars" would send to other Jews in a social environment where, as previously noted, the Jewish marriage pool was very small indeed.[38]

Mikveh Israel's hierarchy was uncertain about whether to emulate New York's stance or to grant Nathans' desires. After all, he was a respected and affluent member; as of 1780, he was the fifth-richest Jew in town with property valued in excess of £39,000, who, in all other matters, "does keep up as far as we know to our rules and contributes toward the support of our congregation." So conflicted, they turned to the London rabbinical court for advice. The issue was a "Business of importance to Jewdaism [*sic*]," they wrote, and "there was no Haham [rabbinic leader] or Beth Din in any congregation on this continent." It is not known if the London tribunal answered this question and if so, what was its decision. What is certain is that in 1794, a year after Nathan's tendered his application, Mikveh Israel's records indicate that he and his former mistress were married under congregational auspices, undoubtedly to Josephson's consternation.[39]

Just a few years earlier, Mordecai M. Mordecai's comparable change of religious heart had also brought him into conflict with the unyielding Josephson. Not unlike the youthful Nathans, in 1782 Mordecai had showed a hard side when he informed the Philadelphia synagogue, based on a questionable hearsay report, that a fellow Jew, "Ezekiel Levy, contrary to our laws, had shaved on a Sabbath in Baltimore." Interestingly enough, Mordecai was not exercised about the shaving itself, which is in its own right a violation of rabbinic law. But then again, from portraits of early American Jewish worthies, it is evident that even the most observant of contemporary Jews — Josephson included — honored this regulation in the abuse. In any event, scant years later, in 1785, Mordecai began to manifest a more lenient or understanding side. Though surely not intermarried like Nathans, Mordecai showed abundant sensitivities toward those who had found spouses who were non-Jewish. The positions he took and the ways in which he acted upon them raised the hackles of Josephson and his tightly doctrinaire confreres at the helm of Mikveh Israel.[40]

The first case involved his alleged performance of a Jewish marriage ceremony sanctifying his niece's union with a non-Jew. The couple had been wed previously in a Christian ceremony to the great consternation and damnation of the bride's father. Hoping against hope to bring some degree of peace within the now distraught Jewish family, the girl's mother brought Mordecai, "the man much learned in Jewish law," into the picture and to their home in Easton, Pennsylvania. Now on the scene, Mordecai reportedly conducted the Jewish rites. Most significantly, there was no indication that Matthew Pettigrew, the groom, had converted or was interested in becoming a Jew. The most Pettigrew might have done was "to affirm in what is stated therein" in the Jewish marriage contract regarding his obligations to his wife under Jewish law. When Josephson and other Mikveh Israel officials got wind of these highly questionable actions, Mordecai was subjected to a congregational trial.

Mordecai vociferously denied the allegations and asserted that no such nuptial proceedings had ever taken place. While he was at it, the defendant upbraided his judges as "not sufficiently qualified scholars," excoriated his relative Barnet Levy, who had testified against him, as an impermissible witness because "he defiles the Sabbath and eats treif foods aside from many other character shortcomings," even as Mordecai generally characterized the inquest as an "inquisition." While the historical record is hazy about whether Mordecai actually took Jewish law into his own hands and played loose and fast with its teachings, from his actions just a year later, it is certain that his sympathies were with embracing the intermarried couple.[41]

In 1785, Mordecai reentered the fray against Josephson et al. when he acted on his own to provide an intermarried Jew with a proper Jewish burial. This was the previously noted incident in which Moses Nathans, while still a

Figure 1.1. A beardless Manuel Josephson (1729–1796).
Courtesy of The Jacob Rader Marcus Center of the American
Jewish Archives.

member in good faith, had agreed with Josephson and his colleagues to have Benjamin Moses Clava buried "in a corner of the *Beth Hahayim* [cemetery] without ritual ablution, without shrouds and without funeral rites." Through this decision an implicit, if not explicit, warning was tendered — it was hoped — "to every scofflaw who marries a gentile women," a ruling that was to "remain in effect for future generations."

Disregarding this decision, Mordecai did what he believed was right. He and some of his friends, a group whom Josephson characterized as "heedless," "impudent," "irreverent," or "light-minded people," buried the deceased as a full-fledged co-religionist.

Josephson was outraged that a fellow and otherwise pious Jew, like Mordecai, would ignore a synagogue ruling that he perceived reflected what the Torah taught. But even beyond that patent abuse, what his former compatriot had done — in Josephson's view — vitiated the message that those who upheld the commandments wanted to send to those in the community who saw themselves bound to the halacha. Leaders like Josephson were determined to assert the authority of Jewish law in a libertine America where "evil people pay no heed and come to the synagogue, because according to the law of the land they cannot be excluded." Facing the unhappy fact that "the congregation here has no power to discipline anyone except for the minor punishment of excluding them from a ritual quorum," when they had the chance to push their point — as in the burial case — "the need is great to make an impression on the public . . . to close the breach as much as possible." But, to their great chagrin, the Mordecai group had undermined their effort to pressure communal conformity, if only on the most fundamental level.

Josephson's frustration was articulated in a letter that he helped write to Rabbi Saul Loewenstamm of Amsterdam,[42] seeking support for this position. We do not know how the distinguished Western European rabbi responded to this request for backing. What is evident is that when the unyielding and influential Josephson died in 1798, there were few congregational colleagues prepared to rise up his fallen standard. At the time of his passing, the old rules were still in effect at Mikveh Israel. The synagogue's second constitution continued to provide that intermarrieds would lose their membership in the congregation, forfeiting their rights and privileges. But just seven years later, a rather vague statement was adopted, directing the hazan to gain the "consent and approbation of the Parnass" of the synagogue before converting and then marrying a Christian woman to a Jewish man. By the 1820s the synagogue was unqualifiedly accepting of all co-religionists. Thus, when hardliner Levy Phillips *proposed* a by-law — in other words, sought to reverse a trend — denying synagogue honors to "a Jew or Jewess whom marries a Christian and the son of a Jewess who is not made a Jew according to the Law of Moses," his motion was voted down.[43]

At approximately the same time, Philadelphia's and America's first Ash-kenazic congregation, Rodeph Shalom, opened the door even more widely to the out marrying in its midst. When established in 1795 — as the German Hebrew Society — and incorporated in 1802, this new synagogue had some old-school rules regarding observance. For example, its semiprofessional cantor and ritual slaughterer, who also owned a clothes store, was rigorously monitored. Once, he was brought up on charges of incompetence, but was ultimately exonerated. More importantly, on the crucial question of burial accommodations for intermarried couples, the synagogue leadership in 1811 made its position abundantly clear when it denied permission to a woman to have her "only son who had died" interred "in accordance with the Jewish rite in the congregational cemetery . . . because she had not married in accordance with the law of Moses and of Israel." The commit-tee's terse, harsh conclusion said it all: "we could not give our consent that such a son be buried in our cemetery." Fifteen years later, the congregation reiterated its stance, albeit with one remarkable caveat. It then resolved "that all subscribers except Aaron Dropsie who may have married, or who may in the future marry contrary to the Jewish Rites, shall not have, nor be entitled to any honors or privileges in our synagogue." The synagogue's resolution does not specify why this most affluent of members was given special consideration, but it has been suggested that class and financial considerations were involved in this special case. However, Rodeph Shalom did not countenance Aaron's young son, Moses Aaron Dropsie, being granted a Jewish education — after all he was the child of a Christian woman — until he reached the age of informed consent and personally converted to Judaism. As it turns it out, Moses A. Dropsie did precisely that — he stud-ied assiduously with Rev. Isaac Leeser, Philadelphia's most outstanding re-ligious leader of his time — and became both an observant Jew and a sup-porter of his mentor's many Jewish religious and educational initiatives.[44]

In 1828, three years after Rodeph Shalom nodded affirmatively toward the Dropsie family, it determined that all prior rules regarding excluding the inter-married "be rescinded and that all persons belonging to the Congregation should be entitled to all the privileges and honors customary . . . provided they train their children according to the law of Israel and follow the law of circum-cision and other Jewish rites." In opting for this lenient, accepting policy, synagogue officials may have wittingly or unwittingly gone beyond what Jewish law permitted. Nowhere within that declaration was there a requirement that Christian mothers be themselves converted to the Jewish faith.[45]

During these years other, and very different, sets of social circumstances that arose within their own core constituencies caused synagogue leaders to reconsider another thorny question: were their long-standing, man-made synagogue rules that had no explicit status one way or another within Jewish law as inviolate as the halacha?

For example, though the halacha provided that women were to sit in their own section during services, sequestered from men, was there any reason why women could not be provided with unobstructed sight lines to observe the rituals that the men performed? While rarely accorded membership status—they belonged in the synagogue as part of their fathers' or husbands' privileges—wives, mothers, and daughters attended public prayer services in significant numbers, sometimes more frequently than men. This phenomenon in America was a remarkable sociological change from the European past, where women very often did not attend services at all.[46]

But in the United States, partially as a reflection of their personal piety and partly to emulate their Protestant sisters, Jewish women went to the synagogue in significant numbers. Rebecca Gratz, one of Philadelphia's most involved and articulate Jewish women of the early nineteenth century, described the socioreligious scene at Mikveh Israel this way: "We all go Friday evening as well as on Saturday morning — the gallery is as well filled as the other portion of the house." What she failed to note in this letter to her brother was that when women arrived at services, there were not enough chairs in the balcony available for them. These women often battled among themselves over who got the available or best seats in the house. Even those who were seated could not have been satisfied in being unable to watch the activities below them in the men's section of the sanctuary.[47]

While some dissenting voices were heard within the men's congregational board rooms about the religious implications of women observing the proceedings so closely—and even more to the point of men watching women watching them during services when their focus was supposed to be on prayers—suitable accommodations were made particularly as synagogues moved to new buildings. Although the sources are silent as to whether women pushed for amelioration of this unhappy situation, several of that era's synagogues made architectural adjustments, and the "open gallery" came into vogue. These moves seem less connected to male sensitivity to female religious issues and more to the leaders' projection that Jews would look bad in the eyes of Christians who might happen by and witness Jews, as one visitor put it, relegating their women "of whom some were very pretty, stood up in the gallery like a hen coop." In churches of the time, balcony seats were the province the indigent, including indentured servants or blacks. The styles of the new buildings, whether in New York, Newport, or Charleston, also reflected the congregation's hiring of gentile architects to envision their edifices. These professionals were engaged as part of a Jewish strategy to project style and class to the general community around them. The Christians, who did the drawings, conceptualized Jewish space along the lines of the American churches that they were familiar with and attended.[48]

During this same time period, in 1825 to be exact, another dissatisfied group rallied at Shearith Israel to make its leaders more responsive to the feelings of Jews who shared the trustees' ostensible strict religious values, but who felt disenfranchised within the stately congregation's social and procedural structures. Their explicit request was simple enough and at face value was not particularly controversial. They merely asked for "the use of our place of worship and the *Sephorim* [Torah scrolls to read the weekly portion of the Law] on the Sabbath mornings during the summer months" and they even reassured the "officers" that any charity monies pledged during their devotions would "be given to the clerk of the congregation and be added to the usual bills."[49]

Behind this initial call, however, was a demand for a more populist and egalitarian service for men with a heavy emphasis on "the study of our Holy Law and the better to extend a knowledge of its divine precepts, ceremonies, and worship among our brethren generally and the enquiring youth in particular." In the petitioners' opinion, the search for personal honor and status had obscured the holy mission of creating a "dwelling of the Living God." In their view, a congregation of committed Jews did not need an entrenched leadership to "create distinctions" — so often based on wealth and lineage — as "each member [could] fulfill the duties [of ritual life] in rotation, having no Parnass or Hazan." Lurking not far removed from the scene was also an implicit critique of the leniency then being shown toward transgressors of the halacha within the congregation; the dissidents' sense was again that the synagogue was losing its way. These spoken and underlying issues all came out after the unhappy young people were denied the chance to debate their fundamental and fundamentalist grievances. The board, unwilling to even begin to countenance moves that smacked of disunity within their midst and undermining of their authority, summarily "resolved unanimously . . . that this [initial request] can not be granted." For those resolved to maintain their synagogue's traditions, just the idea of an alternate service threatened to "destroy the well known and established rules and customs of our ancestors as have been practices for upwards of one hundred years past."[50]

Given short shrift, the petitioners quickly made their own institutional statement, founding the Chevra Chinuch Nearim [Society for the Education of Youngsters] to promote not only Jewish training for young people, but also to provide a place where every man could study, pray, and garner synagogue honors and leadership status, so long as they upheld the commandments. It would be a society restricted to the pious alone. "No person," its constitution dictated, "can be a member . . . unless he strictly adheres to our religion as regards the observance of our holy Sabbath and holidays." An additional "requisite" was that the fellow "possesses a good moral character." Soon, this Society would coalesce into Congregation B'nai Jeshurun, the city's second congregation.[51]

While Shearith Israel's officials could not have been happy with these affronts to their prerogatives, they had to have respected the religious values of these dissidents. That was not the case, however, in Charleston, where the leaders of Beth Elohim just a year earlier in 1824 had faced down their own protesters. In this encounter, it was a group of dissenters whose personal religious practices were questionable that pushed for religious reforms of the Orthodox synagogue ritual.

Charleston was the "blessed community of three hundred Jews" that Rebecca Samuel fled to in the early 1790s, when she had had enough of Petersburg, Virginia's lack of "Yehudishkeit" [Jewishness]. In this South Carolina city, synagogue leader Philip Cohen boasted that "the religious rites, customs and festivals of the Jews are all strictly observed." At least that was the religious lifestyle of Beth Elohim's early nineteenth-century president, Nathan Hart, who was renowned as "conspicuous for his exemplary devotion to long-established forms . . . who constantly and strenuously advocated the observance of the Ceremonial Law." While the sources again do not permit us to say for certain that every one of his brother trustees was as pious as Hart, the congregation did have the strictest of rules for conducting its services and dealing with deviants of all sorts — be they intermarried, Sabbath violators, or even proselytes, particularly if they were "people of color." That latter restriction had nothing to do with the halacha and everything to do with the racial mores of their Southern society. At that time, 87 percent of Charleston's Jews owned slaves, slightly less than the percentage of whites.[52]

In 1824, forty-seven community people — some of them paid-up members of the congregation, others in arrears, three intermarried fellows who could not qualify for membership, and mostly the younger men in town — publicly critiqued and petitioned the leadership for changes in the way those in charge managed Beth Elohim and conducted its services. The cohort's greatest concern was with the Orthodox congregation's myopia toward the religious needs of disinterested Jews — beginning, most likely with them — part of "the rising generation."[53] The dissidents clearly were up in arms over "the defects which are apparent in the present system of worship" which had contributed to "the apathy and neglect which have been manifested toward our holy religion." Here was the first case in America where Jews who led their religious lives unbridled by the halacha — the group's leader, journalist Isaac Harby, for one, was at most an infrequent attendee at synagogue — desired more than just admittance into an Orthodox synagogue. They wanted their needs and their religious values officially accommodated.[54]

In their view, the services were too long. They were conducted entirely in Hebrew, the holy language that was unintelligible to so many young people. No time was set aside for an English language discourse to explain the

Figure 1.2. Interior of K.K. Beth Elohim synagogue. 1838 by
Solomon Nunes Carvalho. Courtesy of the Jewish Heritage
Collection, Addlestone Library, College of Charleston.

weekly Torah portion to the assembled. Too much time was wasted in a noisy and often unbecoming manner when the leaders sold synagogue honors that, the petitioners asserted, brought no honor to the synagogue. Some proposed changes certainly were in no way contrary to the halacha. Jewish law permitted the cantor to repeat in the vernacular, in this case, English, "such part of the service as may be deemed necessary." A sermon or Torah discourse can be offered as an element in the service, even if historically the rabbi or lay leader did not ordinarily speak every week. Rabbinic tradition honored the idea of quiet and decorum in the synagogue.

However, in one very fundamental way, the reformers' proposal violated rabbinic tradition, auguring to bring nonhalachic, ritual practice into an American synagogue's life. They called for the shortening of the services. In doing so, Harby and his followers recognized the following communal reality: there was but a three-hour window for prayer on Saturday morning, 9 AM to 12 noon. The rest of the day may have been for work or Saturday recreation. Committed, as they surely were, that the service be "conducted with due solemnity" and needing to add new attractive elements to bring in people, they were suggesting that cuts be made in the old order of devotions. Though not specifying which prayers were to be taken out, they "recommend[ed] that the most solemn portions be retained, and everything superfluous excluded." Those "principal parts" would be read both in English and in Hebrew.[55]

Challenged on both halachic fronts and on the way they ran their synagogue, the "miscreated front among our people," as an Orthodox opponent would subsequently characterize the memorialists, were denied even a hearing on their submission. The troublemakers were told in no uncertain terms that Jewish tradition "prescribed a certain fixed mode of service established at the destruction of the second Temple." No innovations would be considered at this Orthodox congregation.[56]

But, the trustees could not prevent the insurgent members from leaving their synagogue altogether and joining with outsiders in establishing their own Reformed Society of Israelites. Perhaps on one level, some old-timers may have said to themselves, good riddance to those who did not share their religious values, even if some of the dissenters were their own sons. Others may have been chagrined about their inability to control the local religious situation. No matter, this early experiment in American Reform Judaism lasted but nine years until 1833 where a combination of social pressures from among those who wanted the young men and their families returned to the congregational fold and the departure of Harby from Charleston brought the offending minority back into Beth Elohim.[57]

Still, the victory of those who initially stood against change proved to be short-lived. Less than a decade later, in 1840, they found themselves in the congregational minority as old and new change makers both, under the leadership of Reform Hazan Gustav Poznanski, voted to install an organ in the sanctuary for use on Sabbath and holidays. This unambiguous deviant move, from a halachic perspective, drove those in town who still cherished the old-time rules out of Beth Elohim. This remnant founded Congregation Shearith Israel, literally the "Remnant of Israel." The name they chose for the new synagogue constituted their parting shot at those who now dominated the scene. Their message was that they were the only true Jews left in Charleston. However, they knew in their heart of hearts that by this time, the Orthodox synagogues that the most committed Jews once dominated were no longer alone in a religious environment that clearly was out of traditional control.[58]

## 2

## AMERICAN CHALLENGES AND
## JEWISH CHALLENGERS

Beginning in the 1820s and continuing for more than a century, European Jews were a people on the move. For some, the migration took place within their home province, from the village of their birth to the teeming, rapidly industrializing cities. One estimate of the peregrinations within Central Europe suggests that in 1840 almost all the Jews of Bavaria lived in small towns. Seventy years later, eight out of ten southern German Jews called Munich and the other large, regional cities their homes. For others on the go, the transition from traditional village to modern urban center required a change of passport as former Russian and Lithuanian Jews exchanged subject status under the tsar for the hope of citizenship in a more enlightened Germany. Still other travelers left a region whose own political status changed as northwest Poland, Poznan, fell under Prussian suzerainty from the end of the nineteenth century to the beginning of World War I. Legally these Jews were Germans even if culturally most long remained traditional in East European habits, mores, language, and religious practice.[1]

The most common of immigrant impulses, the search for a better economic life for themselves and their families, put many Jews on the road.

More footloose types, possessed of a compelling wanderlust, packed their bags and took off for the bright gaslights of the city. But more often than not, government rules hastened, when they did not dictate the decision to move. In Central European provinces like Bavaria, cynical regulations fixed the number of Jews permitted to reside in a given hamlet and limited the number of Jewish marriages allowed in a town. Facing up to their inability to even contemplate living a normal life, Jewish young men and women left their parents' homes forever. The end of their journey might be Berlin, Frankfurt, or Vienna, or even Paris or London. As the century progressed many of the disenfranchised also looked to America. Concomitantly, under the tsar's heavy hand, harsh edicts forced entire Jewish shtetl [small town] populations to pull up stakes. Those dispossessed were directed to the cities of the Pale of Settlement. While in mid-century Russo-Poland tens of thousands followed instructions, more determined types left the entire world of tsarist abuses behind them — including fear of intermittent pogroms — and looked westward to lands of freedom, including the United States.[2]

For those contemplating an onerous ocean voyage, a monumental technological improvement — the introduction in the 1850s of cheaper, safer, and quicker steamship transportation — brought the New World within reach. Now the journey, with all its encumbrances, took but ten to fourteen days, instead of six weeks on a sail ship when the winds were blowing well and on course. By 1880, America absorbed some quarter million European Jews; a polyglot mixture of Bavarians, Bohemians, Prussians — many of whom who were really Poznan Poles — and a goodly number of Russians, the vanguard of an even larger post-1881 migration.[3]

While all immigrants who ascended the gangplanks were anxious about what the future held in store for them, devout Jews on board felt an additional, spiritual trepidation about taking off to America. On his long ocean voyage from Hamburg to New York in 1847 on the two-masted brig Colibri, twenty-five year old S. E. Rosenbaum of the Bohemian village of Goltsch Jenikau wondered if he had made the right decision. His self-described "travel mania" coupled with "a longing for freedom" had propelled him first to leave his parents' home for Prague, then eventually to Lamstedt in North Germany, and ultimately to Hamburg before "the crazy thought" dawned upon him "to go to America." But this still-pious young man worried about his ability to maintain his fidelity to traditional Jewish life. While comforted somewhat through his faith that "what will happen to me in the Land of Freedom, I leave in the hands of God . . . who helped me up to now and will help me further too," he noticed that many of his fellow Jewish passengers did not share the depth of his religious values. While some immigrants did gather occasionally for a minyan — he served as the group's cantor — few of them abstained from "the bacon [that] is not for me; I prefer bread, butter and cheese." He also could not help but reminisce about how back home "young and old hurried to the shul" to observe the Jewish fast day of the 17th of Tammuz (commemorating the breaching of the walls of Jerusalem that led to the destruction of the First Temple in 586 BCE). However, "on ship, no one here" — presumably other than he — "has fasted."[4]

The hundred or so Jewish men and women who, in 1839, gathered "from the neighboring parts of the Bavarian and Saxon frontiers" to embark on their transcontinental trek felt considerably better than Rosenbaum about both their present situation and their future religious possibilities in America. They had thought through and planned well their effort not only to leave their homeland but to quickly "found a small Jewish community together in America." Toward that end, they carried on board a Torah scroll, a megillah, a shofar, and enlisted in their group "such persons as are qualified for the exercise of religious functions as slaughtering, circumcision . . . religious teachers etc." They also made "the necessary arrangements in Hamburg in advance" — perhaps stocking up with some sort of kosher provisions — "so that they may live during the voyage undisturbed in their religion." Some seven years later, in 1846, a dozen Jews from Oberdorf in Baden-Wurttemberg were similarly and confidently disposed. Encouraged by letters from "kinsmen and acquaintances who preceded them a number of years" earlier that all was more than just well in the new world, they carried with them a "Torah . . . which they solemnly consecrated" in the local synagogue "before their departure." By that time, some ships bound from Hamburg to America made it well known that "those who wish to eat kosher on the voyage" could "pay a trifle extra and get kosher meat, a separate stove, where passengers could take care of the cooking by rotation." Accommodations "were also made for other ritual needs on board ship."[5]

Reports indicate that such observant Jews made it to these shores "with their old-country piety" intact. They had their "*Shabboth* lamps . . . and on Friday evening before the beginning of the Sabbath would light them, then offer a consecrative prayer, and after that would not touch fire." There was a "congregational oven to which all who belonged brought their pots and kettles on Friday afternoon. The oven was heated, the pots placed in and the oven doors sealed with clay in order to retain their heat, and kept closed until Saturday noon, when they came to get them. The coffee for the Sabbath morning was kept hot on ashes on top of this oven." To help them through the holy day they found that seemingly omnipresent gentile assistant, the Shabbes Goy, to ignite a light or a fire when needed.[6]

If these Jews started out with the best of intentions and initially upheld their regimens of personal observances, they nonetheless quickly discovered that American challenges awaited them. In the larger, older seaboard Jewish cities, an infrastructure existed to provide the requisite kosher foods or religious ritual objects or important communal facilities such as ceme-teries and mikvehs. Their committed colonial predecessors had to seen to that. There were also Orthodox synagogues of long standing available for them to attend. However, the foreigners frequently balked at affiliation for several reasons.

As devout newcomers, fresh off the boat, they were ill attuned to Ameri-can realities and uncomfortable with the religious laxity apparent among synagogue-goers. These Jews also did not feel at ease with congregational policies that increasingly countenanced Sabbath-desecrators and even wel-comed intermarrieds. Moreover, social and economic class issues lurked right beneath and above the surface, engendering hard feelings. The immi-grants resented the often high-handed attitudes of the entrenched syn-agogue leadership. But ultimately these problems with the religious status quo were not of great moment. A solution was readily at hand although their moves destroyed the local community's already tenuous history of unity. The pious new Americans could and did march off on their own, start their own congregations, and pass synagogue legislation that reflected their re-ligious values. They could pray together in the style of Ashkenazic worship that reminded them of the way they had lived as Jews on the other side of the Atlantic. That was the complicated story line in the emergence of Congrega-tion B'nai Jeshurun in New York in 1825. Once a large town had two syn-agogues, most notably in 1820s–1840s New York, it was a relatively non-controversial matter for it to harbor many. By the end of the 1840s, the Dutch, Bohemian, English, German, Polish, and old Sephardic–Ashkenazic Jews of Shearith Israel each had their own congregations. There were then some fifteen such synagogues in the city and the future would bring many more.[7]

Of far greater, enduring concern for the punctilious was the often frus-trating question of how rigorously supervised were foodstuffs or religious articles and facilities that they required, and how well trained and scrupu-lous were the functionaries who made available essential goods and services. When the newcomers pressed on these issues, they were reminded, really to no one's surprise, that they were a minority among those with whom they resided. Those around them demonstrated little concern about correct Jewish practices.

On the question of meats, for example, very often properly slaughtered beef was sold both in Jewish butcher shops and in general markets. A con-cerned consumer had to rely upon a special seal that designated a large side of beef as kosher. However, when a gentile butcher sliced the cut down to size, he might either inadvertently or intentionally mix the kosher and non-kosher products. Such was the unhappy experience of a shopper who, in 1863, reported that "on entering the butcher's shop . . . there are several heads of cattle offered for sale, some kosher (at least marked so), others *terefah* and as long as they are not cut up we may distinguish one from another." However, it then fell on the erring shoulders of the "butcher boy [who] tells you that this or that piece, though not marked, is part of the kosher cattle." Meanwhile, "the shop is filled with . . . hogs, oysters, crabs and clams."[8]

Then there was the long-standing question of Jewish slaughterers' skills. These workers varied in their degree of expertise and commitment to doing their jobs correctly. In 1840, a London-based rabbi and shochet tendered a blanket indictment of the abilities of those who were on those boats to America. "Not even one halacha they know or understand the Hebrew language. They only study a few laws orally in the vernacular and then go overseas to become a ritual slaughterer until they die." And to make things worse, he averred, the new land is a place "with no rabbi or Talmudic scholar to supervise them."[9]

Though Rabbi Abraham Sussmann may have been somewhat overheated in his criticism of those who plied his trade in the new country, he had a point about lack of oversight in mid nineteenth-century America. By that time, the system of controls that the early congregations used in efforts to maintain rigorous standards had broken down. A century earlier, slaughters had occasionally been brought up on charges of incompetence. But now as the cities came to house not one, or two, but many congregations, each with its own designated shochet, each with its own strictures, quality control suffered. One observer of the "market" scene in Philadelphia noted that in a situation where many Jewish establishments issued their own seals, the possibility "that frauds can take place under such mismanagement is clearly apparent." "Notorious" perpetrators constantly plagued consumers.[10]

To make the situation even worse, as private entrepreneurs discovered kosher eaters, Jews and gentiles, scrupulous and corrupt, hired their own slaughterers. These employees were loyal to their bosses and may have been ready to cut corners. Such was the dismayed viewpoint of a costumer who testified in New York "that there are men seeking and obtaining employment in the above sacred office [of shochet] without any congregation being consulted, or moral qualification or capability. . . . Indeed the whole system is out of control." Another dissatisfied householder complained that "the butchers, Christians as well as Jews, are made the only judges of . . . qualifications"[11]

Some valiant efforts were made to standardize the anarchic kashruth industry. For example, New York's Association of United Hebrew Congregations Shechita Board, established in 1863, attempted to insure that slaughterers knew what they were doing to enable buyers to trust the authenticity of a kosher label. But the organization soon foundered. First, it failed to force independent butchers and abattoirs to follow its strictures. More importantly, only a minority of kosher eaters cared deeply about unquestionable standards. Others who preferred, but did not demand, punctiliously prepared meats, were reportedly "careless" or "indifferent" toward the strictures of the rabbinic dietary rules. Many were content just to eat meat from kosher animals, and asked no questions about the butcher's halachic expertise. Others within the community cared not a wit about kosher laws, except perhaps to disdain pork products. The obliviousness of most Jewish customers included myopia toward the irreligious behavior of some slaughterers themselves. "People continued to buy from their favorite butchers whether Jew or gentile, licensed or unscrupulous, including whom kept their shops open on the Sabbath." One offender, it was said, tried to finesse the halacha with the stratagem of hiring a Shabbes Goy. This Jew was "seen by his customers reading his prayers in a back room and although he will not cut the meat himself he gives directions to his man to do so." Clearly unimpressed with that butcher's cutting corners with the Sabbath rules, the association was eventually moved to say "very plainly rather buy of a Christian who sells meat killed by an authorized shochet, and bearing his seals, than of a Jew who violates the Sabbath." Although they called upon "our congregations . . . [to] again take action on this question," deep down they knew the ultimate source of the endemic problem: the sociology and economics of kashruth did not favor the strictly observant who could not impose their religious wills on anyone.[12]

All was also less than well for the punctilious when it came to having at hand rigorously supervised seasonal ritual objects and special Sabbath and holiday foodstuffs. Here too, a dedicated minority found itself very much alone in its anxieties over whether the phylacteries that they donned or the mezuzahs that adorned their doors or the citrons that they purchased for the harvest festival of Succoth or California wines for the Sabbath and holiday table were 100 percent kosher. For all their impressive developments, even the established seaboard cities were miles, if not a continent, away from international centers of Jewish life or American west coast wineries. There were always reports filtering into the communities that this or that imported object or product was somehow or somewhat suspect. Questions even arose when a local technological innovation that augured to make the performance of a central and popular commandment easier not only for them, but for all Jews who wanted this product, came to the fore.[13]

A large proportion of American Jews — both then and now — observe the mitzvah of eating matzah on Passover with care, if not with relish. Many may not necessarily abstain totally from leaven during that eight-day period. Still, that gastronomic tradition looms large in their consciousness even as the foodstuff lays low in their digestive tracts. When machine-baked matzah were introduced in New York in the 1840s, that most basic Passover product became more readily available and cheaper. Most Jews did not debate whether these matzahs were up to the strictest halachic standards. But the more pious were concerned. Lay leaders of the B'nai Jeshurun congregation wrote to British Chief Rabbi Nathan Adler — they included in their briefs diagrams of the machinery — to ascertain its permissibility. Adler approved of the new method per se. The issue for him, as for those who followed his ruling, was whether proper ongoing supervision could be assured.[14]

As the middle decades of the nineteenth century progressed, those who cared, particularly those fortunate enough to reside in the major Eastern cities, could turn to sage religious guides to answer their questions about the detailed matters of observance and religious status. In those established areas, the 1840s–1850s were years of transition as a small group of quite learned immigrant Orthodox rabbis complemented, and then superseded, the last of the prominent cantors cum rabbis who previously had assisted the observant American crowd. Most notably, Reverend Isaac Leeser, spiritual leader of Philadelphia's Mikveh Israel, exerted influence from the time of his arrival in Philadelphia in 1829. Late of Westphalia, Germany, by way of Richmond, Virginia, Leeser would earn national renown, most notably through his monthly *The Occident and American Jewish Advocate,* for his efforts to keep wavering American Jews attached to Orthodox ways. But he was also attuned to the needs of a core observant constituency within his local bailiwick and constantly spoke out about the seemingly endless abuses of the kashruth industry. In 1867, for example, he went after those "who kill cattle and poultry for the use of Israelites who violate the Sabbath," admonishing his community to stay clear of those who "so offend."[15]

Abraham Rice, who arrived in America from Zell, Germany in 1840 as this country's first ordained rabbi, was even more focused and perturbed about the problems that the pious faced. From his perch in Baltimore, he not only rendered a wide variety of decisions from rulings on the kashruth of imported French cooking oil, to how to properly install plumbing in a mikveh, to that seemingly perpetual question of whether an uncircumcised child of an intermarried couple could be buried in a Jewish cemetery. He and his supporters routinely defined who was a Jew very strictly. He also was totally in character when he publicly lamented the misdeeds of the unscrupulous who "cause Israel to eat that which dieth of itself." Unkosher meats, the works of these offenders of the faith, he said, are "deeds of evil and corruption in their hands."[16]

Rice's colleague in the Orthodox rabbinate, Bernard Illowy, migrated to this country from Kolin, Bohemia in the early 1850s and secured temporary teaching and preaching posts at two New York synagogues, beginning a peripatetic American career that would take him over close to twenty years to other jobs in Philadelphia, Baltimore, and Syracuse and to pulpits as far south as New Orleans and to the larger midwestern city of St. Louis. Notwithstanding his almost constant movement, the faithful in his several towns looked to him for guidance on issues ranging from kashruth to proper cemetery practices. In one decision suggestive of endemic American problems, he attempted to address the Sabbath problem among local butchers through a decree prohibiting slaughtering on Friday afternoon out of fear that the meat would be put up for sale on Saturday.[17]

While congregants respected their rabbis' and cantors' knowledge and authority in purely religious realms, this did not mean these leaders had more than the most tenuous power over their undisciplined communities. Quite the contrary, and Orthodox rabbis were hardly alone as all American Jewish clergy labored under controlling synagogue boards and disgruntled members. Rabbi Max Lilienthal reported back to Germany in 1848 that in the United States, congregations of all stripes quickly "get tired" of their religious officials who are given but one-year positions and then "must submit to a new election every year." Inevitably, Lilienthal observed, in these "extremely precarious" positions, the "functionaries . . . acquire enemies" that lead to tensions and often firings. He advised those considering Jewish posts in America to think twice before "exchang[ing] a permanent position in their fatherland for a precarious annual position here."[18]

Lilienthal knew what he was talking about. In his first rabbinical stint in New York, where he served three Orthodox synagogues simultaneously, he ended up discharged for failure to respond to a congregant's complaint and for unspecified insults to the board of trustees. He was let go despite the fact that in his three years in their pulpits, he had greatly advanced the possibilities for the Jews around him to observe the commandments. He had organized a Talmud study group, took his turn trying to bring order to the kashruth industry, and attempted to address the knotty question of *halitza*, biblical levirate marriage. The rabbi even proposed the establishment of a rabbinical court for the out-of-control country. Still, Lilienthal remained an employee who could be fired summarily, even by those who would defer to him reverently when it came to strictly halachic issues.[19]

Although the unhappy rabbi did not identify the influences that contributed to his and his colleagues' dilemmas, most likely their congregants had learned how to disrespect the clergy by taking cues from those who headed up America's longest-standing synagogues as well as from Protestant churchgoing neighbors. In both religious "traditions" in the United States, the trustees strictly controlled the purse strings of their spiritual leaders and otherwise showed them who the boss was. In all events, those Jewish laymen in charge showed sure signs of assuming American values in these power relationships when they unabashedly treated a religious authority as just another person on the payroll. In the Old World, congregants were never so contemptuous of their rabbis.[20]

Sometimes, rabbis had themselves to blame if they failed to maintain communal respect even in the circumscribed ritual realms where they were the acknowledged leaders. In-fighting over who was more correct in halachic decision making lowered their prestige and raised questions about the viability of the halacha in America. For example, beginning in the 1850s, the earliest rabbis from the tsarist empire arrived in New York, attracted their own committed coteries, and soon began battling among themselves over slaughtering procedures. In the most dramatic if convoluted case, Rabbi Joseph Moshe Aaronsohn of Salant, Poland took on the equally learned Rabbi Judah Mittleman of Lvov and Warsaw for his staunch support of shochet Aaron Zvi Friedman's practices and behaviors. In time, Rabbi Joseph Ash of Semyavich, Russo-Poland joined in on Aaronsohn's side and against Mittleman. Both groups of antagonists corresponded with European sages to support their positions. Rabbi Mittleman received letters of approbation from the rabbis of his hometown of Lemberg. Aaronsohn communicated with five distinguished Polish and Russian Jewish scholars and the head of the beth-din of Jerusalem, Rabbi Samuel Salant, who hailed from Aaronsohn's place of birth. Ongoing controversies splintered the ranks of those who cared the most about Jewish law within the country's city with the largest Jewish population.[21]

For all of the challenges devout Jews faced back east in maintaining their traditional religious practices, their problems paled in difficulty to those who ventured out west and took part in this country's manifest-destiny adventure during the middle decades of the nineteenth century. The American Jewish population spiked substantially and its demography changed dramatically in the years that preceded the Civil War. From a small Atlantic enclave of perhaps 3,000 souls in 1820, the national community grew to approximately 150,000 some four decades later. While New York maintained its place as the largest American Jewish city — it had captured that title from Charleston in the early nineteenth century — by 1861 more Jews lived west of the seaboard than on the east coast. Moving out west did not only mean trekking out well beyond the Mississippi River. Jewish settlements could be found all over the widths of New York State and Pennsylvania on to Ohio and into Indiana, Michigan, and Illinois. Road building facilitated migration, as did the network of canals that was constructed in Erie-Ohio, Illinois, Michigan, and Indiana. Most important, the rise of east–west railroad lines from the mid 1820s to the 1850s hastened transportation. Seemingly every town and certainly every growing city on the commercial road toward California had its share of pioneer Jews. In the Golden State, Jews were among the hardy and adventurous folks caught up in the excitement and sweep of the late-1840s gold rush, positioning San Francisco as the largest early far-western Jewish community. During this time period, Jews could be found in more than 1,200 localities in thirty-seven states and territories coast to coast, although, again, urban destinations rather than rural territories or the very transient mining camps of the time attracted the overwhelming majority of Jews.[22]

Jewish migration to middle and western America continued unabated after the Civil War as the national Jewish population approached one-quarter million in 1880. By 1878, San Francisco, with its 16,000 Jewish inhabitants, outstripped all American Jewish cities other than New York. Chicago was home to as many co-religionists as Baltimore. Cincinnati matched up well with Philadelphia. St. Louis had almost as many Jews as Boston. In the last two decades of the nineteenth century, there were no fewer than twenty-six cities — east and west of the Alleghenies, and north and south of the Mason-Dixon line — that could boast of Jewish populations of more than 1,000. There was also a place for small-town Jews in this mix. One well-reasoned estimate has it that there were "134 cities and towns in the U.S. with Jewish communities of at least 100, but less than 1,000 in the late 1870s."[23]

In almost all places and cases, an immigrant Central European peddler was the first Jew to appear in a frontier town. He was that courageous fellow who after amassing just enough capital back east, through pluck or from relatives' help to start him on his way, brought consumer goods to the hinterlands and developed a clientele. The tenderfoot relied "upon the advice of those who were here before him," was "supplied with 'Yankee notions,'" and a wholesaler "instructed [him on] what to call things and how to offer them for sale." As the small-time entrepreneur progressed economically, he could benefit from the services of a one- or two-horse wagon. Those just starting out carried their packs on their backs and persevered daily and mightily. In time, such a person might specialize in servicing customers for luxury needs, supplying watches for men and jewels for their wives. Eventually, if he were successful or just stuck it out over the long haul, this businessman would settle down in town or be among the first residents in an outpost, perhaps becoming that locale's first dry goods store owner. There, such entrepreneurs sought to build upon their earliest successes.[24]

Jewish peddlers struggled as they sought to rise out of poverty through the back roads of America. At least one immigrant met a tragic end on the outskirts of Lancaster, Pennsylvania, as he tried to grasp the first rung of economic advancement. In 1839, Lazarus Zellerbach, age twenty-seven or twenty-eight, a "pedlar of Dry goods, Jewelry and German Silver" who had come to America some four years earlier from Balz on the Rhine River, was accosted on a deserted roadway en route from Pittsburgh and suffered multiple lethal wounds. Many more Jews who traversed the wilds of the frontier in search of a livelihood were robbed or had very high licensing fees extorted from them in order to ply their wares. All small-time merchants had to cope with the difficulties of just making a sale as well as the loneliness and the anxiety of long-term separation from home and hearth.[25]

Perhaps in part as a coping mechanism, some of those who went out on their own kept diaries of the experience or subsequently recorded memories of their adventures and trials. Though the happy-ending conclusions of many of these documents recounting the travails of the road may be questioned, what these authors have to say about the difficulties of starting out in America possess a strong degree of verisimilitude. One veteran vendor would report on that "utterly frozen" night in Easttown on the banks of the Delaware where he found himself at the less than tender mercies of a tavern owner and patrons, some of whom made it abundantly clear that they had no use for Jews. The peddler denied his religious identity to avoid a confrontation, made his sales, and moved on. Another unhappy merchant wondered whether he was really "living" as he "plod[ed] through the remote country, uncertain as to which farmer will provide him with shelter the coming night." A dream of "fortune" back in Europe, he lamented, had led him to "depart from his home," only to find himself "in the cold and icy night, treading his lonely way through America."[26]

The peddlers' religious values also suffered amid these unsettled situations of constant movement and lack of companionship. It was not as if those who contemplated this adventurous career on the frontier had not been warned in advance. For example, as early as 1816, on the very cusp of this new period of migration, the head of Philadelphia's Mikveh Israel congregation advised a newcomer to stay back east rather than test himself in the Ohio territory. Levy Phillips warned Joseph Jonas that "in the wilds of America, and entirely among gentiles, you will forget your religion and your God."[27]

As always, there were men on the road who cared little about whether they could secure kosher food from a friendly farmer, or whether local laws and regulations put Sabbath observance in jeopardy, or if an unmarried man could someday and somewhere settle down with a Jewish wife. Jewish peddling was an almost exclusively male occupation.[28] In a distant replay of the early colonial period, the undeveloped and disorganized Jewish frontiers of this new land offered those who were so often all alone multiple scenarios for breaking with their religious pasts. Those who wanted could easily toss "religious duties and observances overboard as burdensome ballast." And many did. At least, that was the observation of Moldavian Jewish traveler, I. J. Benjamin as he surveyed and wrote about Jewish life during the late 1850s– early 1860s in the American wilderness.[29]

On the other hand, there were those who made extraordinary efforts to keep up with, even if they did not precisely follow, their ancestral traditions.

Take, for example, this almost legendary saga of two young men who were peddlers in northern Westchester County, New York, in the early 1840s who were determined to "hurry . . . to the city on a holiday to be there for the service." Starting out at 4 AM the morning of the festival "at a farm house" upstate, they hustled seven miles to Sing Sing to catch a steamboat down the Hudson. When they missed their connection by a few minutes, they had "no alternative [but] to walk" toward the city to meet up with a streetcar that would deliver them downtown. Unfortunately for these intrepid travelers, while they "tramped and tramped" toward the station, they got there only after nine o'clock PM "when the last car had left." Evidently, they would have boarded the train after sundown in violation of a holiday precept. But, no matter, they were not going to spend the holiday in Harlem, which "was then a suburb" of Manhattan. "Impelled," as they were, "by the religious fervor and devotion instilled under the parental roof" — or at least a degree of such commitments — the young men traveled by foot "the remainder of the distance which in all made fifty-six miles and in consequence, of over-exertion were compelled to take to their beds for three days."[30]

Then there were those who were deeply grieved about their inability to lead strictly observant lives amid so many environmental difficulties. From 1842 to 1843, Bavarian immigrant Abraham Kohn articulated the utter despair of a peddler who was unable to live as he would have wanted while he was in constant transit. In his classic statement penned while trekking through "the icy cold winter of New England," he confided to his diary, both about himself and "thousands" of other guilt-ridden "young strong men [who] forget their Creator . . . [who] pray neither on working day nor on the Sabbath . . . hav[ing] given up their religion for the pack that is not their backs." Ashamed that "one must profane the Sabbath, observing Sunday instead," Kohn hoped that God "knowest my thoughts . . . knowest my grief when on the Sabbath eve, I must retire to my lodging and on Saturday morning carry my pack on my back, profaning the holy day, God's gift to His people." So distressed, he prayed in "the open field" which was his "temple," that a forgiving "Father in heaven comforts me and lends me strength and courage and endurance for my sufferings."[31]

Perhaps Kohn derived some additional consolation — beyond what God might offer him — when he came across other peddlers who bemoaned similar religious fates. Once, for example, he met up with a fellow immigrant named Marx, an acquaintance from Kohn's home region in Bavaria, who "in pursuit of [his] daily bread" was "compelled to profane [the] Holy Sabbath." Marx reportedly told Kohn mournfully that he was able to "observe the Sabbath less than ten times" in three years in the new country. Knowledge of what Marx suffered through only caused his interlocutor to wonder whether "this is the cherished liberty of America."[32]

Ultimately Kohn, Marx and many other Jews who were isolated just did their level best to keep the commandments whenever and wherever they could. At points where even the smallest groups of merchants found themselves together, they tried to spend the Sabbath as a community at rest. The fellow who knew the most about the procedures of Jewish law led the prayers. There is also a recorded case of a peddlers' cemetery where colleagues took care of that most fundamental and nonreciprocal act of lovingkindness. It was the first Jewish institution in a small town in Mississippi.[33]

These Jews' desires to observe Jewish traditions, again as conditions allowed, became even more apparent when the successful ones set up stores and shops in small towns. There were constant calls sent back east, seemingly from everywhere across the country, for personal and communal religious needs. Jews needed the services of a mohel for their infant sons. In some cases, that scion was the blessed culmination of a relationship that began as a chance encounter between an established entrepreneur's daughter and a peddler who was taken in "after a week's work for the Sabbath." By welcoming in a road-weary guest, parents not only fulfilled the mitzvah of hospitality toward the wayfarer but also hopefully set the table for their child marrying a fellow Jew.[34]

In other cases, children were the joyous result of men and women reuniting after long absences when a fledgling merchant was able to bring his wife to the town where he had set up shop. In 1854, for example, a year after her husband Joseph had set off for St. Paul, Minnesota, Amelia Ullmann faithfully followed him to the upper Midwest. There, as "a devoted mother," she endured "the inconveniences and miseries . . . in my efforts to be my duty." She would report to her diary that "every drop of water used had to be carried across the prairie from a well in a livery stable. . . . My child was ill much of the time and from lack of proper nourishment; for good, wholesome food was difficult to obtain. Fresh vegetable[s] and fruit were unknown."[35]

It is unknown what the Ullmanns' core religious values were, save for a fleeting reference to Amelia being "weary of bacon" as a foodstuff staple. But if this couple was concerned that a male child be circumcised, given their isolation from centers of Jewish life, when their little fellow arrived, they — like so many frontier parents — might have had to be patient and flexible about the "rabbi's" date of arrival. As in the colonial period, given the difficulties of transportation, many boys from outpost families did not formally enter the covenant on their eighth day. When that all important functionary arrived, he might be asked to perform this mitzvah not only on Jewish children, but on those who had issued from mixed marriages. That long-standing tradition too, of intermarried couples identifying with Judaism on the most fundamental level, continued on the frontier. Here again, in situations so reminiscent of the seventeenth and eighteenth centuries, these American Jews married out not due to any antipathy toward their ancestral faith, but because they had found a Christian loved one.[36]

Many frontier Jews also wanted matzahs and other kosher foods. As once-remote groups grew, efforts were made to recruit permanent jacks-of-religious-trades. One semi-scientific estimate claims that from 1850 to 1860 some thirty-five communities all over the United States either had "a professional shochet . . . at work or . . . advertised" for one. Thirty-six more came on board or were sought over the next decade. The ideal candidate could also perform circumcisions even as it was assumed that this more learned fellow could lead services.[37]

As always, Sabbath observance continued to be a problem; exigencies of work were a critical problem with the holy day that was honored in the breech except among the minority who were pious. Nonetheless, one such observant Jew who found himself in remote Pueblo, Colorado, waxed optimistic that now, under his leadership as shochet and mohel, in a place where "we have no Synagogue and the Sabbath is not observed," the future was bright. "Ere long," he prophesized, "it will be in my power to inform you that, even in Pueblo, the Jews observe the dietary enactments [and] honor the Sabbath day."[38]

Along the same lines and putting aside Benjamin's harsh evaluation that nonobservance was rife out west, his travelogues also reveal all sorts of efforts to uphold semblances of religious observances and to bring formerly isolated Jews back together. "No matter how indifferent and cold our fellow Jews are toward their religion," he once observed, "nevertheless they are never so estranged from all religious feeling that it is a matter of total indifference to them where they bury their dead." In fact, Benjamin observed that for most Jews there was a distinct hierarchy of observances — beyond according a friend or relatives a proper Jewish funeral — that captivated them. "New Year's and the Day of Atonement [had] still some meaning for them." Their emotional ties were rooted, he recognized, in "all the dear, slumbering memories of the past awoke and wished to live again." In places where "during the rest of the year, no one thinks about performing Jewish ceremonies" — the "cemetery is practically all that discloses the presence of Jews" — "public services are held" on those holiest of days. Dietary laws, particularly Passover food traditions, also retained much popular importance even if the same Jews erred when it came to "related laws and precepts." The unknowing might bake the unleavened bread "of the flour usually offered for sale in the market, no attention being paid to the regulation for grinding flour." It also made no real difference to them that they purchased matzah "at great expense, but along with it ate the usual food." Stumbles over halachic details were not particularly important to many Jews who, on the other hand, prized those pieces of Jewish religious life and custom that retained fond and powerful memories.[39]

Recollections of what religious life had been like for them back in the old country also dictated the nature of the ritual that they would be comfortable with gathering to pray. Such emotions and predilections meant that, almost invariably, they would worship according to the Orthodox rite. While the immigrants' decisions to move to America coincided with an era of tumultuous changes in Jewish religious life in Central Europe, the maelstrom of new ideas and practices in the old country did not influence most Jews who chose American futures. These newcomers opted for Orthodoxy because it was the only form of Judaism that they knew.

Liberalization of ritual and reinterpretation of theological doctrines of varying sorts took place in Germany as Jews attempted to present their faith and traditions in a modern, attractive way to the gentile world. Their twofold goals were to convince those loath to extend the bounties of emancipation to Jews that their religious confession did not preclude staunch loyalty to the Fatherland. Moreover, they desired to show that the Jewish religious way of life was not archaic, but rather possessed universal qualities. These new religious movements also said to those within their community who chafed from their marginal status in the larger world, that they had necessary roles to play as Jews in the progressive spread of ethical monotheism within their contemporary times. These ideas and emotions were refracted in the ritual of German Reform and Historical School synagogues in their languages of prayer, in the wording of their prayer books, and in the general ambience of congregational devotions.

However, not unlike the emancipation struggle itself, that was a class-based and geographically centered endeavor. So too, the excitement concerning the liberalization of Judaism was largely confined to certain groups and particular places. Acculturated, achieving, and aspiring German Jews, often newly ensconced in the burgeoning cities, cared greatly about formal entrance and ultimate integration into general society. Emancipation issues mattered less to their poorer cousins, be they denizens of Bavarian villages and hamlets or within the Polish provinces under Prussian control, who still struggled to eke out subsistence livings. Berlin or Hamburg or Frankfurt or Breslau — those dynamic, growing urban centers attractive to the upwardly mobile — hosted great religious discussions and innovations. But less-worldly, rural folks who pulled up stakes did not migrate to these locales. Rather, those who had little exposure to liberal Judaism in the old world headed off to America. Thus when newcomers gathered to pray in this country, their forms of prayer resembled, in all essential ways, the Orthodox synagogues of their European villages. They really knew of no other options.[40]

The first Jews to organize a synagogue in St. Louis, the United Hebrew

Congregation, made it clear in its original Constitution that prayers should never be performed otherwise than among the Polish Jewish *Minhag Polin,* Polish custom. [The words were written in Hebrew.] This [stipulation] "shall never be altered or amended under any pretense whatsoever."[41]

Though the leaders of this shul evidently aspired to maintain Old World ways, they moved to assure such continuity in an American manner. After just a brief time in the United States, they already were acculturated enough to record their desires in a "constitution," an American legal form. In other words, even as they were becoming accustomed to this country's surroundings, when at prayer they still wanted to maintain ties to their European pasts.

In Louisville, Kentucky, where reportedly most of the founders "had been but recently identified with the strictly Orthodox congregations in their European homes," not only did the traditional ritual obtain, but members were also very concerned and bickered incessantly about the reliability of both the shochet and the local kosher butcher.[42]

Synagogue life in Cincinnati began formally in 1824 when its first twenty Jewish residents, primarily of Central European extraction by way of Great Britain, established Congregation B'ne Israel. There they prayed "according to the form and mode of worship of the Polish and German Jews," with one minor variation. One of "the original founders" recalled very late in his life that when they first joined together they were "all young people . . . not so prejudiced in favor of old customs as more elderly people might have been." And "since some of their wives had been brought up in Portuguese congregations" where the style of Orthodox worship allowed for "considerable chorus singing" among women as well as men, "the sweet voices of the fair daughters of Zion" were heard, albeit from their side of the mechitza. Soon, however, with the arrival of "large emigrations of our German brethren" who were not attuned to that tradition, "the voices of the ladies were effectively silenced." In the succeeding decade and a half, as additional groups of German Jews arrived, the most recent newcomers came to see the acculturating B'ne Israel crowd — the so-called "English Congregation" — as insensitive to their religious values. Accordingly, they established their own Orthodox synagogue, B'nai Yeshurun, and pledged that they would "worship therein according to the rites, customs and usages of the German Jews."[43]

In Chicago, the first fledgling attempt at synagogue life dated to 1845 when no more than ten men gathered on Yom Kippur. Prayers that day perforce were intermittent; services were halted whenever one male worshipper left the small, rented room. Some of these same participants formally committed themselves two years later when they established Kehilath Anshe Maarav. There, reportedly, "the ritual was transplanted in its entirety from the old country, the *Minhag Ashkenaz* being the prayer book in use." As an unmistakable signpost of fidelity to Orthodoxy, the women worshippers,

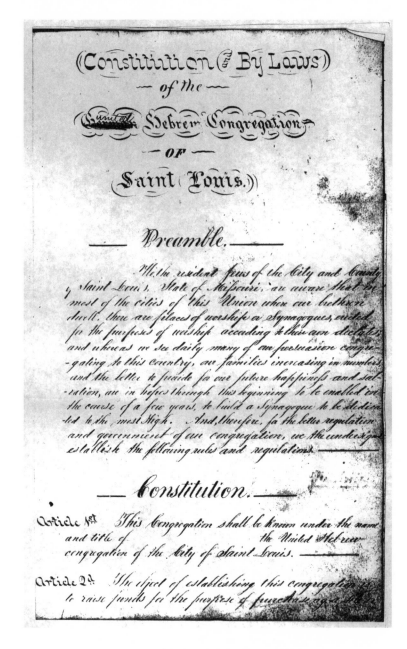

Figure 2.1. Constitution and By Laws of the United Hebrew
Congregation of St. Louis (1841). Article 3rd notes the synagogue
ritual in Hebrew as "Minhag Polin." Courtesy of The Jacob Rader
Marcus Center of the American Jewish Archives.

lot for the erection and building of a place of worship,
for persons belonging to our persuasion: to pay for
the lot already purchased for the interment of the dead,
and the purchase of a few copies of the holy Pentateuch
and such other books and furniture as is needful and
customary, to have in all Synagogues; to bury at
their demise, all persons professing Judaism, providing their estate shall pay for the funeral expense
if they are able to do so.

## Article 3d

The prayers shall never be performed otherwise than among the polish Jews. מנהג פוליש
This section shall never be altered or amended under
any pretence whatsoever.

## Article 4th

Any person may become a contributor
to this congregation.

## Article 5th

Any male Hebrew by paying into the hands
of the proper Officers for that purpose elected the sum
per month, specified in the by-laws, shall be
considered a congregator. He shall be entitled to
all honours and privileges in the Synagogue, during
service, but shall have no voice at any of the general Meetings.

## Article 6th

Any person having resided at least one year
either in this State or the State of Illinois, and is known
to be a man of good and moral character, may by
applying for membership be elected by a majority
of the members present: providing always, he
shall have been a congregator at least one year.

who attended as regularly as did their men, occupied the rear seats of the one-floor building.[44]

In Milwaukee, an Imanu-Al Cemetery Association, formed in 1848, morphed some two years later into Imanu-Al, the city's first congregation. Although the word around town was that all its founders "wish for us to repeat the same *piyutim* [liturgical poems] in the same order exactly as their fathers did," the handfuls of members soon battled over precisely which filial Orthodox customaries should be used in reciting the prayers. Each faction wanted to evoke memories of their particular region of Central Europe. In short order, Milwaukee had three synagogues, two following the Polish tradition, the other cleaving to the German minhag.[45]

Out in San Francisco, I. J. Benjamin noted that the city's oldest synagogue Shearith Israel, founded in 1849, "follows the correct Polish minhag and is strictly Orthodox." To his pleasure, as an observant Jew, Benjamin found that a decade or into the congregation's existence, "the service is still conducted in the true Jewish manner, as our ancient ancestors used to conduct it."[46]

But were the shul attendees that Benjamin met up with in the Bay Area as pious as he? It is impossible to determine how many of the peddler-now-merchant founders of the San Francisco, or other immigrant congregations, rigorously maintained their religious traditions while on the road or if they came back to strict personal observance when they got off the trails of the American frontier. All that can be said is that they surely demonstrated deep dedication to building Orthodox synagogue life.

Take, for example, the case of Joseph Jonas, Cincinnati's "first Jew." He was the man who had been warned before he left Philadelphia that he would forget his religion and his God in the American wilds. He did neither. Rather, he subscribed to the notion that it was "the duty of every member of the Jewish persuasion, when separated from a congregation to *conform as near as possible* to the worship and ceremonies of our holy religion." Upon arrival in the Queen City, he dedicated himself "to be a nucleus around which the first congregation might be found to worship the God of Israel in this great western territory." With no rabbi or cantor, he would frequently lead the prayers and served two terms as B'ne Israel's president. For all of his commitments, he discovered lay leadership to be quite a frustrating experience, causing him to once complain: "the more I do for my congregation, the more I am insulted and abused." While all of these communal activities and positions suggest strongly that he was among the more devout Jews in the area, it is not known how meticulously Jonas practiced what Orthodox Judaism taught.[47]

Regarding Abraham Kohn, the renowned and frustrated peddler who asked for God's comfort and courage while he trudged through America, there is one indication that while he was a community builder par excel-

Figures 2.2a–c. Photos of Dilah Kohn,
Abraham Kohn, and Isaac Kunreuther.
In Hyman L. Meites, ed., *History of the
Jews of Chicago* (1924).

lence, he was not overwrought about the observance of kashruth. Kohn turned up in Chicago in time to be one of the founding members of Kehilath Anshe Maarav. In fact, the story of that synagogue's organization has been linked to his concern for his frail mother, Dilah, whose "scrupulous observance of the dietary laws . . . resulted in her refusal to partake of meat . . . because it had not been slaughtered by a properly accredited shochet." She survived on a "precarious diet of bread, and potatoes" much to the alarm of her son and other family members. Kohn's solution was to help bring a congregation into existence that would support an approved slaughterer. His action surely speaks to his high degree of filial piety but does not evidence his own level of personal observance. He undoubtedly adopted a devout demeanor when his mother was around. But how concerned had he been about the availability of kosher meat before she joined him from Europe? In his calculus of religious concerns, the Fifth Commandment, to honor one's parents, may have loomed much larger than adherence to the rules regarding kosher food preparation.[48]

Having said this, there is also a historical tradition about the Chicago synagogue's founders — perhaps Kohn included — that recalls that on Sabbaths and holidays "most members clos[ed] their places of business and post[ed] signs in their windows reading 'Closed on Account of Holiday.' "[49]

It is evident, however, that those who headed up many of these frontier Orthodox synagogues — whatever their personal level of observance — were very tolerant of those who did not rigorously follow Orthodox Judaism's cardinal rules. Perhaps they reasoned that it would be more than just hypocritical, but downright impossible, to restrict synagogue honors or even membership — as those back east had done — to Sabbath observers when they themselves who sat in the front of their synagogues did not always follow the strict demands of the halacha. In these environs, seemingly even the most pious, who prayed that their fellow Jews might conform to their religious standards, did not perceive pressure and exclusionary tactics as an effective stratagem to promote observance. No one wanted to narrow the tent of worshippers. In some communities, even intermarried Jews were counted within the fold. On the other hand, those in charge demanded that the men who led the service and community ritually — the shochet or the shamash or the hazan, for example — had to be pious beyond question. Thus, in St. Louis, it was allowed early on, in 1841, that "any male Hebrew" who paid his membership fee, would "be considered a congregater [*sic*]" and would "be entitled to all honors and privileges in the Synagogue," no questions asked, seemingly even of intermarrieds. However, when the shamash was, in 1850, seen in a barber shop on the Sabbath, he was summarily discharged.[50]

The unrivaled hegemony of old-time Orthodox religious values within these congregations did not last. Invariably, as the founders and members adapted to American ways, advanced economically, and broadened their circle of acquaintances, many became dissatisfied with their erstwhile immigrant congregations' look and some of its practices. There was a common apprehension that gentile friends and associates might happen past their synagogues as the Jews were in prayer and find that the styles of worship were totally different from their own, if not altogether strange. Hence, Jews rising toward the middle class were determined to make their houses of worship resemble in appearance and ambience their neighboring Protestant churches. The Charlestonians had felt the same way in the early 1820s. But now with new groups of acculturating Jews feeling that old ways could not coexist well with Americanization, such fears appeared all over the country.[51]

The South Carolinians' even more profound concern — that the youth of their community were disaffected from synagogue life — also loomed extremely large among this new era of change makers. The children of Central European immigrants took on the language, work habits, and overall lifestyle of this country faster than even the most adaptable of their parents. These youngsters had even more non-Jewish friends. Thus attuned, they manifested little interest in connecting to European-style religious life. If these young people had any interest in associating with fellow Jews, they were increasingly finding their ways to the smoke-filled, drink-laden, and gambling venues of social clubs. They surely stayed clear of synagogues and also were not particularly enthusiastic about the Young Men's Hebrew Associations' salubrious, secular Jewish settings.[52]

Not all of the remedies proposed and implemented to these multigenerational religious dilemmas were inimical to Orthodoxy. When it came to creating a more refined, classy atmosphere at services, the halacha hallowed, when it did not demand, decorum during prayers. Rabbis had always countenanced recitations in languages other than Hebrew, although the holy tongue was preferred. The logic of the nineteenth-century American Orthodox synagogue leaders was unassailable: a worshipper who could follow what is going on would most likely be silent and reverential in the sanctuary. Conversely, it is unquestioned that the sometimes riotous scene that obtained when old-time commercial practices — including the auctioning off of ritual honors to the highest bidder — which slowed down and disfigured services had no halachic standing. Moreover, it was an unqualified faithful act when Jews built a commodious synagogue for God to comfortably dwell within their midst, even if the external architecture, steeple included, made it resemble a church.

However, Jews violated Orthodox strictures when men and women sat together in the sanctuary or when a congregation installed an organ for use on the Sabbath day or holidays and recruited a mixed male–female choir to complement the instrumental music. When new synagogues ordained that men not wear prayer shawls or yarmulkes during services, the congregations not only broke with the halacha but also with folk practice. It was an enormous cultural step for a Jewish man, whatever he did religiously outside of the synagogue, to appear in God's house bareheaded. When modern prayer books that liberal rabbis of Central European extraction wrote and edited were substituted for the siddur, prayers were recited that articulated non-traditional visions of Jewish history and destiny. No longer were these Jews petitioning — as their ancestors had for nineteen hundred years — that their people be restored to Zion and in a messianic age witness the rebuilding of the Temple and the restoration of the sacrificial cult. Rather, at those moments of devotion, the men and women in their pews were asserting, at least to God, that they had found a permanent home as Jews in the blessed United States.

The moment and extent of acquiescence to change, however, differed along a long expanse of time and from synagogue to synagogue, with some congregations deviating dramatically from Orthodox norms and others acting more conservatively about transformation. For example, relatively few congregations wanted their men not to wear hats. There was no step-by-step pattern for communities saying good-bye to old-time strictures. Sometimes influential Reform rabbis had their say in the process and rooted their ideas in considerations of Jewish history and theology. Yet very often the lay leaders made their moves on their own without necessarily taking a distinct ideological stance. The abandonment of certain Orthodox rituals during services did not necessarily mean, however, that congregants were anxious to set aside all of the demands of Jewish law. A synagogue that tinkered with the liturgy might well have had a shochet on its payroll to provide the kosher meat that the members still desired. Moreover, those who desired more alterations in synagogue life were not necessarily less observant in their personal life than those who were comfortable with fewer shifts in the way the congregation presented itself. An individual could be both very devout in personal religious behavior and an advocate for change in the Orthodox ritual. Though the halacha required both punctiliousness in lifestyle and fidelity to the way synagogues had long operated, sometimes a desire to appear in the public religious realm much like their neighbors' did won out, while back at home traditional practices held sway. On the other hand, an unbreakable emotional tie to old-style synagogue services might have precluded some Jews from countenancing change even if in their private lives they felt increasing unbound to the commandments

Examine, for example, the case of Michael Putzel of Easton, Pennsylvania. In the 1850s, he was a prime mover for the modernization of services at

Brith Sholom, and when his entreaties were rejected, he was instrumental in founding the competitive Congregation Emanuel. His mission was to establish in town "a regular religious worship with a view of conforming . . . to the circumstances which surround us, and the age in which we live." Yet this "reformer's" personal Orthodox credentials were impeccable enough that he retained — at least for a while — his post as shochet of his erstwhile Orthodox congregation. Conversely, many of those who resisted major transformations coast to coast were persons who, as one contemporary critic put it, "do not lead a Jewish life but read the olden prayers." Their devout moments might even have been confined solely to the time they spent in public prayer. On balance, however, as the middle decades of the nineteenth century unfolded, the vast majority of once Orthodox synagogues shifted in their religious orientation, although again the changes over time were of varying degrees and intensities.[53]

In Chicago, Kehilath Anshe Maarav moved toward Reform early in its second decade of existence when a majority of members voted to adopt the prayer book used in the Hamburg Temple. As the congregants replaced the traditional Roedelheim siddur, introduced a choir, and enforced decorum, prideful statements were made that now the synagogue was putting an end to "out-of-place ideas."[54]

At almost the same time, Reform in Cincinnati advanced immeasurably with the appointment of two eminent spokesmen for liberal Judaism. Rabbi Isaac Mayer Wise, destined to be that movement's most renowned national advocate even as he aspired to lead all American Jews, came to B'nai Jeshurun's pulpit from Albany, New York, in 1853. Max Lilienthal, that erstwhile Orthodox rabbi late of New York City who would now cast his lot with Reform Judaism, was appointed to B'ne Israel in 1855. In the two years before his colleague's arrival, Wise attempted to minister to both congregations, but local communal jealousies reportedly undermined that scenario. In Wise's first years, an organ was installed and the congregation readily adopted his prayer book *Minhag America*. The second days of holidays were soon abolished. Two millenia earlier — back in Second Temple days — when the exact start of holidays was still determined through observation of lunar cycles and with Diaspora communities uncertain as to precisely when the priests in Jerusalem officially declared the beginning of a festival, the rabbis added an additional day of observance outside of Palestine to assure that the faithful observed a full complement of holy days. Though by the nineteenth century Jews had long come to rely on calendars, additional days for Succoth, Passover, and Shavuoth remained a requisite part of Orthodox teachings. If nothing else, that continued practice made a distinction between Jewish life in the Land of Israel and the Diaspora. Wise wanted no part of this distinction. However, still in keeping with Jewish tradition, two days of

Rosh ha-Shanah were observed. Perhaps here, though calendars made it possible to know for certain when the Jewish New Year started, the power of folk tradition prevailed. Jews continue to show special reverence for what are called the "Days of Awe." In a comparable vein, it would be more than another decade and a half before the B'ne Jeshurun board resolved that it was "not unlawful to attend divine services with uncovered head."[55]

Over at Lilienthal's synagogue, a mixed choir was introduced early on in his tenure. In a few succeeding years, "an entire change of . . . mode of service" was deemed "necessary to impress the minds of the rising genera-tion of the veneration and respect that our holy cause demands." Practically, this meant the installation of "family pews [and] an organ" and the elimina-tion from the liturgy of "all expressions such as 'release from bondage' and the like." The rabbi and his followers wanted all to know and anyone who might ask that they, as Americans, had already been freed from oppression. They did not need future Divine intervention because they were already immensely comfortable in this country. The congregation also implemented a triennial cycle of Torah readings that accommodated its worshippers' Saturday work obligations and recreational plans. For millennia, congre-gants had followed their readers as they annually worked their way through the entire Five Books of Moses even if that recitation contributed to the long length of Sabbath morning services. Other ritual and ideological changes would soon follow.[56]

In St. Louis, at its United Hebrew Congregation, discussions first ensued in the mid–late 1850s "to revise the prayers so as to omit what can be dispensed with." However, the change-makers did not cast themselves as reformers but resolved concomitantly "to preserve and advance the path of *Orthodox Judaism* . . . to strive to the utmost of their ability to uphold the purity of their faith as they have received it from their own fathers." While the synagogue would not long remain unalterably Orthodox — for example, by the early 1860s, the cantor would have a mixed choir, including some Christian voices, assist him in the prayers — a number of very traditional practices were retained. As late as 1881, men and women sat separately and the siddur was still in use. When they finally followed through on a prayer-book reform initiative, their liturgy of choice was from the more traditional *Avodat Yisrael*, a collaborative effort of rabbis Marcus Jastrow, Benjamin Szold, and Henry Hochheimer and not Wise's *Minhag America*.[57]

Shifts in allegiances of so many varying degrees and speed — like these in the Midwest — became a national trend and phenomenon. Even in New York, which had been home in the mid-1820s to some immigrant Jews who initially cleaved staunchly to the old ways, changes took place in the older synagogues, affecting the ritual traditions once cherished. When they began their synagogue, the founders of Congregation B'nai Jeshurun had wanted to build an Orthodox community focused on Jewish learning and prayers; it was not to include those who did not uphold the commandments. As late as the mid-1860s, its long-standing leaders could still boast that "the minhag is German and Polish as established in England and the congregation is Orthodox" even if the classy rabbi, English-born and -trained Morris J. Raphall, did institute some shifts in the social demeanor of congregational life. His and his cantor's donning of clerical gowns during services only punctuated his drive toward making the service more respectable. But the tides of more profound change proved unstoppable at B'nai Jeshurun. By 1875, "the institution . . . would have family pews, a choir of men and women and organ music in the service."[58]

During this same era in New York, change of a grander and more radical nature occurred—in much shorter order—within another German religious group that originally had called itself the Cultus Society and conducted Orthodox services. When organized in the mid-1840s, on the intersection of Grand and Clinton Streets on the Lower East Side, congregational protocols called for the separation of the genders during prayers—men sat in the front of the storefront quarters, women in the back — and for the use of the siddur and the observance of all the traditional holidays. The innovations that it countenanced, like the recitation of some hymns in German or a weekly sermon, or an all-male choir, each designed to make the devotions intelligible and edifying to those not conversant with the traditional services, were hardly breaks with the halacha. This synagogue would have a long way to go before it would become one of Reform's flagship synagogues, Temple Emanu-El of New York.[59]

But these transformations within so many independent American synagogues, each possessed of multiple opinionated voices, did not come easily. When push came to shove, a Jew who "felt pangs of conscience" about his days as a peddler when on his "trips" was "forced to accustom" himself "to other than Jewish food," who did not then observe the Sabbath and even "frequented more and more Christian churches and Christian society" might "come forward as [a] true zeal at all congregational meetings" to oppose changes "merely to show that [while] they yield to the harsh necessity of making a livelihood, but otherwise they are observant Jews." In one case, at a meeting in Louisville early on in its synagogue history, one overheated member made it clear that he would personally go to great extremes to prevent "every attempt at reform." He threatened to "burn down the synagogue if an organ were put in." Others within the congregational mix might position themselves on the side of changes as if to be "justified in their transgressions." Still others there could vote in favor of reform while they would be sure to stay clear of the ferocious firebug. Meanwhile, a final significant contingent of community people might be simply "indifferent" about how worship took place, one way or another.[60]

Just these types of splits within congregational ranks frustrated Bernard

Felsenthal when he attempted in 1857 to promote a plan of "edification, instruction and improvement through worship" at Adas Israel in Madison, Indiana. In the winter of 1856, Felsenthal responded to an ad for a Jewish jack-of-all trades that the congregation posted in *Die Deborah*, the German language newspaper of Isaac Mayer Wise. The young man was soon hired as communal shochet, hazan, and teacher of Hebrew, German, religion, and Bible. Arriving in town, Felsenthal, a teacher and not a rabbi albeit possessed of a distinct affinity for liberalizing Judaism, found a community that had grown dissatisfied with the Orthodox service even if members still personally observed many traditional strictures. By virtue of location, all of the kosher eaters in town put up daily with the often sickening smells of hog food odors. Pork slaughtering was a major local industry, one that earned Madison the nick-name of "Porkopolis."[61]

However, as Felsenthal would report to *Die Deborah*, several times in the past services had been cancelled due to lack of attendance. The teacher attributed this malaise to the all-too-long Sabbath service being incomprehensible to those — probably members of the younger generation — who did not know Hebrew. Moreover, he believed that even those who understood what was being said did not resonate to "notions, views, hopes and wishes" — like the ancient desire for the restoration of sacrifices in a Holy Temple in Jerusalem — that made no sense to the modern Jew.

Felsenthal's solution was a modest revision of the Adas Israel's ritual, with one noteworthy exception. To assure that a minyan would be more easily and consistently attained, Felsenthal went far ahead of his time and called for including women in that religious quorum. Such a makeover, he believed, would not only bring adults and children back to the synagogue but would send a message to the Madison community that its Jews were faithful to a "lofty Israelite religion, the most beautiful on the whole wide world," possessed of great "virtue and morality." He prayed that this uncommon change along with his amendments to ritual — such as including English and German prayers in the services — would "show the world that we here in Madison, though few in numbers, [are] great in our intentions and full of holy zeal for our divine Judaism." Here as with all reform initiatives, Felsenthal proffered a dual message of continuity for Jews and acceptability for these acculturating Americans within a larger society.

Most of his congregants disliked Felsenthal's proposals. Some thought his changes deviated too far from the tradition, while others wanted even more radical breaks with past practice. At a meeting where his plans were discussed, one outraged traditionalist questioned out loud whether a "goy" (lit., a gentile; fig. an ideological Jewish opponent of Orthodoxy) like Felsenthal "should . . . be teaching Judaism to our children." To begin with, this antagonist was unequivocally opposed to counting women in a minyan. On the question of using Hebrew vs. vernaculars in the service, he further averred that the holy language alone should be used since "whole worlds depend on a single word. . . . The existence of whole worlds is conditional on each vowel, the angels of Heaven employ each little stroke. [These] new fangled things — they are all sins."

Others within the group took diametrically opposite positions. One, whom Felsenthal characterized as a "radical," proposed doing without Hebrew entirely during the service, even when the Torah was supposed to be read. In response to this suggestion, a third voice, one of moderation or compromise, argued that Hebrew surely had its place in the prayers since it "is indeed one of Jewry's embracing bonds linking co-religionists around the world with one another." Another member in the room was perturbed that these noisy ideological debates were interfering with his interest that evening. He would have much preferred a card game among these competitors to a discussion of religion.

Felsenthal and his interlocutors could not arrive at an agreement about the triennial Torah reading cycle nor on many other issues. In Madison, Indiana, no consensus meant no change. The Orthodox stance prevailed — at least at this juncture — much to the consternation of Felsenthal. Frustrated, the ambitious teacher cum rabbi left in 1858 to lead a more responsive Jewish group in Chicago. Adas Israel, in the meantime, would not really move toward Reform until 1869. Then it adopted Rabbi Wise's *Minhag America* prayer book.[62]

Orthodox factions also did not go down without a fight in Chicago, where none other than Abraham Kohn led the major struggle. When talk of modifications started at Anshe Maarav in 1851, six years into its existence, Kohn supported "mild changes" — undoubtedly alterations in etiquette and procedures — that did not violate the halacha. This stratagem, however, designed to head off more "radical reform tendencies," so outraged Rev. Isaac Kunreuther, the very shochet whom Kohn had brought to town in 1847, that this most unyielding of Chicago Jews resigned his communal post and retired to "private life" and business where reportedly he "clung to orthodox customs and traditions, many of which had been abandoned by members of the congregation." Six years later, Kohn carried the cudgels for Orthodoxy as he opposed Leopold Mayer, his fellow founder of Anshe Maarav. Mayer had changed his religious ways and was the most articulate advocate for congregational reform. The two battled it out in congregational meetings and within the pages of the *Israelite*, Wise's well-known English language weekly. Ultimately, Mayer's side prevailed on the aforementioned question of prayerbook reform even though Kohn contended his opponents had stolen the election, "paying for such members as were in arrears with their dues, in order to get their votes." Perhaps the winners had learned from the corrupt world of Chicago politics how to manipulate a democratic process to achieve their ends. It was another benchmark of Americanization.

Soon after the defeat, some of the disenfranchised supporters of Orthodoxy — primarily those of Polish extraction who had never really felt comfortable socially in the "Bavarian" Anshe Maarav — simply left the synagogue and founded their own Kehilath B'nai Sholom. But Kohn fought on from within, possibly because he discerned a spirit of moderation and compromise among the victors. One of the winners had written magnanimously after the triumph that "the reform party does not desire to keep up hard feelings and wishes to retain the cooperation and the good will of all members." Kohn's strategy now was to financially support the appointment of a learned, English-speaking rabbi late of Dublin, Ireland, to put a modern but traditional face on the synagogue. While the appointment of a Rabbi Meyer Mensor did not fulfill its "promise of being able to reconcile the varying religious viewpoints," the delay that Kohn's move engendered caused those impatient for greater religious change to go off on their own and establish the Israelite Congregation Ohabey Or, also known as the Israelite Reform Society. In short order, its founders — including Leopold Mayer — tended an offer to Bernard Felsenthal, who had just come away unhappily from Madison, Indiana. Thus, in less than three years Chicago had gone from having one Orthodox congregation to being home to three synagogues, two of varying degrees of the Reform persuasion and one that was Orthodox.[63]

As just seen here in Chicago, the formation of breakaway synagogues among disgruntled and/or disenfranchised Orthodoxy sympathizers was the most common response to Reform congregational triumphs. The names these angry losers gave to their synagogues often reflected residual animosities. We saw this already in Charleston in 1840 where the battle over Beth Elohim ended with the traditional dissidents calling their synagogue, Shearith Israel, the Remnant of Israel. So too in Cincinnati, when Lilienthal declared that Tisha B'Av — the fast of the Ninth of Ab that commemorates the destruction of the Temple in Jerusalem — should be changed from a day of national mourning to one of rejoicing because that central event in Jewish history liberated the Jewish people and faith to spread ethical monotheism around the world, the traditionalists within B'ne Israel had enough. In 1855, they founded their own Shearith Israel.[64]

In 1871, Orthodox Jews gave up more than a decade of struggle to hold back reforms at the Baltimore Hebrew Congregation and established Congregation Chizuk Amuno (lit., strengthening of faith), letting everyone know just how devoted they were to maintaining traditional ways. Their erstwhile synagogue, the city's oldest, had been founded in the mid-1830s and was Abraham Rice's pulpit from 1840 to 1849. Frustrated with the low level of observance among his flock, Rice then left the rabbinate — he would subsequently earn a meager livelihood as a merchant — only to return for a brief stint in 1862, the year of his death, during an era of congregational turmoil. Three years earlier, in 1859, the incumbent rabbi Henry Hochheimer had attempted to substitute *Minhag America* for the siddur and proffered among other innovations the concept of a confirmation ceremony for girls. The residual Orthodox majority rebuffed his initiatives. His efforts blocked, and unwilling to fight on from within that synagogue, Hochheimer resigned only to soon secure a post at another, more receptive local congregation. Hochheimer would serve in the Eden Street congregation for the next thirty-three years. In the course of that time, he would collaborate with Marcus Jastrow and Benjamin Szold on their own modern prayer book. Meanwhile, back at Baltimore Hebrew, Bernard Illowy held the rabbi's post for Orthodoxy for two years — 1859–1861 — and, of course, Rice returned in 1862.[65]

However, as the decade of the 1860s progressed, renewed calls for changes were heard within synagogue ranks. Among the modifications that were contemplated was the organizing of a mixed voice choir. Determined to maintain "the custom of the Orthodox German Jews from time immemorial," the traditionalists moved to take their opponents to court. As Jews who had become comfortable with this country's legal system, they were certain that they would receive at least a fair hearing. In this regard, these litigants were quite different from their European Jewish counterparts who long retained their historic fear of standing before "gentile" courts. Besides which, even if they had an American beth-din to hear their appeal, neither they nor the Jewish jurists had any power to force opponents to follow its directives.[66]

In any event, the petitioners' position was that the transformations afoot were in violation of its constitution on file with the State of Maryland that stipulated that no amendment might be made in religious rites without a two-thirds majority vote. No such definitive decision had been made. However, before Justice William S. Pinkney could rule on this motion, an agreement to disagree was reached among Baltimore Hebrew's feuding Jews. Undoubtedly, some financial arrangements were reached as elements within the divided congregation went in fundamentally different religious directions. Still, on its way out, the Orthodox group made sure everyone knew that they were deeply committed to the strengthening of the faith.[67]

The Chizuk Amuno battlers were not the stereotypical poor immigrants looking back at the Old World, who knew little of this country's ways while trying to hold off insurgents who were more acculturated and affluent than they. We have already seen that they knew how to turn to American courts for redress. Rather, like their opponents, they had achieved significant levels of economic and social mobility. Neither religious faction, made up primarily of merchants, some clothing manufacturers and a few professionals who were all comfortable as Americans, wanted a religious home that smacked of the social ways of the past. Where they differed was over the fundamental question of whether Baltimore Hebrew, in trying to attract Americanized Jews to its synagogue, should project a modern and Orthodox image or should stand comfortably within the rising tide of Reform Judaism. The Chizuk Amuno people made a definitive statement about the modern cultural outlook that they wanted within their Orthodox congregation when, in 1876, five years into its existence, they hired the first American-born rabbi, Henry W. Schneeberger. A local lad who had succeeded, Schneeberger assumed the pulpit possessed of an undergraduate and master's degree from Columbia University, Orthodox rabbinic ordination from the modern Orthodox seminary of Esriel Hildesheimer in Berlin, and a Ph.D. from the University of Jena. It was projected that this well-rounded intellectual and spiritual leader would both influence the Jews and impress all others in town. They would be proud that when he preached the Torah's teachings these lessons were adroitly integrated with contemporary philosophical thought, articulated with perfect English diction.[68]

Although maintaining religious common cause with like-thinking Jews had its spiritual rewards, a fear remained among these once-dispossessed Orthodox dissidents that liberalizing tendencies eventually would also challenge the religious fidelity of their new congregations. To avoid this potential catastrophe and to ensure future Orthodox minority rights, Chizuk Amuno legislated sagaciously that "no change or alteration to our daily prayers . . . ceremonies and customs whatsoever shall be made," if but one member objected. Its constitution also boldly announced that "should any member offer a motion or resolution to change . . . he shall ipso facto forfeit his membership." In this regard, the Baltimoreans emulated a spirit and strategy that New York's Shearith Israel had implemented some time before to ensure that newly affiliating insurgents, who might possess neither the religious sentiments nor the sense of history of indigenous members, would not outvote old-timers. They created a committee to look into the religious opinions of potential members. Subsequently, a rule was passed that members had to be affiliated three years before they could be considered synagogue electors. Only electors could enact ritual changes.[69]

But these few victories—or holding of the line for Orthodoxy—were largely offset nationally as more often those within a congregation who preferred the traditional ritual ultimately surrendered to the reformers in their midst. Isaac Mayer Wise observed just this phenomenon in Milwaukee. In the late 1850s, the three formerly immigrant congregations melded into B'ne Jeshurun, founded under Wise's reformist influence. As far as "the few hyper-orthodox who are dissatisfied" with the "sincere and lasting union" were concerned, Wise allowed that "they take too much pride in the new temple that is free of debt and feel too profoundly the benefit of union, that they should think of separation." Besides which, the Cincinnati rabbi observed, "their number is too small to form a congregation, and so they will submit." When the congregation subsequently moved toward mixed pews, an organ, and a mixed-voiced choir to accompany the hazan, Wise further reported that "the old men are not as stubborn as elsewhere, so as to object to choir, organ, and a divine service agreeable to modern views."[70]

As most American Jews of this era struggled through their religious dilemmas, trying to make Judaism more compelling for themselves and their children, the Orthodox rabbis and influential hazans on the scene adopted a range of strategies in advocating for traditional behavior. Some of these spokesmen's plans turned out to be resistant while others were accommodating of American challenges and Jewish challengers as they attempted to face up to two interrelated realities: masses of Jews were simply not interested in surrendering their personal religious autonomy to any demands for conformity that Orthodox leaders might seek to impose on them. In other words, there was an ever-declining pool of pious Jews whom they could comfortably influence to stay on the halachic straight and narrow. In addition, forms of non-Orthodox religious life armed with their own formulas for identifying as both Jews and as Americans were constantly growing in popularity.

Abraham Rice of Baltimore was the arch-resister of the mid-century period. He made it clear from the outset that his mission was nothing less than "to establish pure Orthodox faith and to prevent the entry of Reform," a message that resonated only with the devout in town. He took a harsh position toward Sabbath desecrators within his flock, ruling, early on at his Baltimore Hebrew Congregation, that such miscreants would be denied the privilege of being called to the Torah. But he could not make his proclamation stick in a community of declining traditional religious values. In time, circumstances forced him — if his board did not — to modify his stance. He did, however, admonish the congregation not to respond with an "amen" to a violator's Torah blessings. Significantly, four years after Rice left his pulpit in utter frustration; his undisciplined congregants removed any and all restrictions on Torah honors. Additionally, the Hebrew Congregation's laity then ruled that only Sabbath desecrators who lived "in the city" could not serve as synagogue officers. That call, it has been said, gave a pass to peddlers, for example, who were observant when at home in Baltimore but who could not follow Sabbath restrictions while on the difficult roads out of town.[71]

By that time, Rice had long rued the day he had come to this country with his lofty agenda. The year that the rabbi resigned, he wrote back to his religious mentor in Germany, Rabbi Wolf Hamburger that "my mind is perplexed" whether "it is even permissible for a Jew to live" in this libertine, irreligious land. "I am tired of my life. I often think of leaving and going to Paris and put my trust in the good Lord."[72]

Rice, the paradigmatic resister, did, however, evince accommodationist-style sensitivity in one noteworthy area. In 1851, he wrote to Isaac Leeser that he supported the latter's translation of the Bible into English as a Jewish educational device for those — particularly young people — who knew no Hebrew and were uncomfortable reading or speaking their parents' German vernacular.

When it came to the rise of Reform Judaism around him — which he described as "sparks scattered from the burning" of German Judaism that "are already kindling a flame in our dwelling" in America — Rice was an unrelenting polemicist and unyielding opponent. In a most dramatic, if unenforceable act, against its ideological stances, in 1850 Rice excommunicated Isaac Mayer Wise for publicly denying the expectation of a personal messiah and of corporeal resurrection. Wise instead prayed for a universalized messianic era of goodness and peace. Rice would take his own stance as the "duty" of "a true Israelite, to show . . . the iniquity of these doctrines and to warn them not to go in these paths," even if in a religiously voluntary America his action had no practical effect. He could assert the authority of the Torah's teaching as much as he wanted, but he had no power to bring down Wise. Rice certainly had no interest, some five years later, in joining Wise — whom he would later describe as a "wicked individual" — at a conclave in Cleveland ostensibly designed to arrive at an American minhag and understanding of the halacha to which all Jews could comfortably relate.[73]

Rice's contemporary, Rev. Isaac Leeser, on the other hand, tried to make Orthodoxy appealing to the wavering. He frequently advocated adjustments that would modernize and popularize Judaism, in ways that sometimes resembled what the reformers were doing, but without, in his view, doing violence to the halacha. For example, this prolific writer's first book, *Instruction in the Mosaic Religion,* which appeared first in 1830 — a catechism that laid out fundamental Jewish beliefs — derived from a work that an advocate of Reform in Germany had produced. But, ever the Orthodox loyalist, Leeser substituted traditional teachings about national restoration to Palestine and bodily resurrection for the new radical theology. Leeser's production of Hebrew–English editions of the Sephardic and Ashkenazic siddur (1837, 1848) and his completion of the first Jewish version of the Bible in English — a fifteen-year project that ended in 1853 — demonstrated how he reached out to the religiously unlettered and uncommitted among his people. Disturbed over missionaries' successes among disaffected Jews and about the nasty remarks conversionists made about his faith, Leeser, in 1845, organized an American Jewish Publication Society "to dispel ignorance among ourselves ... and enable the Israelite to put many a work in the hands of his Christian neighbor [to] dispossess him of any prejudice."[74]

As an advocate for improvement of Jewish education among the younger generation, he supported modern Sunday School initiatives in his city of Philadelphia and was almost a century ahead of his time in recognizing the unparalleled value of American day school education as a builder of Jewish identity. Early in the 1840s, he dreamed publicly of an advanced theological seminary in this country where "young men are to be educated ... fit for the office of Hazan, lecturer and teacher; and young women be educated for the high calling of female instructor." In the last year of his life, 1867, he actually witnessed his Maimonides College come into existence. He prayed that it would produce modern Orthodox "candidates for the ministry" — trained in traditional Jewish subjects and possessed of rigorous exposure to the sciences and humanities — able to communicate with Americanized congregants.[75]

In his ministerial role at Mikveh Israel, Leeser saw great value in the weekly sermon so that again "the untaught may learn and the learned may be fortified in faith." For him, it was "an incongruity that words of instruction formed no part of our regular service." Indeed, when in the pulpit, he was not beyond occasionally chastising his community harshly for being "contaminated by the iniquity of unbelief, by the boldness of open sin." He would then say that "the whole regeneration of Israel rests on the basis of the precepts and commandments which we have received as the will of our Father in heaven."[76] But while these precepts and commandments were unalterable in his view, he was totally dedicated to adjusting the sociology of the synagogue to modern sensibilities. Thus, while someone like Rabbi Rice would have preferred that his congregants remain silent in prayer — as the halacha dictates — he was not nearly as concerned about decorum as was Leeser. However, this modern minister to Jews understood that the people in the pews would resonate to a classy, stylish service.[77]

From his bully pulpit as long-term editor of the *Occident and American Jewish Advocate,* Leeser consistently railed against Reform initiatives that shattered halachic barriers. Though a believer that Judaism may be "re-formed ... upon correct principles," Leeser told his readers that what Wise and his followers were doing was a "deforming" of Judaism. They were, to his mind, in effect creating a new, foreign faith. He averred that radical change did little to solve the endemic problems of Sabbath desecration and emptiness of synagogues and spiritual life. Indeed, it was the *Occident* vs. the *Israelite,* from the late 1850s through much of the 1860s, as each editor canvassed the country for supporters of their understandings of the faith. Beyond those journalistic forays, this battler for Orthodoxy also went so far as to appear in Wise's own synagogue in Cincinnati. There, as he reported, in front of "eight hundred or perhaps near a thousand persons . . . in the lion's den," Leeser boldly told Wise's followers that "if you mean to follow those who call on you to accept their dreams as your guides through life, better burn the law then let it stand here forsaken."[78]

Nonetheless, quite unlike Abraham Rice, Leeser was willing to entertain finding common cause with Wise when his ideological antagonist, in 1855, organized a conference to create a synod "to preserve the union of Israel." When he made his pitch for broad-based attendance, Wise—despite his prior ritual deviations—initially indicated that he was willing to accept Orthodox interpretations of Judaism. Leeser really could not avoid exploring this intriguing offer. After all, as early as 1841 he had called for precisely this type of meeting that he prayed might bring some order to religious life under the sway of the halacha, upgrade the quality of Jewish leadership, and help create Jewish schools all over the United States. In 1848, so anxious was Leeser to bring the disaffected Jews in America together that he had permitted Wise to publish a call for what turned out to be a stillborn unity conclave in Albany, New York. Hence seven years later, Leeser "deem[ed] it [his] duty" to encourage others who were part of "the orthodox section" to consider attending because "many subjects besides reform can and ought be discussed at such an assembly."[79]

Leeser came away from the Cleveland Conference disillusioned about the possibility of creedal uniformity that could help the estranged Jews of America find their way religiously; he was also more adamant than ever in his objections to Reform. It has been said that that the Cleveland meeting though "originally intended to unify American Judaism, ironically marked the beginning of a new era of religious divisions." In any event, during the remaining decade of his life, Leeser continued to attempt to influence his fellow Jews through his newspapers, published sermons, and other writings and would find allies only among those who stood, like him, for Americanized Orthodoxy.[80]

Bernard Illowy shared Leeser's appreciation of the realities of American Judaism and was prepared too to make all appropriate accommodations. Keenly aware of the strides Reform Judaism was making everywhere in the 1850s–1860s as he occupied positions in such hotbeds as Wise's and Lilienthal's Cincinnati and Rabbi David Einhorn's Baltimore, Illowy attempted to simulate what his opponents were doing in his Orthodox synagogues. But his responses were always within the halacha. He preached every Sabbath either in English or German and emphasized the need for decorum, going so far as to support the levying of fines upon noisy congregants. Most remarkably, he developed a confirmation services for youngsters of both sexes that closely emulated what other Jewish movements were doing.[81]

Also in line with Leeser, Illowy roundly criticized Wise's theology in print

—usually in the *Occident*—but was willing initially to grant the reformer's unity plan the benefit of the doubt. Illowy was an original signatory to the Cleveland Conference call, but he backed away when he came to fear that "he would be in the minority and overwhelmed by the majority of Reformers who would be present." However, in the wake of the gathering, Illowy was not nearly as antagonistic to Wise as was his Philadelphia colleague. If anything, he held out hope that the "shepherds of Israel" who attended the conclave would follow through on their earlier overtures to the Orthodox. His hopes would not be realized.[82]

What Illowy ultimately had in common with all mid nineteenth-century Orthodox rabbis and hazans in America is that they were, in the end, unsuccessful in stemming the tides of mass disaffection from Judaism and of ritual and ideological change in this country's congregations. Some leaders, like Leeser, did better than others with the forces for change within their local congregation, although he had ongoing difficulties with his board, primarily over nonhalachic contractual issues. Leeser left Mikveh Israel in 1851 and made his greater mark outside the pulpit. His successor Rabbi Sabato Morais would have a better go it with his trustees while he succeeded, during his forty-six year tenure at the Philadelphia synagogue, in keeping the old traditions alive and unamended. But that synagogue and its sister congregation, Shearith Israel, under the mid–late century ministries of the refined and English-speaking Revs. Jacques J. Lyons and Henry Pereira Mendes, were exceptions to the rule.

By the 1870s, almost all Americanized congregations had turned away from Orthodoxy. But neither the victorious reformers nor the shrinking constituency within Orthodoxy's tent could claim that they had come close to solving the problem of disaffection that haunted Judaism's survival in this country. However, in the decades that followed, the calculus of allegiances was destined to change with the arrival of a new wave of immigrant Orthodox Jews, some of whom were profoundly observant. Most others were not, but they still situated themselves squarely within a now expanding Orthodox tent. In short order, these newcomers would emerge as the Jewish religious majority in America even as they and their children struggled to find their own ways of maintaining their religious identities within a free America.

# RELIGIOUS DILEMMAS OF A *TREIF* LAND

Massive Jewish migration from tsarist Russia and other parts of East Central and Eastern Europe was well underway before Rabbi Israel Mayer ha-Cohen Kagan — known by his nom de plume as the Hafetz Hayim — rose to call for a halt to such perilous travel. For him, the danger was spiritual rather than physical. Though progress had surely been made over more than two centuries, making America hospitable to those who wanted to maintain the religious traditions of the Old World, for the revered rabbi of Radun, Poland, settlement in this libertine country was still fraught with danger to devout Jews. In the years prior to his admonitions, other distinguished East European rabbis had already sounded their alarms. As early as 1862, the Galician rabbi Joseph Saul Nathanson of Lemberg had warned that "dedication to the Torah is weak" in that far-off land to where so many "patently unknowledgeable people are migrating." In Lithuania in 1890, Rabbi Isaac Jacob Reines observed sadly that over the course of time, even the most pious people who came to the United States ended up losing their "fear of God and their religious ways." But it remained for Rabbi Kagan to articulate the most definitive warnings and directions.[1]

In his plaintive work, *Niddehei Yisrael*, which appeared in 1894 and was addressed to the "dispersed and wandering Jews in distant lands," Kagan went beyond calling upon the faithful on the move to make heroic efforts to keep the Sabbath, observe kashruth, and follow the laws of family purity in that "curse[d]" place where "desecration of the Torah" was rampant. He instructed those who would listen to him that, in the end, "the only one proper solution" for those desiring "to live properly before God" was to not settle at all in America. For him, the only observant immigrant who was even conceivably worthy of praise was that rare "God-fearing man" whose presence in this barren land might "strengthen religious life." Perhaps here, in his parenthetical note, he was referring to the hundreds of rabbis from his part of the world who ventured across the ocean to minister to the spiritually benighted immigrant masses. However, on balance, he continued, if a "proper person" had made the tragic mistake of emigrating, "he must return to his home where the Lord will sustain him. He must not be misled by thoughts of remaining away until he is financially wealthy." For only back in Poland and Russia, he believed, could a Jew live the right type of religious life and "bring up his sons in Torah and piety."[2]

It is impossible to determine how many Jews actually heard his definitive message, but evidently several million East Europeans did not follow his commands. By the time Kagan spoke out, some tens of thousands of former denizens of the Pale of Settlement, Romania, and Hungary had already made America their home. Only a fraction of those who settled here ever considered the idea of going back. As previously noted, during a veritable century of Jews on the move, refugees from East European lands were crossing the Atlantic as early as the 1820–1830s. Moreover, the migrants who started their long journeys westward just from the year 1881—when random violence in parts of the tsarist empire began to punctuate the economic miseries that had long been the Jews' lot, to the moment when Kagan cried out—were but the initial wave of an uninterrupted population relocation that would continue and crescendo until the World War I made the trek across wartorn Europe extremely dangerous. In the thirteen years before Rabbi Kagan made his plea, approximately 370,000 Jews arrived in America. In the succeeding twenty years, an additional 2.1 million sought freedom here. Migration to the United States would peak in the years 1904–1908 when approximately 650,000 Jews entered the new land. The flow of these immigrants would resume again in the decade after 1910, ending only when onerous United States immigration regulations, promulgated in the early 1920s, called a halt to Jewish newcomers approaching this free country's shores.[3]

Rabbi Kagan was correct about one thing. The hope of breaking the cycles of poverty that had long threatened Jewish existence drove so many to leave for America. Pogroms surely had their place in group- and family decision making as certainly those whom mobs victimized in Warsaw and Odessa (1881) or Iaşi (1899), or Homel and Kishinev (1903) could attest. But these traumatic moments — or fears that the disorganized rioters would someday come to their hometowns — only magnified the daily struggle for sustenance and survival. The numbers show that over the course of forty years — 1881–1921 — more Jews left Galicia and Lithuania where there were very few violent outbreaks than from Ukraine, the site of several of the most infamous pogroms. The greater enemy ultimately was the restrictive, discriminatory government policies that stifled Jewish lives and exacerbated the economic vicissitudes suffered by so many as their home countries modernized and industrialized. Occasional famines, diseases, and other acts of God only added to their miseries.[4]

Through the eighteenth century, Russian tsars did not countenance sustained Jewish settlements in their territories. Peter the Great, for one, reportedly allowed that he would "prefer to see in our midst nations professing Mohammedanism and paganism rather than Jews [who] are rogues and cheats." It was his "endeavor to eradicate evil, not to multiply it."[5] Only the political force of circumstances brought those whom these rulers had never tolerated under their dictatorial sway. From 1772 to 1795, hundreds of thousands of Polish–Lithuanian Jews became Russian subjects as the Polish Commonwealth was partitioned among the Prussian, Austro-Hungarian, and Russian empires. Substantial territorial adjustments after the defeat of Napoleon and the Congress of Vienna in 1815 brought additional Jews under tsarist control. Anxious to keep the previously unwanted minority apart from Holy Mother Russia, a Pale of Settlement was established as early as 1791 to segregate the annexed Jews. The new acquisitions were held within the outer periphery of the Russian domains, within its fifteen most western provinces and the ten provinces of what became known as Congress Poland, basically the former Duchy of Warsaw.[6]

Within the Pale, Jews were never left alone as they bore the dual afflictions of an attenuated medieval antisemitism — their rulers and much of the populace hated them for theological reasons — and the incursions into their lives of modern state initiatives to change the way they conducted their lives. For example, beginning with Alexander I (1801–1825), who desired to make these subjects productive, Jews were frequently forced out of the countryside where they previously had worked among the poor peasants and were directed to the settlement's expanding cities. While these ukases were intermittent and sometimes repeated — Russian officials did not always follow through well on their commands — the required relocations caused both economic and social turmoil within the oppressed minority.[7]

Under the even harder hand of Nicholas I (1825–1855), Jewish life turned appreciably darker in Russia. The most grievous decree was the drafting of Jewish men and boys into the tsar's military for twenty-five years of service. Those unfortunates who were over eighteen were immediately inducted into the army. Youngsters, aged twelve to eighteen, were inducted into special cantonist brigades in which they were harshly educated and resocialized. Jews in that army were stuck in a totally different world from the colonial American militia that Asser Levy wanted to be a part and even from the French and German forces that counted Jews among their ranks. Elsewhere, the barracks were a place where Jews could prove that they were manly and loyal citizens in free societies. Under the tsars, those conscripted were constantly pressured to abandon their Judaism, and were effectively compelled to become Russian Orthodox subjects. To make matters even worse, the leaders of the kehillah were assigned the heart-wrenching duty of selecting the young men who would be slated for induction. Impressionable teenagers usually went first, to the great pleasure of tsarist officials. In the worst of cases, *khappers* ("catchers") in the Jewish community's employ literally kidnapped children as young as eight or nine. The horrendous choices that Jewish officials made did little to inspire continued popular confidence in that long-standing institution. All told, 70,000 Jews suffered that grievous fate — 50,000 were minors — over three decades.[8]

Given these very difficult sets of circumstances — with the military threat to life, limb, and souls looming largest — the reign of Nicholas I witnessed Jews in flight from Russia to Central and Western Europe. Some traveled as far as the United States. For those who ventured to move, the logic was inescapable: if they were destined to be uprooted, why not live their new lives in the cities of Prussia or France or America? Though former tsarist subjects may well have been roaming free in this country in the 1830s–1840s, they certainly were here as of 1852, when the Beth Hamidrash, the first Orthodox synagogue under East European auspices, was founded in New York. Two years later, in 1854, a Lithuanian rabbi named Hirsch Levine who came to Charleston, South Carolina — where his wife's family, also of Lithuanian extraction, already resided — was instrumental in founding Congregation Brith Sholom. The multiethnic synagogue that emerged in the Palmetto city also included some Germans and even one or two "Hollanders," even if they all prayed according to some sort of "Polish *miniek*" (minhag). None of them felt comfortable praying at the Sephardic and acculturated Orthodox Shearith Israel, and the Reform Beth Elohim was totally out of the question. During this same decade, rabbis from the lands of the tsars, such as Aaronsohn, Ash, Friedman, and Mittleman made their presence known in the New York metropolis, immersing themselves in kashruth problems and other halachic issues.[9]

Ironically, as much as they suffered the uncompromised despotism of

Nicholas I, it was under the somewhat more enlightened policies of his successor, Alexander II (1856–1881) that the immediate stage was set for large-scale migration. Here the Jewish story intersects with that of all Russian subjects in the Pale and beyond. Almost everyone had to cope with fundamental transformations that their tsar brought to society. Reacting in large measure to his father's defeat in the Crimean War at the very end of Nicholas I's regime, Alexander II pushed his country to take its place on the continent as a competitive, modern, and industrialized nation. High on his agenda was the construction of railway links and the development of an efficient and productive factory system in the growing cities of his domain. For Jews, the good new was that as the tsar, in emulation of the West, bowed slightly toward liberalization of his regime and approved the entry of some of them into the Russian heartland for trade and even settlement. Among these privileged elements, there would be those who dreamt the dual dreams not only of economic success but also of integration and ultimate acceptance. But for more inhabitants of the Pale, Alexander II's policies had multiple adverse affects.[10]

The emancipation of Polish serfs in the early 1860s — one of Alexander II's most enlightened moves — contributed immensely to this growing concentration of competing and struggling peoples in the cities. There, Jews and gentiles alike tried to figure out how their prior artisan, production, and handicrafts skills or trade occupations could work in these new environments. Ultimately, one favorable result of these pressures for change was that many Jews acquired warranted industrial skills — most notably proficiency in the factory-based needles trade — that would in time hold them in good stead in America. But, while still in Russia, they suffered grievously, as did all of those around them, in making personal peace with the new conditions.[11]

While Alexander II's commitment to industrializing and urbanizing his country long continued, his flirtation with liberalism did not last beyond the first decade of his twenty-six year reign. For Jews, sustained repression coupled with the difficulties of city life exacerbated their lot. Although upon ascending the throne Alexander II abolished his father's demand that Jews serve for twenty-five years in the military, this tsar's drafting of Jews to help him fight the Russo-Turkish War of 1878 presented an additional crisis for Jewish families. And Jews, like everyone else, suffered grievously from a famine in Lithuania from 1867 to 1869 and a cholera epidemic in 1869.[12]

In 1881, violence through pogroms — though intermittent and localized — was added to the negative equation of Jewish life under the tsars. In the aftermath of his father's assassination that year, Alexander III cracked down on all forces for social change within his domain. For Jews specifically, the May Laws of 1882 had additional deleterious effects. This legislation forbade any Jewish settlements outside existing locales and stopped them from

conducting business on Sundays and Christian holidays. Under these regulations, an unfortunate Jew who might have left an old town for only a few
days might be defined as a newcomer and denied return home. The only
mitigating aspect of tsarist activity was that while Russian rules prohibited
out-migration without exit permits, bribery helped ease the move past
checkpoints. Experienced and daring border smugglers did their part, too,
in getting their co-religionists on to Germany. But then again, such a pass
was far from a sign of benign lack of oversight. Rather, it was in keeping with
tsarist adviser and Russian Orthodox religious antisemite, Constantin Pobe-
donostsev's alleged statement that the solution to the Jewish question in
Russia was that one third would die, a second third would be converted, and
a third would migrate.[13]

A comparable set of hateful governmental policies punctuated with
spates of physical attacks and unforeseen economic disasters moved late
nineteenth-century Romanian Jews to their country's borders. Although
this host country had long harbored Jews, they were hardly welcomed and
barely tolerated. In the mid-nineteenth century, Bucharest's long-standing
ill treatment of Jews was so well known in the West, that in 1870, a sympathetic President Ulysses S. Grant dispatched Benjamin F. Peixotto, a leader
of American Jewry's most important fraternal organization, the B'nai B'rith,
as his envoy to protest the offending country's activities. A year later, in
1871, the situation worsened for the Jews of Ismail who weathered a pogrom
that arose out of a blood libel accusation. In 1878, while the Romanian
rulers promised the great European powers at the Congress of Berlin that in
return for full independence, they would respect the rights of all peoples in
its midst, Jews continued to be "foreigners without protection." Jews could
be summarily barred from peddling in towns and cities, as they indeed were
in 1884. They could be expelled from some villages, as happened in 1899.
Then there were the recurring nightmares of physical attacks, like those
that Jews of Iași endured also in 1899, the same year when all Romanians
suffered the beginnings of a two-year failed harvest and "severe depression," another act of God that was blamed on the Jews. Afflicted and disgusted with their lot, some 30 percent of Romanian Jews fled to America
between 1881 and 1914. These 75,000 immigrants constituted percentage
wise the largest single group of Jews to leave an East European locale during
this long era of migration.[14]

The traumas of economic modernization, but without such robust and
horrific oppression, underscored the story of Jewish out-migration from
Eastern Hungary — most notably Galicia — the once Polish territory that was
under the Austro-Hungarian Empire's control. As of 1867, Jews in that
region possessed the emancipated rights of citizens, even if spokesmen for
antisemitic political parties and local enemies continued to articulate nasty

words about Jews. The intensification of ongoing poverty was the major story in their lives. Railroads that quickly brought city products to consumers in small towns put Jewish shopkeepers out of business. Co-religionists who worked as drivers and as coachmen became obsolete. Local artisans found that they could not compete with larger urban-based manufacturers. In the overcrowded cities, where competition was extreme and wages low, the economic status of the Galician Jewish worker was actually worse that that of their Polish and Ukrainian Jewish counterparts. These conditions led approximately 30,000 Jews to immigrate to America in the 1880s. Some 60,000 followed them in the 1890s. All counted, about 150,000 from all Austro-Hungarian locales — not just Galicia — settled in the United States in the first decade of the twentieth century.[15]

Once Jews began contemplating leaving their homelands, several forces made the still-wrenching decision somewhat easier. As previously noted, as of the 1850s, steamship travel reduced the cross-Atlantic time to ten to fourteen days. The costs were affordable even if poor passengers had to cope in their steerage holes with "sickening odors, vile language . . . screams of women defending themselves, the crying of children . . . and practically every sound that reached the ear, irritated beyond endurance." Jews also had to trek first across Europe to major port cities such as Hamburg or Bremen. For Jews living under the tsar, Alexander II's railroad works linking the empire with the West helped in this regard. German, Austrian, English, French, Swiss, Dutch, and Belgian Jewish relief organizations also ably assisted their brethren transverse the continent. Their efforts were born both out of humanitarian concerns for their own kind and from a desire to make sure that these afflicted co-religionists continued on to America. Finally, and possibly most significantly, as the years went by an ever increasing number of Jews left for the United States because relatives and friends had already ventured there. Those who came first wrote back, factually or fictionally, about their successes in the free land, sent remittances, and created a chain of migration that would continue for four decades.[16]

If the multitudes of emboldened immigrants, driven in their economic pursuits, did not listen to Rabbi Kagan's admonition to remain in, or to return to Eastern Europe, did they hearken to his demand that they be scrupulous in their observance of Orthodoxy's pillars as they wandered toward America? To hear the rabbi's contemporaries tell it, here too his laments fell on deaf ears. Using powerful and evocative metaphorical language, they decried the disloyal actions of those immigrant Jews who emerged from their steerage quarters to throw their tefillin overboard as they crossed the Atlantic Ocean. For these critics, the voyage was a turning point; the beginning of the end of fidelity to Judaism and the dramatic head start on the road to disaffection and assimilation. "Like Jonah of old who boarded a boat to Tarshish," prior to his legendary encounter with that big fish, fleeing "from before the face of the Lord," so were these travelers depicted as making a statement, in the midst of their passage to America, that they now wished to put the religious values of their ancestral past behind them.

When Lithuanian rabbi Moses Shimon Sivitz settled in Pittsburgh, he recollected homiletically and decried dramatically the behavior of those who "fled from God while still on the boat that first stopped praying and then committed their talis and tefillin to the deep." Tragically, for him, modern Jewish migrants could have emulated the most ancient of Jewish travelers, their forefather Abraham, who "left his home and birth place, but who, instead of distancing himself from God's call, accepted the yolk of the Commandments even more completely." But such was neither the mindset nor the destiny of the Russian Jews coming to America. As Sivitz saw it, even those "upright" individuals who, at first, resisted the sirens of secularization while at sea, soon succumbed to the tide of disaffection as they witnessed "their wives and children . . . straying from the ways of their fathers."[17]

Sivitz's colleague, Rabbi Alexander Z. Levin of Detroit, who also hailed from Lithuania, would assert that the contemporary Jonahs' trek away from faith began even prior to their setting off from their homes in the Russian Pale. He lamented that they agreed to "sell their souls" while still in the "land of their birth." Those who pulled up stakes knew that in America there was no religious order or control, and they looked forward to taking part in this libertine world. Thus they hurried to "flee to Tarshish" (i.e., New York), like the disloyal biblical figure, Jonah, had done. As soon as they crossed the border, their "desecration of the Sabbath" and "their shedding of the yolk of the Commandments" was imminent as these Jews sought new identities. It remained for these defectors, while on their long ocean voyage, to make it known to all that they had "turned their back on the Torah." The dispatching of their tefillin to the deep was another emphatic way of demonstrating their utter disaffection from their religious pasts.[18]

But were not these rabbis on board who witnessed such blatant transgressions also subtly distancing themselves from their own pasts? While no one would dare suggest that they did not keep up with traditional ritual practices, there was that ban which Rabbi Kagan had placed on migration to America. Some rabbis on the move would have answered charges that they were breaking with the authority of a great Torah sage by projecting themselves as among those special-case Jews, "God-fearing men," whom the senior rabbi prayed might against all odds "strengthen" American Jewish religious life. Others would have asserted that they were conforming to the authority of equally renowned and respected rabbis Chaim Soloveitchik and Isaac Elchanan Spektor. Although these leaders' views were the minority position among European sages — most colleagues were sure that since the Judaism of migrants would founder on foreign shores it was no place for the devout — Spektor made clear to many of those whom he personally had ordained that they were obliged to do their utmost to reclaim those on the move away from Judaism. Here again, the halachic tradition that a Jew must not only be pious but also be concerned with the religious behavior of others was surely in play. Rabbi Soloveitchik went even further in his charge. Not only "had the needs of the time . . . thrust an obligation" upon rabbis "to ameliorate Judaism" in America, but he also projected this presently treif country as potentially "a secure refuge for our people." This optimist looked at the freedom that Jews enjoyed in the United States, contrasted it with what tsarist oppression was doing to his people in Russia, and prayed that his rabbis would not only "ameliorate Judaism" but would also be the vanguard who would "build a secure refuge for our people and our Torah." They could construct the next great Diaspora Torah center until "the redemption to Zion would occur."[19]

Not all of the migrating rabbis had such lofty goals. Ironically, they left Eastern Europe for the same fundamental reason that motivated those whom they criticized: they were out to obtain a better standard of living for themselves and their families. While this motivation surely did not sit well with Rabbi Kagan — and perhaps Spektor and Soloveitchik, too, may have raised their eyebrows about such unheroic attitudes — the reality was that many Russian rabbis were unable to provide for their families. In some cases, when communities lost large segments of their population to Western European and American migration, those who remained — often the poorest Jews — were unable to support their rabbis. And competition was keen for the better posts in larger cities. For many of these impoverished religious leaders, the pains of poverty transcended whatever pangs of guilt they may have suffered about their decision.[20]

It is unlikely that most rabbis who left knew of Rabbi Pinchas Michael's feelings about their pragmatic decisions. But had these migrants known of his sentiments, they would have been warmed that at least one fellow rabbi understood the predicament that they shared with so many other Jews. Michael, of the small shtetl Antopol, had reportedly told those of his flock who considered emigration to "travel to America, there you will make a living." Of course, he was also quick to tell them in no uncertain terms to "preserve the Sabbath." Rabbis on the move could only hope that this calculus of concerns would prove prophetic. They prayed that they might do well in America and witness not only their families but all those around them observe that most cardinal of Jewish teachings.[21]

As these rabbis and other devout Jews contemplated the mixture of economic and religious motivation that had brought them on board, there certainly were those in steerage who did throw their tefillin overboard. But at most only one half of the Jewish population could have acted that way. At that point, women did not have that ritual item in their possessions. To properly engender this story—though rabbis of that time would not have spoken in these terms— the females would have disposed of their candlesticks, symbolically rejecting a positive commandment that the tradition imposes upon women. We will have more to say soon about other acts of religious disloyalty, like men shaving their beards and their wives disposing of their wigs and scarves on board.

There also were many Jewish men who did not bring tefillin aboard nor carry this holy object in their knapsacks when they left their former homelands. Jewish secularists and radicals of varying stripes also traveled westward. Adumbrations of enlightened attitudes and behavior patterns entered the Jewish scene as early as the 1840s during the last decade of the evil regime of Nicholas I. In the hopeful first years of Alexander II's reign, as the tsar spoke and moved toward westernization and modernization, decidedly nonobservant elements were among the increased number of privileged and progressive ones who came to fervently believe that worldly, productive Jews could eventually find their place in a new and egalitarian Russia. They became devotees and expositors of what became known as the Eastern Jewish Enlightenment, the *Haskalah*. As that monarch and his successors turned reactionary, such Jews eventually were part of those in Russia who argued that the only solution to oppression was the overthrow of tsarist absolutism and the reordering of society along radical social, economic, and political lines. These viewpoints brought Jews — usually young student cadres — into a myriad of agrarian radical, anarchist, and socialist cells and parties. After 1881, a few of these aggressive, modern-thinking people determined that the solution to their problems and the dilemmas of all Jews would never be solved in Russia or in any Diaspora setting including the free and attractive United States. They cast their lot with incipient Zionism and made Palestine their ultimate destination.[22]

By the time they decided to leave Russia—either because they had given up hope that change was imminent or because the tsar's police was chasing after them—many of the men who had once dreamed either of freedom and acceptance or who conspired for revolutionary change had long since dispensed with that morning commandment of donning phylacteries. Women of these political and social dispositions did not have to put that mitzvah behind them since the halacha had never required them to allocate time every day for prayer. But if they had become Sabbath desecrators, most likely it had been a long time since they had taken moments out of Friday night to light candles. As secularists on board, these men and women also would not have been careful about what they ate even if kosher foods were available on board. If some of them had among their belongings a Jewish book that meant the world to them, it would not have been a Bible but a dog-eared edition of Karl Marx's works in Yiddish or Russian. A few misplaced Zionists—who deferred migration to that barren Middle Eastern locale— might have clung dearly to Leo Pinsker's *Auto-Emancipation* or later on to Theodor Herzl's *The Jewish State* as they progressed toward a different Zion, America.[23]

Upon arrival in this land, if the most profoundly radical among these migrants remained true to their secular faith—some might have thrown Marx's works overboard, giving them too a head start in adjusting to America—they might have expressed dissent from religious Judaism in the most obnoxious of ways. Among the most noticed outright rejectionists were Jewish anarchists who, beginning in the late 1880s, organized and participated in Yom Kippur balls where the solemn religious Kol Nidre service was parodied through song, dance, and drink. At their gatherings, the ancestral faith was lampooned as a welter of "stupidities cooked up long ago . . . in order to mislead the poor worker, all the better to exploit him." Their stances earned them the opprobrium of religious enemies who returned the radicals' volleys. These most unrepentant of deviants were denigrated as "the outcasts and dregs of our people [who] propagate their despicable opinions to besmirch the faith of Israel." Though these antagonistic atheists had their say, most immigrant Jews did not maintain such radical antireligious values.[24]

Nor were the majority of Jews who left for America resolute assimilationists who consciously committed to separating themselves from their fellow Jews as completely and as quickly as possible. For these turn-of-the-twentieth-century counterparts of Solomon Pieterson —who came to America in Asser Levy's time and quickly gave up the totality of his ancestral past—public disregard for mitzvoth was only the most visible sign of disregard for any sense of Jewish identity. Those within the East European period of migration who disdained all religious connections also had no interest in attending Yom Kippur balls or in any other way linking themselves with alternative, radical forms of secular Jewish allegiance.

The religious values of most immigrants of this period, rather, can be better symbolized—using the rabbis' metaphor—as Jews who carried their tefillin or candlesticks on the long trek to America but over the course of time utilized them with ever decreasing frequency. They certainly did not angrily commit these sacred objects to the deep. If anything, while drifting away from many religious practices—even as they continued to follow many others—these Jews harbored more than a modicum of residual guilt when they failed to perform specific mitzvoth. Most remained deeply attached to Orthodox traditions even if the force of circumstances often precluded them from fulfilling all religious commitments.

For some Jews, the decline in observance began well before they actually considered taking that first step toward America. While the Jewish small town of the turn of the twentieth century was still known as that place where Jews "lived under strictly orthodox conditions," a contemporaneous student of international Jewish city life observed, from a fact-finding trip to Eastern Europe, in "Russia, Poland and Romania . . . many Jewish workers at work on the Sabbath." He would suggest somewhat hyperbolically that "conditions in Eastern Europe were approaching those observed among the Jews in western countries." Rabbi Isaac Margolis of Druzgenik, Lithuania, did not concur completely with Dr. Maurice Fishberg's conclusion that Eastern Europe was becoming as bad for Judaism as America. Still, he did allow that the many who lived a spiritually decrepit existence in the new world of freedom had started on their road away from tradition while in the oppressive world of the tsars. The social pressure that was so robust in the shtetl, where it was said that "if one should dare in a little town in Russia to keep his place of business open on the Sabbath, he would probably have to close it the rest of the week," simply no longer obtained in the more open, burgeoning, and confusing cities of the region.[25]

The many stores and businesses open on the Sabbath in a place like Lemberg [Lvov] caused another on-the-scene reporter to encounter two distinct types of Jews living different existences in the same urban locales. "The old-fashioned *frum* [punctiliously observant] Jews go their way and their modern counterparts go their own way, with each acknowledging the others' actions as natural phenomena."[26] While those who stood on the modern, less observant, side of the Jewish streets frequently separated themselves from traditional strictures, they in no way considered themselves as separate from other Jews. Nor did they—unlike the secularists and radicals—ever question the validity of biblical and rabbinic prohibitions against their actions when they worked on the Sabbath day.

Other Jews broke with their religious past on the boat to America, but had palpable misgivings about their actions. So, while Rabbi Isaac Margolis, that rabbinic expatriate who was less than content with the way Jews were living their religious lives in Lithuania, reported with disgust about his shipmates who "desecrated themselves with the bread and soup of the gentiles," he also could not help but notice that some of these transgressors were "embarrassed by their actions particularly when they got to know the rabbi on board." They did not eat treif in his presence.[27]

Still others took their first tentative strides away from traditional behavior upon arrival at Ellis Island. Reportedly, while Jews at this point of immigrant disembarkation ate the kosher food that the Hebrew Immigrant Aid Society provided, they neglected to ritually wash and to recite the blessing over bread nor did they say the grace after meals.[28]

Ultimately, however, it was the lures of America itself that transformed so many newcomers into what one devout critic would call the "*Poshe Yisrael,*" [sinners of Israel]. On the cultural level, the Jews' desire to look and act like other Americans caused men and women to change their appearances and dress, sometimes in violation of the halacha's codes. In this regard, the metaphor for the abandonment of tradition was the image of men shaving their beards as soon as they settled in the immigrant Jewish quarter. Another version of this act of disaffection with the past has the men emerging from steerage clean-shaven as their boat passed Lady Liberty in New York harbor. Meanwhile, their wives upon their first encounters with America immodestly took off their head coverings forever. An alternate reading of this transformation has wives joining their husbands on deck, anxious to toss their scarves or kerchiefs overboard as families decided to begin a new life in America.

In Eastern Europe, the biblical prohibition against the cutting of a man's scalp and the rabbinical regulation that instructs married women to display what is deemed as sexually alluring uncovered hair only to their husband in private comported well with Jewish men's and women's disinterest in looking like the gentiles among whom they lived. In America, the integrated-minded did not want to look different.

Then there were Jews who made good-faith efforts to resist these temptations whether on board or upon arrival but who eventually gave in to social pressure. To hear an early twentieth-century sociologist tell it: "Many a young man who was firm in his religious convictions, while in his native village" steeled himself against the "laxity prevalent" and the "temptations and allurements of the free country only to succumb . . . in his struggle and renounced his Judaism when he first submitted his chin to the barber's razor, at the entreaties and persuasions of his Americanized friends and relatives." The same may be said about women who also faced pressure to appear like all others.[29] Where, however, these dramatic depictions of religious decline proved to be inaccurate was in the categorical assertion that the clean-shaven men and the kerchiefless women *renounced* their Judaism. Rather, in so many ways and through so many practices, these Jews displayed a deep desire to remain within their people's wide religious tent.

Jews without beards may still have used their tefillin — at least occasionally — and they constantly identified with other Jewish traditions in a myriad of ways. Married women could have appeared in public sans scarves but may have confirmed their continued affinity for the faith every week when they lit Sabbath candles in the kosher homes that they monitored scrupulously. Anecdotal evidence also suggests that a goodly percentage of immigrant women utilized mikvehs — at least upon arrival — on a regular basis. As always, the very private nature of this family law precludes uncovering hard numbers on patterns of observance here. But this much is known: in 1884, the *New York Tribune* reported that some fifteen downtown synagogues maintained mikuchs. In 1905, another Jewish social worker observed that the "religious rites and customs [of mikveh] are carefully observed by the older generation who are pious." In time, many of them would come to "perform" this commandment in ways that the halacha did not prescribe. They would become physically clean — but not ritually pure — after immersion in their private bath tub; that is, if they were fortunate enough to live in such an up-to-date apartment. Or they would resort to the healthy settings of the public bath houses that American reformers, intent on cleaning up the newcomers, established in their neighborhoods. The point is that in the process of moving from lands of oppression to a world of personal and religious freedom, American Orthodoxy's new rank and file both affirmed and discarded their religious cultural traditions in different ways and to varying degrees.[30]

In the end, the greatest challenge to traditional observance was the drive to succeed economically. In so many ways, the pressures that this new era of immigrants felt were not unlike those Jews had always faced in this country. Whether that person was an eighteenth-century colonial merchant or a mid nineteenth-century peddler or a sweatshop laborer, there was no law stopping Jews, if they were so committed, from staying away from their workplaces on the Jewish Sabbath and holidays. But only the most devout of individuals would forego the chance to advance themselves — taking an extra day off — given the unavoidable reality that Blue Laws dictated that their shops, stores, and factories had to be shut on Sunday in civic recognition of the Christian Sabbath. In Eastern Europe, when Jews worked on the Jewish Sabbath — in those locales where their own communal mores permitted such violations — they did so largely to survive economically. In the new world, Jews labored on holy days to both survive and advance. One observer of this difficult scene, at the turn of the twentieth century, estimated that 95 percent of the Jews who worked on the Sabbath violated tradition out of economic necessity.[31]

An early twentieth-century immigrant poet set this scene, both metaphorically and dramatically, when he wrote of the masses of Jewish workers "trampl[ing] with their weekday boots the train of [the Sabbath queen's] bridal gown." Radical Jews, to extend the imagery, would have intentionally kicked mud in the Sabbath Queen's face. But they were not the downtown community's rank and file. In his neighborhood in Boston, Ephraim Lisitzky would also note matter-of-factly, "very few Jews observed the Sabbath."[32]

From New York, at approximately the same time, a Christian muckraker offered a comparable impression of what he characterized as "the disintegration of the Jews." Ray Stannard Baker wrote of a conversation with a

"Russian Jew" who told him that "from the time I entered the shop my religious interest began to decline . . . I ceased going to the synagogue first only on week days, later on Saturday as well." Two concomitant sociological studies offered hard numbers that quantified the extent of the religious problem. A report from 1912 showed that only one-quarter of Jewish workers in New York did not labor on the Sabbath. A year later, in 1913, a second study revealed that nearly 60 percent of the stores in a Jewish neighborhood on the Lower East Side were open on Saturday. Perhaps, as significant, the customers whom these shopkeepers serviced were in the majority also Jews, a factor that only added to the decline in the Sabbath atmosphere of the downtown neighborhood.[33]

Saturday work was also the lot of immigrant Jews who ended up in America's small cities and towns where they serviced a largely Christian clientele for whom Saturday was the big shopping day. In Johnstown, Pennsylvania — the Jewish population as of 1910 was between 700 and 750 — workers in the steel mills and coal mines received their paltry checks that day and went off with their families to buy their week's provisions, often at Jewish markets. Speaking of his immigrant father's and that generation's mindset, one memoirist recalled succinctly that they "came to America without anything to make a better living and worked very hard to give it to their families." Sabbath work, he said, was a "necessity."[34]

In other localities, where Jews also were a very small minority, an additional business psychology stratagem pointed to keeping a store open on the Sabbath. In Wichita, Kansas, Jewish merchants feared that their gentile customers might view them as bizarre and thus not worthy of their trade if they closed their stores on Saturday. Moreover, for these small entrepreneurs, it would have been, reportedly, a "mortifying experience" to explain the ins and outs of Jewish practice to their clientele. On the other hand, a memoirist from a small town in Texas recalled that while not working on the Sabbath was tantamount to committing "economic suicide," storekeepers where he came from were sure to shut their doors on the High Holidays. To do otherwise would show "a lack of self-respect." Did not the Christians around them celebrate Christmas and Easter? Should not Jews also honor their most important religious days? However, in observing their specific traditions they probably ended up having to explain to intrigued neighbors what Rosh ha-Shanah and Yom Kippur were all about. In another part of small-town America, in Benton Harbor, Michigan, Jewish businessmen made everyone know how important the central fall holidays were to them; their community's newspaper reported that "local Jewish stores which annually celebrate the event will be closed Thursday and Friday." These same emporia were open on the Sabbath to not lose a key shopping day.[35]

By contrast, although the hard numbers are not really there to cinch their assertion, local Jewish tradition from Charleston has it that the Sabbath work problem was not nearly as robust in that city due to a unique set of business circumstances. Recalling the situation from a somewhat later time —the 1920s—another memoirist has contended that "Charleston was probably in the forefront of all cities in the United States with the number of Jewish merchants, at least percentage wise, that kept closed on the Sabbath." Why keep your business open on Saturday, local conventional wisdom argued, if your steadiest non-Jewish customers, like those who worked in the local phosphate factories or navy yard, did not get paid until work ended *late Saturday night*? The hour at which gentile customers were paid, whether in Johnston or Charleston, made much difference in determining Jewish Sabbath work patterns. In addition, since in that southern town Sunday closing laws were often not strictly enforced, business people did not quite feel the pressure to work on Saturday that was so acute elsewhere. What these storekeepers did with their free time was another matter entirely. Some may sanctified these hours. They may have attended the synagogue, studied or read, or simply congregated with friends and relatives in sedentary realms, observing a real day of rest. Others may have seized upon this opportunity to travel, to have time for recreation, or to take part in all sorts of secular entertainments.[36]

At the same time, both in Charleston and elsewhere, less fortunate Jews who were compelled to work on the Sabbath demonstrated an otherwise deep devotion to keeping that day holy. In thousands of immigrant homes, the Sabbath Queen still ruled as the family gathered around the table for a traditional Friday night meal at sundown or when the father could get off from his job.[37] Preparations for welcoming this regal guest began some twenty-four hours earlier as, for example, Thursday night–Friday afternoon gained the reputation in the New York Jewish quarter as the busiest shopping time of the week. Here immigrant women took the lead and played the major role in creating a Sabbath atmosphere. Beyond purchasing the best they could afford of culinary delicacies, "in the ghetto," wrote an observer of that downtown scene, "Friday . . . is a day of agitation, of scrubbing, cooking, baking." A sanctified scene prevailed all Friday night as favorite religious songs were sung at dinner, quiet conversation enhanced the holy atmosphere, and no gas or electric lights were turned on or off unless prior arrangements had been made with the local Shabbes Goy to come by at the right times. Just as in earlier periods of American Jewish history, these friendly gentiles were useful enablers of their neighbors' religious traditions.[38]

Saturday morning did witness the breadwinners—fathers, mothers, and possibly older children—reluctantly don their work-a-day shoes, but not before admonishing those they left behind to continue to observe the Sabbath at home. Many men said their traditional Sabbath prayers at a minyan

Figure 3.1. The tradition of Jewish-owned stores in
Charleston, S.C., closed on the Sabbath continued into the
mid-twentieth century. Courtesy of the Jewish Heritage
Collection, Addlestone Library, College of Charleston.

conducted very early in the morning before the long day of labor began. They did so in a neighborhood synagogue before the lucky ones who did not have to work arrived for more leisurely devotions some hours later.[39] Heartfelt rituals also were performed in the work places themselves. Hence, many of these Jews did not come close to renouncing their Judaism. One otherwise observant immigrant Jew spoke for so many when he told his children in their small Pennsylvania town that he deeply regretted laboring on the holy day but did so only "to make a good living for his family." This pattern of religious behavior, as we have seen, would long endure within twentieth-century American Orthodoxy.[40]

Then there were those within these neighborhoods and communities who hallowed the start of the quiet Sabbath evening with prayers and perhaps with religious song before leaving their sacred home precincts for the decidedly secular environs of the local Yiddish theaters. While they prioritized Jewish popular culture over religious observance, some of these ticket holders may have squirmed in their orchestra or balcony seats as they felt guilty about their presence in such a place. Conflicted, they projected their ambivalence upon the thespians who, in their view, were *really* violating the Sabbath.

Hutchins Hapgood, another muckraker who lived among the downtown poor, captured this interesting slice of immigrant life with the following report:

> The Orthodox Jews who go to the theatre on Friday night, the beginning of the Sabbath are commonly somewhat ashamed of themselves and try to quiet their consciences by a vociferous condemnation of the actors on the stage. The actor, who through the exigencies of his role, is compelled to appear on Friday night with a cigar in his mouth is frequently greeted with hisses and strenuous cries of "Shame, shame, smoke on the Sabbath!" from the proletarian hypocrites in the gallery.[41]

Perhaps some of these angered and embarrassed Orthodox theatergoers may have purchased their tickets before the Sabbath to peremptorily assuage their consciences. They would thus avoid handling money and be only in violation of the spirit of the Sabbath; a gray area in the halacha. Still, they were far from truly pious in that guise or demeanor.[42]

At the same time, there were Jews within this religiously diverse downtown community who cared even less about the call of the traditional Sabbath rest. As suggested previously, some immigrants who had begun to succeed economically and who did not have to work on the holy day transformed Saturday from a day of rest to an occasion for shopping and recreation. Neighborhood Jewish storekeepers were more than ready, willing, and able to court unabashed consumers. However, these miscreants, too, did not completely renounce their Judaism. Though the weekly Sabbath cycle did not move them, certain critical days in the Jewish calendar — most notably Passover and the High Holidays — laden with the full power of historical memory moved them toward observance.[43]

Again women were the foremost advocates for preserving ancestral traditions as they literally scrubbed the streets to rid their quarter of all leaven before Passover. They also saw to it that their families possessed the requisite matzahs, wines, and dishes for the Festival of Freedom. Annually, vendors of such foodstuffs and items made fortunes. These proclivities also were not lost upon other Jewish merchants who were there to assist customers in looking fashionable in commemoration of these holidays. In an interesting twist of traditions, weeks before these central religious moments in the spring and fall, suit and dress sales were held in downtown emporia, sometimes on the Sabbath, to avail Jews of the opportunity to be seen in the proper clothes for these holidays.[44]

For the classier set among these immigrants, the place to be seen with their new gear was within, or just outside, the landmark synagogues of the larger cities' downtown areas. These were congregations that had been established as early as the 1850s–1860s as incipient East European elements first arrived in America and created their "Russian," "First Hungarian," or "Romanian" shuls within the midst of the Central European majority. Anyone who had come even earlier from these lands had to make due with attendance in a "German" congregation, so long as its ritual was strictly Orthodox. By the 1890s, congregations like New York's Beth Hamidrash Hagadol of Norfolk Street or Kehal Adath Jeshurun of Eldridge Street, or Chicago's Anshe Kanesses Israel — the so-called "Russiche Shul" — on Clinton and Judd Streets or the Ohave Sholom Mariampol of Canal and Liberty Streets — or even Charleston's Brith Sholom had enough affluent members committed to their cause to raise hundreds and then thousands of dollars to build commodious structures. These synagogues remained Orthodox in ritual. Still, efforts were made to have the services project an emerging stylish American ambience. The well-heeled worshippers were instructed to be quiet during prayers and to control all forms of spontaneous and indecorous behavior. They were expected to smile appreciatively at the quality of the melodious flourishes that the well-trained cantors offered, accompanied by their choir of male voices. By these same 1890s, the competition among the better-off within the immigrant communities to brag about having the best cantor around to both inspire and entertain the fancy-suited men and women in their respective pews was so robust that a salary war ensued nationally. Congregations romanced candidates with sweetheart annual contracts worth thousands of dollars.[45]

The majority of poorer and less acculturated immigrants offered their

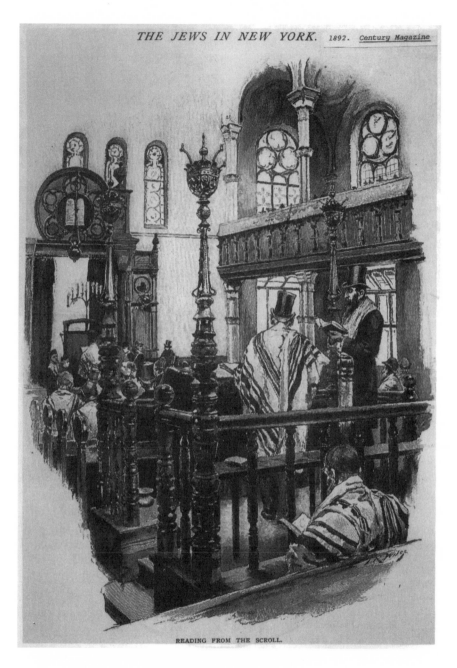

READING FROM THE SCROLL.

Figure 3.2. Services at Kehal Adath Jeshurun in the
1890s. From Richard Wheatley, "The Jews of New York,"
*Century Magazine,* January 1892.

prayers in their neighborhood *landsmanshaft* synagogues. These small store-front congregations — hundreds could be found in the larger cities of America, and many small towns that housed East European Jews also had their share — were the Jews' fundamental religious and social institution. They grew out of a basic human need and desire that all newcomers possess to connect with, learn from, and assist those from the same hometown in their initial encounters with a new, still foreign land. An immigrant's very presence in this country or in any specific American locale may well have been due to an earlier arriving *landsman*'s communication to those still back in the old hometown about the promises and wonders of America. Upon arrival on these shores, later comers usually sought out fellow Jews for help in finding housing, employment, and possibly above all, psychological succor in dealing with this strange new world. When they desired to pray with a minyan of like-minded Jews, they wanted, if at all possible, to worship and socialize in a synagogue that reminded them of the specific minhag and social ambience of their past religious life. Certainly by the 1880s, all immigrants — except those who found themselves in the smallest of American towns where regional differentiations could not be made — could choose to pray just as they once did in their specific home town or *gubernia* (province). As they acculturated and made enough money to own their own seats, they might have felt more comfortable in a landmark congregation. But for starters in America, they were more than satisfied being within the "*Kehillah Kedosha* [The Holy Congregation] of the People" from their erstwhile city or shtetl.[46]

These shuls were open for prayers three time a day, seven days a week, but were often half-filled Saturday morning as so many worshippers went to work. But they were packed solid to their unsteady rafters on the High Holidays as a palpable sense of religiosity permeated the ghetto. Then a combination of nostalgia, awe over the days of judgments and, again, a desire to be among (and to be seen in the best finery they could afford) their fellow Jews brought all those who clearly had not renounced their Judaism to the shul. In these places, the Jews' prayers were so heartfelt and sincere that even a hard-boiled freethinker like the socialist newspaper editor Abraham Cahan could not help but describe reverently the "sighs and sobs of the Days of Awe, the thrill that passes through the heartbroken, talis-covered congregation when the shofar blows."[47]

Comparable spates of frenetic religious activity, and with it a discernible degree of seasonal piety, also obtained in the smaller locales where some East European immigrants ended up. For example, at Shearith Israel in Wharton, Texas, an agricultural town on the Gulf Coast, some seasonal worshippers from outside the area bedded down on "cots or roll-away beds in the synagogue's community hall," so as not to transgress through traveling on the holiday. In Fort Worth, where Congregation Ahavath Sholom's leaders found it difficult to secure a minyan on many Sabbaths, additional chairs had to be rented on the High Holidays, where "tickets sold (for $3 a family)" for nonmembers. These Jews — like their big city brethren — were on the scene not only to pray but also to be seen by other Jews. So robust was the social context there that synagogue officials were reportedly less than pleased when worshippers took some of the rented seats out of the sanctuary and sat around and gossiped.[48]

Back in the metropolis, the demand for seats often exceeded the capacity of its immigrant synagogues, leading to the emergence of a cottage industry of "mushroom" or "provisional" synagogues. However, to the great consternation of many neighborhood people, all too many of these "Temporary Halls of Worship" contributed to the "the abuse of religion," as "self-styled . . . irresponsible . . . Holy-day Rabbis" often bereft of proper credentials rented "halls and sold tickets of admission." In one of the more grotesque examples of public exploitation, in New York in 1901 a placard was supposedly placed "in front of the Grand Central Palace which announce[d] the services that will be held there during the coming Holy Days, by the 'famous Tompkin Brothers.' " To a critical observer it appeared "very much as if a circus has come to town" with "its . . . famous troupes of performers" with the "Talith and the Sacred Shroud . . . prominent among the 'costumes' worn by the 'stars' in these performances." Adding "to the disgrace," there was "some broken-down 'rabbi' who, for a consideration . . . lends his name to these sacrilegious proceedings." Meanwhile, seats at those Yiddish theaters not cannibalized for such "services" were reserved — as the show went on at both matinee and evening performances — for those Jews who had only the barest of connections to their ancestral religious past.[49]

While these devotees of the Yiddish theater found their places guiltlessly on and off the aisles on Second Avenue, back in the synagogue Jews who, at first blush, would seem to be unlikely synagogue-goers swelled the ranks of the faithful. Much to the chagrin of their ideologically true leaders, rank and file members of the Arbeter Ring (Workmen's Circle), whom the rest of the year identified with varying forms of atheistic socialism, felt the tugs both of their people's longest-standing religious traditions and of more immediate personal demands. Some who never really abandoned their belief in God, even if they habitually did not follow the commandments, "went trembling and shaking to shul to pray, due to fear of judgment." Though free to live as they chose, they were far from liberated from the ancient belief that on those momentous days, a Supreme Being evaluated the actions of all people over the past year and determined who would live and who would die. Others who were not so afraid of the Almighty showed up to maintain harmony at home. In some immigrant families, a husband might be enamored of Marx's teachings, while his wife remained true to the Torah of Moses. One observer of this family scene put it so well when he explained that "the smart man understands that it is easier to give in to the wife and go once or twice to shul . . . rather than not go to shul and always fight with the wife." Still others fidgeted in their seats next to their parents, drawn to services solely out of respect for their elders.[50]

The proclivities of such "Yom Kippur Jews" or "three-day-a-year Jews" so offended the most radical elements in their neighborhoods that their "treasons" were characterized as "betrayals" and as hypocrisies, leading to calls for the effective excommunication of those who acted periodically in a religious manner.[51] Later on in the Arbeter Ring's history — in the early 1920s — even greater calumnies had to have been heaped upon those members who took their twelve-year-old sons out of their radical Yiddishists school and sent them to an Orthodox Talmud Torah so that they might be prepared for their Bar Mitzvahs.[52] Others who were more tolerant of diversity within their own secular midst welcomed all who stepped foot into the often half-filled fraternal lodges. Though they could schedule their cultural events around their members work schedules — Sabbath labor was not a problem for them — not unlike downtown religious leaders, they also competed against the theaters and other amusements that took folks away from their secular activities. The inclusionary sorts may have also understood the following ultimate reality about mass immigrant passage into America: Jews who carried Marx's writings with them on board to this country may have also found room in the knapsacks for a Bible, as well as for tefillin and candlesticks. Situations and conditions on the ground in the new environment would determine how dedicated they would be in their religious life and how committed they would be to their progressive causes.

Amidst the multitudes of immigrants who made partial peace with Jewish tradition as they strove to adjust and succeed in America, there was a coterie of deeply devoted Jews who rigorously kept the commandments. They were the men who carried their tefillin with pride from shtetls of the Pale to American cities and donned them without fail every weekday morning as Jewish law prescribes. These were the married women who not only used their candlesticks weekly but persisted in frequenting the mikveh as that tradition provides. In some cases, the sagas of those who dedicated themselves to strict observance took on almost legendary qualities as in the case of some Minnesota women who reportedly in the winter "would go to Lake Geneva and break through the ice to immerse themselves" since there was no ritualarium around.[53] Then there is the example of Harry Fischel of whom it was said struggled for forty years — from his first days in the United States through his emergence as one of New York's leading immigrant real estate magnates — to uphold the principle that this country's lures of economic opportunity did not "require" that a Jew "forget about God . . . religion and especially about the Sabbath and dietary laws." According to his biographer, this Orthodox Horatio Alger from the small Lithuanian town of Meretz was thrust into the metropolis in 1883 at age eighteen and was immediately told, in no uncertain terms, that he had to "work everyday including the Sabbath and eat what you can." But Fischel would not follow the crowd, persevered, and ultimately made a substantial fortune with what he unquestionably believed was God's help.[54]

Few Jews possessed of Fischel's strict religious values were as successful as he. But statistical speaking, as of the second decade of the 1900s, some 40 percent of the downtown storekeepers who kept their shops closed on Saturday and the approximately 25 percent of the ghetto's Jewish laborers who absented themselves from their workplaces on the Sabbath seemed to have tried.

Piety of a different sort was on display daily among that minority of Jews who set aside time for regular Torah study. These commitments were far from lost upon that perceptive ubiquitous outsider Hutchings Hapgood, who reported that "the sweatshops are full" with those who "in addition to their ceremonies at home, form Talmudic clubs and gather in tenement house rooms, which they convert into synagogues." Those whom Hapgood called "religious fanatics" — though with more than a measure of respect and admiration — were, he said, "Orthodox Jews" who look upon "all these regulations" that the Torah and rabbinic law prescribed as "privileges." They were a breed apart from the other "Orthodox Jews," whom the gentile journalist encountered at the Yiddish theater on Friday night. Meanwhile, one outspoken immigrant rabbi who was otherwise disgusted with the irreligious scene all around him, found some consolation in the evident commitment of both "the great merchants, men of substance and wealth" and the "people who support themselves with difficulty by the work of their own hands" who "study together" and "learn as a congregation, and in smaller groups . . . deliberately and sharply." Still, Rabbi Moses Weinberger could not help but wonder: "Will their children follow in their ways? Will they enjoy, as their fathers did, God's holy Torah and the wisdom of our holy rabbis of blessed memory?" The pessimistic Weinberger "doubt[ed] it very much."[55]

Though habitually pessimistic, Weinberger surely had a point. As pious Jews like he surveyed the scene in their immigrant neighborhoods, they saw much to offend their religious sensibilities. Many fellow Jews ran past them on their way to work on the Sabbath. Others sauntered by to shop or to engage in secular amusements. Kosher meat was abundant; however, there always was the squabbling over its proper control. Mikvehs dotted the local landscapes but no one knew how many people in the neighborhood actually utilized them. For most folks, public baths took care of the personal hygiene issues and served as a substitute for the ritual purity that only the Jewish religious founts could provide. But for devout Jews — rabbis and lay leaders alike — the largest concerns centered on the future religious identity of the next generation. Ultimately, a simple lack of acculturation would keep the majority of immigrant Jews connected, at least in an attenuated way, to their ancestral roots. They would never lose their desire to be counted within their people's religious tent. The same could not be said of their children, who were fully enamored with American attractions and values and who preferred the lures of the street to any religious involvement. Moreover, they were subject to intense, ongoing pressures to become fully one with this country's ways — from the public schools they attended, and to the afternoon settlement house centers they frequented. Even those scions of the most pious families were not immune to the call to acculturate fully at the expense of what was revered in their parent's home.

Thus, while the late 1880s witnessed the beginnings of concerted efforts, from a variety of quarters, to address the religious challenges that undermined immigrant Jewish observance, the largest thrust of Orthodox Jewish activism centered on preserving and retrieving the younger generation. In setting out on their missions, leaders and their organizations had to decide to what extent American mores and values and this country's modern socializing practices could be deemed kosher in fostering identification with Orthodox Judaism. Some came to the battle convinced that the only tack was staunch resistance to new ways. Others reluctantly made the judgment that such policies were not truly feasible if they hoped to attract more than just the most devoted of religious youngsters. Still others opined and acted in a fundamentally different way. Convinced that America was too powerful a force to fully overcome, they welcomed much of this country's way of life into their midst and trumpeted the compatibility of Americanism and Judaism.

These accommodationists also welcomed assistance from other Jews who were not Orthodox but who possessed significant financial resources to move their efforts forward and whom, they believed, had no designs to pervert traditional faith. Meanwhile, within this Orthodox mix, there were those who did not countenance openness to religiously unreliable sources. In their own contrarian ways, they opted for go-it-alone policies in meeting threats to their community. It is to this process of how pious Orthodox activists of varying stripes, operating out of their New York bases, addressed the problems of Americanization that we now turn our attention.

# STRATEGIES OF NEW YORK'S
# ORTHODOX ACTIVISTS

Wherever they settled in the United States, devout immigrant Jews from
Eastern Europe were severely challenged to find ways of observing past ways
and of perpetuating them among their children. But in most localities they
lacked the numbers of like-minded Jews — a community of the committed —
to do much more than to struggle to hold their own families close to punctilious practice. Not so among the pious of New York. Though they constituted a minority of those who settled in the hundreds of thousands on the
Lower East Side and in packed neighborhoods elsewhere in the metropolis,
there was a critical mass of the faithful in place that was more than merely
committed to holding fast to religious traditions. If galvanized, they might
work as a group to convince all others to follow their lead. Such was their
halachic obligation to bring others closer to what they believed and practiced. They strategized that what they would do in the city could well stand as
a model, a vanguard, for upholding Orthodoxy throughout the country. At
least that was the viewpoint of activists among the devoted downtowners who
in 1886 responded aggressively to Rabbi Weinberger's call to find means of
bringing Americanizing youngsters back toward ancestral teachings. With

the establishment of a small elementary, all-day school for boys in the immigrant quarter, they made a first concerted public attempt to fight back against the dynamic forces of acculturation and disaffection among their neighborhood's youth. Through their efforts, a battle was joined to break the by-then fifty-year hold the public schools had vigorously maintained upon the personal and religious identities of Jewish children throughout the country. Their creation of Yeshiva Etz Chaim was enough of a "marvel" that a gladdened Weinberger cried out in joy: "Hurrah! What pleasant news . . . I can hardly believe my eyes."[1]

From the moment that the city's public schools rid themselves in the early 1850s of their "gross sectarianism," Jewish parents had sent their children en masse to these free institutions that promised to teach all youths how to be good Americans and advance in this free country. Jews elsewhere in America did likewise when their schools dropped their explicit Christian missions. But those mothers and fathers who signed the admission papers did so at a price to the youngsters' faith commitments. It was not so much the daily readings from the King James Version of the Bible that caused problems. In fairness to many school officials, such texts were adopted not so much to inculcate specific Christian theological teachings, but rather to have their faith's central figures help instill proper national and patriotic attitudes and behavior among Jewish students. The larger difficulty was with what these pedagogues said implicitly, if not explicitly, about Jewish religious culture, practices, and traditions. The languages, usages, and customs of the minority group were routinely disparaged as inappropriate for those whom it was assumed wanted to be members of a "homogeneous people." All told, "the little fellow" — or for that matter the little girl — ran "plump against a system of education and a set of influences which are at variance with those traditional to his race and with his religion." Here again, Hapgood captured a community's predicament so well when he observed that Jewish youngsters were taught, in no uncertain terms, "to prefer Sherlock Holmes to Abraham."[2]

If these forces were not powerful enough, once the secular school had its way, having captured the regular school day — those hours from 9 AM to 3 PM — to inculcate its values, what time remained to teach Jewish learning and loyalty to impressionable youngsters? The culture of the street also beckoned youngsters with its own slang versions of English as well as its new heroes, such as the local neighborhood tough, another totally different role model from the revered rabbis of their parents' past. Varying types of supplementary forms of Jewish education — that attempted to pick up the slack — would be hard-pressed to compete for youthful allegiances.[3]

Early on in the era of public school hegemony, Isaac Leeser already had sounded the alarm when he warned Jewish elders that "the Jewish child soon observes," in these hostile environs, "when mixing with others, that even in America his religion is ridiculed and heartily despised by the great majority around him." He sought to *re-create* all-day Jewish schools "to separate the seed of Abraham that dwell among the gentiles that their faith might never lose aught of its purity." An incipient Jewish parochial school system that dated back to the eighteenth century, when all education was undeniably sectarian, had been effectively put out of business as the secular public school movement advanced. But Leeser's calls fell on deaf ears. Back in the 1850s, wherever Jews dwelled, they were enamored with the opportunities these schools promised for their children. They perceived a better secular education available than in the small, inadequately financed, and often poorly run Jewish schools. They also liked the free tuition. Unlike immigrant Catholics who built enduring parochial schools because they balked at the Protestant religious forms that were insinuated into their children, Jews desired the most minimal of differentiation from the Christian American majority. So, even when Jewish parents were fully cognizant of the affronts to their faith, they put up with the Bible readings, the nasty remarks, and the Christmas and Easter pageants — which were cast as American national, seasonal celebrations — that were part of their youngsters' program of going to school in this country.[4]

Etz Chaim offered a very radical solution to the public school challenge. Not only would that institution separate its charges from gentiles and Christian-style schooling, but this school would also position itself against the very tide of Americanization that engulfed Jews all around them. Students there would be indoctrinated into a very different world: the universe of their ancestors' past. These founders and teachers prayed and worked that in keeping with old-time East European ideals, their sons would emerge as outstanding Torah scholars instead of great American success stories. Perhaps they also labored assiduously to prove to those who might have personally admonished them about leaving the Old World that America was not nearly as barren a spiritual wasteland as it had been so often depicted.

With the European past that they remembered and idealized as their guide, they developed a curriculum that called upon students, as they grew in their Torah learning, to engage for six–seven hours a day in the traditional study of the Bible, Talmud, and Codes, leaving but two hours for English-language instruction along with studies in Yiddish and Hebrew language arts. The very inclusion of the teaching of the secular may have been but a concession to the letter of a New York State Law of 1874 that required that "all parents . . . shall instruct their children, or cause them to be instructed in spelling, reading, writing, English grammar, geography and arithmetic." While it is impossible to determine how strongly the students stuck to their books, it is certain that in line with its educational design, little time was left for pupils to imbibe the deleterious-to-tradition culture of the streets. In keeping faith too with how they recalled religious training from their own youths, no provisions were made for girl's all-day education. No such model then existed among Orthodox Jews in Eastern Europe. Their daughters would have to make the best of the bad situation within the co-educational public schools.[5]

Almost immediately after they opened its doors in 1886, some of Etz Chaim's founders joined with other like-minded Jews in a grand effort to project their religious values well beyond just their own faithful followers and to influence the larger Jewish population around them. Their Association of American Orthodox Hebrew Congregations composed of devout representatives from some of the fifteen largest congregations on the Lower East Side attempted to "rouse" their "brethren" from their lethargy to create a great Torah center in America, to capitalize upon the "liberty to observe our religion, to study, teach, observe, perform and establish our Law" which until then had been "neglected and held in low esteem." For them, there was a "battle" to be "waged" on neighborhood streets to "keep the next generation faithful to Judaism in spite of educational, social and business influences which in America are so powerful to make our sons and daughters forget their duty to the religion in which their ancestors lived and for which those ancestors died."[6]

Garnering interest in, and support for, Etz Chaim loomed large in their plans. But other "abuses . . . which have been a reproach for us and a weapon for the enemies of Judaism" also needed "correct[ion]." For example, insufficiently trained rabbis, or just plain imposters, who made a mockery of the holy regulations of marriage and divorce had to run out of business. There was no authority to check a religious functionary's ordination certificate. The long-standing question of who controlled kashruth also appeared high on their list of problems requiring immediate attention. Even worse, there were those outright criminals in their midst who intentionally purveyed unkosher meats and sold them to unwitting consumers.[7]

The market for kosher foods among Jewish immigrants — not only the most devout — was extremely robust. Although maintaining kashruth was not only a chore but an economic burden upon poor customers — properly prepared meats always cost more than treif cuts — Jews held on longer and stronger to that cardinal Orthodox teaching than they did to the Sabbath observance which succumbed to money-making necessities. Perhaps it took a certain advanced degree of acculturation for most East European Jews — other than some radicals who might eat pork just to make a point — to walk into a patently unkosher meat market or to saunter into a gentile-owned restaurant and order the day's bill of fare. The kosher kitchen in tenement dwellings also bespoke a desire, particularly among women who also scoured the streets before Passover and made sure that matzahs were on the table, to maintain an observant home for their families, even if on the morning after their scrupulously prepared Friday night dinner their husbands, and possibly they too, went off to work. Unscrupulous entrepreneurs recognized these tendencies and took full advantage of the sometimes naïve housewives' continued calls for kosher meat. Such scandalous conditions unquestionable gave ammunition to those "enemies of Judaism."[8]

But above and beyond dealing with any other specific condition that the libertine American world had wrought upon Judaism, the association's leaders again saw as their overriding mission to stop "our children and grand-children [from] straying." "For many are they," as the group's first broadside expressed it, "who stray like sheep, listening to shepherds who bid them drink from broken cisterns that hold not the true water of life." What was needed, they divined, was the importation to these shores of a charismatic, dynamic rabbinical leader who would lead a religious renaissance in America's largest Jewish city that would serve as a model for the entire nation.[9]

Talk about the possibilities of such a position had been rife among downtown's most devout elements for more than a decade before the association made its move. Back in 1878, with frustrations mounting about the seemingly never-ending problems with the ritual slaughterers, a call had been sent to Rabbi Meir Loeb ben Yehiel Michael, better known as the Malbim, of Romania. But this Torah scholar died before he could consider any American offer. Anxious now to not only revive that initiative but also to expand its purview, the association placed advertisements in Russian Hebrew newspapers, and letters were sent to leading Torah figures internationally, most notably Rabbi Isaac Elchanan Spektor. After much solicited and unsolicited advice from European authorities and some competition among potential candidates — Rabbi Spektor's own son, Zvi Hirsch, was for a while up for the post — a respected rabbi with a reputation as an influential preacher, Rabbi Jacob Joseph of Vilna, was elected. Rabbi Joseph's ardor for this position stemmed in large part from his sharing Rabbi Spektor's feelings that American Jewry badly needed assistance. He also had significant financial problems that the association promised to ameliorate; paying off his debts was part of the transcontinental contract negotiations. In 1888, he assumed the rarified position of Chief Rabbi of New York City.[10]

Rabbi Joseph championed the association's mission to his utmost. He frequently visited the yeshiva, encouraged both students and teachers in their holy labors, and undoubtedly spoke warmly to them and whomever else would listen of the glories of that past Old World civilization that in the public schools and elsewhere so many other youngsters were curtly told to forget. He exhorted the Jewish masses from his pulpit to observe the Sabbath and took to the streets to upbraid Jewish employers who demanded

Saturday work out of poor co-religionists. In 1894, he headed up a Sabbath Observers Association with "the goal . . . to arouse the employees in the branches of commerce and manufacturing to keep the Sabbath, to try to find bosses that rest on the Sabbath and to find them workers and servants that are Sabbath observant." In an effort to bring light and integrity to the dark and dirty kashruth industry, he appointed a group of reliable meat inspectors and dictated that a tag certifying kashruth be placed on every chicken slaughtered in his domain. This monitoring was to be done gratis as a service to consumers.[11]

The rabbi's efforts and all of the lofty goals of the association came to naught. On Sabbath mornings only the most devout who would not work, and the privileged few who did not have to labor, heard his pulpit pleas. A more religiously diverse crowd might have come to his community-wide Saturday afternoon talks. He often would alternate weeks among the synagogues that supported the association. But the masses who might well have come to hear him out most likely did so *after* they had finished working. His street protests, though loud and heartfelt, yielded few positive results.[12]

Rabbi Joseph suffered an even crueler fate in the kashruth area as the parsimoniousness of some leaders of his own association leaders proved his undoing. While he was hired to lead a religious revival, his lay bosses sought ways of offsetting his substantial salary. Thus, *they* decided to assign a one-half cent per chicken surcharge on every slaughtered chicken in Joseph's domain. This levy, which raised cries of *korobke* (an infamous tsarist tax on kosher food) from radicals, did much to alienate the larger immigrant community from the chief rabbi. Toward the end of this career, the rabbi and his son even had some vocal confrontations with women protestors who decried Joseph and his son's complicity in the setting of what they deemed the high cost of kosher meat, even without the onerous surcharge. "Since when," inquired a socialist newspaper editorialist, "is there a partnership between those who give rabbinic endorsements in the Chief Rabbi's name and those . . . meat handlers. . . . The Chief Rabbi's son is merely a salesman for the [Meat] Trust." Reportedly, the women activist once accosted him with cries of "Trust-Kosher Korobke" as he passed within a protest zone.[13]

The seemingly never-ending kosher meat–korobke issue also led, in part, to the emergence earlier on in Joseph's tenure of two additional and competing chief rabbis in town. These opponents gathered their own groups of pious congregants and not-so-devout butchers around them. When he initially set himself up in the metropolis, Rabbi Joseph had reached out to Rabbi Joshua Segal — the so-called "Sherpser Rov" — who had preceded the Chief Rabbi to America to occupy a distinguished post on Joseph's rabbinical court. But the ambitious Rabbi Segal, of Galician and Hasidic stock, looked askance at the Lithuanian Joseph's invitations and brought together some twenty other congregations and handfuls of butchers who declared him "Chief Rabbi of Congregations of Israel of New York." In 1893, another contestant, Rabbi Chaim Jacob Vidrowitz arrived from Moscow and did both incumbent chief rabbis one better. He put together another group of small Hasidic synagogues and had them call him "Chief Rabbi of America." When contemporaries asked—or so the story goes—who authorized him to be religious head of all American Jews, Vidrowitz replied: "the sign painter" who helped hang out his shingle. And "why Chief Rabbi of America?" as the tale continues, "because it would be well nigh impossible for all the Jews of America to gather together to depose me." In a humorous way, this new-comer's whimsical aside spoke to the endemic problems of voluntarism, disunity and lack of control that always undermined religious life in a large and wide-open America. Not only could lay people practice whatever they chose to observe, fearless of any binding censure, but rabbis could promote themselves unabashedly in any way they saw fit.

Both Segal and Vidrowitz who contributed to making Joseph's life miser-able in the rough and tumble world of kashruth supervision were no less scholarly than their opponent. While still in Russia, Vidrowitz published the works of Rabbi Mendel of Lubavitch and numerous scholarly Torah articles of his own. As a rabbi in America, Segal wrote a significant halachic work, in 1901 producing *Eruv ve-Hotzaah,* a tract that argued the permissibility of carrying on the East Side on the Sabbath. His position was based on the reality that water bounded the Jewish quarter on three sides and that the fourth side was considered legally closed, creating an enclosed "private" environment by virtue of the elevated railroads with their raised columns that ran north–south on Manhattan Island. Reportedly, the "Hasidim who followed him carried their taleisim on the Sabbath" as they publicly punctu-ated their loyalty and respect for his sage opinions. More than a century later, this influential book is still consulted as part of an ongoing contempo-rary debate over the halachic reliability of the so-called "Manhattan *eruv.*"[14]

But whatever concerns Rabbi Joseph had in holding off these competitors paled in significance to his problems in advancing the association's highest objective. He was unable to convince immigrant families to disdain a public school education for their boys. Despite his vocal encouragement, Etz Chaim's student body grew ever so slowly in the 1890s. By decade's end, it enrolled at most one hundred or so boys in its eight grades and made no impact upon the wider Jewish community. Only those families that were most committed to a decidedly separatist philosophy even considered the yeshiva as an option. Even among those who were exceedingly devout and who dutifully signed on to the association's plans and cast their lots with the chief rabbi, there were some Jews who had second thoughts about Etz Chaim's mission. While they subscribed to transplanted strict Old World religious values and would have personally been thrilled if their sons became great Torah scholars, they were concerned, nonetheless, that this school was ill-equipped to prepare youngsters to live in the new country.[15]

Downtown Orthodox man of letters, Judah David Eisenstein, who would serve as the unofficial historian of the association, thought that "necessity impels us . . . to know the language of the land grammatically . . . so that we may mingle with the people among whom we live." It is impossible to determine whether, having said that, he would have kept his own son, Isaac, out of Etz Chaim. As an elementary school pupil, his boy was enrolled in public school almost a decade before the yeshiva opened its doors. To complement — or to offset his child's secular training — Eisenstein arranged for a "private teacher for him to spend a few hours daily in Hebrew studies until he succeed[ed] in his study of the Written and Oral Torah and all books of our sages." Eisenstein boasted to his grandfather, Esriel Zelig, who was still in Europe that he would "spare neither money nor effort" to ensure that Isaac "may be an example to the children of his age in this country." That was his pragmatic plan for combating the public schools and his solution to raising up a new generation of deeply-observant Jews in America.[16]

Just a few years later, with Etz Chaim up and running, Rabbi Israel Kaplan and his wife perceived its educational design as a barrier to their own son's achieving the dream that they harbored for his future career. Upon arrival in New York in 1888 to serve as Rabbi Joseph's colleague on the chief rabbi's rabbinical court, Israel and Anna Kaplan, after just the briefest of initial of exposures to the public schools, enrolled their young son, Mordecai, in Etz Chaim. He remained, however, in the yeshiva for at most a year, before he was withdrawn and sent to public school for the remainder of his elementary education. At age fourteen, he would matriculate into the "sub-freshman class" — basically the high school — of the City College of New York. Anna Kaplan, and perhaps Israel too, had the ambition for their son that he might some day be elected chief rabbi, not of New York, but of the British Empire. So disposed, they reasoned correctly that since the English monarch was not a Yiddish speaker, it would behoove Mordecai, as a fundamental part of his training, to learn how to speak the King's English.[17]

Eisenstein and Israel Kaplan's desire for their children to be exposed to the wider worlds of knowledge was also due, in part, to their own affinity for the Haskalah while they were still in Russia. While most Jews in the Pale and elsewhere who became enamored with secular teachings and training — as a conduit for hoped-for future integration into tsarist society — ended up drifting away, or fleeing from, traditional Jewish practice, some Orthodox students were also caught up in that modernist movement's net. Eisenstein indicated in his memoirs that "at the age of fourteen, the spirit of knowledge began to stir within me and aided by youth of my age I studied extensively the Bible and books of the Enlightenment in pure Sacred Tongue, and we corresponded in the Hebrew language." Beyond that, "with the help of a Christian teacher," Eisenstein "studied Russian and German and the rudiments of the sciences."[18]

Not the typical yeshiva student of his time, Israel Kaplan was inquisitive about the world of secular culture outside his Lithuanian Torah center. While at the Volozhin Yeshiva, he seemingly was persistent enough to gain approbation for his outside readings from a school administration that generally frowned upon students' exposure to the messages of the Haskalah.[19] He earned "privileges [within the yeshiva] not accorded to other students. He was permitted to read something of modern Hebrew literature and journalism."

This future downtown rabbi also was unconventional, both for New York and Russian Orthodox Jews, in his attitude toward education for girls. While still in Europe, he had insisted that his daughter, Sophie, attend the heder —the traditional school—in their hometown of Swetzian because, reportedly, "that was the only way she would have the opportunity of learning Hebrew and understanding the Bible." Kaplan, like Eisenstein, put significant stock in the singular sentence that was tucked into the association's initial broadside—even if that principle did not fundamentally influence its activities. It allowed that "honor, *enlightenment* and culture can be combined with a proper observance of religious duty . . . to create an intelligent Orthodoxy."[20]

The decision that the Andron family made—who were also devout and basically loyal to the association's agenda—to devise their own and competitive institutional alternative to Etz Chaim was not based on their earlier flirtation, while, in Europe, with the Jewish Enlightenment. Rather, their move, in 1901, to organize an elementary yeshiva that was more open to secular education was due to a troubling development that the family encountered in its own dealings with the problems of the public schools. Reportedly, when one of the Andron youngsters who had been sent to a public school only to "return one afternoon in late December asking . . . for money toward a Christmas party," his parents immediately started raising funds from friends and associates to start the Beth Sefer Tifereth Jerusalem. At their school, an attempt was made from the outset to offer a secular education to pupils, approximating what immigrant parents liked about the general curriculum proffered at the religiously unreliable public schools. In time, its leaders would arrogate for the school the title of the "first Yeshiva in America where students," that is, boys, "received a synthesized program."[21]

In the end, for Eisenstein, the Kaplans, and the Androns, whose institution would be renamed the Rabbi Jacob Joseph School, after the chief rabbi's death in 1902, an unregenerated yeshiva system modeled totally along the lines of the East European past was a wonderful and holy ideal. But these pragmatists recognized that they, and the school, were in America where even devout Jews had to make some adjustments to reality as they raised their youngsters. Their realism, however, went just so far. Another quarter century would pass before anyone either in Eastern Europe or in America would conceive of an all-day Jewish educational program for girls that would provide them with both secular education as well as extensive religious schooling under one roof. Until that time, the daughters of the devout — like all other immigrant girls — would put up not only with the annual Christmas problem but with the daily dismissals of Jewish tradition and practice that took place in the public schools. For their training in the faith, they would have to look, as always, to their mothers or to some sort of supplementary schooling to transmit Judaism's traditions.[22]

In the meantime, while unwavering compatriots within the association may have raised their eyebrows privately even at these small steps out of line in altering how boys were socialized in America, Eisenstein, the Kaplans, and the Androns remained respected members of the core of pious down-town Jews. Rabbi Joseph was silent about these changing attitudes among his colleagues and erstwhile supporters as he struggled unsuccessfully amidst dissenting abattoirs, butchers, and opposition rabbis. All told, when Rabbi Jacob Joseph died at age fifty-one, a broken man from all of his travails, none of his or the association's lofty initial objectives had been achieved.

The Agudath ha-Rabbanim (the Union of Orthodox Rabbis of the United States and Canada) set out to solve in a harder-edged way the same problems that had confounded Rabbi Joseph and the association. Talk of such a North American-wide organization of transplanted East European rabbis began in July 1901, when a call went out from a group of stalwarts ensconced in pulpits within such diverse locales as Des Moines, Detroit, Philadelphia, and Boston to fulfill a divine "obligation to unite and form a union of Orthodox rabbis" to take on "the constant desecration of the Torah all around them." Months later, in May 1902, at a planning meeting in Boston an agenda of concerns was drawn up and a tentative date was set for a large July rabbinical conclave in New York. The sobriety of this call was matched only by the somberness of the fifty-nine delegates from thirty American cities and Montreal and Toronto as their deliberations began. As fate would have it, the meeting was convened on the day after Rabbi Joseph's funeral. Yet the mourners persevered in their work that focused — just like the association had — on upgrading Jewish education through the yeshiva, calling and demanding greater punctiliousness in Sabbath observance, fighting for better and always honest kashruth supervision, and rooting out of "unqualified persons" who "pose as rabbis." Perhaps, on this final front the focus of their animus was upon those "Holy-day Rabbis" who manned those entrepreneurial "Temporary Halls of Worship."[23]

In many respects, they picked up where Rabbi Jacob Joseph left off. They pledged that "attempts must be made to establish proper kashruth supervision, particularly regarding the slaughter, inspection and sale of meat." Efforts were extended to centralize and rationalize oversight in every city where a member resided. Local rabbis were told to be aggressive in monitoring the manufacturing of all kosher products. The examinations included wines, Passover liquors and matzahs, and religious articles that utilize parchment like tefillin and *mezuzot* [door post amulets that contain the *Shema,* the fundamental Jewish creedal prayer]. They called upon colleagues to support one another, especially when one rabbi "finds it necessary to publicly disqualify a butcher for violating the laws of kashruth." It was hoped that "no other rabbi [would] reinstate the butcher."

However, just like Vidrowitz and Segal, whose independence haunted Rabbi Joseph's efforts, so too the rabbis' union would be ultimately unable to bring so many colleagues into line. Those who declined to affiliate, who perhaps were as scrupulous in their religious work, had little interest in surrendering their authority in controlling numerous abattoirs and butcher shops — a major source of income — to any powerless ecclesiastical combine. As American voluntarism again held sway, this group of rabbis could set forth its set of principles and procedures for proper behavior and jurisdiction. But it could not force dissenting colleagues to follow its rules.

On the no-less-daunting issue of Sabbath desecration, the Union of Orthodox Rabbis did more than merely exhort the Jewish masses to observe the holy day. It called for communal sanctions against certain miscreants, according them no benefit of religious doubt. People were "warned . . . not to buy bread baked on the Sabbath." Harsh declarations were made that "not only is purchasing such products considered aiding a sinner, but it is practically certain that there is also non-kosher oil and shortening in the baked products." In a more positive vein, the rabbis' union called upon its members to find — as Rabbi Joseph once tried — "employment for workers desirous of observing the Sabbath" and to "try to influence owners of factories to employ Sabbath observers."[24]

These rabbis' ideal educational construct was the transplanted Old World-style yeshiva, embodied first in Etz Chaim and subsequently at the Yeshiva Rabbi Isaac Elchanan. This upper-level Torah institution, established in New York in 1897 and named appropriately for the Russian religious leader who smiled upon America as a destination for the faithful, took its post–Bar Mitzvah age and young men more deeply into the world of the Torah. Its methods and educational design followed those hallowed in the great yeshivas of Lithuania. As its most favored institutions, members of the rabbis' association were called upon to raise monies for Etz Chaim and the Yeshiva Rabbi Isaac Elchanan, and their organization claimed control over the schools. The Agudath ha-Rabbanim's constitution read that teachers [who] "must be God-fearing and their deeds in accordance with the Torah," would instruct students in Yiddish, the language of the children's parents. Before being allowed to enter a class room every teacher had to have "a certificate of approbation from one member . . . and two pedagogues . . . testify[ing] to his religious devotion and teaching abilities." A "supervising committee" was empanelled to be on hand to assure that Torah study "is properly organized so that yeshiva students will truly succeed in their endeavors." Success meant proficiency in the ways of the Talmud alone. To monitor further goings-on at the school, the rabbis' union called for the "yeshiva committee" to "supervise the secular subjects taught. . . . Only necessary subjects should be taught by qualified instructors." Every effort was to be made to prevent teachings and actions that would suggest that the "yeshiva [is] simply . . . a stopover before [students] pursue advanced secular studies." That sort of "attitude," it averred, "will impair [students] accomplishments in the yeshiva."[25]

For all of its bold-lettered intolerance for those who transgressed the Sabbath and its staunch affinity for ideal educational ways and means, the Union of Orthodox Rabbis was also grudgingly realistic about religious conditions in the United States. In the case of the Sabbath problem, recognition of business factors that undermined observance led it to countenance cooperation — the creation of a united front — with some unlikely allies. At the very moment of its creation, the rabbis' association reached out to Jewish labor unions, many of whose leaders shared little, if they did not actively oppose Orthodox religious values. The deal that the Agudath ha-Rabbanim *proposed* — the rabbis were the initiators of the scheme — was that "when there is a strike," they "should influence the workers to include the right for Sabbath observance among their demands." As a quid quo pro, if the unionists agreed, "the rabbis will pressure the owners and employees to comply with the requests . . . the just demands . . . of the union."[26]

Perhaps more remarkable was its tacit recognition that the rarified yeshiva system that they supported was not, and could never be, for all Jewish youngsters. To begin with, the Agudath ha-Rabbanim implicitly acknowledged that this ideal school, situated as it was in Manhattan amid multitudes of Jews really could not serve as a model for other locales. Even more significantly, in reaching out even to those parents and youngsters living in the metropolis who perforce would only attend an afternoon, supplementary Jewish school, they went so far as to grudgingly take a lesson on educational method and structure — albeit without attribution — from no less a source than the public schools, that great enemy of Jewish identity.

As previously noted, once the public schools captured the 9 AM–3 PM slot in the lives of Jewish children, religious education was only left with the late afternoon and weekend hours at its disposal. Generally, supplementary schools did not fare well in their unequal competition against the lures of street games, the more organized fun and recreation at settlement houses, and the demands that some parents put on their poor children to do their "home work"; that is, assist their elders in their interminable in-house sweat-shop labors. The yeshiva was available as an educational option for New York boys who lived on the Lower East Side. But, as we have seen, even if the most pious of Jews built it, most people in the community did not support it. In smaller Jewish cities, where no critical mass of highly devout families existed, yeshiva education was inconceivable. That last reality of American Jewish life could not have been lost on the forty of the original fifty-nine members of the rabbis' union who were not from the New York area. A series of totally disor-ganized and atrociously run independent heders — one-room Jewish school-houses — was the basic alternative there both in New York and elsewhere.

The worst among these ephemeral institutions were situated in "unbeliev-able places; above stables, at the back of stores, in cellars, in garrets, and in similar well-nigh impossible locations." Some of the teachers had been in-structors in Eastern Europe who having come "to this country too late to make adjustments" continued in the "only occupation which they knew in the land of their birth." The best among them, whom one unsympathetic critic described as "earnest" yet "medieval men . . . zealously" tried "to impart unwished-for knowledge to the unwilling youngsters of the New World." Others who manned the heders were, reportedly, just "ignorant men who spend their mornings in peddling wares and in plying some trade, and utilize their afternoons and evenings for selling the little knowledge they have to American children." The scene "in the home of the self-appointed 'Rebbi' was often chaotic. While one pupil drawls meaninglessly, the Hebrew words of the prayer book, the rest play or fight, with the full vivacity of youth." When the Jewish boy and his parents — these schools too generally were only for males — "compare[d] this school to the highly devel-oped public school, Jewish education suffers greatly by the comparison."[27]

An incipient, more modern Talmud Torah system that arose in the de-cade prior to the Agudath ha-Rabbanim offered some glimmer of hope for a much better brand of supplementary Jewish school. The Machzike Talmud Torah, founded in 1883 and housed in a commodious building on East Broadway, quickly earned itself the reputation among its supporters as "the pride of the East European Jews on the East Side." There, systematic instruc-tion "was granted to poor children gratis in the Hebrew language and litera-ture." As an additional incentive, shoes and clothing were also provided, courtesy of a women's auxiliary called the Malbish Arumim Society (literally "clothing the naked," a most basic mitzvah). Funding came from charity boxes and door-to-door solicitations within the community. Though im-pressed with their work, the rabbis' union felt that the school and four other

Talmud Torahs established in its wake — two situated in the neighborhood and one each up in Harlem and over in Brooklyn — could do even more to attract students.[28]

Here, in a partial bow to the ways in which the public schools ran their operations, the organization spoke of the need "to draw up a proper curriculum" for "the various levels of study," making clear that "important topics must no longer be left on an ad-hoc basis." They also recognized the need for "a graded system of study so that teachers will no longer have various levels of students in one class," a message here to both the heders and the Talmud Torahs. They also assented that when "*necessary* for the clarification of the topic, the teachers may also use English [and] in areas where only English is spoken, it may be the basic tongue." Thus, although Yiddish was a preferred language, the teachers had to know the language of the new land. These latter strictures spoke to the experiences of rabbis who struggled in communities, remote from the metropolis, including Omaha, Louisville, Kentucky, Denver, Bangor (Maine) or Hazelton (Pennsylvania). In those locales a Jewish school certainly could not survive without English instruction of the traditional curriculum.[29]

In addition, while the rabbis never gainsaid the initial Etz Chaim model as an ideal educational institution — that for the present was only in New York — it aligned itself with the Rabbi Jacob Joseph School's pedagogic initiative when it called for the engagement of "graduates from the normal schools in the employ of the City of Boards of Education" to moonlight in the all-day yeshiva. It was hoped that the best types of teachers, those who were sensitive to the religious values of the students and of the Jewish school, would respectfully introduce a greater modicum of general studies training.

Finally, the rabbis' organization, in its pragmatic mode, also went on record in support of "evening schools for those youths who work . . . by day." Realistically, these pupils were not candidates for the yeshiva. The Agudath ha-Rabbanim also approved of systematic education for another overlooked groups — girls — when it called for the establishment of "Hebrew schools" for them. Seemingly through this latter proclamation, they acknowledged yet another significant social circumstance. Mothers caught up too in the whirlwind of work and adaptation to new environs could not be counted upon to be the sole — or even the primary — transmitters of religious training for their daughters. Some sort of formal educational mechanism, at that point still undefined, had to be put into place.[30]

While the East European rabbis' association grudgingly acknowledged that American realities had to be heeded, at the same time a second group of American Orthodox rabbis and their devout lay supporters appeared on the scene, armed with an avowed accommodationist approach to reclaiming religiously wavering immigrants, and especially their children. Their initiatives that also were hatched in New York were designed, too, to serve as models for Jews throughout the entire country. This second set of Orthodox activists came together first in 1886 — the very same year that the downtown association was founded — when the spiritual leaders of America's oldest congregations such as Henry Pereira Mendes of New York's Shearith Israel and Sabato Morais of Philadelphia's Mikveh Israel joined with Baltimore breakaway Orthodox synagogue head Henry W. Schneeberger and a handful of like-minded leaders in supporting the creation of the Jewish Theological Seminary of America. There, they prayed, a new generation of young "teachers-rabbis" would be "educat[ed], train[ed] and inspire[d]" to use their "knowledge of Jewish learning, literature, history, ideals and Jewish science" to reach the wavering masses of American Jews.[31]

Though ministering to immigrants and their children who were disaffected from Old World religious traditions long proved to be the school's calling card, ironically the Seminary was initially called into existence because of a strident challenge to Orthodoxy articulated some hundreds of miles away in Pittsburgh, Pennsylvania. In 1885, a group of Reform rabbis, meeting in the Steel City, ironed out a set of ideological protocols that envisioned a denationalized and deritualized form of Judaism. Its teachings were high on advocacy of universal ethical values and very low on performance of traditional mitzvoth.[32] This radical platform came on the heels of an almost as troubling manifestation of Reform power, and even arrogance, that had taken place some two years earlier in Cincinnati at the graduation celebration of the first class of rabbis trained at Hebrew Union College. At a gala gathering, shellfish was served at what became known as the "treif banquet." This menu choice punctuated to halachic-minded erstwhile supporters of Isaac Mayer Wise's institution that a school ostensibly designed to train leaders of all Jewish religious persuasions was aggressively insensitive to those who retained affinities for the traditional mitzvoth.[33] These double barreled actions — the dinner and then the platform — caused rabbis like Henry Hochheimer, Benjamin Szold, and Marcus Jastrow who, until the mid-1880s, still believed that as modern thinkers they could have some common cause with moderate reformers in the promotion of religious unity policies, to abandon such quixotic dreams. In short order, these progenitors of twentieth-century Conservative Judaism in the United States allied themselves with the Americanized Orthodox group in the creation of the Seminary, as a major institutional response to Reform Judaism in this country.[34]

But as the Seminary slowly swung into action, revulsion over Reform and any concerns the Americanized Orthodox had about *their* common cause with Conservatives, paled in significance to the transcendent mission of addressing the religious needs of those newcomers from Eastern Europe. Accordingly, a curriculum was designed to produce young rabbis — most recruited from within the immigrant masses themselves — who would have both a familiarity with traditional texts that elucidated the questions Jews always asked, along with a strong grounding in modern secular and Judaic disciplines. To be worthy positive influences upon their own kind, the young men and women who came to be called "the rising generation in Israel," these future rabbis had to be exposed not only to Torah and Talmud but also had to be comfortable with the realms of history, sociology, psychology — particularly of the pastoral kind. They furthermore had to be proficient English public speakers and be able to boast of college credentials.[35]

In the Seminary's early years, New York's Bernard Drachman was a role model for these American Orthodox rabbis in the making. Born in the metropolis in 1861 and raised in Jersey City, in a family of Central European extraction, he initially was ticketed for a career in the Reform rabbinate. As an undergraduate at Columbia College, he also studied at the Temple Emanu-El Theological Seminary, preparatory to travel to Berlin for advanced training in the school that the renowned Reform theologian Abraham Geiger had founded. However, upon arrival in Europe, he made an ideological hard right turn and enrolled in the Judische Theologisches Seminar, the Historical School — or Conservative — rabbinical school identified with its foremost ideologue, Zechariah Frankel. Returning to America in 1885, possessed of both Breslau ordination and a Ph.D. from the University of Heidelberg, he proceeded to prove his Orthodox bona fides when his first congregation, Oheb Shalom of Newark, New Jersey, voted over his objection to allow mixed seating during services. Unwilling to accept this deviation, he resigned. But that act of fidelity to the halacha left him in a quandary and for a while unemployed. At that time, he would later recall, "there was no room, no demand in America for an American-born, English-speaking rabbi who insisted on maintaining the laws and usages of Traditional Judaism."[36]

Drachman was right. In late 1880s America there were few Americanized synagogues that were still Orthodox. Baltimore's Chizuk Amuno — a notable exception — hired its own local scion, Henry W. Schneeberger. If they could afford a rabbi, the many immigrant Orthodox shuls wanted a Talmudic scholar or a Yiddish-speaking preacher to whom they may, or may not, have listened. These immigrants could not relate to Drachman.

Fortunately, for this rabbi in search of a pulpit, he found employment at a then idiosyncratic congregation, in Yorkville in 1889, in the uptown reaches of Manhattan. The Jews in that shul's pews included successful and acculturated immigrants of East European background who had risen out of the poverty of downtown life well before most others on the Lower East Side. They wanted a spiritual leader whose style, training, and sensibilities bespoke the beginnings of their newly found comfort with American culture and whose message, preached in English, talked of the compatibility of Orthodox Judaism with the modern world and resonated with their Americanized children. It also helped, in securing the rabbi's selection, that the major financial force behind Congregation Zichron Ephraim was Jonas Weil, Drachman's father in law.[37]

Most importantly, for the greater future of American Orthodoxy, from his position as Dean of the Faculty and Professor of Biblical Exegesis, Hebrew Grammar and Composition, and Jewish Philosophy at the Jewish Theological Seminary—he basically did it all at the fledgling school—Drachman shared with his students his affinities for secular knowledge and wide-ranging Jewish studies and the wealth of experiences that he was deriving as a congregational rabbi. They, in turn, took his instructions and orientation into the field as this first generation of Seminary alumni prepared to meet the challenges of addressing the religious dilemmas of their fellow second-generation Jews.[38]

These young rabbis-to-be advanced their in-service training appreciably, beginning in 1898, when many of them participated in the youth-wing activities of the newly established Orthodox Union. This congregational association of synagogues, closely aligned with the Seminary, had as its primary mission the protection and promotion of "Orthodox Judaism whenever occasions arise in civic and religious matters." Its other announced agenda was to "protest against the teachings of Reform rabbis not in accord with the teachings of the Torah." But the Orthodox Union really had little to do with the advocates of the Pittsburgh Platform. Rather, the rabbis and lay people who headed up the association spent much of their time downtown trying to establish, through new congregational and educational forms, a type of Americanized Orthodox Judaism that would bring the children of immigrants back toward their ancestral traditions. Rabbis such as Drachman, Mendes, and Schneeberger were always around to lend guidance and sage advice. Harry Fischel, one of the successful and still devout lay leaders, offered his viewpoint and financial support. However, in many of this union's early initiatives, it was Seminary men — and later its women who studied in the school's Teachers' Institute established in 1901 — who were the foot soldiers in these battles against disaffection.[39]

The Orthodox Union was very concerned, for example, that while landsmanshaft synagogues meant much to newly arrived immigrants as sanctuaries providing the ritual and social flavor of the best of the old side, they said less and less to the Americanized immigrant and nothing good at all to their youngsters. For a synagogue to be attractive to those weaned or schooled on this country's cultural values, it had to countenance its worshippers' realities and proclivities.

The Jewish Endeavor Society, founded in 1901, under the Orthodox

Union and run primarily by Seminary students, did just that through its "dignified services" designed "to recall indifferent Jewry back to their ancestral faith." At its "young peoples' synagogues," organized first on the Lower East Side and then in Harlem and Philadelphia, a weekly sermon on themes relating to the American Jewish experience was standard. Recognizing that most public-school educated youngsters had minimal Jewish training and were unfamiliar with the Hebrew liturgy, these congregations instituted supplementary prayers in the vernacular. Congregational singing in English and Hebrew was encouraged as a way of assuring a decorous American-style service. For Seminary students, these activities provided invaluable internship opportunities that would hold them in good stead throughout their future professional careers. Their teachers and role models like Drachman and Mendes were often available as guest lecturers, what we might today call "scholars-in-residence."[40]

None of these social changes or innovations in synagogue life did any violence to the halacha. If anything, the Endeavorers evidenced staunch fidelity to Orthodoxy's central creeds as they were certain to use the traditional siddur in all services and were sure to separate men and women during prayers on either side of a mechitza. At the same time, they espoused a pragmatic Orthodoxy that was tolerant of the transgressions of their potential congregants. Recognizing the reality that Jews worked on the Sabbath, regardless of any and all rabbinic admonitions, they scheduled their "model" services for late afternoon on Saturday after the workweek ended. Particularly in the summer months, when the sacred day lasts well into the evening hours, it gave Endeavorer leaders several hours to influence their congregants toward greater future observance.[41]

Meanwhile, the parent organization, the Orthodox Union, as a good American advocacy or lobbying group, did its utmost to address the difficult conditions that contributed to irreligious behavior. True to its mission of "protecting Orthodox Judaism . . . in civic matters," it spoke out against the practice of holding State Regents, school, and civil service exams on Saturday; protected Jewish children who were punished for skipping school on Jewish holidays; and constantly butted heads with the legislative system, which retained discriminatory Blue Laws.[42]

The Endeavorers declined toward the end of the first decade of the twentieth century as their generation of Seminary students graduated. From their pulpits, they began to take the Orthodox Union's New York-initiated ideas to other communities. However, the Endeavors' spirit lived on at the Seminary and was formally reconstituted in 1913 when the Young Israel movement was established, primarily by its students. Its congregational ritual and style was the same as the Jewish Endeavor Society, with one additional programmatic innovation. After the Sabbath ended, they transformed the *melave malkah*—a traditional gathering for song food and words of Torah to "escort" the Sabbath Queen appropriately out of Jewish midst—into a synagogue social. Its goal was to keep Jewish boys and girls away from the down and dirty downtown halls and the almost as troubling Christian and radical-run parties that were then part of ghetto life. Confronting these social evils, no one asked halachic questions about religious modesty issues. A decade or so later, the devout East Bronx couple, whom we previously profiled, became part of that social scene.[43]

During the twentieth century's first decade, Seminary students—and here we are speaking of both the men in the rabbinical program and the men and women in the teacher-training track—also played important roles in advancing the Orthodox Union's modern Talmud Torah initiative. From its inception, this American Orthodox organization acknowledged that the public schools' power and influence over Jewish immigrants and their children could not be resisted. Yeshiva education—whether in its transplanted mode or incipient modernized form—was not a popular alternative. Moreover, supplementary Jewish education was still largely the province of the poorly trained, less motivated, and badly funded *melamdim* (teachers). Drachman articulated well his group's multilayered solution in 1902 when he first called upon the public schools to grant Jewish youngsters what later would be called "released time," an "an ideal program . . . during the day when children are awake and interested," to imbibe a modicum of Jewish religious culture. But his greater dream for the disaffected children of immigrants was "a great system of Jewish *public schools* housed in their own buildings and equipped with all pedagogic requirements to supplement the general public school system." There, he prayed, Jewish boys and girls on an equal basis would be instructed, primarily in the English language, "to perform all the duties, to think all the thoughts and to feel the emotions that are the historical heritage of those of the household of Israel." In keeping with the child-centered educational philosophies regnant at that time, Drachman judged success in his youth reclamation work not so much in the amount of content pupils absorbed, but rather if students and graduates showed an ongoing interest in connecting to the type of Americanized Orthodoxy that he and his Seminary disciples were proffering.[44]

So disposed, during that first decade of the new century, leaders of the Orthodox Union supported the growth of a string of modern Talmud Torahs both on the Lower East Side and in other larger Jewish concentrations in the city, effectively building on the Machzike Talmud Torah's good start. The Uptown Talmud Torah was one targeted institution.

During its first decade of existence, 1892–1902, this school, situated in a poorly ventilated three-story building with inadequate sanitary facilities, was like so many disreputable heders in the city, although its principal Rabbi

Moses Reicherson was personally a reputable Hebraist. In a sympathetic profile of this intellectual, the always supportive Hutchins Hapgood described Reicherson as a "submerged scholar" who "no matter what his attainments and qualities" was unknown and unhonored "amid the crowding and material interest of the New World." This being said, the reality still was that he and his four-man faculty were unable to generate much enthusiasm for an old-style curriculum that taught only the "Aleph-Beis [Alphabet], siddur and Chumash [Pentateuch]" among American-born youngsters.[45]

The Uptown Talmud Torah's fortunes changed dramatically when, in 1903, it began to resonate to Drachman's visions even if the American Orthodox rabbi did not actually participate in the actual modernization of the school. Now a conscious determination was made that while it was impossible to "make a Hebraist" out of each Jewish child, they all could be taught to love their religion and to follow its precepts.[46]

David A. Cohen, a counterpart and colleague of Harry Fischel's, headed up the lay backing of these initiatives. According to a newspaper group biography, this Orthodox Union leader and his associates were "leading men of the Jewish race . . . over 50 years of age who had been in this country 25–35 years and who from early youth trained to be intensely Orthodox, yet so thorough is their Americanization that they saw at once the possibility of a combination of the Hebrew school with the modern educational institute with all its accessories."[47]

Notwithstanding the Orthodox Union's jaundiced views about the Pittsburgh Platform, in seeking monies for its endeavors Cohen and his compatriots reached out to major communal figures, including Jacob Schiff and Louis Marshall, leaders with strong personal ties to Reform Judaism. Early on, Marshall was invited to join the Orthodox Talmud Torah's board of directors. Marshall readily acceded, primarily because he was in favor of most communal initiatives that augured to lift immigrant youngsters off the streets and away from the deleterious influences of radicalism and criminality. This vision also brought him during that era to chair the board of the Seminary, again with the goal of having the right type of rabbi minister among the youngsters of downtown. By 1910, the Jewish Theological Seminary's formally constituted Teachers' Institute was located in the Uptown Talmud Torah's building.[48]

Schiff entered the Uptown Talmud Torah picture in 1910. Like Marshall, he too was mightily concerned with the proper behavior and the upbringing of the Jewish youth of the poor. In joining he averred that he had no issue with the American Orthodox ideology. His major concern was that the mode of instruction had "to conform to approved modern methods and ideas of pedagogy and hygiene and maintain . . . activities looking toward the Americanization of our Jewish youth."[49]

It was within this same spirit of conviviality that Schiff and Marshall, among other German American leaders, invited the Orthodox Union to join the New York Kehillah, the New York Jewish Community. This citywide umbrella organization was called into existence as a Jewish response to an antisemitic allegation made by New York City's Police Commissioner Theodore A. Bingham about Jewish criminality on the Lower East Side. Revolted and concerned about their people's image and status, Marshall, Schiff, Felix Warburg, and Daniel Guggenheim, among other German American leaders, wanted all local Jewish groups—immigrant and established Americans alike—to work together toward solving the communal problems that could give voice to a prejudiced Christian observer of Jewish life who overstated the extent of a real communal pathology.[50]

The Kehillah thus saw as its largest mission the mitigation of the incidences of lawlessness among downtown youths. Having youngsters in good Jewish schools that taught all of the correct moral values in an American way—the same rationale that brought Schiff and Marshall into cooperation with the Uptown Talmud Torah—was immediately judged high on the organization's list of priorities.[51]

The Orthodox Union lent its support to the Kehillah beginning in 1909, albeit with some reservations, arguing that this initiative should be given a chance if the "Kehillah can help not merely Judaism but Orthodox Judaism." Doubtlessly, they agreed with the organization's plan to make the Talmud Torah system a bastion of both Americanization and Judaism. Had not Drachman's idea of a "Jewish public school system," earlier in the decade, anticipated this motion? The Union likewise appreciated the promise of financial support that would bolster their still fledgling ring of neighborhood schools. And, on a personal level, they trusted that Schiff, Marshall, and Rabbi Judah L. Magnes of Temple Emanu-El, who chaired the movement, had no designs to interfere with the Orthodox Judaism that would be taught in the schools. Fischel saw the major benefactor of New York Jewish education, as his role model in communal affairs, and his faithful biography has submitted that around town he was "not undeservedly hailed in many quarters as the Russian Jacob H. Schiff." So disposed, Fischel, Drachman, and Mendes were among the half-dozen Orthodox Union leaders among the charter members of the New York Jewish Community's twenty-five-man ruling executive committee.[52]

For all of their vitality, Orthodox Union efforts in the field of modern Jewish education did not sit well with all elements within the local Orthodox community. In some instances, those who were just as committed to solving the heder problem simply did not trust "German" money. When, for example, David A. Cohen first pushed for educational changes at the Uptown Talmud Torah, people on his own board openly questioned whether, with the Marshall–Schiff crowd around, these structural, social, and method-ological changes would not ultimately endanger the essence of traditional faith. Their opposition caused an angered Cohen to respond that these dissenting members were "reactionaries" who through their "blind, unrea-soned prejudice based on four hundred years of ghetto life" could not comprehend that "nobody had any designs whatsoever upon their beloved Orthodoxy."[53]

Other opponents contended that the introduction of modern pedagogic practices challenged basic Orthodox teachings. Harry Fischel encountered this fundamental question of the appropriateness of avant-garde Orthodox educational initiatives when in 1914 he purchased — innocently enough from his point of view — a slide machine for use in teaching Bible stories at the Uptown Talmud Torah. He had assumed the school's helm after the untimely death of Cohen some three years earlier. Outraged that the show-ing of these slides constituted a violation of the Second Commandment of "making no graven images of God," one unidentified parent of a pupil took independent — and illegal — action and surreptitiously ripped out the wires of the new device. Remarkably enough, an editorialist for the unyielding Orthodox Yiddish daily the *Morgen Zhurnal,* rather than pillorying the van-dal, went after Fischel and his cohorts for their blatant insensitivity. The writer effectively accused "the official philanthropists, public providers of the larger Jewish world" of forgetting their East European roots, of having become as high-handed as the renowned establishment figures whom they emulated. The paper advised that "the very best plan" for the community was "to leave the Jewish religious education in the hands of the religious parents."[54]

Stung beyond words by this and other such criticisms, Fischel soon re-signed his post, and in a letter to his "mentor," Jacob Schiff, unburdened himself with the charge that his opponents were "of the old-fashioned type who believed that the only way to give children a Jewish education is by teaching them in the same way as they were taught twenty-five years ago in Russia." But it was more than just that: class and status issues and perhaps jealousies toward those — like Fischel — within the Orthodox community who had succeeded in America, and who now consorted with the Germans, stoked the fires of controversy.[55]

While Albert Lucas, Secretary of the Orthodox Union, never joined this chorus of criticism of his organization's leaders, he nonetheless believed that their association with the Kehillah's most prominent spokesmen was sorely misguided. Lucas came to this contrarian point of view after a decade of frustrating experiences as head of its antimissionary task force which Lucas called his Jewish Centres' Association.

Early in its existence, the Orthodox Union recognized that Christian activists who took careful note that immigrant youngster were falling away from their parents' religious roots attempted to make capital in Jewish souls. Some of these evangelists were open in their conversionist designs; others were more circumspect, earning themselves opprobrium as instigators of "masked institutions." In either case, the English-born Lucas, who grew up in a country where conversionists were also a long-standing problem, saw as his mission the organization and supervision of "religious classes . . . in downtown synagogues in which girls as well as boys are taught the Jewish religion in the English language exclusively; purpose, to counterpart the Christian missionaries." There, the most modern of educational techniques that he could afford would be used. One of his prime targets was the famous critic of downtown living conditions, Jacob Riis, whom Lucas attacked for secretly having designs on Jewish youngsters' religious identities.[56]

To accomplish his plan, to "offer bribe for bribe, and spend dollar for dollar in order to hope of any permanent success," Lucas appealed for funding to Fischel and the other East European moneyed people associated with the Orthodox Union. Drachman and Mendes lent their moral support. But Lucas also hoped that Marshall and Schiff—who had backed other antimissionary efforts in the past—would also champion his cause. However, to his greater consternation, these most prominent New York Jews failed to resonate to his appeals. Perhaps Lucas's style of protest deterred Marshall and Schiff; Lucas organized noisy street demonstrations to drive the missionaries out the neighborhood. Whatever their motivations, their demurrals convinced an angered Lucas that these Reform Jewish leaders were soft on conversionists.[57]

Lucas's fears were confirmed for himself when the agenda of the Kehillah was promulgated and antimissionary work was relegated to a tertiary status among pressing communal concerns. And when he saw that the Orthodox Union's delegates were significantly outnumbered on the New York Jewish Community's executive committee, he was convinced that his organization had been co-opted. He certainly understood that as presently constituted his *issue* would never receive the attention he believed it deserved. After a rearguard action to pack the Kehillah with many more additional Orthodox delegates failed, Lucas and his group of dissidents withdrew their already minimal support for the endeavor, and struggled alone in their antimissionary campaigns for much of the next decade. But Fischel, Drachman, Mendes, and others from the Orthodox Union stayed with the Kehillah. Their affirmative persistence was based on their recognition that the missionary problem was but a troubling subset of the larger dilemma of mass disaffection from Judaism. In their view, far more young people were losing interest in their ancestral faith than were becoming interested in affirming Christianity. Confident of their ability to work with the Schiffs and Marshalls for the common good, they cast their lots with programming that they hoped would promote the popularity of Jewish education.[58]

While American Orthodox leaders pursued their many activities, the East European rabbis in America, and their small groups of pious lay followers, were of several minds over whether to consider these efforts worthy attempts to bring the disaffected back toward Jewish practice or to condemn them as unwarranted departures from tradition. Ambivalence, for example, toward the Seminary as an Orthodox institution dated back to its very founding. To begin with, some downtown critics attacked its curriculum and approach to producing rabbis. One of the first Orthodox periodicals on the Lower East Side scoffed at what it characterized as the low level of expertise in Talmudic learning that Seminary students achieved. *Ha-Ivri* once claimed that the most advanced rabbis-in-training covered in the course of an entire academic year but seventeen pages of the Talmud and only a portion of Rashi's commentary. Rashi was the prime medieval expositor of traditional texts. Perhaps even more damning, the weekly asserted that these undereducated rabbinical school graduates who were supposed to lead a battle against Reform Judaism were under the tutelage of professors lacking in commitment to the traditional teachings of the Torah. Among the founders of the Jewish Theological Seminary were Conservatives, like Szold and Jastrow, who held modern views of the origins and authority of traditional sources.[59]

A reporter for the *Yiddishe Welt,* another organ of downtown Orthodoxy, seconded *Ha-Ivri's* negative assessment of the Seminary's work. For this correspondent, "that there is naturally a great difference between rabbis who graduate from a Volozhin yeshiva" — symbolic of the best of the world of Talmudic learning — "and those who graduate from the Jewish Theological Seminary" was a gross understatement.[60]

Judah David Eisenstein, too, had reservations about some of the Conservative rabbis associated with the organization of the Seminary. He also feared that, if not monitored and controlled properly, the rabbinical school might drift away from its mooring in Orthodoxy. In his view, the faculty had to be faithful to Orthodox traditions "and be sure not to break with even the most minor mitzvah of the commandments of the Torah."

However, the ever-pragmatic Eisenstein also believed strongly that the Seminary could be "good, useful and warranted" for American Judaism, if it hewed closely to the mission of producing acculturated Orthodox rabbis who could serve the needs of the next generation of Jews. In a moment of pure candor, this spokesman for the Association of Orthodox Hebrew Congregations averred that, unfortunately, many of the East European rabbis who came to America — whose scholarship he unquestionably revered — were really unable to relate to the outlook of native-born Jews. On the other hand, if properly imbued with staunch commitments to upholding Orthodoxy, graduates of the Seminary could fulfill the calling of ministering with passion and effectiveness to downtown's wavering youths.[61]

Eisenstein's colleague in downtown communal affairs, Eliezer Robison, principal of the forward-thinking Machzike Talmud Torah, went even further in his approval of the Seminary's efforts. He stated that it was "the only seat of learning in this country whose graduates are looked upon as worthy of occupying the high position of Orthodox rabbis."[62] Less articulate members of the Association of Orthodox Hebrew Congregations shared some of Eisenstein's and Robison's sentiments. They financially backed both their own chief rabbi plan and the Seminary program. For them, it was possible to pay homage to the hallowed East European past, and to pray that the chief rabbinate could turn the tide of disaffection from Judaism, while at the same time look favorably upon an American Orthodox effort. Some pious downtown young men — such as Israel and Anna Kaplan's son, Mordecai — who perceived themselves as in the vanguard of a viable American Orthodoxy put their faith in what the Seminary had to offer. They enrolled in that institution. We do not know what these committed students thought of the heterodox views of some of their teachers. But it is certain that they signed on faithfully to the practical outreach training for which that school was becoming known.[63]

The founders of the Agudath ha-Rabbanim never questioned the personal religious values of Drachman, Mendes, and their Seminary disciples or any of the people who lined up with the Orthodox Union. Years after its organization, a house historian for the East European rabbis' group would recall with praise that "the first students who graduated from there [the Seminary] were full-hearted for the faith of Israel and its Torah."[64] Still, they did not judge these young rabbis, or their teachers as colleagues, worthy of admission to their group of well-trained Talmudic scholars. They were "rabbis," deficient in Torah learning. Often that English word was transliterated in the Orthodox press to differentiate them negatively from the truly learned *rabbanim* from Eastern Europe who were members in their organization. More importantly, while the Agudath ha-Rabbanim grudgingly came to grips with American realities, some of its most revered leaders were highly critical of American Orthodoxy's embrace of modern methods.[65]

Rabbi Jacob David Willowski was perhaps the most famous antagonist of even innocuous sociological change. He caused a major stir when, in 1904, this man whom the Agudath ha-Rabbanim honored as *zekan ha-rabbanim* (most distinguished of rabbis) attacked the very use of English in Orthodox rabbis' sermons. This outstanding rabbinic scholar from the Russian town of Slutsk, best known for his telling epigram that "America is a treif land where even the stones are impure," happened to be in America that year. He was "on tour" raising funds for his publication of a new edition of the Palestinian Talmud with his commentary when an Americanizing congregation, Kehilath Jeshurun in the Yorkville section of upper Manhattan, approached him to help officiate at High Holiday services.[66]

Less than a year earlier, this synagogue had appointed erstwhile Endeavorer and Seminary graduate Mordecai M. Kaplan as its English-speaking minister, replacing the Yiddish-preaching rabbi Meyer Peikes, whom the congregants perceived as unable to relate to the younger generation. In a bow toward tradition, coupled with some pressure from the Agudath ha-Rabbanim and the ambivalence toward change that the congregation would soon demonstrate, the young designee was called alternately "minister" and "superintendent of the religious school" but not "rabbi," since he did not possess Orthodox ordination. But before Kaplan, the membership rainmaker, who was charged to attract more young people to the shul could even get his feet wet, some old-line worshippers, within the conflicted congregational mix, decided that with the awesome High Holidays approaching, Kaplan had to be complemented with a rabbi who would remind them of the piety of the past. In other words, as Americanizing Jews, they did not want men like Peikes as permanent fixtures. Still, the High Holidays were special. Whatever the congregants' religious values were throughout the year, the Days of Awe still possessed a power to move these Jews back toward ancestral roots. Having a distinguished visitor in the pulpit contributed to the reverent atmosphere they hoped to create in the sanctuary. Hence, an invitation was tendered to a rabbi who would personify faithfulness to all that was holy.[67]

Willowski acceded to the call. Some three-quarters of a century later, Kaplan would suggest that the entrepreneurial rabbi's interest in Kehilath Jeshurun had much to do with the fact that its "members happened to be the only Jews in New York who were both learned and rich enough to purchase his commentary."[68] In any event, when Willowski came aboard, he made the controversial demand that in his presence all sermons — both his and Kaplan's — had to be delivered in Yiddish, the language of "Torah, faith, ethical instruction and discipline" for the raising of devout Jewish children. For the *Ridbaz*, the acronym by which he was known, English "sermons contain no guidance . . . simply make the Jewish people like the rest of the nations . . . and open the gates leading our brethren to Reform Judaism."[69]

Remarkably, the hard-nosed senior scholar did not object to the young American Orthodox rabbi's presence with him on the pulpit, a resistant move that he might have contemplated in light of his organization's condemnation just a few months earlier of the Seminary's new leaders, Professors Solomon Schechter and Louis Ginzberg. In no uncertain terms, the East European rabbis' group had, in June 1904, excoriated the famed orientalist Schechter and the noted modern Talmudist Ginzberg as "expounders of the Higher Criticism which is anything but Orthodox" who would not have "a share in the world to come."[70] Through this decree, the Agudath ha-Rabbanim made its own clear differentiation between the so-called Old Seminary of the Drachmans and the Mendes's and the newly reorganized school that was then beginning its long road toward emerging as the flagship institution of twentieth-century Conservative Judaism. Willowski's most minimal form of recognition of Kaplan failed to mollify the Seminary graduate. In a pointed rejoinder to those whom he was unhappy with in the congregational family, Kaplan argued that "Judaism need not and must not be afraid to meet and absorb all that is good in modern culture."[71] Here the young American Orthodox rabbi drew his line of demarcation between his worldview and that of the Agudath ha-Rabbanim.

It was with a spirit of negativism worthy of Willowski that most Agudath ha-Rabbanim members declined the Kehillah's invitation to join its umbrella organization. Here again, it was a question of trust within an Orthodox group toward those who did not share their religious values. Fears were expressed that this American institution that unreliable Reform rabbinical and lay leaders inaugurated would "undermine the Orthodox institutions of the Jewish Quarter." Rejectionists had little faith in Magnes's assurances that the "autonomy of all member organizations would be observed" and that his organization's evolving plan would actually help Orthodox Jews deal with critical problems of specific relevance to them, like the never-ending problem of kashruth supervision.[72]

In stark contrast, Rabbis Philip Hillel Klein and Moses Sebulun Margolies —known by his acronym Ramaz—who were no less distinguished figures within the Agudath ha-Rabbanim, stood apart from Willowski and his compatriots' oppositional positions. Through their deeds far more than their words—they were not particularly articulate about the reasons behind their affirmative stances—these leaders, both as congregational rabbis and as communal stalwarts, approved of American Orthodox pedagogic techniques, respected Orthodox Union rabbis as colleagues, and perceived real benefits accruing to Orthodox life through careful cooperation with the Kehillah.

Perhaps Klein's diversified educational background, highly unusual for a member of the presidium of the Agudath ha-Rabbanim, was the key to his accepting attitudes. Though the Hungarian-born scholar received his earliest Talmudic training at the feet of his father, Zeev Zvi Klein, a disciple of Rabbi Moses Sofer (the renowned arch-opponent of traditional Jewish reconciliation with the changing, secularizing world), already as a teenager Klein was ill-disposed toward the notion that "innovation is prohibited according to the Torah." That was the strictest of constructions of the halacha that Sofer preached. At age fifteen, Klein began studying with Rabbi Esriel Hildesheimer, arguably the foremost advocate for flexibility and modernity within Central European Orthodoxy, while his teacher still resided in Eisenstadt, Hungary. Like his mentor who set off for Berlin where Hildesheimer established his Orthodox rabbinical seminary, Klein, too, ultimately migrated to a more cosmopolitan setting, in his case, Vienna. There he studied secular subjects and taught in a yeshiva as he earned ordination at the age of twenty-one from Hildesheimer's institution. This precocious and widely engaged student then went on to encounter secular studies on the highest of levels, earning a Ph.D. from the University of Jena, prior to his migration to the United States in 1890.[73]

Fortunate enough to secure upon arrival the position of spiritual leader of the First Hungarian-American Ohab Zedek Congregation of Norfolk Street, a growing and prestigious immigrant congregation, Klein also aligned himself at its very outset with the founders of the Orthodox Union. He served on its committee on resolutions and was honored with the privilege of delivering the opening prayer to the delegates at that group's second convention in 1901.[74] Though not a charter member of the Agudath ha-Rabbanim — possibly his modern training from Hildesheimer and his advanced secular degree troubled some of its most hidebound members — once on board, he quickly rose to prominence as a member of the rabbis' presidium, a post that he held throughout the first decade of the twentieth century. Still, he maintained very close contacts with the Orthodox Union, that organization which many of the East European rabbis in America habitually disdained.[75]

Klein worked with Americanized Orthodox rabbis first in 1905 when he joined hands with Drachman and Mendes to restart Rabbi Joseph's failed efforts to promote Sabbath observance through a Sabbath Observers Association. Drachman renamed the organization the Sabbath Supporters Association, and together these rabbis, with a small group of lay supporters, organized mass gatherings and street rallies as a political movement might do to garner the allegiance and to inspire constituents. They also publicly pilloried storekeepers who opened their stores on the holy day, and through its Yiddish, Hebrew, and English monthly, the *Shabbes Zhurnal*, called upon those whom one historian has called "the reluctant Sabbath desecrators to express their ideological affinity for the Sabbath."[76]

Even more significantly, Klein demonstrated his affinity for Seminary–Orthodox Union rabbis in 1909 when he agreed to work with Drachman as his rabbinical associate when Ohab Zedek moved up to Harlem and started to attract both new immigrants and more acculturated and second-generation Jews to the synagogue. Unlike Willowski's difficult relationship with Kaplan, there was no dispute over how Torah messages would be delivered from their pulpit. Klein preached to the older worshippers in Yiddish and

Hungarian; his younger colleague held forth in English. As Klein cooperated comfortably in this professional relationship, Drachman returned the favor. He recognized his senior's multiple talents as both "a rabbi of the old ghetto-type, on par with the great Talmudists of Poland and Russia, but he was a university graduate as well." When the Kehillah was created, Klein joined with Drachman and Mendes as members of the Committee of Religious Organization.[77]

A first glance at Ramaz's rabbinic resume, both prior to his arrival in the United States in 1899 and in his first half decade here, would have given no indication that he might partner with Klein in supporting American Orthodox efforts. Born and raised in Kroza, Russia, he was exposed neither to a gymnasium education or university training nor to the ideologies of modern Orthodoxy emerging in Central Europe. He attended yeshivas in his home town, Bialystok, and Kovno and served as a rabbi in Slobodka from 1877 to 1899 before migrating to America and settling in Boston. The draft agenda for the founding of the Agudath ha-Rabbanim was drawn up in his New England home. As late as 1904, Willowski seems to have perceived him as a kindred spirit. It is no coincidence that concurrent with the confrontational Ridbaz's visit to Kehilath Jeshurun that the congregation — at Willowski's suggestion — tendered an offer to Ramaz to be its permanent old-school rabbinical complement to Kaplan, the congregation's youthful minister.[78]

However, in the Yorkville setting Ramaz displayed very different religious stripes. He got along very well with Kaplan. They divided their clerical labors in a manner akin to the Klein–Drachman relationship. Many years later, Kaplan recalled that Ramaz's "function was to preach in Yiddish on Sabbath and holidays, while I would not only preach in English on these mornings, but also headed a five day a week afternoon Hebrew school . . . met regularly [with] a young men's group . . . and led daily an elderly group." Kaplan was pleased that Ramaz's appointment did not isolate him from the older, more traditional elements in the synagogue as he was the prime attraction for the youthful folks. In general, Kaplan remarked retrospectively that he and Ramaz "functioned in a very friendly way with each other."[79]

On his own broader communal fronts, Ramaz, soon after his arrival in town, added his considerable weight to the Sabbath Supporters Association that Drachman championed and Klein supported.[80] Beginning in 1908, he served on the board of education of the Uptown Talmud Torah and by 1911 had become head of that group which included Rabbi Israel Friedlander of the Solomon Schechter-era of the Seminary, as well as Schiff and Marshall. The presence of Harry Fischel, his influential congregant, as president of the modern educational institution during precisely this same time, could only have increased his ardor for this endeavor. Given this range of associations, it was almost natural that Ramaz would resonate to the Kehillah's appeal, particularly to its special offer to the Orthodox community.[81]

As a strategem toward bringing every Jewish group under its umbrella, the Kehillah called for the creation of a Vaad ha-Rabbanim (Council of Rabbis) within their city-wide construct, "a committee of recognized and authoritative rabbis for the control of the whole matter of kashruth and shechita and other religious matters." Such rabbis would be recognized as the officialdom in charge of "all matters such as kashrus [*sic*], milah, mikveh, etc." An infrastructure was being proposed, albeit from an unexpected quarter, that augured to fulfill many of Rabbi Jacob Joseph's dreams — with funding to boot. Here was a possibility of ensuring all the requisites for perpetuating a pious community in America. The trusting Ramaz and Klein worked with Drachman and Mendes within the Kehillah's Committee of Religious Organization to broker that deal; consequently, twenty-three of the forty-six New York–based members of the Agudath ha-Rabbanim joined the Vaad ha-Rabbanim of the Kehillah.

The Vaad lasted within the New York Jewish Community but two years, 1912–1914. The relationship foundered over the rabbinical membership's desires to wrest control over the most controversial item on the Kehillah's plate — Jewish education — from the Magnes-led group. One of its specific complaints was that "session or time allowed for daily instruction by the [Kehillah's Education] Bureau, for the schools affiliated with it, was insufficient for effective religious training." But beyond that cavil lay the reality that for most East European rabbis in America, the yeshiva was still the ideal format. Supplementary education, even when run properly, was a grudging necessary evil. For the Kehillah, the modern Talmud Torah system was the warranted American Jewish institution. If the East European rabbis had their druthers, more time, effort, and certainly funding should have been directed to the yeshiva. The most that the citywide organization would say to the Vaad was that it "would at all times welcome every recommendation made to it," but it would "not bind itself to same."

The decline in the Vaad's rank-and-file stake in the Kehillah posed a major dilemma for Klein and Margolies, who had to decide whether their ultimate allegiances lay with their East European colleagues or with their American friends. Conflicted, the two politically astute rabbis, acting in a manner almost akin to neighborhood ward "bosses" who wished to retain the allegiance of multiple constituencies that differed ideologically with one another, moved first to countenance their Agudath ha-Rabbanim compatriots' concerns. In August 1914, both resigned from the Kehillah board. Klein cited "poor health" and complained that the committees that he served upon did "not call upon [his] specialized sphere of knowledge." Ramaz reportedly alleged that "in all matters pertaining to religion [that] should be referred to the Board of Rabbis to be acted upon . . . the Board of Rabbis was ignored."

However, Klein's and Margolies' formal departure from alliance with the Kehillah did not end their personal participation in Americanizing efforts. In their own heart of hearts, they seemed to believe that this country's social ways and means had to be accommodated. Klein worked harmoniously with Drachman through the 1920s, up in Harlem. Ramaz continued to serve on the Uptown Talmud Torah's board of education as that school became one of the New York Jewish Community's flagship institutions. He cooperated well with Kaplan's successors, Schechter-era Seminary graduates Herbert S. Goldstein and Elias L. Solomon, who ministered as English-speaking rabbis in the Yorkville synagogue.[82]

Bernard L. Levinthal, an unofficial chief rabbi of Philadelphia who oversaw some six congregations, was, however, this era's most ambivalent, conflicted, and perhaps hypocritical immigrant rabbi. On the one hand, Levinthal, who came to the United States in 1891 after having studied in yeshivas in Bialystok, Vilna, and Kovno, said and did much to sustain the argument that he was "the most Americanized of the strictly Orthodox rabbis in the country." He reportedly averred that "a rabbi is a rabbi of all Israel, not merely Orthodox, Conservative or Reform" and that in communal affairs, a leader has "to stand above all positions and denominations." So disposed, Levinthal, like Klein, could be both a member of the Agudath ha-Rabbanim's presidium and a supporter of the Orthodox Union. He also was both a leader of the Federation of American Zionists and a charter member of the German American, Reform-dominated, and decidedly anti-Zionist American Jewish Committee. While the Orthodox Union had its concerns about the hegemony of the American Jewish Committee within the Kehillah, Levinthal had no such fears.

But this same Rabbi Levinthal could be downright antagonistic toward the Seminary and its graduates, resistant to a fault. He was one of the driving forces behind the Agudath ha-Rabbanim's 1904 excoriation decree against Solomon Schechter and Louis Ginzberg. It also has been alleged that it was Levinthal's influence that moved Kehilath Jeshurun to designate Mordecai Kaplan as merely a minister and not a rabbi when he was first appointed. In that latter posture, Levinthal acted much like the arch-resister Willowski. But his apparent profound antipathy toward a school that trained modern American rabbis did not mean that he objected to his own son, Israel, enrolling for precisely that type of training at the same Jewish Theological Seminary. Perhaps, Levinthal's ultimate problem with Schechter's institution was not so much ideological but stemmed from the Philadelphia rabbi's overriding desire to be a power broker, to have a say about how and where rabbis served American Jewish communities.[83]

This maelstrom of diverse Orthodox ideas, activities and personalities —
from the Seminary youth synagogues, through the Agudath ha-Rabbanim's
grudging acceptance of some American realities, to the emergence of Klein,
Margolies, and Levinthal as East European-trained leaders who embraced
American ways — had a major impact on the road the Yeshiva Rabbi Isaac
Elchanan treaded in entering the communal battle to influence second-
generation Jews.

As previously noted, when organized in 1897, this America-based institution modeled along the most rarified of East European educational lines had
as its sole mission the production of a new generation of young Torah scholars who would continue the legacy of Talmudic erudition that was the hall-
mark of the great centers of Old World Jewish learning. In keeping with this
singular agenda, the school provided its acolytes with no formal seminary-
like training in the practical sides of being a rabbi in this country. If pressed
about this conceivable lacuna, its teachers and supporters might have replied
that all a rabbi needed to know to be successful both in his scholarship and in
addressing contemporary communal needs was contained in the worlds of
the traditional texts. The yeshiva was, thus, from the founding of the Agudath
ha-Rabbanim, its most favored institution. Some of its members were its *roshei
yeshiva* (teachers of Talmud). All Agudath ha-Rabbanim people were asked
to raise whatever monies they could for the fledgling institution. The rabbis'
organizational constitution spoke strongly about the God-fearing type of
person who should do the teaching. Thus, it had to have been a moment of
great joy, if not glory, for the rabbis when in 1904 the first men to finish their
yeshiva training were ordained under the direct authority of the Agudath ha-
Rabbanim that manned its board of examiners. They had proven — at least to
themselves — that a Torah center in America could produce a young leadership cadre dedicated to fulfilling Rabbi Joseph's and their own fondest
prayers. These graduates, loyal to their teachers, would without questions or
qualifications do their "duty" to promote "the religion" — as the immigrant
Orthodox Association had first put it — "in which their ancestors lived and
for which those ancestors died."[84]

However, not long thereafter, rumblings for change were felt within the
institution. Its high-school and college-age youngsters made it known, in
very specific terms, that they wanted more out of their yeshiva education.
Some planned on pursuing secular careers once they finished their period
of intense Torah learning and felt strongly disadvantaged in their future
competition with fellow Jews and all others. Their advanced Jewish school
provided only the most minimal of general educational training. Had not
the Agudath ha-Rabbanim warned against words and deeds that might suggest that "the yeshiva [is] simply . . . a stopover before students pursue
advanced secular studies?"[85]

Others within the student body were aggrieved because they wished prep-aration to be more than *just* learned *rabbanim* in America; they wished to serve as effective rabbis in this country. Notwithstanding the received truth harbored in the yeshiva's universe that all knowledge was contained in the Torah texts, these young men could not help but notice that other fellows from the neighborhood, students who were as pious and as motivated as they, were receiving invaluable preparation for their calling at the Jewish Theological Seminary. In many cases, it was literally their friends and rela-tives who were manning Endeavorer activities, garnering through these in-ternships the modern skills that would hold them in excellent future stead. The yeshiva boys might have been proud that they learned more of the Talmud than the Seminary students. But, their uptown counterparts — the Seminary was then situated a mile or so north of the Lower East Side — were studying how to relate to Jews in America. Unhappy with the educational status quo, those seeking eventual secular careers and they who dreamed of positions as American Orthodox rabbis petitioned for change. Initially, the heads of the yeshiva turned down their request cold.

Rebuffed, docile students "submitted" and sheepishly "devoted their en-tire day to yeshiva studies." Other classmates, whose dreams of secular ca-reers could not be so easily chilled, packed their bags and checked out of the school. One student, who had hoped someday to be a rabbi, came to realize through his attempts to deal with the anti-English stance that what he really wanted out of life was not the pulpit but a calling as a humanist. Ephraim Lisitzky, the future American Hebrew poet — he would eventually write about the sad travails of the Sabbath Queen in Boston — "sadly and dejectedly . . . sailed back" to New England. Still others who were determined to be Ameri-can Orthodox rabbis joined the opposition and enrolled at the Jewish Theo-logical Seminary. With role models like Mendes and Drachman around, the move was not a dramatic ideological shift but a sage career move. Finally, there were those who remained on Henry Street and environs and fought their teachers and directors for a systematic study of the secular and, more broadly, for a new definition of the yeshiva's mission.[86]

For close to a decade, and through two student strikes, those "tainted with socialism" — to borrow an administration canard — "battle[d] with the fa-natics." That was the way the students spoke about their opponents. In the course of these times of struggle, support from, among others, Harry Fischel and the *Yiddishes Tageblat,* that forward-looking Orthodox daily, heartened the protestors. The *Morgen Zhurnal,* the always unyielding Orthodox organ downtown, took the school's side. Perhaps more significant, the support of rabbis Klein, Margolies, and Levinthal both bolstered the youngsters' spirits and heightened the credibility of their demands. As the school moved ever so slowly — with frequent reneges — to allow the yeshiva to become "an institution of Torah and *hakhma* (secular knowledge) . . . according to the spirit of the times," the school's installation seriatim of Klein, Margolies, and Levinthal as temporary presidents was one sign of its good will.[87]

While the yeshiva's drift, slow and tortuous as it was, toward becoming the modern Orthodox theological seminary the students desired, could not have sat well with the most narrow-minded members of Agudath ha-Rabbanim, by 1915 their organization's pragmatism ultimately directed acquiescence. After all, if concessions were not made, more disciples would not only be lost to the wide secular world, but the brain drain of some of the yeshiva's best and brightest would continue to end up in the heretical hands of the Schechters and Ginzbergs. If the East European–trained rabbis deigned to explain their tacit affirmation of the secular within a world of Torah, the inescapable reality was that analogous currents were coursing even through the old world of Orthodoxy that they had left behind.

As early as 1882, Rabbi Isaac Jacob Reines had argued at a rabbinical conference in St. Petersburg, Russia, that yeshivas had to introduce the study of Russian and secular sciences into their curricula. Reines argued that the Enlightenment, Jewish and general, and other modern ideological and political movements were making a deleterious impact both on their student bodies and the larger Jewish community. Thus, he reasoned, for their cloistered institutions to remain a viable force, and for its graduates to effectively communicate within a changing community, accommodations had to be made.

The majority of the Russian rabbinate did not approve of these far-reaching ideas. Reines's suggestions were consequently tabled; his early attempt that year to create an enduring yeshiva in Lithuania was pilloried and undercut financially. Still, the modern-thinking rabbi and others of his opinion persevered and some twenty years later, in 1905, at the same time that battles were starting to rage at the New York yeshiva, Reines succeeded in establishing a modern yeshiva in Lida, Belorussia. His students were trained there in "Hebrew language and literature, the language of the country and in general disciplines as taught in the secondary schools."[88]

The Lida experiment may have helped some rabbis on this side of the Atlantic come to grips both with their own presence in this treif land and with their still idealized view of the Orthodoxy on the old side. Even more importantly, Reines's efforts had to have helped them concede that if Torah-strong Eastern Europe perforce produced a Lida yeshiva in response to the modern world, could less be expected from an Orthodox institution in America? Finally, the great respect that many within the Agudath ha-Rabbanim's rank and file personally possessed for Rabbi Reines may have eased greatly their acquiescence to what they could have called the transplantation of Lida to America.

In the years between his initial foray into yeshiva-building and his incipient efforts in Lida, Reines emerged as a leading ideologue and practical tactician for religious Zionism. Most importantly, in 1902 he was instrumental in the founding of the Mizrachi movement, an independent Orthodox body within the budding Zionist cause, dedicated to serving as a watchdog organization against the pervasiveness of secular ideas and activities within the Jewish national movement. Agudath ha-Rabbanim members were for the most part Mizrachi men. Their respect for their teacher of Zionism may have well carried over to other aspects of his creed. In supporting change in New York, they acknowledged that movements and ideas clearly inimical to their definition of Judaism — including Schechter's Conservativism — had to be fought on their own grounds, even if in remodeling their school, they were supporting a yeshiva that no longer totally resembled the Torah institutions they remembered from Eastern Europe.[89]

The actual implementation of far-reaching change at the New York yeshiva awaited, however, 1915 and the arrival of Rabbi Bernard Revel. This unusually talented and intellectually curious Talmudic scholar possessed all the right qualities to stand as the consummate role model for projecting a synthesis of Torah and secular vistas within the Orthodox institution. Born in Kovno in 1885, young Revel earned a reputation as a budding Talmudic luminary at the Telshe Yeshiva where he was ordained. But, Revel's purview went far beyond the ells of traditional learning. While still in Russia, he demonstrated an interest in the Haskalah. Family tradition also has it that given "his multi-faceted personality and profound grasp of historical event," the rabbi also flirted with some of the teachings of the Jewish Labor Bund, that decidedly nonreligious, socialist expression of Judaism. Actually, Revel's presence in the United States had much to do with his need to flee tsarist authority during the 1905 unsuccessful Russian Revolution after a controversial political piece that bore his a name landed him for a brief time in a Kovno prison cell.[90]

Upon arrival in New York, Revel found the early, downtown yeshiva hospitable to his interests in continuing his rabbinic learning. Simultaneously, New York University met his desire for intensified secular studies. He graduated with a M.A. in 1909. Revel's quest for advanced academic Jewish studies then brought him to Philadelphia, where he earned a doctorate in Karaitica from Dropsie College. He also studied American law and other humanistic disciplines at that city's Temple University and the University of Pennsylvania. When called to his post at the Yeshiva Rabbi Isaac Elchanan, at the age of thirty, Revel had achieved, through his own perspicacity, what the supporters of change at the school wanted to provide succeeding generations of American Orthodox rabbis. Here was an esteemed rabbi who possessed both the Talmudic pedigree of the past and the modern perspective needed for the future. It also helped in bringing Revel aboard that he had married well. Sarah Revel's family, the Travis immigrant Jews from Latvia, who made their money in oil businesses in Tulsa, Oklahoma, sent much-needed financial support to both Revel and the always indigent school.[91]

While making dramatic changes at the yeshiva was his ultimate goal, the new president began with a sage conservative move. He brought in esteemed East European rabbinical colleagues, as roshei yeshiva, to bolster the core Talmudic program. Then, in building an academic Jewish studies track, Revel hired fellow Orthodox Jews whom he knew, or was aware from the old side, to teach his young men subjects such as Jewish history, philosophy, and philology. To help Revel introduce secular worlds to his disciples, he engaged the two grand older men of American Orthodoxy, Rabbis Mendes and Drachman. The former was installed to teach homiletics; the latter became professor of pedagogy, and "acted in various instructional capacities," teaching both Hebrew studies and the German language. To Mendes and Drachman, the reorganization of the yeshiva represented a new beginning for the concept of the Orthodox seminary that had loomed large when the Jewish Theological Seminary began some thirty years earlier. Revel also found a post for that long-time supporter of Orthodox seminaries, Judah David Eisenstein, who taught *midrash,* rabbinic homiletic excurses on the traditional Torah texts.

Looking further ahead, in 1916 Revel moved to organize the Talmudical Academy, the first Orthodox high school in this country that proffered both traditional Torah studies and a State of New York approved general education curriculum. With that school in place, a recruitment strategy for producing young men comfortable with their Orthodox backgrounds and worldly perspectives was now in place. Some of the graduates would go on to advanced Torah study and eventually to rabbinical ordination. Others would emerge from the yeshiva prepared to compete with all others for jobs and positions in American businesses and professions. The system that the student protestors had called for, a decade or so earlier, was now implemented Finally, Revel announced that he was ready to establish the Society of Jewish Academicians; an American Orthodox think tank to bring scholars from varying Torah and academic disciplines together to ponder solutions to the major social and religious questions of the time.[92]

Even as Revel strove, through this entire flurry of activity, to make his yeshiva competitive with the Seminary, he was far from personally antagonistic toward that other institution or its leaders. While the Agudath ha-Rabbanim excoriated Schechter for his heterodoxies, Revel corresponded with this major figure in the world of Jewish science. In 1907, he asked Schechter for an academic recommendation as a part of this young Orthodox rabbi's quest for advanced academic Jewish studies. Revel also was comfortable enough with the views of many of the members of the Seminary's faculty that he invited them to join his planned Orthodox Society of Jewish Academicians. There even is some evidence that suggests that Revel was so close to the Seminary's intellectual elites and to the Seminary's ideas, that in 1916–1917, as his plans at the yeshiva moved frustratingly slow toward fruition, that the yeshiva president—with some prodding from the Travis family—may have contemplated either merger of the yeshiva with the Seminary or alternatively, becoming president of the Jewish Theological Seminary. In all events, by the end of the second decade of the century, the Yeshiva Rabbi Isaac Elchanan, temporarily renamed the Rabbinical College of America, operating under Revel's system, began to produce young rabbis prepared to address the Jewish religious problems of their times. The calling of Rabbi Joseph H. Lookstein to a rabbinical post at Kehilath Jeshurun in 1923 was one sign of the Orthodox school entering the lists as a viable trainer of American rabbis. Prior to his appointment, Ramaz had Seminary men, Mordecai M. Kaplan, Herbert S. Goldstein, and Elias L. Solomon as his pulpit colleagues.[93]

However, notwithstanding all of these Jewish retrieval efforts—from the incipient yeshiva, to the chief-rabbi scheme and the Agudath ha-Rabbanim, and from the Orthodox Union's avowed Americanizing efforts, to the Revel-run school taking cues from all Jewish forces around it—the reality remained that the majority of American Jewish immigrants and their children were oblivious to all initiatives. If these New York–based plans were to be a model for the entire nation, they were far from successful models. Two studies that the Kehillah sponsored in 1917–1918 offered stark statistics about mass disinterest in religious life in the metropolis. Mordecai Kaplan found that "the synagogue has lost hold on more than one-half of the largest Jewish Community in the world." As discouraging, one in four Jews who attended services did so in the so-called "provisional synagogues," basically entrepreneurial enterprises, "improvised place[s] of worship" set up "to accommodate the large number of Jews who, no longer connected with the regular synagogues," the majority of which were landsmanshaft Orthodox shuls, where they "still want[ed] to worship with the rest of the Jews on the two most important Jewish holidays of the year—Yom Kippur and Rosh ha-Shanah." Despite his own and so many other's efforts, Kaplan observed ruefully that the "synagogue owes its existence more to the momentum of the past, than to any new forces created in this country that make for its conservation and development."[94]

Dr. Alexander M. Dushkin, one of the educational professionals most committed to the Kehillah's Talmud Torah work, likewise reported unhappily that after nearly ten years of modernization efforts, "less than 24% of the estimated number of Jewish children of elementary school age" received any form of Jewish education, including the "private teachers" and the "one teacher schools, or 'Chedarim.' " On the secondary school level, counting the newly established Talmudical Academy, "hardly one percent" was continuing their Jewish schooling into the teenage years.[95]

A lack of acculturation would keep the majority of immigrant Jews still connected, if in an attenuated way, to their ancestral roots. So many of their Americanized children, on the other hand, disdained all religious involvement. Only the scions of the most pious of families opted for yeshiva education — that is, if they did not rebel against their parents.

When all was said and done, once the public school day ended, most youngsters wanted to run free rather than attend even the most innovative Jewish schools. If these kids were ever rounded up in a Jewish "after-school" venue, typically it was within at a settlement house or at the Young Men's Hebrew Association. These outlets were designed to remove impressionable youths from the delinquency of the streets. But these supervised play and recreational places, while under nominal Jewish auspices, provided little in the way of substantial Jewish religious educational instruction.[96]

Facing up to the dilemma that the best of the Americanized shuls and the most progressive of schools had yet to staunch the tide of disaffection, Kaplan, while reporting glumly on the synagogue attendance problem, brought his special brand of creativity, influence, and leadership to three new Orthodox institutions. These were the next efforts to create environments where youngsters who had their hearts set on playing might be moved to study and to pray. In each instance, the game plan involved the creation of a multifunctional synagogue complex where those who liked athletics or dances or art classes or club meetings would be welcomed. While they were on the premises, subtle efforts would be made to convince them of the value of a Jewish education and of attendance at Orthodox services.

The Central Jewish Institute was an extension of the modern Yorkville Talmud Torah and an appendage to Kehilath Jeshurun that Kaplan's student at the Seminary, Herbert S. Goldstein, rolled out in 1916. A year or so later, with the help of his father-in-law Harry Fischel, the ambitious Goldstein brought the idea that the sanctuary could be approached through diverse social and cultural portals to neighboring Harlem. At his Institutional Synagogue, the target audience was "many of those . . . attracted to . . . its diverse activities [that] would not be apt to go into a synagogue per se." The logistical strategy was that those with nonreligious interests on their minds would naturally "pass the Synagogue hall and cannot help dropping in for services because it does not require an extra effort, as he or she follows the path of least resistance." Then in 1918, Kaplan returned to the active rabbinate when he accepted a call from, among others, some erstwhile Kehilath Jeshurun congregants to head up The Jewish Center on Manhattan's newly emerging community on the West Side. Though in accepting this post the unconventional rabbi acceded to the Orthodox ritual that was to be observed at the outset at the new synagogue, Kaplan believed that in time through dint of his personal charisma and intellectual acumen he would turn The Jewish Center into a spiritual laboratory for the promulgation of his new vision of Judaism. But only a few close associates and congregants then knew of his Reconstructionist ideas.[97]

By Kaplan's own account, his personal, troubling observation of Jewish young adults playing baseball in the streets on a Sabbath afternoon while their still-devout elders listened to a rabbi drone on in a shul about some traditional text ("there were no young men among the listeners") helped quicken his and his supporters' pace to create a model synagogue. The formula called for the "translat[ion]" of the synagogue into "a synagogue center . . . where all the members of the family would feel at home during the seven days of the week. There they could sing and dance and play. . . ." In many ways, Kaplan's gauge of how well The Jewish Center was doing was the extent to which the "athletikers," as he was wont to call young athletes who frequented the institution, found their way from gym or pool to the sanctuary. A "happy Center combination" took place when "two youngsters were overheard while walking into the gymnasium, humming to themselves with delightful unselfconsciousness, the *Meleh Elyon* melody [a prayer from the High Holiday liturgy] sung a few minutes earlier on the floor below."[98]

In the succeeding decades — the so-called interwar period — many American Orthodox rabbis, as well as their Conservative counterparts, followed Kaplan's lead and embraced the New York–initiated Synagogue Center activities as they confronted even more difficult times for American Orthodoxy. During the 1920s–1930s, the minority of pious immigrant Jews literally died out. With the virtual close of the gates of immigration in the immediate post–World War I period, no new large cadres of strictly observant Jews were permitted to come over here to bolster the ranks of faithful immigrants. While the yeshiva community that began on the Lower East Side in the 1880s and was now situated primarily in Brooklyn, New York, survived and advanced among a staunchly dedicated second generation, and while an incipient modern Orthodox day school movement began during these years, in the end, the youngsters who were involved constituted only the smallest percentage of America's Orthodox Jews. More generally, Jews identifying as Orthodox in America were largely oblivious to the demands of the halacha. They may still have shown up at central Jewish times and occasions and events within Orthodox synagogues. But they, otherwise, demonstrated little interest in the observance of cardinal traditional teachings. They would come to synagogue centers more often to play more than to pray. It was an era where Orthodoxy was still numerically strong — it maintained a very large tent, if only when compared to other American Jewish movements. But the religious commitment of those who affiliated was very weak.

# CRISIS AND COMPROMISE

In 1921, the United States Congress passed legislation that ended a century of constant, unrestricted Jewish immigration. According to the Emergency Quota Act, "the number of aliens of any nationality" eligible for admission in "any fiscal year" was "limited to 3 per centum" of that group's foreign-born presence in this country as of 1910. The emergency, said restrictionist Representative Alvin Johnson of Washington state, was that America was "being made a dumping ground" for "the dependents, the human wreckage of the war," and radicals of many red stripes who, it was alleged, were receiving their marching orders from the newly created Soviet Union. After more than thirty years of a national debate over immigrants and persistent questioning about whether they could, in time, become productive, loyal Americans, the nativists and racists won. The law limited immigrants from such low quota entities as Poland, Romania, and Russia to about 50,000 in 1921–1922, down dramatically from 120,000 the prior year. Three years later, the situation worsened for those who might seek these shores when the Johnson-Reed Act pushed the determining year for "national origins" back to 1890 and reduced the quota to 2 percent per country. Under this measure, designed to keep out East European Jews and Italians, fewer than 11,000 Jews entered the United States in 1924. Over the seven years that immediately followed the implementation of this legislation, fewer than 75,000 Jews were admitted, about 10 percent of the numbers who settled here in 1907–1914, the years just preceding the start of World War I.[1]

These new realities provoked great concern among the editors of the *American Hebrew,* a "National Jewish Weekly." They wondered out loud whether the "landlocked" Jews of America, now on their own and bereft of the "diverse infiltration of European Jewish religion and culture," could "adjust," drawing upon both "American sources" and its own "spiritual springs." Though uncertain about what the future held, these commentators were confident that, come what may, at least American Judaism would be devoid of "every vestige of the Old World distinctiveness," having "dispensed with those externalities which constituted the heritage of ghetto days," the "extreme East European orthodoxy" of the past. But what the newspaper people prayed for — an end to the "extreme East European orthodoxy" of the past — was precisely what concerned this country's most pious Jews.[2]

Looking back on the prior forty years, veterans of the Association of Orthodox Hebrew Congregations initiative and founders of the Agudath ha-Rabbanim would have had to admit that only modest gains had been made in upholding the banner of transplanted Orthodoxy. To make matters worse, beginning in the 1920s the inevitable march of time started to deplete its ranks of activist first-generation Jews. Rabbi Klein died in 1926. By 1929, more than half of the charter member of the Agudath ha-Rabbanim had expired. In 1936, Rabbi Margolies passed on, too.[3]

It was also significant that Orthodoxy's immigrant constituency, which would occasionally hearken to religious importuning, particularly when it was feeling guilty about its breaks with the halacha, was also leaving the scene. If that actuarial reality was not grievous enough, a new second generation was coming into its own during this interwar period, with ears deaf to calls to return to tradition. The children of the immigrants, who never showed a particular proclivity to follow ancestral teachings, were on the streets as early as the first decade of the twentieth century. But their era of predominance — both in their numbers and their religious attitudes — began in the 1920s.

Evidence of its disaffection from Orthodox practice appeared over the course of the next two decades both to sociologists and to rabbis. Surveying an unhappy scene as early as 1920, the Orthodox Union's Rabbi Henry P. Mendes — an old hand at evaluating troubling religious situations — reported that "it is perfectly true that Sabbath desecration is painfully noticeable in the Middle West, the West and the South, where Reform Judaism is so powerful. But it is also true of the East, where Orthodox Judaism has its strongholds." Orthodox Union synagogues stood generally half-empty week after week, packed only on the High Holidays. Such was the case from Stamford, Connecticut, to Brownsville, Brooklyn, where scholars found in the first instance that "only three times a year [did] the synagogue fill all of its pews." In the inner-city locale, another survey revealed similarly that "only nine percent of adult males . . . attended synagogue with any regularity."[4]

Comparable patterns of observance also obtained in "Easttown," an unidentified city situated some sixty miles from the metropolis. There in 1931–1932, a Jewish community was observed where "religion played a relatively small part in the life of the Jewish family as compared with the aspects of making a living, marrying and educating one's children" secularly. In that community, two-thirds of all Jewish families affiliated with the synagogue, with the predominant proportion signed up with the Orthodox congregation. But only 1 percent attended services regularly during the year.[5]

The sources also suggest that those "one-percenters" were, as one memoirist has recalled, "people who did not work on the Sabbath, but they didn't work on any other days of the week either. They were too old or too frail to work so they became de facto Sabbath observers." Others in that group included those who might have owned the family business. They absented themselves from work, leaving their stores "in the hands of their children or hired help." During the Great Depression, many of those who would have liked to have been more observant, young and old alike, found the pressure to work at a job any job, even on the Sabbath, compelling. During that time of economic crisis, other Jews who may have blamed God for the family's financial predicament became ill-disposed to frequent God's house to thank the Almighty for providing them with all of the necessities of life. One young man who grew up in the 1930s has related that "with the Depression, things changed with my father even in religious practice. Before, he never failed to take us to the synagogue every single Saturday. After the crash, he didn't seem to care anymore." Indeed, many Americans of every faith suffered from similar bouts of what has been called "spiritual depression" and stopped going to their houses of worship. Then there were those who stopped attending shul because they were embarrassed by their inability to maintain their synagogue membership. Some impoverished families had no money even to pay for Rosh ha-Shanah seats. Exigencies like these led to the return of the less than savory "mushroom" synagogues, with their money-hungry "rabbis" at their heads who tendered cut-rate High Holiday seats.[6]

The religious values of those within the younger generation who had moved beyond their parental homes were cause for even less communal optimism. While surveys of interwar Jewish college students enrolled from upstate New York to New England to Chicago to even North Dakota indicated that they felt Judaism's "code of ethics" spoke to them, most "young men and women," it was found, "observe few of our customs" and were decidedly less interested than their elders in the "preservation of existing religious organizations." This pattern of disaffection from ritual life was even true in Brooklyn, which, as we will see, was the hottest bed of devout Orthodox behavior during this era. There, as one early community chronicler put it, while "the pious Jew every Rosh ha-Shanah . . . chants . . . 'penitence, prayer and charity can avert the evil decrees,' . . . the Jew today, for the most part, considers his communal obligations from the point of view of charity." Though giving to the unfortunate, especially during a time of national economic calamity, was surely a mitzvah par excellence, otherwise these Jews "ignore[d] every obligation of Judaism." Despite efforts to strengthen the appeal of modern Jewish education, most of its messages were lost upon youngsters as they matured. This next generation neglected more of the core traditions that their parents routinely observed, most notably in the area of kashruth.[7]

Remarkably, choosing to not eat kosher foods took place at a time when it was becoming easier than before to follow those commandments and to do so in an American way. By the 1920s, Jewish women who had always assumed the responsibility to maintain traditional practices in their homes found a willing ally in Madison Avenue. Companies that produced such staples as flour or baking powder or even mustard and biscuits made it known through advertisements, published recipes, and cookbooks that their products were available and produced according to strict halachic specifications. As always, entrepreneurs, Jewish and otherwise, capitalized on wives' and mothers' desires to have just the right foods on the table for Passover, that longest standing of traditions. Maxwell House coffee, reportedly, caused a stir at many seder meals when it introduced a new "tradition" of drinking coffee rather than tea at the end of the sumptuous holiday banquet. A decade or so later, the company would print its own Haggadah to insure a "unique relationship between a product and a people." While there was still a robust market for kosher foods — especially at holiday time — a decreasing segment of the Jewish population remained committed to that fundamental tradition.[8]

As with so many other religious strictures, when it came to food, the halacha was broken or abridged in many ways and to varying degrees. "Practically all of the Jewish people," one kosher advertising promoter observed, "have a natural, inherited repugnance toward certain distinctly *non-Kosher* [or *treyf*] items, such as lard — because of a centuries-old antipathy from a religious standpoint toward pig and products derived therefrom."[9] Some young men would not taste their first morsels of pork products until they were drafted or enlisted in the United States Army during World War II.

# Crackers baked with lard are "TRAIFFE"!

Even though you do not see it, many crackers are baked with lard. But it is easy to be safe. Just be sure to serve Sunshine Kosher Crackers. They are baked with a Kosher vegetable shortening. That makes them "parve."... And besides this fact, they are crisper, flakier and more flavorful!

 Sunshine Kosher Crackers are made under the supervision of the Union of Orthodox Jewish Congregations of America, whose representative, Rabbi E. Goelman, appointed by Rabbi M. S. Margolies, is always present at the baking of the crackers to see that they are kosher in every respect. These kosher crackers can be used with meat or dairy dishes.

*Rabbi Herbert S. Goldstein*
*Honorary President*

WAX-WRAPPED . . .
ALWAYS OVEN FRESH!

**FROM THE "THOUSAND WINDOW BAKERIES" of LOOSE-WILES BISCUIT CO., Long Island City, N.Y.**

Figure 5.1. "Crackers baked with lard are 'TRAIFFE'!"
Advertisement for Sunshine Kosher Crackers, *Jewish Forum*
(March 1933): 1.

Then they ended up "eating ham for Uncle Sam," as that was the food placed in front of them in the mess hall. At that critical moment, Jewish G.I.s had to decide whether they wanted to stand out among their fellow soldiers by eating so differently or to swallow this most unkosher food as a sign of fellowship and patriotism. Some fellows caught in this pickle rationalized that "you're gonna learn to be a soldier and that's it" as they took their first disgusted bites. Only a minority of the devout-in-uniform held out.[10]

Deeply observant soldiers either avoided eating meat altogether or prayed that a salami would arrive from home or that the Orthodox chaplain would have enough in his stash to share. Passover was a particularly vexing time, as so many other Jews wanted a piece of the rationed matzah. During the rest of the year, the basic staples that the devout consumed were fruits, vegetables and, if they were lucky, "eggs boiled in their shells" when that delicacy "happened to be on the menu." The most punctilious would carefully scope out the mess hall, finding a seat where the soldier's back would be against the wall, so that no one would see him unceremoniously place a yarmulke on his head as he quickly downed his meal. Army protocol generally prohibited "wearing a uniform cap or helmet in any mess hall." No one seriously considered petitioning for any sort of "kosher food kitchen" at a camp or base. One "Orthodox G.I." would later explain that such an accommodation "would be feasible only if there were separate Jewish units. Nobody wanted that. There was to be no 'Jewish brigade' in the U.S. Army."

As far as the Sabbath was concerned, those committed to the halacha in such difficult environs were at least sure to avoid "voluntary desecration . . . for private, non-military purposes." Here too the fortunate ones were those who might find a gentile comrade in arms who was willing to swap "Sunday duty" to allow a Jewish friend "to be off on Saturday." But those who proposed trading places did so in such a way as not to gain any advantage from the arrangement. Nobody wanted to be "accused of using religion as a means of 'gold-bricking'." Similarly, daily prayers were said both rapidly and partially to avoid holding up the unit from its daily regimens.[11]

While still civilians, however, most future Jewish G.I.s and their sisters, girlfriends, and future wives blithely ignored the rabbinic rules regarding how biblically approved fish, meats, and poultry were prepared, opting for what became known as a "kosher-style" style cuisine. For many Jews, eating unkosher "out" — that is, away from home — was the way to go even as they were sure to eat kosher foods in their mothers' kitchens and were very scrupulous in their food observances during Passover. That holiday still loomed large in the religious calculus. Perhaps, as significant, when they transgressed, as so many Jews from kosher homes did, they harbored "no personal misgivings" or any worries about their "status as Jews." All told — although definitive numbers are hard to come by — as of the mid-1930s, it could be estimated that only 15 percent of America's Jews strictly followed kosher laws. Twenty percent honored "some of the laws some of the time," while two out of three disdained "all of the laws most of the time" although many in the latter group of miscreants may have stopped short of eating pork.[12]

To make matters worse for those concerned with this major decline in observance, if members of the younger generation attended their local Ys or Jewish Community Centers — those other nominally Jewish institutions that competed with synagogues and Talmud Torahs for youthful allegiances — they would find in their precincts little that recommended pious behavior. Though its national leaders averred that those who were its young members imbibed "the rich cultural heritage of the Jewish group" and were "prepar[ing]" themselves for "Jewish living in America," the reality was that "too little attention [was] paid to the development of the religious side." The worst offenders were those Ys and JCCs whose lunchrooms and restaurants were not kosher and which kept all of its facilities, from its offices to its gymnasium and pool, open on Saturday, taking no cognizance of the Sabbath day.[13]

More than anything else, what kept that disaffected second generation together as Jews — at least within this country's largest cities — was their residential propinquity in their urban neighborhoods. Housing discrimination played its part in promoting group persistence as Jews found homes together in the new settlement areas to which they flocked before the Great Depression. Other ethnic groups' desires to live in largely homogeneous enclaves where they could hold on to their own turf also helped to segregate Jews. In an era where social antisemitism restricted Jewish integration in university education and elite occupational realms, the minority group's members also found each other on an ongoing basis in schools or at the workplace. Given this set of circumstances, even Jews who ordinarily did not attend a synagogue might end up in its sacred space on one occasion. They would be in the sanctuary on their wedding day to a fellow Jew who had also grown up in that predominantly Jewish neighborhood, attended the same school, or worked in the same job. Though Orthodox rabbis of that era had to have been pleased with such endemic endogamy, they also knew that they were now ministering to a generation whose involvement with their faith was born mostly of nonacceptance in the outside world rather than any staunch commitment to the values of the Torah.[14]

In keeping with its by now long-standing traditions, the rabbis and lay leaders of the Orthodox Union — increasingly the graduates or supporters of Revel's yeshiva, but a few still from the Jewish Theological Seminary community — eschewed excoriations. Rather, they labored to impress upon the wavering that their presence within Orthodoxy's tent was still greatly desired, and went out of their way to convince their listeners to make good-faith efforts to conform to halachic teachings. On the Sabbath question, for example, in a 1936 radio address, Rabbi Herbert S. Goldstein asserted to those who might listen to him that "just because a Jew thinks he is forced to give up this or that part of his faith is no reason for his retreating completely from the banner of tradition."[15]

At almost the same time, the Young Israel synagogue of Newark, New Jersey, made it clear that all it requested of worshippers was their discretion in not flaunting their nonobservance to pious regulars in its pews. In a printed guide to "Synagogue Etiquette and Procedures," it softly admonished that "on Sabbath and Holidays, the display of pocketbooks, the jingling or open display of money . . . and driving to the synagogue" — all unqualified violations of rabbinic strictures — were "indeed violations of *good taste.*" The guide's further call to "respect the traditions of our people and our sacred writings" carried only the implicit suggestion that such blatant, public breaks with the law were offensive to fellow, more committed Jews around them. Rather than speaking sternly of halachic violations, the message was that it was just poor etiquette to behave inappropriately in public religious settings[16]

As an outfit with designs to be national in scope, the Council of Young Israel Synagogue organizations, with its network of twenty-five congregations in the New York metropolitan area and five cities elsewhere in the country, maintained the same open approach to potential affiliates. The Sabbath desecrator certainly could be called to the Torah. However, lay leadership was reserved exclusively for the observant. Of course, when the holy day ended, all members would cut in on each other at the always popular Saturday night synagogue socials.[17]

In comparable lenient lockstep, the Rabbinical Council of America, founded in 1935 basically as the rabbinical alumni association of men ordained from Revel's institution, also approached is "half-baked" and "confused" laity with the softest of touches. It recognized the world of non-observance of the Sabbath all around it and did not question the religious lifestyles of those who showed up at services. All men in their pews could be called to the Torah. In dealing with its rank and file, the most that its Committee on Traditional Observances impressed on its members was the need to "*urge* congregants to refrain from attending movies or going shopping on Sabbath," "to *encourage* parents not to allow their children to work or shop on Sabbath" and to "*insist* . . . that handbags and purses not to be brought to synagogue on the Sabbath." The organization's Halacha Committee did determine, however, that the privilege of leading the services had to be reserved for Sabbath observers as was the high honor and responsibility of acting as a mohel.[18]

On the kashruth front, the Americanized Orthodox leadership's point of emphasis was the compatibility of halachic teachings with the most up-to-date American thinking. The health benefits of kosher consumption was at the heart of an article that Professor David Macht wrote in a volume on Jewish traditions and practices that the Orthodox Union sponsored in 1930. His editor, Rabbi Leo Jung, Kaplan's successor in the prestigious Jewish Center pulpit, who effused high culture and dignity, introduced the piece with the traditional teaching that "according to the Torah, the purpose of the dietary laws is to sanctify us and assure our racial and moral integrity" even as he asserted proudly that "Macht's genius for research . . . continues to uncover their inherent hygienic value." This distinguished physician and pharmacologist, with a medical degree from Johns Hopkins University—one of this country's few academically accomplished, pious Jews—made the case that kashruth "has proved to be of remarkable, combative resistance to various diseases." Indeed, the researcher warned that "modern pathology has shown that oysters" — among the most treif of delicacies — "and various mollusks are carriers of many deadly germs such as the typhoid bacillus." He suggested, perhaps hyperbolically, that "other animal foods forbidden by the Torah have been known to produce undue and excessive excitement of the sexual passions."[19]

The leaders of the Women's Division of the Orthodox Union offered a comparable, if less explicit, understanding of the power of kashruth in arguing for observance. Through its books, magazines and, above all cookbooks, this organization, founded in 1923 and long headed up by Rebecca Fischel Goldstein, Harry's daughter and Herbert's wife, delivered the messages that "nothing defines the Jewish character as much as the dietary laws . . . abstinence from foods permitted to others develop[s] and strengthen[s] self mastery and control." Borrowing a page from Macht's book, they were also sure to aver that the kosher eater lived longer and healthier lives. Perhaps as important and indicative of its modern strategy to reach acculturated Jews, the Women's Division emphasized that the skilled and creative observant housewife, a culinary "artist" in her own right, could prepare kosher dishes that were as classy and classic American as any treif chef. Though recipes teaching the uninitiated, or forgetful, how to make the traditional fare that their parents liked so much had their honored place in these interwar cookbooks, advice on how to whip up foods that ordinarily appeared only on unkosher tables — if just the right ingredients were substituted — was the highlighted feature of these guides.[20]

Health, comfort, and contentment were likewise at the forefront of appeals by Orthodox Union spokeswomen to other Jewish women to observe the laws of family purity. Here the challenge was, to begin with, to dispel the general perception that these procedures were an "archaic custom" of no value to the modern Jewish woman. Though here, again, numbers on actual mikveh use are hard to come by, the sense is that even in homes where other religious regimens were rigorously followed, "where milk and meat are separated and *chametz* [leaven] removed before the Passover holiday, mikveh is not observed." Contributing to the dereliction was the dirty, unsightly, and unsanitary appearance of many of these long-existent ritual pools that were totally unattractive to Americanized women who had fine bathing facilities at home and who would never venture into an unhygienic venue.[21]

The Americanized Orthodox answer to widespread female avoidance of the mikveh was to project the traditional observance as a way toward improving family life. Again, "abstinence," in this case periodic sexual separateness, was held up as a "safeguard against the disadvantages, dangers and pitfalls of married life." The beautiful looking mikveh guides emphasized "renewal, fulfillment and purification."

Turning to science, as Dr. Macht had done for kashruth, advocates argued that those who frequented the mikveh experienced a lower incidence of gynecological diseases than did the general population. On a far more positive note, they asserted that "healthy Jewish offspring," ready and able to "cope with life's many problems" issued from "healthy, physically fit mothers . . . and the law of monthly separation." Finally, the women of the Orthodox Union made a major push to clean up the site of monthly immersion, renamed in some circles as a "ritualarium." The modern mikvehs were touted as a "Jewish Women's Club," complete with all the amenities of the local beauty salon.[22]

These ministrations on behalf of kashruth and family purity laws and, as always, advocacy for Sabbath observance may have raised the consciousness of those who wavered in their observance. They surely elevated the spirits of the committed who could now feel more modern as they continued to observe the commandments. But the reality was that for all of the zeal of these efforts, they were rearguard actions. Particularly in the area of kashruth, they basically constituted prophylactic measures designed to keep the still-kosher kitchen in line with halachic standards. The phenomenon of "eating out," with all of its complexities — ranging from the dilemma of whether to eat cooked kosher fish prepared in treif pots to the question of dining on unkosher plates with the wrong type of silverware — was not really addressed. The most that was done was to inform the public about praiseworthy kosher eating establishments, restaurants and hotels with their "refined home-like atmosphere . . . [which] encourage not only the aesthetic, but also the vitally religious needs in Jewish life."[23]

However, for so many Orthodox rabbis, the depressing sight of those rows of half-empty seats that they preached to week after frustrating week more than offset whatever progress was made in stimulating some congregants' greater commitment to the mitzvoth. Perhaps as pernicious, these unhappy rabbis also often had to deal with their lay leaders who proposed, in the interest of increasing attendance through putting an even brighter American face on their congregations, that their synagogues alter rituals in ways that violated halachic strictures.

Increasingly during the interwar period, if and when Jews went to synagogue, they expected to sit with their families — husbands, wives, and children together. They also preferred that Sabbath evening services be held at a convenient time. In the case of mixed seating or family pews, these demands bespoke both interests in praying like other Americans did and some respect for gender egalitarianism. Still, most synagogues denied their women leadership in conducting or participating actively in the service. A generation or more would pass before women would possess real power in their congregations.[24]

The call for what became known as the "late" Friday night service — not at sundown, which in the winter months could be as early as 4 PM, but at 8 o'clock — reflected changes in contemporary Jewish work patterns and family life. Particularly in the heady economic days of the 1920s, children of Jewish immigrants who achieved middle-class status ended their five-day workweek on Friday afternoon, but rarely before the sun set. During the Depression, there were innumerable reversals of fortunes that caused the unfortunate to be forced back to the six- or seven-day laboring regimen, if indeed they could find employment. Still, a very popular religious protocol emerged that dictated that their family's Sabbath would effectively begin at home upon the arrival back from work of the major breadwinner — usually the father — from his job a trolley, bus, or subway ride away from his home in the newer better-built sections of American cities. Then after a Sabbath dinner at home, he and his wife and children went out to greet the Sabbath Queen together at their house of worship at the convenient prime time of 8 PM. In many cases, the next morning would be reserved for sleeping in, or possibly for playing out of doors. These Jews resonated to the concepts of Sabbath rest and worship but did not feel obligated to follow the halacha's constrictions of their time and restrictions on their movement and activities.[25]

Attentive to these circumstances, the hundreds of Conservative affiliates with the Seminary-based United Synagogue of America, situated mostly in these new areas, made the popular moves and adjustments in traditional interior architecture and time for devotions. So positioned, from an incipient group of 22 congregations in 1913, the dynamic organization could boast as of 1929 of 229 member congregations. Almost all of them provided family pews. And as of 1933, a total of 95 percent of respondents to a national poll that the Conservative Rabbinical Assembly conducted reported that they proffered "8 PM" services even as most also had a sundown minyan for the more observant and, presumably, older members of their religious community. For many of these rabbis and their supportive lay leaders, that after-dinner slot was not only the best time for assembling the largest number of Jews who wanted to pray and stay together. It was, likewise, a ripe opportunity for additional liturgical, ceremonial, and programmatic innovation all directed toward encouraging occasional attendees to become regular worshippers.[26]

By the late 1920s, there was also sympathy within some Reform circles for a late Friday night service. In response to a National Federation of Temple Brotherhood survey of its constituent congregations, sentiments were expressed that "owing to economic conditions, it is impossible to bring the men to Saturday services, so our strength is used through the Brotherhood to bring the younger element to Friday night services (8 PM) with good results." Recognizing that "persons employed in offices and stores and also those who may work for themselves," many of whom from East European and erstwhile Orthodox stock, "can neither attend Saturday morning nor

Friday at 5:30," advocates called for "Friday night services of one hour with a short sermon . . . [to] permit worship on the Sabbath and still permit one to have the evening for other gatherings and enjoyments."[27]

Issues that energized Conservative and Reform innovators were sources of great anxiety for many American Orthodox rabbis. Predicaments included changes in family work patterns, the nature of home religious life, the way mothers, fathers, and children should pray together as American Jewish family units, and the inviolable nature of the Sabbath's time constraints. All over the United States, whether or not there was a Conservative competitor or Reform alternative in town, congregants wanted accommodations in their synagogues, shifts that violated the halacha. On the seating issue, although hard numbers are hard to come by but perhaps amounted to hundreds of cases, Orthodox rabbis and their congregations acquiesced breaking with the rules to lesser and greater degrees, and sometimes in creative ways. In some cases, change in sanctuary protocols meant the absence of the mechitza, with men and women sitting across an aisle from one another. Elsewhere, family pews were the rule, when ironically, during the High Holidays — the consummate Jewish religious prime time — so many Jews who frequented the sanctuary but three times a year insisted upon that mode of operation. There were also situations in which congregations tried to satisfy all varieties of seating preferences. In a Tulsa, Oklahoma, synagogue, B'nai Emunah, where, according one memoirist, "compromise being the art of the possible . . . [they] wound up with men and women sitting on one side of the building in family pews, and the men along sitting on the other side, with a high curtain between the two sides down the center aisle."[28]

Not unlike the mid–late nineteenth century, sometimes when an established Orthodox synagogue moved to remove its mechitza and/or to switch the starting time of services, resistant forces within and without the congregation attempted to forestall the change. In perhaps the most celebrated case, a minority of disgruntled traditionalists turned to Rabbi Eliezer Silver, a rising and younger leader within the Agudath ha-Rabbanim, for assistance. Together they took on Rabbi Solomon Goldman, a disciple of Mordecai Kaplan, and their dispute ended up in front of an Ohio state magistrate. For Goldman, family pews and late Friday night services at the Cleveland Jewish Center were but the first step toward eliminating all ritual elements that smacked of "antiquarianism" and "Orientalism" as he sought to use his pulpit to promulgate his affinity for his Seminary mentor's Reconstructionist ideology. Silver would hear nothing of these and other halachic deviations — there were thirty-eight in all — starting with mixed-gender seating. He testified in the Court of Common Pleas of Cuyahoga County that the rabbi's actions were "in violation of the Constitution and By-Laws which

establishes the congregation as an orthodox or traditional congregation . . .
a religious doctrine which recognizes the absolute authority of the Five
Books of Moses . . . as well as the Talmud and Torah Codes." The defendant
rabbi demurred, asserting that the congregation was not legally wedded to
Orthodoxy and was a constituent part of a different Jewish faith tradition,
Conservatism, which had its own appropriate sense of the religious right or
wrong. Without attempting to make ultimate sense of these conflicting interpretations of what was traditional Jewish practice, the perhaps perplexed
judge permitted Goldman to continue his efforts within the Cleveland Jewish Center.[29]

When it came to the demand for late Friday night services, many Orthodox synagogues did their best to simulate Conservative and Reform programming, short of violating the halacha. In 1944, Rabbi Oscar Z. Fasman
made the case for the "Friday Night Forum," in a *Guide to Practical Synagogue
Problems* that the Orthodox Union commissioned. It offered a road map for
reaching potential attendees without abridging the tradition. It was clear to
him that the Orthodox synagogue had to offer an attractive way to "mark
the Sabbath in a religious way." Otherwise, the only "contact" that the old-
timers would have with the congregation would be what he called "the three
Y's: *Yomtov* [holidays, probably the High Holidays], *Yizkor* [memorial prayers
said on the holidays], and *Yahrzeit* [anniversary of the passing of a close
relative]." As far as the young people were concerned, it was evident to him
that if their congregations were nonresponsive, the impressionable will "ca-
sually or habitually" end up in "competitive Conservative or even Reform
congregations." That is if they attended any synagogue.

The trick for Fasman was to tweak the Orthodox tradition, ordaining
devotions that stopped short of constituting a formal evening service. Those
prayers would be recited at the proper time by whoever appeared at sundown. For example, besides the rabbi's "formal address," and zemirot led by
a "good cantor, perhaps even with a men's choir," a series of "responsive
readings" in English would be offered, designed "to provide religious nourishment for those who are not completely at home in the traditional Hebrew
service." The evening would be capped off with a social hour.

There was also some talk with these same Orthodox circles of using the
informal hour for innovation in a religious area where the liberal movements had yet to venture, the Bat Mitzvah of girls. It was suggested that after
the formal forum there would be time to congregate over coffee and tea to
"mark the entrance of Jewish girls into their obligations under the provisions of our code." Fasman himself thought that a young woman might be
given the opportunity "to read and translate verses from the Torah portion
of the Sabbath, or she might deliver a short speech suitable for the event."
The reception in her honor within the synagogue's precincts would "help

her feel that her role in Jewish life is no less respected than that of the boys in her family." Such a special forum night, it was reasoned, would "undoubtedly attract members of the family and friends," improving attendance.[30]

While Fasman and others experimented within the boundaries of the halacha, other Orthodox congregations chose to ignore traditional teachings and limits. In 1942, a harsh critic of unconventional Orthodox synagogue practices, Rabbi Isadore Goodman, who was then touring the West Coast, wrote angrily about the "appeasement, compromise and surrender" —words that surely resonated with a World War II Jewish readership— within congregations that "add a Service of sorts late Friday night evenings for the so-called younger set." To make matters worse, since this service was not "in accordance with the 'Din' [Jewish law] or 'Minhag' [custom], [it] becomes a caricature, a cross between an entertainment and a religious display." In his view, the unscrupulous permitted "various innovations . . . mixing of the sexes . . . a mixed choir" and "a microphone for convenience," unconcerned that such electric amplification violated "Sabbath sanctity." For Goodman, "the path to conservatism [sic] and reform [sic] becomes open with the specious excuse that we have to meet the popular desire and compete with the attractions of the Temple."[31]

Such reactions to "popular demands" were not only endemic to Orthodox congregational life in western U.S. outposts, but were also true in New York City, the hub of Orthodox life in America. For example, during the 1930s, the Kingsbridge Heights Jewish Center modeled its late Friday night practices after those of the Conservative Brooklyn Jewish Center and utilized Rabbi Israel Levinthal's — Bernard's son — creative liturgy as its basic worship text. A few miles over, also in the Bronx, at the Mosholu Jewish Center mixed seating was the rule during the High Holidays; there, the late Friday night service was week by week the most attended service.

Down South, in Atlanta, the late Friday night service came into vogue at Congregation Ahavath Achim to meet not only the economic needs of worshippers but also their social desires. Under the leadership of Rabbi Harry Epstein, in 1932 the synagogue began holding services during the wintertime — sometimes at 6 PM and other times at 8 PM, but not at sundown — to permit members "to attend the synagogue after work or before the theatre." Here, not unlike some Reform Jews, there was a palpable desire to attend Sabbath evening worship before going off for a night of entertainment. At these prayers, designed to "bring about greater interest and inspiration," females were allowed to come down from the balcony and sit across from the males as the two synagogue sins were blithely combined.[32]

These congregational proclivities made it difficult, even for Orthodox religious leaders of that time, to ultimately differentiate what went on in their synagogues from that which transpired at Conservative temples. Orthodox Union Vice President David de Sola Pool gave voice to these complexities when, in 1942, he offered the following very candid assessment of his community and of "Judaism and the Synagogue." "Today," he noted, "it is growing increasingly difficult to discern any essential organic difference between Orthodoxy and Conservatism. The main differentiae seem to be that Conservative synagogues permit men and women to sit together, and make more use of English in the services than do most Orthodox synagogues." However, "some Orthodox synagogues use some English . . . and seat the sexes, if not together, at least on one floor." For him, "no logical or clear line can be drawn today" between "the movements as American Orthodoxy no longer mirrors East European life." Indeed, "innovations like the late Friday night evening service or the removal of the women's gallery, or the confirmation of girls or a community seder," practices that "would have shocked the worshippers of a generation ago" are "today . . . accepted in numerous congregations."[33]

Adding to the confusion, wrote a younger colleague, Rabbi Mendell Lewittes, two years later, from his Dorchester, Massachusetts, pulpit, was the reality, to begin with, that "there are many synagogues which are, because of certain practices, considered by some to be Conservative, while their officers and members claim their synagogue as Orthodox." Then there are "graduates of the Jewish Theological Seminary" — continuing the tradition of the young Kaplan and Herbert S. Goldstein — "who profess to be Orthodox rabbis and serve in Orthodox pulpits." Simultaneously, "there are . . . graduates of Yeshiva . . . who serve in congregations leaning toward Conservatism." One further complication; "the United Synagogue of America, nominally representing Conservative synagogues and definitely guided by Conservative rabbis, included within its membership synagogues professedly Orthodox."[34]

In line here too with its long-standing position of tolerance and inclusiveness toward miscreants, the Orthodox Union largely accepted within its national movement synagogues and rabbis that compromised the halacha. By the mid-1930s, Harry Epstein, who was proud of, and not pressured into, the late Friday night service, complete with its mixed seating, was a member of the Union's national executive committee. The Union was also then comfortable with Tulsa's B'nai Emunah, which joined up in 1936. This southern Orthodox congregation maintained its idiosyncratic seating patterns and its popular Friday night "Assemblies." And in 1943, the Orthodox Union sponsored its Southeastern Conference that went even further in judging mixed seating as appropriate within Orthodox congregations. At that conclave, in defining what made a synagogue Orthodox, the resolutions committee determined that "all congregations . . . which conduct their services according to the Shulchan Oruch [sic]" — the sixteenth-century Code of Jewish Law, the standard for Orthodox practice — "particularly using the standard Hebrew Prayer Book, and demanding the proper traditional vesture, such as head-covering, *Talith* and *Tephillin,* shall be eligible for membership in this Conference." However, one of the fundamental "particulars" not mentioned in this protocol was the necessity of men and women sitting separately during prayers as prescribed by that same Code of Jewish law.[35]

The Young Israel movement was considerably more restrictive in its membership protocols. Though all Jews were welcomed into its synagogue mix, only congregations that did not mix the sexes during prayers and separated them by a mechitza could affiliate with that smaller national Orthodox movement.[36]

Tempered inclusion and acceptance characterized the Rabbinical Council's membership protocols. Perhaps, as an organization that was primarily composed of Yeshiva alumni, its leadership harbored sympathies for fellow classmates who might have been pressured into accommodations that violated the halacha. As a group that wanted to represent all Americanized, English-speaking rabbis, it also was hard-pressed to deny affiliation to ordainees of the Hebrew Theological College. Most of its graduates served in the so-called "traditional" Midwestern Orthodox synagogues where mixed seating was a way of life. This newer Chicago-based yeshiva, founded in 1922 with a mission comparable to Revel's school, set out to raise up "modern leaders of Orthodox Jewry" through "intensive study of the Talmud and Codes . . . and mastery of the *Tanach* [Bible] but also a thorough knowledge of Jewish history and literature and a comprehensive grasp of the problem of contemporary Jewish life." Oscar Z. Fasman, that innovative Friday-night forum advocate, and one of the school's foremost early graduates, was fortunate to find his first pulpit in Ottawa, Canada where there were no Conservative or Reform alternatives around and thus he did not have to confront the mixed-seating dilemma. He was destined in 1946 to return to his alma mater as the school's president, taking over from its founder Rabbi Saul Silber, making Fasman the first American-born head of an Orthodox rabbinical school. However, many of Fasman's classmates who battled for Orthodoxy against powerful liberal Jewish religious alternatives in the forty-eight states, more often than not acquiesced on the seating issue. They did so, in some cases, to head off even more dramatic breaks with the halacha in their synagogues. Taking implicit, judicious note of these situations, the Rabbinical Council moved in 1942 to admit all rabbis who graduated the New York yeshiva, the Chicago theological college, or any other recognized Orthodox institute or authority. It reserved national officeholding, however, for those colleagues who served in mechitza-congregations.[37]

The sight of his graduates ministering in mixed-seating synagogues with late Friday night services all over the country was a source of great consternation to Revel and his yeshiva. Still, he too generally opted for grudging acceptance or leniency toward those who violated the halacha in their pulpit careers. Only occasionally did the school move against a graduate who failed to heed established admonitions. Such was the case in 1933, when a rabbi's ordination was revoked because he refused to leave his congregation that had both mixed seating *and an organ*. But more often than not, the yeshiva's leaders lived with ritual deviations.[38]

Perhaps Revel reasoned that to do otherwise would not substantially alter the realities of American synagogue life. As always, in voluntaristic America, religious authorities could do only so much to pressure conformity out of other rabbis and congregations that possessed the autonomy to practice as they pleased. Condemnation decrees might shame some miscreants away from their offending congregations. But it was more likely that excoriations would only drive those pilloried into the welcoming arms of the United Synagogue of America. As it was, during the 1930s, Revel suffered a brain drain of rabbinical students to its arch-competitor, the Jewish Theological Seminary.

There were always discontented students who left the Yeshiva Rabbi Isaac Elchanan to complete their training as American rabbis at the Seminary. During the decade of turmoil before Revel's arrival, the young men on the move were those who chafed at the downtown institution's unwillingness to address their demands to be accorded skills to be effective ministers to their fellow second-generation Jews. The appointment of the dynamic Revel, possessed of a concrete strategic plan to make Yeshiva competitive with the Seminary, staunched the flow. As of the 1920s, his young men were entering the field anxious to serve in those congregations where "they feel the need for an English-speaking rabbi" and who will take either a "Yeshiva man" or a "Seminary man."[39]

The threat that Revel's school posed to its opposition's supremacy was not lost on the Rabbinical Assembly's Placement Committee, which noted in 1929 that "we are no longer the only institution in American Jewry that claims to supply English-speaking rabbis in the traditional field." Its report maintained that while "there is no record of how many of our congregations have been lost to men of other institutions . . . but the number would seem from personal observation high, particularly in the metropolitan area." Facing up to the challenge, it resolved to make "a determined effort . . . to create new fields for Seminary men."[40]

Notwithstanding the Rabbinical Assembly's apprehensions—and perhaps because it rallied its troops—on balance Yeshiva lost far more of the pulpit battles than it won. Often when Revel's disciples triumphed it was because they were willing to accept a lower salary than the Seminary fellow from strapped Depression-era congregations. It also was not uncommon during the last decade of Revel's leadership for his erstwhile students to end up siding with the opposition. Many of these careerists did not perceive themselves as leaving the Orthodox community and becoming Conservative rabbis, particularly in that era when it was so difficult to differentiate one traditional synagogue from another. So close were the two training schools seemingly in their missions that late in the 1920s, there even was serious talk around New York and elsewhere of merging the two institutions.[41]

In this atmosphere, most of those who went off to the Seminary did so simply to earn better livings as American rabbis. Looking back on his decision years later, one former Revel man has recalled that he "did not see himself as joining the Conservative movement. In fact, [he] did not realize that there was a Conservative movement." Another ever-pragmatic student concluded that "Yeshiva's training was out of sync with the American marketplace," while a similarly disposed classmate reminisced that "the only role model they [at Yeshiva] had of a successful American Orthodox rabbi was Joseph Lookstein," who, as previously noted, assumed the prestigious and affluent Kehilath Jeshurun pulpit. There were also unabashed ideological migrants who left Orthodox institutions for theological reasons as they felt a real kinship for Conservative Judaism. One such student left the Orthodox institution and Orthodoxy itself because while still at the yeshiva he "could not accept the premise of 'Torah M'Sinai'" — the most basic belief in the divine theophany on Mount Sinai. He would pursue his future studies as a disciple of Mordecai Kaplan, even if he "did not agree with [his professor's] entire approach."

In the winter of 1940–1941, Yeshiva's chance at remaining competitive, indeed its very possibilities for survival, sustained two enormous blows when, first, Bernard Revel suddenly passed away and months later, its leading *rosh yeshiva*, Rabbi Moses Soloveitchik also died. Although the senior Soloveitchik was quickly replaced by his son, Rabbi Joseph B. Soloveitchik, true stability did not return to the always financially strapped and now leaderless institution until 1943 when Dr. Samuel Belkin was elected president. During this two-and-a-half-year interregnum, Revel's dreams almost died with him. Given these occurrences, the out-migration from the Orthodox school peaked. During the period 1938–1945, some 37 percent of Seminary graduates were former Yeshiva men.[42]

While Americanized Orthodox rabbis struggled for the allegiances of Jews who could choose among a range of similar-looking types of sanctuaries, they nonetheless found common cause with their Conservative and Reform competitors in hatching plans to lure to services an even larger segment of American Jewry that showed no interest in any type of synagogue. Recognizing that the problem of disaffection was larger than any of them, Orthodox Union and Rabbinical Council leaders participated in umbrella organizations such as the Synagogue Council of America. Although its national association eventually devoted almost all its energies to speaking out "on social and international" political issues that worried the Jewish people in America, when formed in 1926 it had Reform, Conservative, and Orthodox leaders in the same room, and on the same page, working together to further mutual religious concerns.[43]

In 1934, for example, Rabbi de Sola Pool headed up the Synagogue Council's Committee on Community Planning, fostering the construction of local councils coast to coast to combat "isolation or competition" among the movements that each engaged in outreach work. From 1933–1935, some of these same individuals worked together, both within and without the council, in an interdenominational "Back to the Synagogue" movement. The plan that officials of the Orthodox Union bought into at "synagogue drive" conferences was to call the Sabbath of Return [*Shabbat Shuvah* of 1935] a "Loyalty Sabbath [October 1935]." The idea was to have "every Jew present and accounted for" in their respective houses of worship, just as Christians were then rallying their own spiritually depressed communicants to "reaffirm . . . faith in God and their fellow men," during the depths of the Great Depression.[44]

Orthodox enthusiasts for "a movement to unite all the forces of Jewry to combat religious indifference wherever it may exist" certainly asserted that they stood "with the first rank against all compromise that might undermine the principle and unalterable truth of the Torah." That lip-service stance and articulation — reminiscent of the Orthodox Union's statements of opposition to the Pittsburgh Platform back at its inception in 1898 — did not preclude them from working, as in the past, with their theological opponents.[45]

Meanwhile, leading East European-born rabbis in this country were, as always, of several minds over how to address the perplexities of American Jewish religious life. Torah journal editor Rabbi Samuel Aaron Pardes, a semi-official spokesman for the Agudath ha-Rabbanim, was most pragmatic as he acknowledged the dilemmas that late Friday night synagogue activities posed, even for the "strictly observant," whom he called the "*haredi* community." Although a relative newcomer to the United States — he arrived here from Chestokova, Poland, just as the immigration doors were closing — he recognized that Americanized Orthodox synagogues were "emulating the 'Temples' around them," the "*minhag Reform,*" where on Friday night "men and women and boys and girls sit together, sing some zemirot and they call that a *tefillah* [prayer service] and then their leaders [Pardes would not refer to them as rabbis] give a talk about the current events in the newspaper." Thus, in a partial bow to the exigencies of the time, he did not unconditionally condemn late Friday night "lectures." Rather, he asserted, as a fallback position, that if such events were unavoidable, it behooved God-fearing

Figure 5.2. "No Disagreeable Odors No Harmful
Ingredients." Advertisement for depilatories, Osten Chemical
Company *Jewish Forum* (May 1932): 145.

Jews to be certain that "men and women not sit together," and he called for
a very circumscribed set of activities, consisting of readings in Yiddish or in
English limited to the themes of Torah and ethical and proper religious
behavior. He also ruled that zemirot, which were totally appropriate for
home use on a Sabbath evening, should not be part of the late Friday night
gatherings. Arguably, in his view not only would the singing of the songs in
shul make the Orthodox synagogue sound like its Conservative counterpart, but perhaps it might cause devout families who traditionally sang these
tunes around their Sabbath table to relegate that bonding religious experience to public precincts — as their denominational opponents had done —
thus undermining one of the most enjoyable Orthodox home customs.[46]

Pardes also addressed a critical tonsorial concern that bristled those devout Jewish men for whom he had the greatest of affinities. These were the
gentlemen who wanted to be clean-shaven Americans without breaking with
the halacha. Just like their fathers who — as previously noted — wanted to
look like their neighbors, they too chafed over rabbinic ordinances that

prohibited the cutting of a man's scalp. Their grandfathers back in Eastern Europe — it will also be recalled — had no such problems as Jewish law comported with their desire to look different from gentiles. Until the late 1920s, depilatories were the only sure option that had unquestioned rabbinical approbation. However, that powder, which came in its so-called Resnikoff box, that carried a label with a late eighteenth- or early nineteenth-century rabbinic responsum approving of its use, was frequently disdained. Even some of most reverent turned away from this method because it burned sensitive skin, caused other dermatological problems. In addition, its sulfur base caused it to stink to high heaven. Fortunately, for all those involved, in 1928 Colonel Jacob Schick invented the bladeless electric shaver.[47]

When the non-Jewish innovator was made aware of his potential Jewish market, he quickly turned to Pardes to garner an endorsement. Years later, Oscar Z. Fasman would assert that he was the essential go-between linking the entrepreneur with the rabbinic decision maker. In any event, Pardes was quick to authorize use of the shaver. The editor-rabbi may have also ghostwritten the Schick company Hebrew advertisement that began running in his journal the very month when he rendered his positive estimation of the product. Customers were told the good news that "a new invention now removes the possibility of committing a transgression. . . . Shaving can now be done in the blink of an eye, without any waste of valuable time and with no chance of harming the skin."[48]

Still, Schick's electric razor did not corner the Orthodox market. As late as 1938, the popularity of tonsorial alternatives that were contrary to the halacha was robust enough among so otherwise pious men inured to "leaving no trace of whiskers behind," that the Gem Safety Razor Company ran a monthly ad of its own, in the American Orthodox magazine, *The Jewish Forum*. In its pitch, Gem disparaged "inefficient shaving instruments which 'top' the beard," and advised its potential customers to "pay a lot of attention to that phrase, '5 O'Clock Shadow' " to "cultivate face neatness — not just in the morning but throughout the day." Although the choice of shaving implement was not acknowledged as such, the option between Schick vs. Gem was a subtle cut that divided different types of observant Jewish men from each other during the 1930s.[49]

Pardes's contemporary and colleague within the Agudath ha-Rabbanim, Rabbi Tobias Geffen, who was born and educated in Kovno, briefly served in immigrant pulpits in New York and Canton, Ohio, before embarking on a sixty-year career in Atlanta (1910–1970). Geffen was even more realistic about American conditions. Widely regarded as the foremost rabbinic decisor south of the Mason-Dixon line, Agudath ha-Rabbanim member Geffen is perhaps best known for gaining knowledge of Coca-Cola's "secret" ingredients and then for convincing the manufacturer to alter its components, making it possible for those Jews who cared about halachic requirements

Figure 5.3. "A New Invention to Avoid a Transgression."
Advertisement announcing the invention of the Schick
Bladeless Electric Shaver. *Ha-Pardes* (May 1932), 32.

and who had a taste for America's #1 soft drink to rest assured that it was
kosher. Here too, an American entrepreneur recognized the value of accommodating the wants of Orthodox Jewish consumers. Geffen even prevailed upon the Atlanta-based firm to adjust its recipe to make it kosher for
Passover. Ashkenazic Jews — those who ancestors hailed originally from medieval Central and Eastern Europe — are not allowed to consume corn-
based foods or drinks, like classic Coca-Cola, on that festival.[50]

Less well-known, except in Atlanta, but even more indicative of his activism toward America's challenges to his flock was Geffen's engagement with
local school boards to protect Jewish children who might have been punished for absenting themselves from the public schools in observance of
their faith's holidays. To address such a critical concern required this rabbi
from Eastern Europe to learn the ins and outs of local school procedures
and politics. Exigencies of Atlanta-wide crises also moved him to countenance his neighboring Reform Rabbi David Marx who headed the decidedly nontraditional Atlanta Temple as a colleague. In the spirit too of the
Klein–Margolies–Levinthal approach to communal cooperation, Geffen
counted the young rabbis of the Rabbinical Council of America, without
question, as valued associates.[51]

But while Geffen maintained his inclusionary stance, the Agudath ha-

Rabbanim was as critical as ever of all other rabbis who ministered to American Jews. In the mid-1930s, Rabbi Louis Epstein of Brookline, Massachusetts, was the prime focus of the organization's ire as he attempted to deal creatively with a vexing problem that troubled so many victimized women of that post–World War I generation: the nightmare of the *agunah,* the so-called "chained woman."

Born in Lithuania, Epstein studied in its famous Slobodka Yeshiva and polished his traditional Talmudic skills at the pre-Revel yeshiva in New York before learning the ropes as an American rabbi at the Seminary, from which he graduated in 1913. After brief stints in Dallas, Texas, and Toledo, Epstein settled in Boston, serving first at its Beth Hamedrash Hagadol from 1918 to 1925. Then in 1925, he started a quarter-century career at Brookline's Kehilath Israel. Epstein saw himself as an Orthodox rabbi and described himself as such to search committees both from the Conservative Har-Zion Congregation of Philadelphia and The Jewish Center, which considered him in the mid-1920s. He publicly endeavored "to lead the way in conducting strictly orthodox services along the most modern lines . . . to make Orthodox Judaism attractive to the younger generation," even if his Brookline United Synagogue affiliate, like so many Orthodox Union congregations of the time, featured mixed seating and late Friday night services. The creative rabbi was already an exponent of the 8 PM time for prayers from his time in Dallas where he reportedly convinced local entrepreneurs "to close the business hours . . . at 6 o'clock to release the tired storekeepers for religious services [later] that night." But it was not so much the style of services that Epstein preferred and oversaw that angered the Agudath ha-Rabbanim. Rather, it was his responsum on the plight of the agunah that was the focus of its unmitigated anger.[52]

For many decades during this period of massive Jewish migration and domestic dislocations, the problem of husbands who disappeared or deserted their wives and families troubled all who were concerned with the dynamics of Jewish family life. Many men were lost at sea on the way to this country. Others who made it to these shores but failed to establish themselves economically took out their frustrations by moving away from their American homes, leaving their presumed loved ones in the lurch. Still others decided to marry American women. As bad as these circumstances were for all families, devout Jewish women felt an additional and most grievous sharp sting. With their erstwhile husbands' whereabouts unknown, the halacha considered these lost men to be still alive and the marriage still in effect, thus preventing women from remarrying or even consorting with another man, since the women did not possess a *get,* the all-important writ of divorce. If this woman were to remarry under American civil law, any children from that religiously adulterous relationship would be deemed *mamzerim* [bastards], basically Jewish untouchables. If a wife disappeared or deserted her family, her husband also was precluded from remarrying. However, the halachic punishments prescribed for such male bigamists are far less onerous and the children would be considered full-fledged members of the Jewish community.[53]

In the 1920s–1930s, in the wake of World War I when tens of thousands of Jewish soldiers from so many different countries, including the United States, failed to return home, the religious problem of M.I.A.s was a real and pressing dilemma. Sensitive to this crisis, Epstein beginning in the early 1930s, in his role first as a member and subsequently as chair of the Rabbinical Assembly's Committee on Jewish Law, to propose amendments to the traditional marriage contract, to effectively allow women, in such distressful circumstances, to write their own writs of divorce. In doing so, he was taking a stance not so much on behalf of the masses of Jews within most Conservative and Orthodox congregations of his time — including perhaps his own congregational flock who were generally satisfied with a civil divorce or a death certificate — but for the minority of devout Jews with whom he strongly identified.

As a Torah scholar who deeply wanted to be accepted within that camp of the committed Orthodox, he deferred unquestionably to what he called the greater wisdom of the "foremost teachers of the day from all corners of Israel" to help settle this nettlesome communal problem once and for all. He was not a radical, at least in his own estimation. Epstein wrote: "I am a callow student who wallows in the dust of the feet of those who raise high the flag of the Torah and I have no desire to question the received tradition." All he asked is that the rabbis, whom he revered, including those who associated with the Agudath ha-Rabbanim, take an active interest, based on his lead, in ending this source of misery that afflicted so many women within their own flocks who held the halacha dear. He sought an authoritative answer.[54]

The Agudath ha-Rabbanim would have nothing of him or of his plans. They perceived his formula, that he swore was so humbly tendered, as constituting not only a perversion of long-standing Orthodox rabbinical rulings, but also as an "insolent" challenge to their status as the decisors of Jewish law in America. The East European rabbis' organization threatened excommunication upon anyone who utilized the Epstein amendment and jumped on the occasion, in pillorying the Americanized rabbi, to heap calumnies upon the Jewish Theological Seminary that produced men who were "utterly unqualified to serve as teachers in Israel." So resolved were these rabbis in their anti-Epstein stance that they compiled a commemorative volume, composed of statements and decisions from the leading Orthodox rabbinical scholars worldwide, to instruct "future generations about what the Agudath ha-Rabbanim achieved in its holy struggle against the new reformers; a war that the Almighty commanded on behalf of the Jewish family."[55]

Graduates of Revel's yeshiva, of Epstein's contemporary generation, fared only a bit better in the eyes of the Agudath ha-Rabbanim who discerned threats to their authority almost everywhere. Though the religious values of these young rabbis were not challenged — at least not among those who stayed clear of mixed-seating congregations — their level of Talmudic learning, and hence their ability to lead and to decide halachic questions, was constantly denigrated. For these rabbis trained in Eastern Europe, the issue of Torah study attainments was more than just an academic determination. The sight of yet another group of Americanized rabbis asserting their halachic expertise had tremendous economic implications. The venturing of Yeshiva men into communities where, for example, lucrative kashruth supervision had long been the sole province of the Agudath ha-Rabbanim associates created competition and controversy.

Such was the issue in 1931, when an Agudath ha-Rabbanim member residing in Portland, Maine, complained bitterly about a Revel man who was hired by a local congregation to "buy his community's chametz" before Passover. Part of the traditional process of removing breadstuffs before the festival has a rabbi buying leaven from his community and selling them to a gentile; the rabbi receives a stipend for his efforts. In this case, the incumbent Old World Orthodox leader who needed such holiday honoraria for his economic survival was outraged and complained to his organization that "this young chick whose eyes have not yet been opened has pushed me aside after my ten years in the community." The challenged rabbi appealed for help, asking, "Please declare his rulings and his ordination nullified."[56]

That same year witnessed an even more troubling incident when, in Massachusetts, a young newcomer from New York "overruled" the chairman of the Council of Orthodox rabbis — an organization that the Agudath ha-Rabbanim backed — in a case involving the supervision of kosher meat slaughtering. Not only did the Yeshiva man declare that the East Europeans' decision was "foolish," but he reportedly "acted as if the Chairman wasn't worth knowing and he boasted that he had no desire to be a member of an organization such as the Agudath ha-Rabbanim."[57]

The energetic and combative Rabbi Eliezer Silver took up his distressed colleagues' cause. Perhaps this leader of the second generation of the Agudath ha-Rabbanim was highly sympathetic to these rabbis' plights because unlike most East European-trained religious leaders, upon arrival from Lithuania in 1906 he had not settled in New York or one of America's larger Jewish cities. Rather, this recipient of advanced Torah training at the yeshivas of Dvinsk, Vilna, and Brisk established himself in Harrisburg, Pennsylvania, where he stayed until 1925. He then moved on to Springfield, Massachusetts, for six years, where not long after his battles with Solomon Goldman in the Ohio courtrooms, he assumed the undivided presidency—replacing its long-standing presidium—of the Agudath ha-Rabbanim. In 1931, Silver assumed a pulpit in Cincinnati, the heartland of Reform Judaism, where he fought the good struggle for his brand of Orthodoxy for the next thirty-seven years.[58]

High on his agenda early on, as a national advocate for his fellow trans-planted rabbinical associates, was to halt Yeshiva graduates' undermining of old-line authority and prerogatives. Silver directed protests to Bernard Revel, urging him to refrain from sending his men to communities that Agudath ha-Rabbanim members led, without the latter's specific permis-sion. In a somewhat conciliatory mode, Silver did hold out the possibility that with the proper additional training, Yeshiva's rabbis could potentially become full-fledged members of his organization. That is, if they could pass the more stringent *yadin yadin* (qualified to judge) ordination require-ments. Associate memberships could be tendered to those who possessed only the *yoreh yoreh* (qualified to teach and to rule in ritual matters) ordina-tion that Revel's school proffered. Toward these ends, in the 1930s Silver actually canvassed these young rabbis in the field—with a twenty-two ques-tion survey—to ascertain how closely their religious behavior and mindset accorded with his organization's. But, whatever their ultimate level of affilia-tion might be, these neophytes would be directed to follow the protocols of the Agudath ha-Rabbanim.[59]

Some Yeshiva and Hebrew Theological College men were none too pleased with the tone and import of Silver's questionnaire that asked, for example, whether they found time to study the Torah regularly and "do you want to be proficient [in Talmudic erudition] like well-known rabbanim?" A recently ordained rabbi from the Chicago school, who had just found a position in Youngstown, Ohio, offered the most vitriolic answer to Silver's missive. Queried about his attitude toward the Agudath ha-Rabbanim, he replied that while he "had heard of such an organization," he was keenly aware that "every member minds the business of his colleagues [which] leads to great shame and disgrace." In his view, "their arguments"—gener-ally over who controlled one or another kosher certification perquisite—"are not for the sake of heaven," and he felt that they undermined popular respect for the rabbinate.[60]

Silver's postures and plans perplexed Bernard Revel. On the one hand, he surely wanted his men out in the field competing for Americanized pulpits. He prayed that his graduates would do so without mixing the sexes during prayers and without violating other halachic strictures. Letters like the one he received in 1929 telling in no uncertain terms that "if we do not get a Yeshiva man, I am quite sure that there will be a Seminary man . . . I feel that the spirit aroused among the younger men is such that they feel a need for an English-speaking rabbi and they will want it satisfied," delivered a clear message.[61] He could not surrender the field through restricting the posts that his men might occupy, especially since the old-line rabbanim were no match for modern rabbis among the masses of the disaffected Jews. On the other hand, as a loyal Agudath ha-Rabbanim member, Revel desired the approbation of his fellow East European colleagues.

Conflicted, Revel adopted a fence-straddling position. He officially was sensitive to the Agudath ha-Rabbanim's policies when specific conflicts arose, but would not let that organization control job placement. He encouraged the Agudath ha-Rabbanim to accept his younger generation as colleagues and he moved to ease that path, in the early 1930s, when he took steps toward developing a curriculum in his school to prepare his disciples for the advanced form of ordination. He also tried to sensitize Yeshiva's students to respect the provinces of their elders.

Nonetheless, as the 1930s proceeded, tensions between the American-trained rabbis and Silver's colleagues only grew worse. Most notably, Agudath ha-Rabbanim members deeply resented the Rabbinical Council's formal arrogation of their prerogatives in the area of kashruth as that decade-long conflict between Orthodox rabbis was raised to an even higher level. For the Americanized, the often chaotic system of sometimes secret agreements where individual rabbis negotiated to oversee a particular product's reliability lowered the public's esteem for the rabbinate when it did not encourage imposters or unscrupulous supervisors. To a certain degree, as early as its own founding in 1902, the Agudath ha-Rabbanim had begun bringing greater honesty, cooperation, and order into kashruth supervision. But some thirty-five years later much work still needed to be done. The Rabbinical Council's solution of concentrating all kosher products under the Orthodox Union's banner made a public statement that the monitoring of this industry was a communal responsibility and not a particular rabbi's sinecure. It commissioned and controlled competent overseers and publicized what became known as the OU symbol as authoritative. In so doing, this bureaucratization and standardization of kashruth denied individual rabbis an important part of their always meager livelihoods. While some of the Council's members who were threatened with the loss of potential sources of income often ignored their own organization's dictates, those Agudath ha-Rabbanim members who were stridently challenged were incensed.[62]

When Bernard Revel died suddenly in 1940, the Agudath ha-Rabbanim launched a major, and ultimately a last-ditch, offensive to reassert its rabbinical suzerainty, through attempting a hostile takeover of Yeshiva. They asserted that as the foremost Orthodox authorities in America, their approbation had both initially and continually given Revel the imprimatur to serve as leader of that institution. They reminded everyone that, during its earliest years, the school mission had been identical to that of the Agudath ha-Rabbanim, nothing less than the transplantation of a Torah civilization to America. They remained, in their own estimation, the "spiritual guardians" of the school. Outstanding Agudath ha-Rabbanim members served as long-time examiners on the very semicha board that ordained Revel's disciples. They thus contended, with the president's demise, that the right to chart the school's future direction reverted to them. Quick to step into the vacuum, Silver and his colleagues declared that they were prepared to administer the institution, through a committee of its choosing. With his men in charge, Silver could monitor the types of young rabbis emerging from school and the pulpits they would assume.

The lay leaders who controlled the school's purse strings balked at this attack on their prerogatives, and politely, but firmly, sidestepped this claim. In response, they first established their own in-house executive committee to manage affairs while they began a protracted search that ended only in 1943, with the election of Dr. Samuel Belkin as president. Belkin would, after World War II, build upon Revel's efforts at the school. But this rebuff of Silver's group in 1940 said immediately to the Agudath ha-Rabbanim that, come what may, the students presently at Yeshiva and their American role models already out leading congregations would not take their marching orders from their organization. If the young rabbis needed halachic direction and career advice, they would hearken to voices within their home institution, from Belkin and soon from Rabbi Joseph B. Soloveitchik, whose impact eventually would be felt on the entire American Orthodox scene.[63]

At precisely the same time that they were protecting their turf and questioning the theological stances of more Americanized leaders, the Agudath ha-Rabbanim's own behaviors and attitudes were subject to harsh, resolute rebukes from another, even more contrarian, Orthodox flank. In 1920, Rabbi Gabriel Z. Margolis, also known as Reb Velvele, organized some 135 like-minded critics into his own Knesset ha-Rabbonim ha-Ortodoksim (Assembly of Orthodox Rabbis) which launched a three-pronged attack against what they perceived as the oligarchic control their opponents maintained over the "politics of kashruth," the Agudath ha-Rabbanim's wrong-headed approach toward secular learning within American Orthodox life, and most emphatically, its heretical misconstruction of Jewish tradition on the pressing question of Zionism.[64]

For the Vilna-born and Volozhin Yeshiva-educated Margolis, who came to the United States in 1907 after a distinguished twenty-seven years as a rabbi in Grodno, White Russia, his Knesset's battle over kashruth control was the culmination of a more than decade-long personal battle against his enemies within the Agudath ha-Rabbanim's presidium, most notably, rabbis Klein and Ramaz Margolies. Projecting himself as far superior to all others in knowledge of Torah and halacha, Reb Velvele consistently accused his opponents of incompetence in their monitoring of kashruth procedures and went so far as to accuse some Agudath ha-Rabbanim members of corruption in their certify- ing of unkosher products. In his view, the Union of Orthodox Rabbis was nothing more than a "union," like the ones the hated radicals endorsed, designed to protect its members and to prevent competent competitive au- thorities from establishing themselves in the United States. Through a series of ephemeral organizations, such as his Agudath ha-Yehudim ha-Ortodoksim (Union of Orthodox Jews) and the Vaad ha-Kashruth (Kashruth Assembly), he spoke out against Klein, Ramaz Margolies, and others' complicity with the New York Kehillah even if the Agudath ha-Rabbanim's official association with that umbrella organization was, at most, temporary. With the establishment of his Knesset, he redoubled his efforts to wrest control of the business of super- vising the kosher meat industry from the incumbents and to assure that Orthodox rabbis did not "receive remunerations for sanctioning articles as kosher and . . . accept perquisites of a questionable source." A decade and a half later, the Rabbinical Council of America — a group with which Reb Velvele would have absolutely no truck — would use almost the same words, albeit in English, to describe their own efforts to clean up the same endemic problem.[65]

The Agudath ha-Rabbanim's initial monopoly in the legal distribution of sacramental wines during the 1920s era of Prohibition further galvanized Margolis and his members. Sensitive to the First Amendments' freedom of religion provisions, the Volstead Act permitted religious groups to use wine for "sacramental purposes." Rabbis, priests, and ministers, designees of their respective "conference, diocese or other ecclesiastical jurisdiction," were empowered "to supervise the manufacturing of wine." Early in the administration of the so-called "Noble Experiment," government officials recognized the Agudath ha-Rabbanim as the sole Orthodox organization entitled to choose rabbinical overseers. Somewhat out of character, when the law was first passed, the usually accommodating Ramaz Margolies has- tened to Washington in an effort to have his organization designated as the sole authority over Jewish distribution of sacramental wines. He sought effectively to freeze out Conservatives and Reformers. In the end, all three major movements had their monitors, and the rabbis of the Orthodox Union took no part in these activities. Their era of involvement in the rough-and-tumble world of kosher monitoring, as we have noted, was a decade away.

Left out of the mix were those immigrant Orthodox rabbis who were not associated with the more established group. Some of the excluded were immediately in touch with Rabbi Gabriel Margolis over the Union's "refusal to share the privilege." Although by law the rabbis involved were not to receive perquisites for their efforts, the possibilities for compensations of all sorts above board and beneath the table were readily available. If nothing else, the word on the streets within this unhappy crowd was that "dealing in kosher wines" constituted a way for Reb Velvele's opponents "to support their impure activities" and to have "weapons in their hands to attack rabbis not in their Union." Quick to pick up the cudgels for his followers and against the Union, Margolis, too, rushed off to Washington and had the Federal Prohibition Commissioner authorize his Assembly as a legitimate entity to distribute permits for sacramental wines.

This official designation of a second Orthodox authority in this realm only exacerbated the tensions between the Agudath ha-Rabbanim and the Knesset. In 1922, the business battles between two rabbinical organizations turned very personal when Ramaz accused his counterpart of complicity in the Menorah Wine Company scandal that had broken out some months earlier. There, a Lower East Side outfit was raided, and a quarter-million dollars of wines confiscated as it was alleged that the company honored fake rabbinical permits, apparently signed by "eighteen and twenty-year old boys."

Perhaps angered by Margolis's constant attacks against him in the struggle over control of meat markets and now Reb Velvele's moves into the wine cellars, Ramaz contended that Menorah's product was, to begin with, not really kosher. How could it be otherwise if his enemy was the kashruth overseer? Ramaz contended that the cynical entrepreneurs had engaged Reb Velvele's services because they figured that the similarity in names of rabbis and their respective organizations would confuse unwitting consumers and government agents. Left unsaid was the inevitable implication that once the wrong people were left in charge, both kashruth and Volstead rules would be circumvented.

Ramaz's allegations about Margolis's malfeasances were not sustained. Meanwhile, Reb Velvele was far from shy in trumpeting that "Washington has recognized the Assembly on the same basis as the other three rabbinic organizations" to issue permits and he invited rabbis and wine dealers to "apply in person to our president, Rabbi G. W. Margolis . . . from the hours of 9 AM to 10 PM." Inevitably, both legitimate rabbis as well as entrepreneurs and unmitigated frauds ended up at his doorstep. Concerned about the looseness with which Margolis seemingly granted authorization, one of his most eminent colleagues, Rabbi Zvi Hirsch Grodzinski of Omaha called upon Reb Velvele to stop issuing wine permits to business people in his town. The Midwestern-based associate reported that "local wine dealers [were] conducting a free-for-all and selling their sacramental wines to Jews and gentiles alike." Such actions, Grodzinski reminded Margolis, made all Jews look bad since it could be claimed that "the requirement for sacramental wine was only a ruse to engage in an illegal wine trade."

But then again, Margolis's corrupt associates were far from the only immigrant Orthodox rabbis contributing to what one contemporary American Jewish newspaper declared constituted a "near national scandal." Although precise numbers of the unscrupulous and the downright criminal are impossible to come by, these bootlegger-rabbis were a known and troubling problem to enforcement officials who had their hands full of all types of shady characters. Indicative of government frustration with the actions of those miscreants who were seen as "violating the law and . . . abusing an honorable trust," James E. Jones, the assistant Prohibition commissioner allowed, in 1925, that such rabbis "were worse that the ordinary bootlegger. . . . The bootlegger admits he is a crook [and] is not cloaking himself with a mantle of authority intended by the law for devout members of a religious faith."

While not condoning the "tempt[ation] to do a little bit of bootlegging" that eventually might lead to "the biggest scandals and a *hillul ha-Shem* [desecration of God's name]," one of Revel's faculty members, Rabbi Samuel Gerstenfeld, who from all accounts was himself never on the take, did suggest that it was "dire poverty" that caused colleagues "to stumble." If such was the motivation for this grievous activity, then it was, ironically, that same desire to survive and to advance economically which caused so many Jews to violate the Sabbath, that enticed rabbis to break with the Torah's ethical code which calls for unqualified adherence to the laws and statutes of the lands within which they resided.[66]

When Reb Velvele was not fighting the good — or ignoring the bad — fight over kosher products, the Knesset platform also gave Margolis a forum to condemn the Agudath ha-Rabbanim for its acquiescence to the ongoing secularization of the Yeshiva Rabbi Isaac Elchanan. From his perch on the Lower East Side, he watched with dismay as Revel hatched plans to expand an educational system dedicated to produce both American Orthodox rabbis and committed laymen comfortable with their religious backgrounds and competitive with all others in the pulpits and marketplaces of America.

In 1916, as we have seen, Revel inaugurated the Talmudical Academy, that high school which provided its charges with a state-approved secondary education complementing high-level Torah training, while keeping them away from the public schools. Now in the early 1920s, the yeshiva's leader began moving toward establishing a Yeshiva College. This initiative would address three intertwined problems that his high school graduates faced as they contemplated the world of American higher education.

As observant youngsters, they knew, to begin with, that even such "Jewish" schools as the City College of New York, known in some circles as the "heder on the hill" (St. Nicholas Heights), or New York University, often referred to in the most uncomplimentary terms as "New York Jew," made no accommodations for Sabbath and holiday restrictions. Students constantly had to finesse the system, if they did not want to run afoul of academic "Blue Laws" that penalized Sabbath-observers who missed late Friday afternoon and Saturday classes. Like their fathers who went off heartbroken to work Saturday morning, many students guiltily compromised their religious practices to advance themselves, to earn their coveted baccalaureate degrees.

The university was also less than a joyous experience for pious youngsters who were lucky enough to find professors who would grant them a pass on attendance or who found less-committed Jewish or Christian classmates who would take notes for them when they missed sessions. If these collegians had hopes of participating in any sort of extracurricular activities, including writing for a school newspaper, singing in a glee club, or playing on a sports team, they knew that the Sabbath question simply disqualified them from the fun parts of college life.

Even those students who found the right teachers and colleagues and cared little for other college activities were often deeply challenged. For some, the demands of secular study and career training conflicted daily with their own desires to continue their intensive Jewish education. If they studied at CCNY or NYU by day, when would they have time for Torah learning? Then there were the theological conundrums that arose in secular classrooms. Whether it was history or philosophy or the other humanities or social sciences, they frequently encountered teaching staffs decidedly unsympathetic to their deeply ingrained religious sensibilities.

Finally, there were those with rabbinical career aspirations who upon finishing the Talmudical Academy would have been content to avoid college altogether, thus avoiding prejudices against observant Jews and their ideas. However, these students also knew that the modern rabbi-in-training, who was bereft of his sheepskin, suffered a distinct disadvantage when it came time to seek congregational employment. The masses of American Jews whom they would attempt to reach, and who episodically attended the Orthodox synagogues of their choice, wanted to know that a college man was addressing them from the pulpit. So they too trudged off to college with heavy hearts, trying to cope with what some commentators in the 1920s called "excessive strains," "pangs of readjustment," or even "the dark abyss . . . of unending conflict," as they were now on their own in the foreign world of academe.

For Bernard Revel, the only solution to these stresses, pangs, and conflicts was to bring the secular collegiate world into his yeshiva. By definition, Yeshiva College would strictly countenance Orthodoxy's unalterable clock and calendar. Although the president did not get caught up personally in the students' extracurricular hi-jinx, he smiled benignly at their efforts not to lose out on a fine college time while staying within the confines of their own environments. Perhaps most important, he did not fear exposing his charges to the wider worlds of knowledge. He asked only for respect for students' religious values from the professors—Jews and gentiles—whom he routinely recruited as moonlighters from CCNY to expand campus intellectual horizons.

On the intellectual level, Revel firmly believed that there was much of worth to be learned "of the beauties of Greece" — that is, modern culture — "in the tents of Shem," the legendary site of the first primordial yeshiva, within his own twentieth-century liberal arts college. Practical speaking, the study of the Torah would take place in the morning, and the yeshiva would become like all other institutions of higher learning in the afternoon. Under this program, those desirous of careers upon ordination as American Orthodox rabbis would be fully credentialed as men of the Law and of the world. All others, similarly trained and inspired, would be prepared to compete for jobs and within professions against all other college graduates. With such commitments squarely in mind, Revel devoted the better part of the 1920s toward fashioning what he would later triumphantly call "the House of God on the Hilltop." The Orthodox alternative to the "heder on the hill" would look down at CCNY from Washington Heights, in a corner of northwest Manhattan.[67]

To Margolis's unmitigated chagrin, when Revel tendered his plans, the Agudath ha-Rabbanim was silent on these dramatic moves. Once the school was established, the incumbent rabbis' association, as self-declared "spiritual guardians" of the yeshiva, would have much to say about drifts within the school toward what it perceived as increased secularization. But by then, Margolis had been on record for a decade with his vision of Rabbi Isaac Elchanan Spektor, the eponym of the American yeshiva, "turning over in his grave if he knew that a seminary had been built bearing his name where [general] philosophy, the humanities and all sorts of meaningless matters were taught." In Margolis's view, the yeshiva had lost its way as it planned to move to a new commodious uptown campus out of sight of the really devout Jews of America who lived with him on the Lower East Side. Minimally, to this outspoken critic, it had become a "*semicha* [ordination] factory" and, at its worst, it was a school that emulated its Upper West Side Manhattan neighbors, Columbia University and the hated Jewish Theological Seminary.[68]

Margolis also departed company decisively with the Agudath ha-Rabbanim in the early 1920s over the religious challenges of Zionism. By that time, these rabbis had compiled an extensive record of support for the modern Jewish national movement that dated back to the creation of their national organization. The planning meeting in May 1902, which led to the association's founding convention some three months later, took place in Ramaz Margolies's home in Boston, where five of the nine rabbis in town were either official delegates to the Federation of American Zionists meeting or even more impressive, were members of its executive committee.

Their presence at this decidedly non-Orthodox gathering in the midst of such Reform rabbis as Richard Gottheil, Stephen S. Wise, and Abraham Radin; Conservative leaders such as Rabbi Marcus Jastrow and Henrietta Szold; and secular Zionists — theologians and leaders whose religious views they routinely pilloried — can only be explained as their keeping faith with the vision and positions of their former European mentors, rabbis Isaac Elchanan Spektor, Naftali Zevi Judah Berlin, and Samuel Mohilever.[69]

All of these respected East European rabbis publicly identified as early as the 1880s with the incipient Hibbat Zion (Lovers of Zion) movement. At the very time that the future America-bound rabbis were their students, Rabbi Spektor and others argued the appropriateness of all Jews laboring together in a national rebirth. These senior scholars acted on their beliefs when they attended Hibbat Zion conferences that also attracted people such as Leo Pinsker, author of the basic political Zionist document *Auto-Emancipation,* a man totally removed from tradition. In the subsequent generation, Rabbi Isaac Jacob Reines, a man whose views also resonated with the Agudath ha-Rabbanim's rank and file, emerged as a prime spokesman for Religious Zionism that stood for Orthodox Jews as watchdogs against galloping secularism within the nascent Jewish national movement.[70]

In Eastern Europe, this approach galvanized into the Mizrachi movement and organization in 1902, but it was a decidedly minority opinion within the Orthodox community of the time. There the regnant ideological position, which dated back to Talmudic times, was that Jews were obliged to remain passively in exile until God willed a messianic return. But in America, Religious Zionist ideas were well-nigh unchallenged within the Orthodox community as the Spektor–Reines tradition ruled supreme among their erstwhile disciples. Even those supporters of Agudath ha-Rabbanim who consistently opposed Americanization backed the modernism explicit in support for the Zionist cause.

Thus it was totally in character for these rabbis to publicly eulogize Theodor Herzl upon his untimely death in 1904. They adopted a "resolution of respect" for the fallen leader and on the last evening of their annual meeting conducted "memorial services under the auspices of the Mizrachi wing of the Zionist movement." On a happier occasion some thirteen years later, the Agudath ha-Rabbanim received news of the Balfour Declaration that promised the establishment of a national home for the Jewish people in Palestine "with great joy and enthusiasm." They reacted to the San Remo Conference of 1920, which legitimized the British Mandate over Palestine with a parade in New York that attracted ten thousand marchers. "How beautiful a sight," one observer remarked, "rabbis, the shepherds of Israel leading a parade with [Zionist] flags at their heads."[71]

Perhaps the Agudath ha-Rabbanim demonstrated its staunchest approbation for Mizrachi through its lack of enthusiasm for the ideology and political agenda of the Agudath Israel. America's East European rabbis were not unmindful of the alliance formed back home in 1912 among Lithuanian heads of yeshivas, leaders of Hasidic dynasties, and German Orthodox rabbis to protest the Zionist movement and show profound disdain for Mizrachi policies of cooperation. At its eleventh annual meeting, in 1913, the American group voted "to establish branches of the Agudath Israel in the United States wherever possible" and to "request that members travel to nearby cities to promote" that organization. But the Agudath Israel that they were advocating resembled the European parent organization in but one way: promoting the growth of holy institutions within Palestine. Their toned-down version of the Agudath Israel mission reflected their subtle desire to maintain the approbation and support of the majority of Old World rabbis without doing too much violence to their Religious Zionist leanings. To do so, the Agudath ha-Rabbanim acted as if the Agudath Israel did not fundamentally oppose Mizrachi goals and objectives. They also did their utmost to convince European leaders of the value of worldwide unity of purpose.[72]

Looking back on its efforts to find middle ground and common cause among disputing Orthodox viewpoints, the Agudath ha-Rabbanim's own devoted chroniclers would opine that "if the Old Yishuv," the pre-1881 settlement of primarily highly pious Jews, "has survived until now, credit must go to [our] rabbis. We have also done much for the rise of the New Yishuv," the Zionist settlements in modern Palestine. "When the announcement came from San Remo, we joined the entire people in its joy; tears welled up in our eyes." In search always of consensus, they concluded, "in our midst may be found both Mizrachi and Agudath Israel supporters, but the Agudath ha-Rabbanim does not interfere in political matters. For us it is clear," they concluded, "if we are to have a Land of Israel, we must have the Torah of Israel, if we have a Jewish people, we must have a God of Israel."[73]

Precisely that sort of maneuvering and positioning infuriated the already disenchanted Rabbi Gabriel Margolis. As a younger man, he had been an early supporter too of Hibbat Zion, feeling that the influence of rabbis like him would undermine the power of the irreligious in the national movement. Two decades later, he was also an incipient Mizrachiite, believing that even if Zionism was not the true redemption, its potential power to unify the Jewish people could bring a positive response from the Almighty. However as non-Orthodox viewpoints continued to dominate the Zionist cultural revolution, Margolis became highly antagonistic to the movement.[74]

As of the decade following 1910, he harbored nothing but contempt for Mizrachi followers whom he asserted backed this irreligious and destructive movement for their own personal gain. Given the references to self-gain during the period of his initial battles royale with the kashruth establishment, his differences with Religious Zionists became another front in his wars against the Agudath ha-Rabbanim. Now, in the early 1920s, Margolis fervently asserted that Zionists were nothing less than false messiahs who violated Talmudic dicta about not rising up against the nations of the world. He believed that the presence of Zionists had increased antisemitism, threatening Jewish survival. He firmly proclaimed that "God will send at the end of days his redeemer to those who wait for him, for him and for no one else. And as he took us out of Egypt, so he will show us miracles soon and in our own days."[75]

For all of his fulminations against the Agudath ha-Rabbanim, Margolis still had to deal with one of the fundamental problems that these opponents and all other American Jewish religious leaders faced. He could not demand or count on unqualified support for his positions among his Knesset followers. The religious voluntarism that undermined rabbinic authority everywhere in America also affected this outspoken critic of the community within which he lived. Though Margolis angled strongly for the Knesset at its 1921 convention to focus on the needs of the old religious community, "to leave rabbis of Palestine the work of establishing Judaism and culture . . . to bring order out of the chaotic disorder among the various representatives who come to America to solicit funds for the old institutions in Palestine," the majority of delegates, at this juncture, were equally concerned with the development of the New Yishuv. Two years later the Knesset seemingly had a change of heart when it expressed support for the Agudath Israel position. But then again, in 1925, the delegate reversed themselves once more and sounded very much like their Agudath ha-Rabbanim counterparts, when at their convention they sent greetings to the secular Zionist Congress then assembled in Vienna. When his position was not sustained at his own group's gathering, an unhappy Margolis may not have been conscious of — and certainly would not have acknowledged — what he had in common with all other Orthodox rabbis during this era of compromises. But he too had to bow on a critical issue and adapt himself to the views of those whom he sought to lead. Transplanted Agudist attitudes, both in the Zionist arena and in other aspects of religious life, would begin to strongly influence Orthodox life only in a subsequent period of American Jewish history.[76]

# 6

## BROOKLYN'S COMMITTED COMMUNITIES

When members of the Agudath ha-Rabbanim and their rivals in Reb Velvele's Knesset stepped back from their internecine rivalries and contemplated the larger, arid religious scene all around them, there was but one place and a single group of American Jews who held out hope that an unyielding Orthodoxy might be long sustained in this country. The location was Brooklyn, New York and the people who heartened these rabbis were the families who were dedicated to raising their sons as isolated as possible from the lures of Americanization. There, in the 1920s, almost forty years after the Association of Orthodox Hebrew Congregations had first struggled to create an enduring, separatist yeshiva system, such a community of the committed came into existence. That outer borough was not immune to the patterns of religious disinterest so rife during the era. One memoirist of his Brownsville neighborhood has recalled that "on our streets one did not have to be religious to be Jewish." Just living among their own kind was a sufficient form of identification. Others "felt a strong commitment to Judaism, but rarely practiced its rituals." They "attended synagogue on holidays, *sometimes.*" Yet at the same time, over in the Williamsburg section of the

184

borough amid the "dance halls and poolrooms for the young" — that attracted more than their share of Jews devoted to the most secular pursuits — there lived an aggregation of "really *baale-battishe* [religiously upstanding] Jews and many *talmidei chachomim* [truly learned individuals]." In this milieu of the meticulous, Sabbath-observant families were the rule, not the exception. There, according to an early student of that time and place, a "representative" family was headed by a father who "did not let a day pass without praying with the minyan in the synagogue" and who "attended a regular s*hiur,* a Talmud study class after his hard, long hours in the sweat shop" and by a mother whose "house was a model of kashruth [where] the Sabbaths and holidays were celebrated with the proper ceremonies." A comparable pocket of piety could be found in that same Brownsville where most Jews stayed clear of religious life. Minorities of highly observant Jews also called East New York and Bensonhurst their homes. In each community, committed mothers and fathers sent their sons in significant numbers to the types of school that the founders of the old Etz Chaim first envisioned. But with just the most modest tweaks of the educational system, the Brooklynites did far better than their predecessors.[1]

Williamsburg's Mesivta Torah Vodaath was the foremost and most comprehensive of some five borough-based schools for boys and young men that placed the highest premium on the transmission of traditional Torah and Talmud learning while discouraging students, as much as they could, from actively pursuing secular studies beyond the high school years that in the 1930s state law prescribed. In the interwar period, nowhere else in the country, not even on the Lower East Side where the dream of the unadulterated American yeshiva movement began, were there so many young Jews studying more of the Torah and less of the secular in such a concerted way. Beginning in the 1920s, first in Williamsburg and then in other Brooklyn neighborhoods, religious havens were created for devout families that migrated from the Lower East Side. A decade or so later, these same settlements would become refuges for those Orthodox Jews who fled Europe during that era's frightening preludes to the Holocaust.[2]

While Torah Vodaath was never officially linked to the Knesset ha-Rabbonim, from the time of the arrival of Rabbi Shraga Feivel Mendlowitz at the Brooklyn school in 1921, a curriculum was developed and vigorously inculcated that was fundamentally in line with what rabbis like Velvele Margolis wanted youngsters to study. The Hungarian-born Mendlowitz came from an environment in which the teachings of Rabbi Moses Sofer still loomed large. As previously noted, Sofer was the foremost arch-resister in Europe of any Jewish reconciliation with the changing secular world. Although Mendlowitz departed slightly from that discipline — he did study of the writings of the German Neo-Orthodox theologian Samson Raphael Hirsch and was thus acquainted with approaches that valued finding spaces within modernity for tradition — once situated in Williamsburg, this man on a mission set out essentially to prove that Bernard Revel and his confederates were so very wrong. As his followers have told it, rather than bow to the idea that to attract and retain students a yeshiva in America had to promise to produce fully integrated graduates, Mendlowitz determined "self-consciously to create a new type of *bochur* [student] in the melting pot of America . . . who would . . . draw from all that was best from the many strands of Europeans life." To achieve his goal, on Bedford Avenue as opposed to Washington Heights, the linkage to the Old World's past would be clear, compelling, and far less-ambiguous. If some strategic retreats and compromises to American realities would be made, they would be the most subtle ones, not what he would deem as the gross accommodations of Revel's endeavors.[3]

The ideal Torah Vodaath student would be the uncommon fellow who stuck to his holy books to the exclusion of outside interests and pursuits. Similar aspirations were harbored, beginning in 1933, when the Chofetz Chaim Yeshiva began making its mark in the neighborhood under its dynamic leader Rabbi Dovid Leibowitz. When he arrived in America in 1929 and signed on with Torah Vodaath, he was seen as a major acquisition for the Williamsburg school. He had already made his mark as a Talmudic star at the famous Lithuanian yeshivas of Slobodka and Radun and had come here on his own quest to spread the unmitigated Torah of Eastern Europe to this country. He reportedly even had the approbation for his move from that renowned critic of migration, the Hafetz Hayim. Perhaps, for the aging Rabbi Kagan, Leibowitz was that rare "God-fearing man" incarnate — of whom he spoke back in the 1890s — whose presence in America augured to "strengthen religious life." Be that as it may, Leibowitz did not stay long in his original post. By 1933, differences with Mendlowitz over "philosophy, personality, outlook and style" caused them to part company. Still, the school Leibowitz established, also on Bedford Avenue — years later it would move to Queens, New York — did not differ appreciably in its effort to create an élan of separatist excellence among its most devoted students.[4]

Not long thereafter, Yeshiva Chaim Berlin, situated in neighboring Brownsville, came completely in line with these brother institutions. Until the 1930s, this school resembled the old Etz Chaim; an elementary-level yeshiva that tried to insulate its young charges from the lures of Americanization through offering only minimal secular education. Now, under the ever watchful eyes of a transplanted Lithuanian rabbinic luminary, Rabbi Isaac Hutner, its mission was deepened. Now it, too, would "aspire to reproduce in this country," as one contemporary student of these Brooklyn institutions observed, "the old type of observant God-fearing Jew devoted to the ancient ideals of learning and piety [who would] exhibit the diligence, sincerity and other-worldliness of the traditional *yeshiva bochur* [along the] model of the *yeshivoth* of Poland, Lithuania and Jerusalem." This school also would be "extreme and uncompromising in its Orthodoxy."[5]

In the meantime, as the last prewar decade drew to a close, Williamsburg acquired a modest distaff counterpart to Torah Vodaath, America's incipient Beth Yaacov schools. The ever-present Mendlowitz played a role in that institution too, getting its start in the neighborhood.

When the Beth Yaacov school movement had been created in Poland two decades earlier, it was revolutionary in providing comprehensive schooling to young women. Under the leadership of a truly exceptional woman, Sarah Schenirer, some of the most pious of the world's Jews faced up to the growing gap in the religious values of their own boys and girls, scions of fervent Orthodox homes. While their young men might be safe from the outside world in their insular yeshivas — although secular voices did permeate its walls — girls bereft of formal Jewish education and more attuned to general culture were drifting away from the traditions. As Schenirer once confided to her diary: "while the fathers of these girls are probably studying *Gemara* [Talmud] and the mothers poring over a *Ze'enah u-Re'enah* [a book of moralistic Bible stories and legends directed for women's Sabbath and holiday reading], leaders of a Polish Jewish girls' club were turning on lights on the Sabbath." Schenirer, strongly supported by the Agudath Israel, offered a concentrated curriculum, all taught in Yiddish, instructing girls in the prayers, the Bible, Jewish laws and customs and hagiography, but not Talmud. That level of higher Jewish learning was reserved, as always, for their fathers, brothers, and future husbands. Upon initial transplantation to America, the Beth Yaakov approach to study was ideal for socializing disciples and devotees into a separatist community. Fired with this mission, the first of its institutions in this country, a fledgling elementary school with 35 students, was organized in Torah Vodaath's Williamsburg neighborhood. Over the next seven years, two other branches were established in East New York and Brownsville, Brooklyn, as borough-wide enrollment rose to approximately 160 students.[6]

While Brooklyn harbored the majority of those with separatist sensibilities, during the 1920–1930s, pockets of such devout families could be found in a number of other American locales. In 1930, soon after Revel's yeshiva departed from the Lower East Side, the Mesivta Tifereth Jerusalem opened its doors on the outskirts of the old downtown Jewish quarter for those who wanted their youngsters exposed to a European-looking Torah center. Almost a decade later, it would become the operational hub for Rabbi Moses Feinstein, destined to earn the reputation for more than half a century as Orthodoxy's most respect decisor of Jewish law in America. Up in New Haven, Connecticut, an ephemeral yeshiva was established in 1928 where students learned "in a European-[style] yeshiva all day and the community helped [it] exist," that is, until Depression-era economic problems and the removal of its most prominent rabbi and most of its students to Cleveland, Ohio, threatened its persistence. In 1933, Baltimore's pious Orthodox could applaud the founding of the Ner Israel Yeshiva, an institution that would soon become an influential fixture in that city.[7]

However, as much as America's transplanted East European rabbis commended families who sent their sons and daughters to these yeshivas, only the most extreme resisters did not grudgingly recognize that these schools were neither in an idyllic nor in an idealized Old World setting. The long-standing reality, which the founders of the Agudath ha-Rabbanim had first come to grips with two decades earlier, still appeared in the secular career aspirations of even the most pious youngsters. It was, for example, impossible to prohibit students from attending high school. Secular training was essential for any young person contemplating a professional career or even desiring to become a bookkeeper or salesperson. In addition, as of the 1930s teenagers were required under state law to attend school to at least the age of sixteen. Yet, the message had to be delivered that even if acquiring secular training to get a better job was understandable, there was no great intrinsic value in exposure to the wider worlds of general knowledge. Quite the contrary, there was more than a chance — if these studies were taken seriously — that what a student learned about sciences or other cultures, faiths, and historical traditions might challenge a pious youngster's Jewish religious commitments. Ever the pragmatist, Mendlowitz, for one, tendered several options to his disciples. Either they could enroll in a public school at night and sit among working people — usually mature adults — who took mandated lessons to secure their own coveted diplomas (these schools, though non-Jewish, were not challenging academic environments that could threaten Jewish values). Or his young men could fulfill their secular school requirements in his own parochial high school, which was established in the 1930s. There a Regents-approved curriculum was proffered but secular studies classes met in a different building, apart from where the Torah was studied. The separation of the sites further demonstrated that what they were learning in the auxiliary rooms was really outside the ells of a yeshiva education.[8]

College training was another matter entirely. No state law forced attendance. And on a real secular campus, the devout would be heavily exposed precisely to those general philosophical, humanities, and other so-called "meaningless matters" — as Reb Velvele Margolis had described secular studies — that troubled the faithful. As these Brooklyn yeshiva heads saw it, Revel's answer of melding "Greece" into "Shem" was no solution. When secular sciences, foreign languages, and literature were taught in the same classroom where the sacred Torah of Moses was imparted, the unpardonable sin was committed of tacitly declaring that secular learning was both compatible and comparable to Jewish teachings. Accordingly, these Brooklyn yeshivas actively discouraged students from entering the foreign world of academe. Their only fall-back position was to turn a blind eye to boys going off again to a night school, be it City College or Brooklyn College, after a full day of Torah training.[9]

If teaching Torah and Tennyson in the same venue was not bad enough, Revel's school was also censured for its modern rabbinical training emphases. The Brooklyn yeshivas refused to complement Torah curriculum with modern Jewish academic disciplines. If history were taught there, it was largely hagiography. If the subject area was philosophy, the teaching uncritically examined the mindset of famous rabbinic thinkers throughout the ages. In fact, at least for Mendlowitz, the quintessential product of his system really was not the rabbi-scholar, trained along those Old World lines, who would make a career out of his Torah acumen. Rather, it was the committed layman who had studied long and hard in his school and then lived his life within Brooklyn's Orthodox midst, making his living with the acceptable practical skills acquired in obligatory general studies classes. Elsewhere, at the borough's other schools, there was a greater commitment to producing graduates who would become educators and rabbis dedicated to promoting an unyielding Orthodoxy. In either case, be they future lay or spiritual leaders, Mendlowitz, Leibowitz, and the others saw their disciples as a legion that stood in their faith commitments more than a cut above those attending Revel's institution.[10]

Mendlowitz's conviction that what he was doing was decidedly on the side of the angels was confirmed for him dramatically in 1938 when he hosted a distinguished East European visitor, Rabbi Elchanan Wasserman of the famed Baranowicz Yeshiva. Wasserman blessed Torah Vodaath's efforts, an approbation that contrasted starkly to Wasserman's public condemnation of Revel's school. He refused to set foot in the Yeshiva Rabbi Isaac Elchanan, declaring it to be "a center of *apikorsus* [heresy] and *sh'mad* [conversion from Judaism] since the writings of Leopold Zunz, Abraham Geiger and Isaac Hirsch Weiss," nineteenth-century German followers of Wissenschaft des Judenthums [Science of Judaism] and Reform Jewish thinkers, were studied there.[11]

Many of these Brooklyn students proudly projected their schools' exalted self-esteem with a swagger that came to the fore in their darker moments when they, too, cast aspersions upon the religious lifestyles of their Washington Heights counterparts. The word on the Williamsburg and Brownsville Orthodox streets was that those at the modern yeshiva were *amoratzim* (ignoramuses) who did not study *lishmah* (Torah for its own sake). Sometimes, even the uncharitable appellation of *stickle shaigetz* (literally a "partial gentile") was hung on those who were perceived as harboring heretical ideas or who it was alleged conducted themselves in a less than punctilious manner.[12]

Perhaps the harshest criticism was reserved for those former Brooklyn boys who broke ranks and moved on to Revel's yeshiva. As always in America, maintaining strict control over followers proved to be the most difficult of tasks. Here, those who "checked out," as the term went, left either because Revel's institution "was the place to be to be trained as a modern Orthodox rabbi" or because they welcomed the conveniences it provided in acquiring advance secular training in a thoroughly Orthodox milieu. Though perhaps no less fervent in their private behaviors than the classmates they left behind, cadres of committed Torah Vodaath and Chaim Berlin students simply did not share their community's full set of misgivings about Revel's educational formulas. Still, such students could find themselves somewhat apprehensive about their decision to cross bridges.

One such aspirant would explain that while "for four years, I studied at . . . Chaim Berlin and I have no complaints to make," still "there comes a time in every young man's life when he has to consider college." Since, he continued, "I've decided to continue my Jewish education," which "to do so effectively entails considerable study during the day, night college holds no appeal to me." Notwithstanding the fact that "most of the reports I have heard about [Yeshiva] were derogatory . . . I wanted both my religious and secular training during the day." He did, however, promise those from whom he sought admission that "I shall enter my new school with unprejudiced thoughts and an unbiased mind."[13] In the early postwar period, many other Brooklyn yeshiva men would follow in this youngster's footstep. They would come not only for secular careerist reasons or the chance to train as budding modern Orthodox rabbis, but also for the intellectual challenge of sitting at the feet of Rabbi Joseph B. Soloveitchik, who would reaffirm and personify what Revel first stood for: the importance of integrating the secular with the religious. Unquestionably, the most famous of these future migrants was a 1945 Torah Vodaath high school graduate named Norman Lamm who was destined to be the third president of Yeshiva.

Still, if Lamm and most of his predecessors remained as devout as they always had been in these new environs, there also were those who fit the stereotyped profile and broke away from their family's religious values while on Orthodoxy's college campus. One visible symbol of tacit dissent was these youngsters' doffing of their hats or yarmulkes immediately upon exiting the precincts of the school. In the 1930s, an imaginative effort was made at Yeshiva College to bring those deviants back into line through an American stratagem. Some student leaders suggested that the entire community begin wearing college beanies with the years of graduation emblazoned on their caps while on the way to and from the school. This appeal to the "collegiate spirit," it was divined, would lead to greater observance of a basic religious tradition. Revel was not impressed with the plan because it seemed to encourage Yeshiva's students to behave like all other American college students. While Revel wanted his disciples to appreciate the "beauties of Greece," he did not want those who would ascend to his "House of God on the Hilltop" of Washington Heights to act like — college hi-jinx and all — those who attended other campuses in this country. The beanie initiative also played into the prejudices of his opponents.[14]

While Mendlowitz and the others were quick to criticize Yeshiva and its students, degrees of heterodoxy could be found within their sacred spaces as well. As these schools grew, they began to attract not only some local youngsters who for their earliest training had attended public schools but also boys from other American cities who were not attuned to the intensity of these yeshivas' religious culture. Perhaps these fellows enrolled reluctantly because their pious parents wanted this regimen for them.[15]

An additional and large group of nonconformists were students who departed from the Torah Vodaath–Chaim Berlin straight and narrow to establish in their spare time close personal relationships with neighborhood boys and girls who stemmed from Jewish homes that were very dedicated to their faith and people but not nearly as observant as the Brooklyn yeshiva crowd.

During the interwar period, Brooklyn, a pocket of commitment and continuity amid an American Jewish world awash in spiritual decline, was also a mecca for unusual families devoted to the goals of modern day-school education. These mothers and fathers desired to see their children live harmoniously as highly knowledgeable and observant Orthodox Jews within, and not without, secular American society. For them, even the best Talmud Torahs did not provide their sons and daughters with sufficiently strong Jewish training. They also did not want their youngsters to be deprived of a solid secular education. Accordingly, these parents sequestered their children, at least through the eighth grade, in all-day, dual-curriculum Jewish schools. There, it was hoped, they would be educated and socialized as "good Americans [and] good and loyal and enlightened Jews." In these institutions, the general studies department was "modeled after the public schools."[16] Thus, they set themselves and their children apart from both their neighborhood's avowed separatists — those who backed Torah Vodaath and Chaim Berlin — and from almost all other American Jews who still believed unquestioningly in the value of a public school education.

The families that sent youngsters to schools such as the Etz Hayim-Hebrew Institute of Boro Park or the Shulamith School for Girls or the Crown Heights Yeshiva and the Yeshivah of Flatbush were, however, not nearly as strict in their personal observance of mitzvoth as those within the Torah Vodaath–Chaim Berlin realm. While it is impossible to ascertain how committed to Sabbath observance and kashruth these people were, one proclivity, noted at the time, was that some day-school parents defiantly objected to their boys being "forced to wear a *Tallis Koton*" to school. This fringed garment, generally worn under a shirt, is mandated according to the halacha as a constant, visible reminder of the obligation to follow the commandments. Even more than the yarmulke, it surely set off Jews through style of dress from their fellow Americans, especially if the fringes were worn outside the shirt. Whatever their feelings about how they appeared to the outside world, these adults also did not want their children subjected to the humiliation of teacher inspections. Sensitive to the heterogeneity within its constituency, in the 1930s school leaders at Etz Hayim accommodated this dissent. Reportedly, "parents who objected could opt their children out by means of a letter."[17]

On a more sophisticated and nuanced level, these families also differed from Mendlowitz's and Liebowitz's supporters in their views of the religious propriety of modern Jewish nationalism. What the parent body and its schools' administration and faculty believed in subjected them to criticism from local yeshiva heads.

To the extent that the dreams and ideas of Religious Zionist thinkers and Mizrachi men and women found a haven among interwar American Jews, it was primarily in these homes and at these day schools that the hopes for an ongoing, Hebrew-speaking, national, and modern Orthodox presence could be found. Precisely, interest in a Hebrew- and Zionism-based curriculum motivated these exceptional parents to enroll their sons and daughters in Brooklyn's modern Jewish educational organizations "to engender in them a love for their people and its cultural heritage and a strong attachment to the Zionist way of life." Their fondest hopes were that these integrative institutions would become "a training ground for future leaders in Jewish life both in America and Israel." Some of these youngsters would find their destiny ultimately in the State of Israel. More would be among the most active American Zionists. These Jews who spoke Hebrew and read Hebrew books and magazines promoted Jewish nationalism as a critical means of group identification in this country and, of course, were deeply concerned with the fate of the Jewish state.[18]

As staunch Agudath Israel men, the old-line Brooklyn yeshiva leaders opposed this mindset and mission. Although deep in the recesses of Torah Vodaath's earliest years, before Mendlowitz strode onto the neighborhood scene, it had been a Mizrachi-related outlet—one early student would later recall "strongly Zionist teachers" and a principal "very learned in Hebrew matters . . . quite modern for that time period," by the mid-1920s none of these perspectives was still countenanced in his school or elsewhere within the staunch yeshiva community. There the Jewish national orientation would not be encouraged and students received, at most, tertiary exposure to the Hebrew language. Religious Zionism was consistently judged as contrary to the thrust of Orthodox tradition.[19]

Co-education at the Crown Heights Yeshiva, which began as an all boys' school but soon established classes for girls, and at the always gender-mixed Yeshivah of Flatbush also did not sit well with the Torah Vodaath and Chaim Berlin leadership. They saw no analogue within a revered Old World Orthodoxy in these educational innovations. Where the most stringent of Orthodox came from in Europe, co-education was the province of Jews of the Haskalah who were often on the road away from tradition. If concentrated education was warranted for girls in the twentieth century, it had to be delivered in the Beth Yaacov manner, a girl's institution that carried the Agudath Israel stamp of approval.[20]

All of these objections were largely lost on considerable numbers of Brooklyn yeshiva students. As teenagers, they socialized serenely with dayschool youngsters with whom they had so much in common as committed, engaged Jews. Particularly on Sabbaths and holidays, Brooklyn's fourteen Young Israel synagogues were the renowned central meetings places for those who went to different schools during the week but shared what one borough youngster called "general convictions." There they met and discussed the compelling issues of contemporary life. If they were also members of the Religious Zionist youth movement, the Shomer ha-Dati, the fate of those living under the British Mandate would be foremost on their mind. At their gatherings, they openly dreamed of someday "work[ing] in Palestine for and under the Mizrachi ideals." Young Israels were also centers for interacting with members of the opposite sex at lectures, socials, and parties, all within the parameter of synagogue life. Other local synagogues established their own independent youth congregations that attracted this cadre of youngsters possessed of strong nationalist and religious feelings. While some officials at Torah Vodaath, "particularly those connected with the Agudah [Agudath Israel] . . . frown [ed] upon association with the Young Israel" and students were "discouraged from, going there," determined dissenters did what they pleased.[21]

During their travels through the Young Israel prayer-, party-, and public-lecture scene and circuit, Torah Vodaath and Chaim Berlin yeshiva boys and Beth Yaacov girls met up comfortably with the final substantial part of Brooklyn's diverse community of committed interwar Jews: the student stars of the borough's own Talmud Torah system.

Like everywhere else in America, Brooklyn's Jewish supplementary schools were the venues where the overwhelming majority of young people, even those from observant homes, received their Jewish education. While most of those who were sent off to these institutions, as always, perceived after-public-school study as a burden that they were happy to dispense with after their Bar Mitzvah — there was no comparable, formal moment of truth for girls — there was a coterie of students who actually liked these classes. Or they had hovering parents who encouraged, directed, and monitored their comings and goings to assure perfect attendance records and diligence. The Jewish religious, nationalist, and cultural values of these insistent families were almost identical to those who sent their children to the incipient all-day Jewish schools. One star pupil of the time has recalled how in her East New York communal school, out of a class of "twenty-five to thirty" fidgeting and disinterested youngsters, she was one of the few "bright and interested [ones] who went along with the teacher." The Hebraist instructor paid scant "attention to the rest" as she equipped those who positioned themselves in the front of the classroom with what this memoirist suggests were Hebraic and Judaic skills "comparable to what youngsters were getting at the Yeshivah of Flatbush."[22]

As high-school students, when frequenting the Young Israel of their choice, they could speak proudly of sticking to Jewish studies within the Marshaliah Hebrew high-school system, which conducted its classes both in the neighborhood and in Manhattan with a strong Zionist cultural spirit, mixing formal training with informal social activities, and endeavoring always to create a sense of enduring community among its charges. A few of these special youngsters could also speak with satisfaction of their own travels to Manhattan as they attended the secondary — the so-called "preparatory" — program of the Jewish Theological Seminary or the more intensely Zionist, but secular, Herzliah Teachers Institute. Here, too, the top Talmud Torah boys and girls, scions of Brooklyn, frequently became friends and associates with day-school products who were also continuing their own Jewish educations in the evenings and on Sundays. By day, they enrolled in local public high schools, where they participated in creating a Jewish student culture in these secular environs and even studied Hebrew, which was introduced as a college-prep, Regents-approved foreign language in 1930. That curricula addition constituted a sea change toward ethnic tolerance within the hierarchy of these Temples of Americanization, a sure victory for advocates of cultural pluralism. On occasion, profoundly nonconformist former students from Torah Vodaath and other Brooklyn yeshivas joined these public schoolers in their Jewish Theological Seminary classes. These renegades, or drop-outs, might well have been fervent in their personal observance. But they checked out either because they did not subscribe to their erstwhile schools' anti-Zionism and unbending religious rules and/or simply had had enough of their institutions' studied separatism. Back again in Brooklyn on the Sabbath and holidays, all of these youngsters coalesced and socialized together as a common-values group at Young Israel services and activities.[23]

While all of those who broke away from the Brooklyn yeshiva world distressed and embarrassed Mendlowitz, they were welcomed within the Yeshiva College–Yeshiva Rabbi Isaac Elchanan community. Revel certainly smiled upon the arrival of fellows with strong Talmudic backgrounds. He also may have observed that their presence in his midst was a measure-for-measure compensation for former students of his own who were lost to the closed Torah environment of Torah Vodaath or Chaim Berlin. During the 1930s, schools in both boroughs battled for the allegiance of the most talented and dedicated budding Torah scholars, even going so far as to raid each other's student bodies. As a Mizrachi-related institution, Revel's school was likewise accepting of day-school products and even of the best Talmud Torah boys. The branch that was available for them, a Teachers Institute, had been grafted on the Elchanan Yeshiva back in 1919, when the Palestine-based Mizrachi leader Rabbi Meir [Bar-Ilan] Berlin stepped in as temporary president during Revel's four-year hiatus from Yeshiva.[24]

The Agudath ha-Rabbanim was never thrilled with a Jewish studies creation whose type was unknown in the European yeshiva world of their past — though these rabbis were still loyal Mizrachiites and remained attached to Revel's institution. The Teachers Institute and the students it attracted were also ever-ready grist for the Brooklyn yeshivas critics' mills. Many of these undergraduates were those off-campus cap doffers whose behaviors contributed to unsavory canards leveled against the school. Nonetheless, the Teachers Institute programs emerged for many as a consummate capstone experience that enabled students to matriculate from the elementary-level day schools — or the best of the Talmud Torahs — through high school in Brooklyn and then on to the college, all within a Religious Zionist educational environment.

One such young man of that time and place of whom Revel was unquestionably enamored attended the Yeshivah of Flatbush for eight years before moving on to James Madison High School. A son of a Hebrew teacher, he spent some of his afternoons tutoring in his father's small Talmud Torah. On other days, he continued his own Hebraic training at Flatbush, where some of his instructors were Yeshiva's Teachers Institute scholars who moonlighted in Brooklyn. For this well-trained youngster, the high-school break from full-time Jewish education ended when he enrolled in Yeshiva College. Here the harmonious melding of family desires, his personal disposition, and early contact with the school made his decision to enroll as an undergraduate a foregone conclusion. Others in his classes like those who, for example, sneaked away from the dormitory on the Sabbath in search of off-limits amusements were not exactly the school's nor their parents' pride and joy. Nonetheless, the Brooklyn haven for committed Orthodox Jews of their many diverse stripes turned out to be the prime feeder community for the fledgling Yeshiva College, with some advancing ultimately to the Yeshiva Rabbi Isaac Elchanan for final training as

American Orthodox rabbis. As of 1935, in the midst of its first decade, four out of ten students who were enrolled in the then-small college came from these observant neighborhoods.[25]

Revel's other arch-competitor, the Jewish Theological Seminary, also benefited from and served as a final training ground for members of this Brooklyn elite. Those on the road to future status as Conservative rabbis and educators included, to Mendlowitz's unmitigated horror, erstwhile members of his own high-school program who had graduated from secular colleges before attending the Seminary. The numbers of such dissidents would have been more robust had some Torah Vodaath men not been turned away due to poor grades or other academic and social considerations. At one high point in the 1930s (1930–1934), Brooklyn boys were one-quarter of those graduated as rabbis from the Seminary that recruited nationally. At the same time, the local Talmud Torahs were the starting point for most of the Brooklyn men and women who chose to train for careers in Jewish education at the Seminary's own Teachers Institute. While these defections nettled Mendlowitz and his compatriots — and also had to have troubled both Revel and those who ran the borough's modern schools — nonetheless during this time period and more than in any other place in America, Brooklyn's Orthodox neighborhoods and institutions produced a cadre of future American Jewish leaders who would make their marks during the postwar era.[26]

But even as Mendlowitz stayed largely on the attack against those who placed much stock in the integration of the secular with the religious within the lives of Brooklyn's and American Orthodoxy's faithful minority, back home in Brooklyn in the 1930s, the leader of Torah Vodaath faced a revolt within his own student ranks among those who attacked his own stances as all-too modern. Presaging attitudes that would garner far greater currency in the postwar period, extremists known as the *M'lochim,* literally the "Angels," rejected all signs of acculturation and practiced their Judaism with uncompromising asceticism. Under the sway of the charismatic Rabbi Chaim Avraham Dov Ber Levine ha-Cohen, known as the *Malach* [Angel], they followed his commands to grow long beards and side curls [*peyes*], to scrupulously avoid wearing "gentile attire," to stop speaking English — Yiddish would be the sole tongue of communication — and to focus their attention on the strictest levels of kashruth and devotion to prayer and meditation. The M'lochim also abstained from all forms of frivolous, injurious-to-the-spirit, secular cultural activities. No radios, no newspapers, and no nights out at the movies for those who were so committed. Though forms of behavior of a distinctive Hasidic tincture were not unknown previously within the community — the Malach was related ideologically to the Lubavitch sect still in Russia — this was, arguably, the first time when these values threatened the religious equilibrium of an Orthodox establishment in America.

But as Mendlowitz contemplated this challenge to his studied modus vivendi with the modern world that he had prescribed for his disciples, he had to have recognized that, in part, he had only himself to blame. In his zeal to expose his students to great Torah figures in the neighborhood, he had introduced the impressionable to this scholar, this "living icon," a "living saint." Frightened that this very different type of nonconformity, "the whole dress, the attire, the *peyes,* the *tzitzit*" — these Jews wore their fringed garments outside their shirts to make a point to the world of their distinctiveness — augured to "convert . . . the school into an ultra-Hasidishe school, something that was foreign and alien at the time," in 1931 he expelled the Malach's followers from Torah Vodaath.

On their own, this cultic community of perhaps several hundred followers remained devoted to Rabbi ha-Cohen and his teachings even beyond the time of his death in 1938. Drawing further and further into their group, they married among themselves and raised their own children in extreme isolation from American culture. Determined above all else to stay clear of contamination, they even failed to make common cause with their closest counterparts, the Lubavitch Hasidim who began arriving in America and settling in their vicinity at the very outbreak of World War II. This miniscule movement would, however, in the decades after the war find an ideological affinity with the Satmar Hasidim as they shared extreme, unmitigated hatred for Zionism and for the State of Israel. In their vitriol — praying that "God Almighty destroy the land" of Israel and the Zionists "without harming faithful Jews" — they would far exceed any of the preaching of a Rabbi Gabriel Z. Margolis or of the positions that the early Agudath Israel occupied.[27]

While the M'lochim's actions and attitudes adumbrated trends that would characterize Brooklyn's most devout Orthodox Jews in contemporary times, others within this truly variegated community also anticipated a totally different development endemic to postwar America. Already in the 1920s–1930s, scions of the borough's most faithful Jewish families began falling away from observance.

Typical of many was the bittersweet family dynamic within that aforementioned "representative" and pious Williamsburg family where the father and mother unfailingly personified devotion to old religious ways. One son and a daughter followed in their parental footsteps, as "good and upright" second-generation Jews. But a second son reportedly wanted to "become a man of the world." As his still-observant brother would later tell an investigator, after "his return from the wars [World War I], he began to mock some of our customs and criticized our rigid observance of the traditional laws." Though respectful while still at home of his mother's deep feelings — the father had passed away — he did not openly violate the Sabbath or vocally object to the family's strict observance of the halacha. Still, "it was only a question of time till he would go his own way."

After marriage to a Jewish girl from Brownsville who evidently shared his declining religious commitments, and then blessed with financial success, the young couple made its way out of the neighborhood and away from Orthodoxy. Their destination was a "swanky neighborhood in Forest Hills," Queens, where, according to his saddened brother, he became "what we at our Shul call a 'high-holiday Jew.' " Most likely the synagogue he then infrequently attended was not Orthodox, If so, in time, he and his wife, and even more likely his children, would became part of that large cohort of formerly Orthodox Jewish families who relinquished that most traditional of religious affiliations in the years following World War II.[28]

# 7

## A MORE FAITHFUL FOLLOWING

It was with measured equanimity that in 1937 the Orthodox Union contended that it represented "the largest Jewish religious group in the United States." Though proud of the size of its movement's tent — then, and subsequently, it floated figures that its affiliated congregations numbered in the thousands (the best real estimates are in the 200–300 range) — those in charge were hardly content with the religious performance of those within its confines. Long-standing patterns of behavior among America's Orthodox Jews were continuing apace. Union lay leader Bert Lewkowitz said as much, just three years later, after a fact-finding tour of this country. In his jaundiced view, there were so many Jews "who do not observe the Sabbath, who do not take their children to any Hebrew school, and do not give them a Jewish home atmosphere [but] consider themselves Orthodox Jews because they have a seat on the High Holidays." In 1943, three years after Lewkowitz's travels, a rabbi from Danville, Virginia, wrote back to the New York Orthodox base with comparable sad tidings. He said that among those to whom he ministered, "practical observance (of the mitzvoth) may have vanished from their lives to an alarming extent. Yet they want an Orthodox shul with an Orthodox leadership." From St. Louis came sobering words from a rabbi who complained about his "at best . . . half-baked laity with a confused and distorted version of Judaism." Adding to this confusion, argued a New England colleague, was the inescapable reality that "there are no definite lines of demarcation which delimit and define . . . our religious life." The signposts that separated Conservatism from Orthodoxy were simply not in place. That predicament only rendered "the position and influence of the genuinely Orthodox rabbi weakened considerably because of this ideological confusion."[1]

Clarity of commitment, if not total identity in practice, could be found within Orthodoxy's Brooklyn heartland and among other small yeshiva–day school communities elsewhere. But as of 1940, fewer than eight thousand youngsters attended all such schools nationally. There were but thirty-five in number and more than 90 percent out of the students were New York boys. Five years later, enrollment figures across the land rose to approximately 1,100. But again, close to 80 percent were from the same established group: male and metropolitan New York. These paltry numbers included the literal handfuls of elementary school youngsters who attended the fledgling Ramaz School in Manhattan and the Maimonides School, in Brookline, Massachusetts, two other unusual Orthodox undertakings that were harbingers of future developments.[2]

The Yorkville institution that Rabbi Joseph H. Lookstein founded and Rabbi Joseph B. Soloveitchik's New England initiative were unique as they were the first day schools to recruit children from families that had to be convinced that core Orthodox religious values, including Sabbath and kashruth observance, were worthy of upholding. At Ramaz, a concerted effort was made to recruit "discriminating" and generally affluent families, who would have been more than happy to see their sons and daughters sit comfortably in the city's elite private schools, through emphasizing that the "academy's" charges would never be disadvantaged socially and culturally. Lookstein would say as much as he sought to rouse his Yorkville silk-stocking community, crying that it was a shame that "hitherto the parochial school has had a special appeal [only] for the children of the middle class and poorer homes." Now it was time to assert "the unalienable right . . . of a child from a rich Jewish home [to receive] a full and comprehensive Jewish education." In subsequent years, when Ramaz's first students moved on to its high school, much would be made of its Ivy League admissions record. Once these youngsters enrolled, families then were cajoled, and sometimes chided, to make their styles at home in sync with the school's religious values. It was suggested to the parent body, for example, that "without any intent whatever to 'preach,' the 'shabbos party' on Friday afternoon [must be] a wonderful prelude to an actual Sabbath-like Friday night. Otherwise," mothers and fathers were warned, on the authority more of psychologists than rabbis, "it is just play-acting and emotional clashes begin to disturb the child." The point was frequently made that "if . . . the parents' omission is no more than laziness, indifference or inconvenience, they might as well begin observing . . . the school's orientation toward Judaism . . . for the sake of their child's educa-tion." Having said that, the school admitted that its formula was suitable not for all potential families. Certainly, Ramaz was not a good choice for those most egregious of dissenters who "disagree with the fundamentals of [the] school's orientation."[3]

In Brookline, the impious religious practices of families within Maimon-ides' midst were not as openly acknowledged. But efforts were made to bring into the day-school fold that hypothetical boy who, if not for its intensive Jewish education, would forget "whatever he learned" for his Bar Mitzvah and would grow "perfectly indifferent to the call of the Orthodox synagogue and other religious institutions." Internal school reports observed that some of these youngsters were not particularly concerned during their summer vacations about wearing "caps or yarmulkes at all times" as well as their tzizith; nor were they strictly observing kashruth and the Sabbath. In pushing harder than Lookstein did toward making those who chose to attend his school toe its religious line, Soloveitchik and his school's lieutenants were equally sensitive to the religious futures and deportment of his community's female students. Maimonides, too, fostered quality education and commit-ment to observance among young women. Moreover, in a move with signifi-cant implications for the future of Orthodox education in America, Soloveit-chik established the precedent of offering Talmud study to girls as well as boys as they matured intellectually. Here, even more that at Ramaz where comparable policies evolved, such equal access to this advanced subject was an institutional desideratum.[4]

In time, the considerations that Ramaz and Maimonides addressed, each in its own nuanced way, toward integrating youngsters from families that possessed differing degrees of commitment to the halacha within the same institutional midst would challenge many communities as day-school educa-tion eventually became Americanized Orthodoxy's preferred mode of in-culcating religious values. But it would still be years before these adumbra-tions would be widely emulated and would ultimately create a larger cadre of religiously devoted Jews. In the meantime, Orthodoxy in America entered the new post–World War II period, with a constituency that was, as in prior eras, numerically strong but weak in religious commitment.

Some fifteen years later, the calculus of concerns among the Americanized Orthodox had changed considerably. By then, Orthodoxy was well on the way to becoming a minority among this country's Jewish movements. Not-withstanding "some official and semi-official declarations or announcements" from Orthodox Union sources that perpetuated, as Rabbi Leo Jung put it, "the myth of an Orthodox majority . . . [a] pernicious illusion because it creates an optimism that is utterly unjustified by the circumstances," the reality was now that when a Jew decided to affiliate with a congregation it was more often than not in a Conservative synagogue. After more than half a century of reigning as American Jewry's premier religious movement, Orthodoxy now found itself in the midst of a battle to retain its very currency among most synagogue-goers.[5]

The newly emerging American suburbs of the late 1940s–1960s were the sites of this struggle over shifting religious allegiances and the eventual narrowing of Orthodoxy's tent. There, in bucolic settings, a revival of Jewish belonging took place as it became a hallowed national value to affirm religion through membership in the house of worship of one's choice. It was one way for this patriotic minority group to line up with their fellow citizens as part of an indivisible nation under the Almighty in this country's struggle against godless communism. It was also vitally important for those Jews who feared assimilation more than ever before, and who abhorred the prospect of intermarriage, to identify themselves and their youngsters with that touchstone institution, the synagogue, in their religiously mixed neighborhoods. For unlike in their prior urban experiences, where Jews lived in their own communities, nearby but often in conflict with their Christian neighbors, now in these suburban reaches, "not only [did] . . . Jews live like others . . . They live[d] with them." In these environs, Jewish allegiances bred on not fitting into America, or nasty memories of gentiles troubling Jews on mean urban streets no longer had relevance. These ways of thinking did not survive the flattening of differences within the younger generation. One 1950s parent understood the dilemma this way: In the city, he observed, "the odds are in your favor. Out here you stack the deck" through linkage to the "social organization of the synagogue." If nothing else, it was widely believed that within this social mix, "the community needs a place for our children and . . . adults need some place to carry out . . . social lives." Or so read a flyer that advertised the founding of a synagogue.[6]

Conservative rabbis were readily on the scene to meet these challenges, offering themselves and their synagogues as leaders and venues for what came to be trumpeted as a fresh start for the "return to synagogue movement." Jewish Theological Seminary graduates promoted the seven-day-a-week Synagogue Center program. It was hoped that their activities would keep youngsters away from the wrong types of interreligious friendships. If the Conservative moment did its job well (or so was the plan), the best of these youngsters who attended their modern religious schools would affiliate with that movement's national youth organization, United Synagogue Youth, and perhaps spend a summer or more at one of its Ramah Camps for a most intensive experience in positive Jewish living. Back home in their sanctuaries, the Conservatives' ritual values bespoke an affinity for the best of Orthodoxy's revered traditions — "leaning toward the Orthodox," as one suburban rabbi explained his actions — while as a middle-class expression of contemporary Judaism, they encouraged full family participation in prayers and ceremonials.[7]

This well-conceived combination of traditionalism and modernization, pitched perfectly for the suburban lifestyle, appealed to a new generation of Jewish adults whose parents had been Orthodoxy's rank-and-file majority. Freed of the nostalgia, inertia, or inherent filiopietism that had influenced their mothers' and fathers' religious choices, they moved smartly into a movement whose leaders — even more than the most tolerant of the Orthodox — did not criticize their personal patterns of observance. All that Conservative rabbis asked of their members was that they be regular worshippers. In its most dramatic decision, Conservatism in 1950 brought the tradition right into the driveways of its constituents. By affirming, under its definition of Jewish law, the religious right of Jews to drive to and from home and synagogue on the Sabbath and holidays, they made it possible for those who might have felt guilty about using their cars on Jewish holy days — that means of travel is a clear contravention of Orthodoxy's understanding of the halacha — to see themselves as legitimately in line with a modern construct of rabbinic teachings.[8]

No less than their Conservative counterparts, Americanized Orthodox rabbis were out on the suburban hustings striving to hold fast to those masses of affiliating Jews. Within many communities, representatives of both the Seminary and Yeshiva University appeared in front of such potential congregants, competing in what became known as "Debate Nights." In recreational rooms and the dens of private homes, spokesmen for both groups tried to convince the assembled, men and women who as youngsters may have spent more time outside their urban Orthodox shuls than within, that their movement's approach to Jewish tradition and American life was the most fitting and desirable. At the end of the gatherings, voters decided with whom they preferred to identify. When taking the high road, Seminary men emphasized the egalitarianism and family orientation that was their movement's calling card. In their darker moments, they attempted to contrast the commodious suburban temples that they envisioned with the less-than-pleasant memories their listeners may have had of the "*shtibls* [small synagogues] of the Bronx and Brooklyn." Usually on the defensive, Orthodox respondents projected themselves to be as socially sensitive and attuned as their counterparts, and they spoke enthusiastically about the good work they planned to do with community youngsters. Perhaps most importantly, they now articulated, as an American Orthodox creed, a sensibility that had long been implied that Jewish tradition neither rose nor fell based on an individual's personal religious deportment. They explained that the quintessence of Orthodoxy did not lie with an individual's personal performance of mitzvoth, though they prayed that their fellows would do more in that private realm.[9]

Tolerant to a fault, these advocates assured questioners, for example, that they understood the religious dilemmas of suburban Jews who might live a drive away from their sanctuary but who wanted to be part of Orthodox synagogue life. A tradition was then evolving among such affiliating Jews of motoring to Holy Day services and parking their cars a few blocks away to avoid red-faced encounters with more observant worshippers who walked to shul. For these accepting rabbis, such fear of embarrassment bespoke a discernible respect for the halacha, an attitude upon which a sensitive spiritual leader might eventually build. After all, these potential congregants tacitly admitted that what they were doing was religiously wrong. Presently, however, Orthodox representatives just asserted that their movement's larger interest was in seeing that when Jews chose to pray and participate in the public arena of congregational life — no matter how they got to services — that they did so in God's most appropriate house of worship. Conservative synagogues, they counterattacked, were but reflections of "the strengths and weaknesses of its founders, a mirror of the people that built them." The Orthodox synagogue, conversely, "stood for something larger ... a model, an ideal toward which all should strive." If, in so doing, the argument went, not all of Orthodoxy's synagogue practices lined up totally with American mores — most notably in its seating configurations — its deviation from conventional norms gave it its strength.[10]

These neighborhood encounters between movements generally retained a civil tone, though the Conservatives usually carried the day. Their advocacy for mixed seating was often the clinching argument, particularly in those instances where the rules of the ballot box stipulated that while both men and women questioned the representatives and debated the issues together, often only the women in the room could vote. They were the ones who traditionally had been "stuck" in balconies or behind a mechitza. Sometimes their opponents prevailed due to the force of their own argumentation, although in one particular instance Orthodoxy won out because of some good old-fashioned politicking. To get out the vote for Yeshiva — specifically on the crucial plebiscite regarding maintaining a mechitza in the synagogue — advocates for Orthodoxy arranged for a babysitting and taxi services for those who would back traditional seating patterns. However, in other early postwar arenas the competition turned nasty when Conservatives attempted to change the way congregations had long conducted their services.[11]

Occasionally, the flashpoint took place when a previously Orthodox synagogue pulled up stakes from its erstwhile neighborhood and followed its members to suburban settings. While the shul was still in the city, there were those who whispered about seating the men and women together and possibly of altering the services through use of instrumental music, enhanced with a microphone. But so long as they were situated downtown, the status quo prevailed. However, now in a new time and place—especially when a congregational building committee considered architectural plans for constructing the sanctuary—louder voices were heard about the necessity for mixed seating.[12]

On other fronts, in still urban locales or in smaller towns, the simple desire of congregants to "bring their shule [sic] up to today's standards" led to strident controversy. In one emblematic case, in Charleston, South Carolina, an outspoken critic of prior practice spoke for many when he asserted that "this is 1945, not 1845 and if conservatism is good enough for cities like Charlotte, Philadelphia, Atlanta, Richmond and New York, it ought to be good enough for Charleston." Addressing the most basic of egalitarian concerns in a highly personal vein, he specified that the synagogue had to address "the complaints," like those "from the women members of [his] family" who were tired of being "put upstairs . . . completely forgotten and ignored" except during the High Holidays in the hot early autumn. Then, the men downstairs heard plenty from their wives who "roasted" in the poorly ventilated balcony. He reported that his own wife "came to the synagogue on the first day of Rosh Hashanah, and it was so hot upstairs that she almost fainted, and she would not return the second day." That situation, he concluded, is "not right and I for one am not going to stand for it any longer." At the core of this demand was a definite desire to reestablish "peace in his house," a most warranted traditional Jewish value.[13]

Articulate representatives of the Seminary and United Synagogue stood behind this and other local advocates for change. Strategically, these Conservatives projected themselves as the true bearers of "modern Orthodoxy" who were determined to help communities create "atmosphere[s] that would be saturated with our traditional habits and customs . . . which will meet the basic needs of the membership, including the entire family." In their most aggressive pose they pledged to help congregations "correct" the "evil" of "those who used the word *orthodox* to cover up abuses, ills and shortcomings and so misrepresented the Synagogue and tradition of our fathers."[14]

In responding to these challenges, the traditionalists within these congregations, with the help of their own Yeshiva and Orthodox Union supporters, initially tried to turn the internal tide of debate. When they failed—and in most cases the Conservatives succeeded in the opening round—the newly disenfranchised resorted to a tactic that Rabbi Eliezer Silver had used in his battles in Cleveland against Rabbi Solomon Goldman a generation earlier.

They sought relief from the civil courts. Once again, Christian magistrates had to wade through reams of halachic argumentation to determine if a particular ritual change broke with the "Orthodox" strictures of congregational constitutions. Often complicating the matter, important national leaders of both competing movements showed up to testify, offering varying interpretations of the tradition.

In most cases, the Conservatives prevailed as the courts themselves, anxious to avoid getting involved in monitoring faith practices in this country, backed away from rendering religious decisions. They were content to say that majorities ruled. Fervent hopes also were expressed from the bench that once all was said and done, "harmonious and unified worship of God" would obtain among warring Jews. But such desires were rarely effectuated. Losers went away angrily from these disputes. In distant replays of nineteenth-century developments, breakaway Orthodox synagogues were established in many communities, splintering Jewish ranks. However, in one noteworthy case in Mt. Clemens, Michigan — a case that would long loom large in Orthodox memories — its faction won out as a state court upheld the "minority" rights of those who "adhere to the established doctrine and practice."[15]

Nevertheless, a win before a tribunal or a victory in a specific congregational referendum did little to halt the flow of members toward Conservatism. In those instances where the Orthodox faction triumphed, the Conservatives built their own breakaway synagogues and became part of a United Synagogue that expanded from approximately 350 member congregations in 1945 to 800 twenty years later. Demographic studies highlighted this "achieve[ment] of primacy on the American scene." In the late 1950s, in both northeastern and Midwestern cities fewer than 20 percent of the Jewish populations still saw themselves as within Orthodoxy's fold.[16]

Still, the Mt. Clemens victory in 1957 had great psychic ramifications. For example, that Midwestern community's strident stance may have well been in Rabbi Jung's mind when he asserted just two years later that if Orthodoxy were destined to be a "minority" denomination, it should at least be a "respectable minority." Now he and his confreres spoke with pride about themselves as constituents of a minority group that "no matter how small our numbers" possessed "inalienable rights." For one of Jung's sympathetic interlocutors, all of this conflict and competition meant that the time had come to tighten the definition of what made a synagogue Orthodox. Describing himself as a member of "a right thinking and just doing minority," this Syracuse, New York, layman suggested pointedly that "instead of having 700 graduates . . . of Orthodox schools . . . who serve congregations concerning some of which there is doubt" whether they conformed to the strictures of the Code of Jewish Law, would it not perhaps just be "better for us to have half that number . . . small but remaining bastions of Traditional Judaism?" For him, the ideal was now synagogues "planned by God-fearing Jews where the Jewish religion of two thousand years is truly lived," not those "erected by modern architects." Reacting in similar tones, Orthodox Union leaders, surveying the field of denominational conflict, asserted that the best news from these fronts was that "the attendant widespread publicity made great numbers of our people aware of the sharp line of demarcation dividing authentic Judaism from the deviationist ideology."[17]

Though some of American Orthodoxy's affinity for fighting back may have been born of a new and general postwar minority group assertiveness — Jews of all types were then taking on their opponents, asserting their rights — much of its vitality had to do with the revival of Yeshiva as a school for the training of rabbis. Soon after Dr. Samuel Belkin assumed the institution's faltering reins in 1943, the school began to extend its purview through what today would be called outreach and in-service programming. Such efforts gave rabbis a sense that they were not alone, neither in a collegial or a material sense. More importantly, the emergence of Rabbi Joseph B. Soloveitchik as American Orthodoxy's ideological standard-bearer and spiritual guide gave the movement a renewed self-confidence. Not since the early days of Bernard Revel was there a leader on the scene who embodied that nuanced message of "synthesis." Soloveitchik went even further in developing a program for the Jew's harmonious — if challenging — engagement with secular culture and modern society, while maintaining allegiance to far more than the core of traditional Judaism.

The immediate beneficiaries of Soloveitchik's wisdom were the young postwar rabbinical alumni of Yeshiva. The man whom they would refer to with affection as "the Rav" [*the* rabbi par excellence] when they did not, in personal conversations called him reverently their *rebbe* [teacher] set authoritative standards for Orthodox rabbis and congregations. He always approved sociological change in synagogue life that stayed within halachic boundaries, and would once opine that it was essential to show the Americanized Jew that it was possible for synagogues to conform to the Code of Jewish Law while at the same time be models of "good behavior, cultivated manners and beautiful sermons as any other American Jewish house of worship." He was also attuned to the battles out on the hustings between his men and their ideological competitors. Thus, he countenanced a go-slow policy in dealing with congregational ambivalence toward separate seating. At the same time, as adviser to and then chairman of the Rabbinical Council's Halacha Commission, Soloveitchik vigorously opposed the adoption or maintenance of other Conservative synagogue practices, such as having the cantor face the congregation rather than the holy ark during prayers, or using a microphone during Sabbath and holiday services.[18]

While American Orthodoxy's aggressiveness buttressed by Soloveitchik's persona did not substantially alter the flow of postwar Jews toward Conservatism, it did have a great impact upon those graduates of Yeshiva and the Hebrew Theological College who ministered in marginal Orthodox congregations. Increasingly, they became men without a movement while they struggled to keep congregants away from neighboring Conservative synagogues even as Orthodox Jewish publications ridiculed "mixed-seating Orthodoxy" as a contradiction in terms. In time some of these congregations gravitated toward the Conservative Movement.[19] For example, Atlanta's Ahavath Achim, Harry Epstein's synagogue, moved smartly into the United Synagogue camp in 1952. At the same time, other, formerly fence-sitting congregations decided to toe Orthodoxy's mark and installed mechitzas. The Orthodox Union was proudest of the thirty affiliated synagogues that between 1955 and 1965 installed mechitzas; a move that one scholar then noted was "the first break in a trend that had been moving in the opposite direction since the nineteenth century."[20]

Still, if Americanized Orthodox rabbis and their national organizations were now more comfortable both with their colleagues' fidelity to the faith and increasingly of one mind on synagogue practice nationwide, much work remained to be done among its residual laity. Many congregations still consisted of a good number of long-term members who then began to be called the "non-observant Orthodox."[21] In many places, attendance at prayers was still a problem even where affiliations held. "The size of a suburban congregation," one on-the-scene Orthodox observer reported in 1961, "bears little relation to the number of worshippers actually at services." He further lamented that "members of Orthodox congregations seem to be becoming lax in kashruth, Sabbath observance and other cardinals of the Jewish faith." In his opinion, Orthodox identification in suburbia was "a mark of social identification, not . . . an act of faith."[22]

As before, Sabbath work presented an unbridgeable dilemma. "The businessman's observance of the Sabbath is a vexing problem," reported the president of a young Orthodox synagogue in New Rochelle, New York. "The retailer is liable to suffer tremendously by having his store closed . . . on the busiest day of the week." For a Yeshiva operative visiting an Orthodox outpost in a New England mill town, the sight of "a line of men's jackets hung neatly on a long row of hooks . . . in shul when there was no one then in the building" brought home to him the sadness and the guilt that Saturday workers of this generation felt about their necessity to labor on the day of rest. "These are Shabbos jackets," the local rabbi explained regretfully. "They belong to the storekeepers who comprise most of our Shabbos minyan. On Shabbos, we *daven* [pray] at seven o'clock. We are finished by nine," permitting worshippers to then put in a full work day.[23]

Perhaps one young Orthodox rabbi on Long Island understood the nature of this constituency best when he included these "preferring Jews" within Orthodoxy's wide tent. For him, the communal agenda was to try to find ways to bring those "of lesser and negligible observance in personal life [but who] retain spiritual allegiance to traditional Judaism" closer to traditional forms of behavior. However, at that point in time Americanized Orthodoxy was only marginally successful in convincing these Jews to be more committed to the halacha. For the most part, Yeshiva's rabbis ministered to a largely older crowd of congregants who stayed on board because they trusted in that movement's aura of authenticity and found greater "warmth" and intimacy in the most traditional congregations then in the larger Conservative and Reform congregations around them. One other consideration: the membership fees in the smaller Orthodox synagogues were also typically lower than in their competition.[24]

The decline in Orthodoxy's popularity among postwar American Jews continued apace through the 1960s. By 1971, for example, only 11 percent of this country's Jewish adults still identified with that form of the faith.[25] Even in its most accepting and accommodating modes, Orthodoxy was not capturing or maintaining hold on the hearts and souls of most contemporary Jews in the United States. But no lamentations or jeremiads were heard within its leadership circles even as efforts continued — as the halacha demands — to convince all Jews of its religious truths. Withal, the movement was more than fulfilling Rabbi Jung's hopes. Beyond standing tall as a "respectable" minority, it was emerging as a self-respecting and sometimes aggressive group, perceiving itself as decidedly on the upswing. By that same year of 1971, even those who had predicted further decline in its impact on the American scene were taking note of its comeback. One leading Jewish sociologist remarked at that moment, "Orthodoxy has transformed its image from that of a dying movement to one whose strength and opinions must be reckoned within any realistic appraisal of the Jewish community."[26] The most satisfying reality for Orthodoxy was that those who chose to remain within its fold were Jews who, with increasing regularity, practiced its teachings correctly and conscientiously both in their homes and their synagogues. Their movement was now pitching a narrower but stronger religious tent. For the first time in American Orthodoxy's history, the pious and punctilious within that community were beginning to outnumber those who were not. The coalescence of a more faithful following was related, in one way or another, to the efflorescence of a growing day school–yeshiva system, that movement's proudest and most important creation in America.

Perpetuating their family values, many of the sons and grandsons of Torah Vodaath and Chaim Berlin's first students continued the tradition of adherence to separatist religious ways. They attended their fathers' and grandfathers' alma maters and other like-minded schools even as the deeply committed switched Brooklyn neighborhoods from Williamsburg to Boro Park. This 1950s urban migration had much to do with such nonreligious concerns as the decline in housing real estate values, the physical deterioration of the old enclaves, and a change in racial composition, all of which conspired to cause these Jews to now seek residences along "tree-lined and high status streets." Their arrival in Boro Park would soon transform the visage of that community from its diverse interwar profile — with its mixture of Orthodox, Conservative, and Reform synagogues, its local YMHA and its Talmud Torahs and one modern day school, Etz Hayim — to an enclave that was trumpeted as "worlds apart in [its] outlook and in [its] conception of Jewish values as well as in their practices and observances" from other American Jews. In that ever-homogenizing settlement area, there were "grocery stores, barbers, bakers, tailors, sporting 'Shomer Shabbos' signs in droves along . . . [the] main business thoroughfares."[27]

By 1960, there were also some suburban locales that were home to Jews who possessed long-standing yeshiva pedigrees. By then, Far Rockaway was reputed to be a "Torah Suburb-by-the-Sea," boasting of being home to some 4,000–5,000 "observant Jews . . . in the 35–45 age range . . . part and parcel of the American milieu [who] migrated to Far Rockaway from such nurturing grounds of American Orthodoxy as . . . Manhattan's Lower East Side, Washington Heights and Brooklyn's Williamsburg and Boro Park."[28]

Joining those entering their second generation of dedication to this intensive form of Jewish schooling were other fervent families who now, for the first time, prioritized providing yeshiva training to their children. Through such enrollments, they redoubled their commitments to perpetuating the halacha and stayed squarely in that movement's tent as prime elements within Orthodoxy's new faithful majority. Previously, throughout the entire sixty years that preceded the end of World War II, there had been many pious parents who would have preferred to send their children to yeshivas but were precluded from doing so for financial reason. Even though the teachers in these schools ostensibly took their own pledges of poverty, the issues of faculty salaries and other costs of education placed these institutions out of reach for many potential families. Some mothers and fathers dealt with this dilemma through solomonic gender-based decisions. Sacrifices were made to enroll sons at the expense of daughters. Or elders found it possible to scrape together sufficient funds to keep their children in Jewish schools through the elementary years, leaving their teenagers to take their chances with their religious identities in the public schools. In so many places in the United States, where they simply were no yeshivas, these determinations were largely moot, unless a move was made to send precocious male progeny to study and live in dormitories in New York.

An atmosphere of understanding among friends and relatives within closely knit neighborhoods mitigated the pangs of guilt these families may have felt about their decisions. No eyebrows were raised in an era when financial crises and exigencies loomed large everywhere. Recalling his youth in just this sort of environment, one postwar Orthodox leader who was by then staunchly dedicated to nothing less than separatist yeshiva education set the scene this way: "When I was a youngster, it was very possible for someone to be an Orthodox Jew without continuing [yeshiva education] beyond elementary school." However, as the twentieth century progressed further, it became, in his view, "unthinkable that one can really be an Orthodox Jew, unless he had at least graduated Yeshiva high school."[29]

What changed was not only the bourgeoisification of those who had previously faced financial dilemmas but, on a totally different plane, their loss of confidence that lessons learned primarily in their observant "homes and ethnic neighborhoods" could combine to preserve among their children a devotion to strict observance. For many families "at mid-century," hopeful expectation ended that "their children's *yiddishkeyt* [Jewishness], as their own, was something deep in the bone and that schools need not — and in all probability could not — instill it." This personal sense of inadequacy to transmit religiosity caused in its wake the burgeoning of yeshiva education as an "intentional enterprise of instruction" dedicated to instilling "a sense of particularity and belonging" within their youngsters.[30]

Perhaps the greatest beneficiaries of these changes in parental priorities were the daughters of the devout. Until then, the vast majority of young women had been relegated to Talmud Torahs if, indeed, these young women were provided any sort of formal Jewish education at all. A select few attended either the modern Orthodox or Beth Yaacov elementary schools, and an even smaller minority, fortunate enough to be in New York, availed themselves of supplementary high school or Hebrew teacher-training programs. Far more than their brothers, these women's Jewishness was rooted in their family traditions and neighborhood atmosphere. They obtained and preserved what has been aptly called "a mimetic religiosity" from watching and emulating their mothers. In the first postwar decades, the gender gap closed somewhat. By the 1960s, females studying in all-day Jewish schools made up more than 40 percent of the student population. Additionally, between 1948 and 1963, some fourteen all-girl high schools were established nationally — six in the New York area — and joined the growing number of co-ed institutions granting intensive secondary Jewish education to teenaged girls. And in 1956, Yeshiva University began offering college-level Jewish and secular educations to young women when it opened its Stern College for Women.[31]

In time, adults and children from families that previously had never considered day-school education for either their sons or daughters augmented Orthodoxy's pious population. But for many within this contingent, it was a long road from interest in all-day Jewish education to commitment to following the halacha. In many cases, fears about their own next generation's religious identity within new welcoming and diverse neighborhoods and the inadequacy of supplementary education initially spiked interest in enrollment. Reportedly, such parents realized "that the great literary and religious heritage accumulated over the ages cannot be transmitted during the shortened hours of the new congregational weekday school or Talmud Torah." For others, a "heightened . . . demand for a more intensive Jewish training" emanated from "the growth of the Zionist movement, the establishment of the Jewish state, the resurgence of Jewish consciousness and the desire for identification with the Jewish group after the rise of Hitlerism." Less openly proclaimed, but part still of the calculus of considerations, were some families' apprehensions of "undesirables" [i.e., minorities of other racial backgrounds] in the public schools, in an era where that educational system began to be perceived as in decline.[32]

Those parents who rapidly acquiesced to the heightened Orthodox values that their youngsters brought back with them from school were praised highly as tales were told, in almost legendary fashion, of children "revolutionizing the religious feelings — and in many instances — the religious conduct of their parents and the spiritual atmosphere of their homes," contributing to "a veritable religious catharsis in the lives of almost 50,000 American Jews." Indeed, "testimonials" were tendered of "heart rending 'confessions'. . . . from parents eager to credit their religious re-awakening to the attendance of their offspring at the local Day School." It was, for one commentator, as if a modern fulfillment of Malachi's prophesy of "the hearts of the fathers being restored to Lord's way *through* the children of our Day Schools" was well-nigh. A most evocative story that was told all around was of a boy "bothered to the very depths of his Jewish heart by his father's Sabbath desecrations" that he "got himself odd jobs after school and managed to buy his father a birthday present," a wool talis. Warmed and thrilled by this act of selfless filiopietism, the father promised to wear it to synagogue every Sabbath. And since that turning-point moment, it was related "he had not been working on Shabbos anymore."[33]

But for all the emotion of sagas like that one, such religious transformations were neither quick, nor all that pervasive. One estimate, tendered in 1952, put the proportion of day-school families that were not overly concerned about how rigorously they or their children performed such cardinal mitzvoth as Sabbath and kashruth "outside of New York (and in many sections of New York)" at 75 percent. These numbers included parents who were "skeptical about the Day School but were willing to try it — and not always for positive reasons" (i.e., unhappiness with the racial mix in public schools). Left unsaid and generally unstudied were the experiences of youngsters from observant homes who, in these heterogeneous day-school environments, chafed at their family's traditional practices and brought their own questions into charged family scenes.[34]

Many of these mixed feelings pervaded the Hillel Academy of Pittsburgh that was founded in 1947. A school community possessed of a wide range of religious values, as of 1955 the institution welcomed not only thirty-five families who observed the laws of kashruth and the Sabbath, but almost twice as many parents and their youngsters who kept neither fundamental principle rigorously. The fervent families in the local mix had the option of sending their children to the neighboring Yeshiva Achei Tmimim, a "European-type" school that stood literally next door, with the buildings adjoining each another. But, they, like the rest of Hillel's parent body, wanted their children to have a general education equal to the best public and private schools. What these Orthodox adults of all persuasions also had in common was a fundamental commitment to inculcating a strong sense of Jewish identity in their youngsters even if a wide variety of personal and family dynamics contributed to their educational decisions.

There were parents — the religiously privileged few — who desired to preserve and protect the values of their own youths. Accorded yeshiva educations, they wanted their children to "get the same education I got." Others saw a Hillel education as a way of avoiding potential conflict within a family between mothers and fathers, and in-laws, who possessed varying religious sentiments. Anxious to "accommodate members of [her] family," one wife and mother explained candidly that "my husband came from an Orthodox background. If my boy went to Hillel, he and his father would have something in common." A very different set of parents looked to the school to compensate for the Jewish education out of which they were "cheated," which left them with a "feeling of inferiority to Christians." They had often felt "embarrassed" when they were unable to "answer the questions of non-Jews." Or, these mothers and fathers wanted to spare [their] child from being rejected as a Jewish minority youngster "raised with *goyishe* [non-Jewish] kids."

However, for most Hillel families, heightened commitment to Jewish identification, and "awareness and belonging" did not translate into radical transformations in religious lifestyles. While day-school education did influence personal practices, "very few homes took on permanently such practices as Sabbath or kashruth observance." Still, almost all parents, even those who did not affiliate with any synagogue, affirmed strongly the teaching to their youngsters of "the observance of traditional ritual." This positive attitude toward following the commandments, even if the home did not quickly fall into line, gave patient pedagogues the hopeful expectation that as the "programs of the all-day schools become more intensified, the effect of the schools on the religious observances of the homes might become more pronounced." Another Orthodox educational strategist divined: "it is not from families such as these that we can demand that the tenor of the home follow the mode of life espoused by the Yeshiva. To make such demands would not win the parent but could well lose the child . . . to the ever present public schools. The best we can do in such cases is to embark on a patient, long effort to re-educate that segment of our parent community."[35]

Perhaps, for Orthodox educators, the most challenging families were those in which the parents hailed from devout backgrounds but had moved away from strict religious commitments as they matured and were liberated from their own elders' sway. Such deviants could be found not only within the most modern day schools but even within a long-standing and old-line Orthodox bastion: the Lower East Side's Rabbi Jacob Joseph School. There, a sample of its alumni from the interwar days, boys who had attended from 1925 to 1949, suggested that fully one-third of those exposed to its educational system — at least through its elementary school — were, as adults and as parents, public desecrators of the Sabbath and holidays. They traveled on these holy days. Forty-seven percent of those graduates described themselves as "less observant than their parents." Still, an overwhelming majority of the former students — including those who had checked out early and others who vocally criticized their own educational experiences — saw "day school education as the superior form of education for their children."[36]

Arguably for these ambivalent alumni, there was no gainsaying how much Judaic knowledge a youngster imbibed in an all-day Jewish environment. A Talmud Torah could not begin to approximate what these students would learn there. But these day-long institutions had to acknowledge the fact that "one need not be especially pious to want to attend" their schools and to welcome with warmth, and without pressure to conform, all children who approached their doors. These men — and their wives too — had to be certain their own children, "who would not dream of missing a favorite Saturday morning television program," could feel comfortable in a new type of Orthodox educational environment. What one such parent of the late 1950s liked about the Yeshiva of Central Queens, a school in which most of the six hundred local and suburban Long Island children came "from homes . . . who were not particularly observant," was that his "child can obtain . . . a sense of inner security, 'sugar coated,' and with few embarrassing compromises concerning school and home environment." He was comforted that his daughter, while still an elementary-level pupil, was able to "reconcile the greater Orthodoxy taught in the school with the comparative laxity at home." For this father, the combination of demeanor and a quality secular education coupled with "pleasure[able] Jewish studies," dedicated to strengthening identification "seem[ed] definitely worth chancing." Among those who ran the school, and who offered among its religious studies not only the "over-towering subject" of Talmud but who allowed "arts, dancing, painting, drawing, singing . . . freely and joyously," the hope persisted that in time youngsters would be comfortable both with the "the do's and don'ts" of Orthodox Judaism.[37]

That modern day-school educators did not easily achieve their goals was evidenced just a year or so later when the religious values of graduates of six "modern" or "integrated" day schools "operated under Orthodox auspices" were examined. In those schools, only a small portion of the male graduates recited their daily prayers and they rarely attended week-day synagogue services. On the crucial question of Sabbath observance, most "abstain[ed] from work . . . [but] disregard[ed] categories of work which fall under the prohibition of the *Shulchan Aruch* [Code of Jewish Law] or under the more recent interdiction of the Orthodox Rabbinate, such as turning on lights and answering the telephone on the Sabbath." These Jews followed the strictures of kosher demands more punctiliously, especially in their homes and particularly during the Passover season. Eight out of ten graduates kept two sets of kosher dishes in their homes and brought in only kosher foods. But they adopted more "lenient standards" for themselves when they ate out or were on the road. Thus, less than 40 percent abstained from eating all foods that were not "absolutely kosher." However, during the eight days of Passover, almost 90 percent followed the strict seasonal "food laws" when dining outside of their homes. Typically, the prime "motivation of the graduates in observing Jewish rituals and religious practices seem[ed] to be the desire to identify with the Jewish people," even if they did not consider that same Code of Jewish Law "as the authoritative guide for Jewish living." In other words, notwithstanding their frequent noncompliance with the halacha's calls, they would be the ones in town who generally offered to be "active in Jewish communal affairs and gave leadership to the organizations with which they are affiliated." Though these statements of Jewish allegiances comforted day-school officials, probably the best news for those who desired more piety of such students was that "recent graduates conform[ed] more to the goals of the Jewish Day School than those who graduated a longer time ago."[38]

Somewhat more upbeat reports about the quality of religious life among day-school families began to reach Orthodox educators at the close of the 1960s. One survey in Greater New York determined that more than 40 percent of those studied were "fully observant" meaning specifically that fathers never did "attend business or work on the Sabbath," nor did mothers "ever shop" on the holy day. The family did not "permit the use of the phone on the Sabbath" and the home was "strictly kosher." The parents were not "lenient about the foods" that their children might "eat outside . . .

home." And the adult male members of the family—those beyond Bar Mitzvah age—"put on tefillin regularly on weekdays." Only 7 percent of those sampled observed none of these commandments As much as these findings must have evoked measured optimism, they also could have been read as a call to further profound pedagogic effort. It was made clear that still "more than half of the parent body of the modern all-day school group" was "not fully-observant of some of the basic Jewish requirements." In other words, much work still remained to be done.[39]

On balance, however, neither the newcomers to day-school education nor the devoted American-born yeshiva families of long standing contributed most to the transformation of Orthodoxy's religious population, profile, and outlook. Rather, a new breed of immigrant Orthodox Jews, refugees and survivors of Nazism and of the Holocaust, were the primary contributors to the emergence of that movement's faithful majority. The uncommonly devout Orthodox Jews who escaped here after enduring the unparalleled horrors of that era did more than just seek a haven in America. Though they differed among each other in many social and cultural senses, members of the so-called "yeshiva world" community, the many Hasidic sects, and the more limited number of followers of Breuer German Orthodoxy that settled in America were all fired with a level of commitment and enthusiasm for Old World ways not seen previously in this free land. Sometimes working together and often laboring apart, they set out to reconstruct the religious civilization they had seen burned before their very eyes. For all of them in their holy quests to recapture the past, yeshiva education, of the separatist variety, was a sine qua non.

Thus in the first postwar decades, these aggressive aggregations of foreign-born Orthodox Jews began building a network of schools designed to keep America out of their children's development to the fullest extent that the law allowed. All counted, their unmitigated interest and concerns spiked the growth of this comprehensive educational system from 95 institutions and some 14,000 enrollees in 1946 to, by the beginning of the 1970s, approximately 67,000 children in 330 schools, within nearly every Jewish community larger than 7,500. Although these yeshivas, too, experienced some defections from their ranks, their graduates on the whole stood as a continuing, if not burgeoning, vanguard of a resistant Orthodoxy through the succeeding decades of the late twentieth century.[40]

Early and anxious to take the lead, in 1941 rabbis Elya Meir Bloch and Chaim Mordecai Bloch "brought Telshe to Cleveland," as one devoted follower described their community's arduous journey from western Russia, through Siberia, to Japan, and over to Seattle, Washington, before they restarted their lives and their yeshiva in an Ohio suburb. Two years later, Rabbi Aaron Kotler, late of the famed Kletzk Yeshiva in Poland, made it to the United States after a comparable escape from tyrannies. Almost immediately, he created his advanced yeshiva in Lakewood, a rural New Jersey community. In 1946, the students and rabbis of the Mirrer yeshiva settled in Brooklyn. Its leaders, Rabbi Eliezer Yehudah Finkel and his son-in-law Rabbi Chaim Leib Shmuelevitz, had taken their wartorn community to Shanghai, China, where they found temporary refuge. After the war, a portion of the school reassembled itself in Jerusalem, while other refugees gained admittance to the United States. In the subsequent decade, the Kamenetz Yeshiva, now of Brooklyn, Beth ha-Talmud Rabbinical College, also in that borough, and the Talmudical Academy of Philadelphia, also boasting of "advanced yeshiva" status and orientation, all sank their roots in American soil.[41]

All of these institutions promoted within their devotees a studied social and cultural separatism from American life that far transcended the hopes of the nineteenth-century founders of downtown New York's old Etz Chaim. Kotler's choice of a venue for Torah in Lakewood, far removed from the assimilatory influences of the metropolis, was in this regard a particularly inspired move. Even more than Mendlowitz's efforts within interwar Brooklyn, these groups de-emphasized the utilitarian or careerist mission of training rabbis. Rather, they prayed that their American-based Talmudic scholars would keep alive the ideal East European tradition of "Torah for its own sake," garnering for them in this country what would have been the lamented Lithuanian Jewry's highest accolades. Rabbi Kotler and his compatriots instilled in their disciples a palpable élan, a confident style and pose, that further reinforced the power of their schools' messages. These sacred values informed the elementary and secondary feeder school system that provided rarefied bastions of advanced yeshiva study such as "Lakewood" with the best mature and focused disciples.[42]

Hasidic groups, products too of the horrific dislocations of World War II, established their own enduring presences. Hasidic groups were not unknown in this country in prior generations. Back at the turn of the century, followers of Rabbis Segal and Vidrowitz had plagued Rabbi Jacob Joseph. In the 1930s, the M'lochim had affected Hasidic lifestyles. But a new era opened, in 1941, when Rabbi Joseph Isaac Schneersohn, the leader of the Lubavitch sect, made Brooklyn's Crown Heights section his home, beginning a process that led thousands of wartime and postwar Russian Hasidic refugees to that locality. In 1947, Hungarian Satmar Rebbe Joel Teitelbaum and his devotees settled in Williamsburg. In many instances, these newcomers replaced the more Americanized Orthodox Jews who were leaving the physically declining neighborhood for other Brooklyn localities or the suburbs. Comparable groups from Romania, Hungary, and Galicia followed their own leaders to the United States, residing in close proximity to one another, seemingly, as always, within Brooklyn's long-standing Orthodox heartland.

It has been said that "members of [Hasidic] courts," be they from Klausenberg to Belz to Munkac to Vizhnitz, among other vicinities, "that had once sprawled from Bratislava to Odessa were now located a few streets from one another or only a brief car ride apart."[43]

As they became ensconced in their respective enclaves, each set up its network of congregations, self-help institutions, and certainly their own yeshivas even as, over time, the propinquity of Hasidic turfs often exacerbated ideological tensions among the sects. These disputes might have been lost on outsiders, except when devotees literally fought with one another on city streets. Contentions between Hasidic courts had been very common back in Europe, but in the past, the canards, excoriations, and bans that were issued were received or ignored from safe distances. Not so in Brooklyn, where most noticeably, Lubavitcher and Satmar militants battled, for example, over the former's extension of outreach, Jewish-proselytizing activities into Satmar's hub. Satmar Hasidim, who proudly saw themselves as the most pious Jews on earth, perceived these emissaries as insolent intruders. Indeed, the question of which group was more devout—which was more the keeper of Jewish tradition—frequently put Satmar and Lubavitcher at loggerheads over the crucial religious issues of Zionism. Satmar Hasidim stood out as vocal and unmitigated opponents of the existence of the Jewish State. Like their cousins, the Niturei Karta in Israel, they rejected any accommodation whatsoever with Zionism—for them it is an apostate form of Judaism—as they projected themselves as the only true-to-tradition Jews remaining in the world. While Lubavitchers often have had profound problems with secularism in Israel, for them the Jewish State is a religiously acceptable reality. Still, for all their internecine differences—not to mention their distinctive types of East European dress, language, and customs—Lubavitchers, Satmarers, and the other America-based Hasidic courts or sects shared a dedication with their advanced yeshiva-world counterparts to prevent the Americanization of their youth.[44]

The followers of Rabbi Joseph Breuer, refugees from Frankfurt am Main who settled predominantly around him in Washington Heights in the late 1930s, were no less determined to transplant their European ways. Yeshiva education for them, too, was the pedagogic modality. However, given their German Neo-Orthodox heritage, their schools and community did not necessarily have to espouse and to live the unyielding separatism so characteristic of their Lithuanian yeshiva and Hasidic counterparts. They were the descendants and disciples of that great nineteenth-century Orthodox rabbi, Samson Raphael Hirsch, who had preached the doctrine of *Torah im Derekh Eretz,* the integration of a Torah-driven life style with the cultural ways of that land. This ideal had translated itself into his community's adoption of the dress code, language, and other social mores of its host society—without gainsaying most of Jewish traditions — all toward the goal of achieving full emancipation and ultimately public acceptance. In transposing their particular ancestral values to this country, they conceivably could have made common cause with the integrationist approach to America and the positive appreciation of secular studies at Yeshiva University. Its uptown university campus was situated just across Broadway in Upper Manhattan from Breuer's yeshiva. However, early in its U.S. experience, the Breuer community aligned itself with the transplanted Lithuanian yeshiva world. That meant, in the pedagogic realm, that educators from the "world of the Mirrer and Telshe yeshivas" would stand in front of their children's classes imparting to a new American-born generation "a negative attitude toward secular education."[45]

But even as all of these newcomers' zeal for their Old World lifestyles clearly exceeded that of earlier resisters, a fortuitous set of conditions and circumstances in postwar America enabled their stances. First, these immigrants benefited from the presence, upon their arrival, of that small yeshiva community of long standing. The Telshe group owed a special debt of gratitude for their very physical survival and presence here to none other than Bernard Revel, whose philosophy of cultural synthesis they would soon roundly criticize. As a loyal alumnus of Telshe, Revel reportedly had "a special place in his heart for the yeshiva." So in 1940, not long before his death, Revel responded to the pleadings of rabbis Bloch and Katz, and extended himself to facilitate the provision of immigration affidavits supporting the settlement of pious refugee scholars in this country.[46]

As yeshiva-world contingents settled in the United States, they naturally coalesced with the extant Torah Vodaath–Chaim Berlin group. Their initial liaison was within the Vaad ha-Hatzala Rescue Committee as they joined forces with the old Agudath ha-Rabbanim in a valiant, if largely unsuccessful, effort to move the reluctant hand of the American government to respond to the extermination of Jews in Nazi-occupied Europe. Perhaps this group's most evocative action took place either in 1940 or 1941, when two Brooklyn Orthodox activists, under the imprimatur of rabbis Moses Feinstein, Shraga Mendlowitz, and Shlomo Heiman, also of Torah Vodaath, drove around the wealthier sections of Flatbush on a Saturday to solicit badly needed funds. For Rabbi Boruch Kaplan, a founder of the Beth Yaacov schools in this country and Mendlowitz's son-in-law Rabbi Sender Lichner, their seeming violating of Sabbath strictures was far from a transgression; they were acting appropriately, within the spirit and letter of the halacha, to save lives in a critical emergency. The sight of these pious Jews in their cars on the holy day made clear to all how desperate the situation was for their doomed brethren. The Vaad's best-known event, its October 1943 March on Washington, brought hundreds of its rabbis to the nation's capital. Meanwhile, behind the scenes and behind the lines, through bribery and other clandestine negotiations, the

Vaad acted on its own — without the support of the American government and other Jewish group support — to liberate fellow Jews from the Nazis, with a particular emphasis on saving their Torah-committed community.[47]

At almost the same moment in 1944, on the domestic front, in a move possessed of the broadest future implications, Kotler joined with Mendlo-witz to create the National Society for Hebrew Day Schools, better know as Torah Umesorah. Here, too, rabbinical representatives of older and newer resistant organizations cooperated to promote yeshiva education in Amer-ica as the most enduring communal response to the stark destruction that they were witnessing in Europe. This vibrant organization initially focused on the funding and development of separatist yeshivas and Beth Yaacov schools. But soon thereafter, the organization, often utilizing faculty mem-bers recruited from the old Brooklyn yeshiva base, extended its purview into the modern day-school world, both within and outside New York. In these latter initiatives, Torah Umesorah made some strategic accommodations toward those whom they sought to woo toward strict observance.

For example, in 1947, Rabbi Kotler demanded that Yiddish be the sole language of inculcating tradition. "Mass assimilation," he declared "among the gentiles will result if we utilize the language of the land. Our Jewish children will then emulate non-Jewish practice." Through that pronounce-ment he went much further than the long-standing Agudath ha-Rabbanim had ever gone in opposing this basic aspect of Americanization. But most likely, he was speaking only about how youngsters from his core yeshiva-world families should be trained. For the National Society approved of — with Kotler's affirmative nod — a multilingual approach to Torah education. English, Hebrew, and Yiddish would be countenanced, with English used most often when Torah Umesorah attempted to strike roots beyond already fervent, immigrant Orthodox communities. Otherwise, they would simply be unable to communicate with the American youngsters. Similarly, when away from its base, Torah Umesorah grudging accepted co-educational schooling. Here the National Society's leaders recognized that most poten-tial parent bodies in the United States would not support single-sex class-rooms that were the norm in yeshiva-world environments.[48]

Most Hasidic groups operated in their own independent realms in oppos-ing Americanization, drawing their strength and inspiration primarily from their respective *rebbes* [leaders] to whom devotees pledged staunch and often militant allegiance. In fact, more than their yeshiva-world counter-parts and far more than earlier committed Orthodox migrants, Hasidic rank and files followed their leaders from their destroyed European home-land to specific American locales. Unlike poor Rabbi Jacob Joseph of the prior century, Hasidic rebbes did not have to seek out inattentive followers in the United States. They settled together with their flocks and maintained their authority and powers. In many senses, chief rabbinates were now established, albeit with one exception. None of these new immigrant leaders, with the exception of the Jewish-proselytizing Lubavitch sect, ever attempted to extend its purview beyond its pious followers.

Arriving as these fervent Jews did during an era in American history where it became increasingly acceptable to be different in the United States also helped them maintain separatist stances. Whereas earlier generations of yeshiva families struggled with their self-perceptions as "freaks" in the eyes of other Americans, these newcomers rode the crest of an American wave that increasingly viewed unusual groups as exotic or even intriguing. The postwar era witnessed the decline of the "melting pot" ideology that hallowed uniformity and demanded immigrant assimilation — including the abandonment of foreign religious orientations — as a dominant American philosophy, if not as an admission ticket to the United States. In its stead the concept of the "Triple Melting Pot" rose in the late 1940s–1950s, as an ideal understanding of the values of the American people. While its teachings that accorded Judaism equal status as one of this nation's three great religions — along with Protestantism and Catholicism — looked somewhat askance at those who maintained Old World cultures, the broadening outlook bespoke greater tolerance for those who were different. Then in the 1960s, this country was on the cusp of its embrace of cultural pluralism. This ideology, which celebrates the heterogeneity of the groups who came here and calls upon them to maintain much of their distinctiveness, had been argued on the public social and political stage even before World War I. But only in the last half century did diversity of all sorts — with these Jews being as idiosyncratic as Americans come — gain wide acceptance.[49]

Blessed with this favorable atmosphere, these unacculturated Orthodox asserted their right to be different and to be accommodated under American law. Under a reconstituted and reinvigorated American wing of the Agudath Israel in America, they battled, for example, to have the legal barriers that undermined the observance of the Sabbath removed as an economic burden. The year 1962 was a particularly good one for those who championed "Orthodox self-determination" as the centuries-old Blue Laws came down in New York State. Reportedly, Governor Nelson Rockefeller was duly impressed with a "sincere demand by religious Jews to regain their rights as citizens and to be permitted to observe the religion to which they were personally committed." Emboldened, they pressed successfully during the next few years, as many erstwhile newcomers became citizens and gained the right to vote to use a focused power at the ballot boxes, to have the state and city governments "arrange an alternate date for a *Shomer Shabbos* to take his Civil Service examination when it is scheduled on a Saturday." A similar enabling piece of legislation, the DeSalvio Bill ended "discrimination against Sabbath observers in scheduling examinations in public colleges." "Orthodoxy's flexing of its political muscles" was felt in other targeted states—Pennsylvania, Ohio, and Michigan—as well as through the federal government's Fair Employment Practices Commission. Perhaps as significant, advocates of Agudath Israel quickly lined up, when they were permitted, for government aid to their parochial schools. In this venue, they did not worry about any implicit abridgement of the hallowed constitutional doctrine of church–state separation. The Agudah's priority was the securing of monies to support their form of a separating school system.[50]

For the Agudah's most experienced political hands, this use of government for parochial Jewish purposes was not only a result of a wise reading of how the American system operated, how well-placed electoral clout could be brought to bear in pursuing specific goals. This stratagem also reflected the Agudah's recent past in interwar Poland where their movement had been a regular political party. There in a nonintegrationist Eastern Europe, they had defended Jewish communal rights and prerogatives against unsympathetic governments and antisemitic forces.[51]

Hungarian Hasidic groups—notwithstanding their European Agudist pedigrees—were not nearly as attuned to the dynamics of secular American politics. However, by the later 1960s, as they too became citizens and possessed the franchise, their potential to swing elections was not lost on local politicians who actively courted their votes. In 1972, for example, Satmar Hasidim of Williamsburg, these most exclusivist of Jews, were easily convinced that they had an uncommon affinity with a Roman Catholic Congressional incumbent whom they preferred over two Jewish candidates. Hon. John Rooney lined up with them on key social policy questions. As a devout religious man, he, like his constituents, opposed abortion and supported government aid to parochial schools. They, who had lived under Soviet tyranny, shared his anticommunist leanings. The Jewish candidates, most especially the renowned anti-Vietnam War activist Allard Lowenstein, opposed conservative political views. Perhaps most important, in his post as chair of a House subcommittee, Rooney routinely assisted Hasidic relatives gain admission to the United States. Given these choices, on no less a day for personal introspection, Yom Kippur [September 1972], the day before a special election was to be held, Satmar officials made it clearly known in their shtibls that their followers were to vote for Rooney. The next day, their man triumphed overwhelmingly.

As the election returns came in, the Rooney camp was far from surprised. Some four years earlier, during a reapportionment struggle, another Jewish candidate had distributed siddurs in the district in a blatant effort to get out "his" group's vote. Rooney's response was to distribute a wedding picture of his Jewish opponent and his gentile wife leaving a church. No comment needed to be appended to that graphic. In future years, another political picture would loom large in metropolitan electoral activities. No New York campaign would be complete without every contending candidate having his or her promotional literature distributed in Brooklyn and elsewhere containing a shot of the aspirant receiving a good-luck dollar bill from a smiling Lubavitcher Rebbe. This currency was no mystical amulet. It was a clear message to the faithful that the politician was worthy of their vote. When this charismatic leader explicitly identified the man or woman he preferred, his legions dutifully followed his directions.[52]

These focused forces — especially the Agudists — were even more aggressive in asserting that their separatist, uncompromising religious ways and attitudes were the only proper Orthodox response to the diverse American Jewish world and pressing world Jewish realities around them. So disposed, these super-resisters could even criticize some of the stances of the old Agudath ha-Rabbanim, particularly its long-standing Religious Zionist orientation. The force of mid twentieth-century world events, especially the Holocaust, precluded the Agudists' total opposition to the State of Israel as a sovereign refuge haven for Jews. Still, they — unlike Mizrachiites — called for Orthodox Jews to chart their own separatist roles in essentially building up an Israel "in accordance with the Torah and the guidance of the sages," with little cooperation extended to its secular government. In time, certainly as of the late 1950s, as the Agudath ha-Rabbanim's own presidium fell under the Council's sway, this political position became normative within the entire resistant rabbinate.[53]

On the domestic front, when it came to the Americanized Orthodox, Agudists were consistently antagonistic to, and sometimes downright disrespectful of, the stances and leaders of the Orthodox Union, the Rabbinical Council of America, and of Yeshiva University. In 1956, the Council of Torah Sages of the Agudath Israel went beyond its routine reviling to demand that these accommodationists cease cooperation of any sort with non-Orthodox Jewish leaders. Eager to assert its ideological hegemony, the Council of Sages proclaimed a ban, under the signature of rabbis Kotler and Feinstein, Rabbi Yaacov Ruderman of Baltimore's Ner Israel, and leaders from Torah Vodaath against continued Orthodox participation in the Synagogue Council of America. When formed in 1926, this umbrella communal organization that brought together rabbis and lay leaders from all Jewish movements had addressed religious problems common to all who were then struggling to bring disinterested American Jews into the congregations of their choice. However, after World War II, the Synagogue Council focused its attention exclusively on the protection of Jews both here and abroad against outside threats. Still, for the Council of Sages, such cooperative efforts were "forbidden by the sacred law of our Torah" because they suggested Orthodox recognition of their Conservative and Reform colleagues' deviant theological understandings of Judaism. Four years later, the long-standing Agudath ha-Rabbanim seconded this condemnation of cooperation when it threatened forfeiture of membership to any of its members who belonged to the Synagogue Council or the like-constituted New York Board of Rabbis. With an eye to telling Orthodox Union and Rabbinical Council of America members how to behave, it declared similarly that "all Orthodox rabbis must also resign from the Board of Rabbis."[54]

The 1956 ban sorely tested the accommodationist commitments of Rabbinical Council members. True, Dr. Belkin and Rabbi Soloveitchik would not support the ban. Two years before the controversial proclamation, Soloveitchik had stated in no uncertain terms that "when representation of Jews and Jewish interest *k'lapei chutz* [toward the outside world] are involved, all groups and movements must be united. There can be no divisiveness in this area." In a most poignant statement on the need for Jewish unity against hostile gentile forces, Soloveitchik had stated emotionally that in "the crematoria, the ashes of Hasidim and *Anshe Maseh* [pious Jews] were mixed with the ashes of radicals and free thinkers and we must fight against the enemy who does not recognize the difference between one who worships and one who does not." Dr. Belkin made his own definitive statement when he appeared with Dr. Nelson Glueck, President of the Hebrew Union College and Dr. Louis Finkelstein of the Jewish Theological Seminary, at the fortieth annual dinner celebration of the newly controversial Synagogue Council of America. But on the other hand, two of Yeshiva University's other revered refugee rabbinical scholars, Rabbi Dovid Lifshitz and Rabbi Mendel Zaks, had signed on to the Kotler–Feinstein declaration. Ultimately, most Rabbinical Council members stood with Rabbi Soloveitchik and Dr. Belkin. Similarly, the Orthodox Union also stayed the course over the long haul, even though, at that critical moment in 1956, the organization's president, Rabbi David Hollander, himself a Yeshiva Rabbi Isaac Elchanan graduate, argued that that his organization had no choice but to submit to what he characterized as a higher Torah law. In dissenting from Soloveitchik's opinion, this American-trained rabbi effectively admitted that the newly transplanted East European Orthodoxy that hallowed separatism and disdained even social concessions possessed a greater legitimacy than the Torah he had learned at the "Rav's" feet. Although Hollander's position never acquired the majority necessary to shift Rabbinical Council policy, these Torah sages' uncompromising attitudes had detached, from the Americanized Orthodox rabbinate, after a generation of struggle for independence that began with its break from the old Agudath ha-Rabbanim, colleagues who were willing to surrender their religious autonomy to a group of immigrant rabbis.[55]

Rabbi Soloveitchik's position on this pivotal question did little to endear him to the new era of arch-resisters. But then again, by the early 1960s, on so many fronts, he was the touchstone counterweight to the views of all opponents of accommodation. His impeccable credentials as a Torah scholar only heightened the frustration and animosity that his critics harbored against him. In 1962, what he represented and they resented was put on public display when an effort was made to humiliate Soloveitchik at the funeral of Aaron Kotler. In keeping with tradition, the Yeshiva standard bearer was prepared to join all of those within the yeshiva world in eulogizing this major Torah figure. But while the Satmar Rebbe and Rabbi Moses Feinstein were among the half-dozen Torah leaders tendered this honor and religious responsibility, Soloveitchik was denied the opportunity to speak. In many ways, this affront anticipated the tensions that would characterize a contemporary era in which so many Orthodox Jews who are united in the dedication to faithfully follow the fundamental teachings of the halacha have confronted one another in a variety of arenas. These internecine battles would take place during an era where living a life as a pious Jew became easier than ever before in American Jewish history.[56]

# COMFORTABLE AND COURTED

The close of the twentieth century witnessed constant improvements in conditions for the maintenance of staunch Jewish religious commitments in America. This very good news for those faithful followers who persisted within Orthodoxy's tent was due largely to their own economic advancement coupled with some communal political initiatives during a culturally pluralistic era in this country. The devout — of all faiths — were often lauded for their reverence. As the new millennium opened, these Jews resided comfortably as a respected minority in the United States. They could dress the way they chose without the slightest fear that neighbors would pass negative or threatening comments about appearing un-American. Elite institutions that had previously looked askance at Jews welcomed Orthodox participants. Moreover, those pious Jews who had become affluent — by dint either of business acumen or professional achievement — were often courted as honored consumers by producers, operators, and entrepreneurs of all sorts ready to accommodate their religious needs.

Consider, to begin with, the lack of religious tension in the life of the son of the Sabbath-working garment industry employee whom I profiled at the outset of this book. This baby boomer has been able, throughout his adult life, to be completely observant of the Sabbath. Setting aside for a moment his own inherited religious values to which he still devoutly subscribes, this professional, a day-school graduate who went on to earn a Ph.D. in communications, has long been able to set his work schedule with all due reverence for Jewish tradition in the educational research field where he is an internationally known leader. His physician-wife, likewise, another day-school success story, neither considers, nor is pressured, to violate the Sabbath. Commenting not on this specific case per se but on the observable general tenor of their times, one contemporary sociologist has remarked that "whereas at the beginning of the [twentieth] century, many Jews were in occupations which made it extremely difficult for them, economically, to observe the Sabbath, today the five-day work week is the norm." He and another colleague have further argued that what they characterized as a "resurgence of Orthodoxy" — among the minority of American Jews who have remained committed to that understanding of Judaism — "has, at least in part, been made possible by virtue of some of the social benefits of the . . . post-industrial era including . . . the shortened work week," and "the liberation of youth from the necessity of work."[1]

In the unlikely event that any potential employer or supervisor might seek to undermine the traditional values of people such as this professional couple, such an antagonist might well find himself or herself up against a mature Orthodox defense establishment that has chalked up an impressive track record of protecting its clients' interests. For more than forty years, since 1965, the National Jewish Commission on Law and Public Affairs, an independent group of "Orthodox laymen, mostly lawyers," has championed the cause of Sabbath-observant Jews whose rights have been abridged. Like their Agudist counterparts, whose incipient efforts they initially emulated, this organization has largely fulfilled the previously unrealized dreams of Sabbath-observer associations that date back more than a century, to Bernard Drachman, Philip Hillel Klein, and Ramaz Margolies. In one effort, typical of many and remarkable only because it touched close to home, some twenty-five years ago this group of activists took on and won a settlement for my brother, when he was unfairly fired from a television news producer's job — an industry that is open seven days a week — for refusing to work on the Sabbath. Giving voice to his position, the commission's representatives made it clear that he was more than ready to trade shifts with gentile colleagues to allow him to have Saturday off.[2]

Employment or career situations do exist where the switching of work times cannot be effectuated. Not every conflict between Orthodoxy's and America's clock and calendar may ever be totally reconciled even in a tolerant host society. Take, for instance, the predicament of those who wish to be "in front of the camera," to be on-the-air news personalities in unalterable prime-time situations. Or consider the young men or women who dream of being observant Broadway performers, opera singers, or big-time sports stars. In each case, the show or curtain rises or the game begins at its appointed time on Sabbath and holidays. While an accepting America is today inured to granting all Jews who desire a pass, or absence, if they choose to observe their High Holidays, the harsh, unyielding economic realities within these amusements and entertainments — and other lines of endeavor — preclude all but the most exceptional and demanding talent from taking off every Friday night and Saturday.

To use sports and observance as the metaphor, it has been more than forty years since American baseball fans, owners, and teammates understood Sandy Koufax's feeling that Yom Kippur was no time for him to toe the pitcher's mound, even if it was during the World Series. This country had come a long way since 1934 when his hometown Detroit and their roaring Tigers demanded that Hank Greenberg compete on the High Holidays. It would be another thing entirely, however, for a contemporary elite southpaw or slugger to find a spot on a roster if he required having Friday night and Saturdays off every week. Wimbledon and the U.S Open Tennis also are not about to alter their traditional Saturday men's semifinals and women's finals competitions.[3]

Notwithstanding these significant barriers, an observant Orthodox Jew almost became vice president of the United States in 2000. In this most rarified case, Sen. Joseph Lieberman's clearly stated position that he would not work on his day of rest while in office — except to protect the country; to save lives in a stark emergency, which is permitted under the halacha — resonated well with many American voters who were impressed with his strong commitment to traditional religious values.[4]

Lieberman and many other Jews who share his religious values fit comfortably within this country's economy, politics, or culture. As just indicated, they have adroitly navigated the rising crests of a flourishing affinity for cultural pluralism that flows through this land. To cite but another prime example of contemporary comfort levels, observant Orthodox students who attend prestigious universities that historically had been unwelcoming to all Jews, but especially nasty to religiously committed ones, today live well and unencumbered on campuses. For example, a major turning point in Princeton University's attitudes and policies took place in 1971 when "Kosher Stevenson," a dining club that followed Jewish dietary laws, opened in its midst. Situated on Prospect Avenue, it was on the very thoroughfare that had long housed the elite undergraduate eating establishments that, in prior decades, had systematically excluded Jews from membership. Princeton's earlier practices had earned it a dark reputation as "among the traditionally most inhospitable if not outright anti-Semitic of Ivy League colleges." In the decade that followed the university's change in dining protocols, Princeton was additionally helpful in assisting "the most Orthodox students . . . remain scrupulous in their observance." By 1985, a trip to an accommodating registrar's office was all a student had to do to "reschedule exams that fall on the Sabbath and holidays." That same year witnessed the rescheduling of the first day of sessions in recognition of Rosh ha-Shanah; a move that almost all Jewish students appreciated. One "*kipah*-wearing" student who noted that moment of change in university procedures reported that in his opinion, "if anything, I think the university . . . bends over backwards to be nice to us," at an institution where "there's a Gemara [Talmud] class [and] there's a religious group of students that have a minyan three times a day."[5]

Still, there were limits to the religious accommodations to which highly committed Orthodox students had become accustomed to at this country's foremost universities. In 1997, most notably, an aggressive group of activists — whom the media would soon dub the "Yale Five" — found out just how far they could push their alma mater to meet their religious needs when they moved for a level of entitlement that would have been unfathomable in prior eras at the Ivy League school. When they asserted themselves, they would find the college's administration unwilling to countenance what, for Yale officials — many of whom were also Jews — smacked of patently unreasonable demands.

By the 1990s, those Jewish Yalies who cared to live pious lives on campus had been privileged for more than a generation to have their food as well as their Sabbath and holiday requirements met at their school. Apart from the flourishing Jewish studies program there — which attracted more than just observant students to its formal curricula — ample opportunities existed for the devout to pursue Talmudic and other religious text learning on their own within the academic community. University officials, notwithstanding some slipups or individual insensitivities, hewed devoutly to a policy of "compassion" toward these committed students, a policy that started to come into vogue in the late 1950s. Here, as at Princeton, until that era of change Yale had its own long and less than distinguished record of suggesting to devout Jewish students that in opting for their school they were seeking seats in "the wrong pew." With barriers in effect, few such students had ventured toward that institution.[6]

Now, however, within a new generation of very observant Jewish undergraduates who were so comfortable at Yale, there was an outspoken cadre that wanted more from the school. Their complaint was that the institution required all unmarried undergraduate freshmen and sophomores to reside in on-campus dormitories, forcing them to cope with co-educational living conditions that offended their religious definitions of chastity and modesty.

Yale demurred; the residential experience within a university community, it contended, celebrates diversity and seeks to undermine all forms of segregation—whether externally imposed or internally dictated. Dormitory living is "a central part of Yale education."

Those in charge averred that no one was out to force devout students to violate the halacha in their personal lifestyles. Dorm authorities could point, for example, to their willingness to provide those who cared with "alternatives to electronic keys on the Shabbat," as using the regular key card on the holy days would constitute a religious violation comparable to turning on the lights. Tolerant school policy also allowed for the use of the Yale meal plan — which every student had to purchase — at the Hillel House's kosher kitchen. No one was suggesting that while in their rooms or on the floors that students abandon their own determinations of what modesty entails. However, in its view, residential regulations would not be abridged just because others "traips[ed] around on the way to the bathroom." Besides which, Yale made it clear that the complainants knew the policies long before these students arrived on campus. The only loophole "relief" for those who felt offended was for the students to pay the $7,000 residential fee and then live off campus, which of course, would add to the onerous tuition burden that undergraduates and their families already bore.

As this dispute proceeded, one of the protesters found another way around the regulations: she married her fiancé in a civil marriage. Then it became the "Yale Four" and their married sister who sued the university, with off-campus support from lawyers and advocates associated with the National Jewish Commission on Law and Public Affairs, the Agudath Israel, the Orthodox Union and a complement of other sympathetic Orthodox organizations. Also acting in character, as part of the then ongoing culture wars in this country, Christian conservative spokespeople such as Phyllis Schlafly were struck by what they saw as another example of odious political correctness on campus, and tendered support for youngsters who had put themselves on the line for "chastity, decency, and modesty." Her remarks were but another example of contemporary cooperative efforts that linked fervent Orthodox Jews with devout Catholics and fundamentalist Protestants on pressing American social issues ranging from right-to-life campaigns to anti-gay rights crusades to advocacy for the mounting of crèches and menorahs in public squares, to even prayer in schools. Seemingly, in pursuit now of an expanded religious mission to see that not only all Jews live according to the halacha but that society in general conform to "strengthened religious values," Orthodox Jewish activists struck remarkable alliances. Setting aside — at least in these venues — deeply held theological antipathies toward Christianity and millennia-old memories of mutual animosities, these traditional Jews entered into common causes with observant gentiles. To the dismay, however, of this Judeo-Christian coalition and of the Yale Orthodox petitioners, the university prevailed both in the initial court proceedings and in subsequent appeals that dragged on for four years. The judges were ultimately most impressed with the argument that Yale's dorm policies should have come as no surprise to these students when they applied to Yale, particularly since there were other schools available where single-sex housing was an option in campus living.[7]

While Yale and the specific students involved moved on after this struggle ran its protracted course, the incident revealed some fault lines within Orthodoxy's pious constituency. The protestors' activities did not receive unanimous approbation from among those within the Orthodox community who were as dedicated as they were to such halachic basics as Sabbath observance and the following of dietary principles. Even within Yale's own community of committed Orthodox Jews, there was a sense that the activists had overstepped their boundaries. An alternate view was that it was entirely possible to "live within the restrictions of modesty . . . attainable at the dorms," as reportedly a "clear majority of Orthodox Jews at Yale" did comfortably. In some critics' darker moments, there was an articulated view that the Yale Five were not merely at odds with the school but were also implicitly criticizing the actions of their confreres, who lived observant lives in the co-ed environment without feeling compromised, as "not as Orthodox as some would have them be." For one Jewish observer, what was happening at Yale was just the latest chapter in their own culture wars that pitted, "ultra-religious Jews . . . and the modern Orthodox Jew," where "there is no position more comfortable than being 'more Orthodox' than thou."[8]

On the other hand, one staunch supporter of the Yale Five used his bully pulpit, both in another Jewish newspaper forum and subsequently in his blog, to criticize those "Modern Orthodox, including rabbis, who are unsympathetic to the claim advanced by the Yale students" for their "shame-[ful] . . . example of how when they are forced to choose between the imperatives of modernity and Torah standards, they go with the crowd and abandon the latter."[9]

However, whatever their disagreements regarding dormitory domesticity, there have been no splits within the ranks of pious Jews when opponents have attempted to undermine their rights to live how and where they choose off campus. Ironically, during this era of unparalleled American toleration, those committed to strictly observant lifestyles have faced their greatest residential difficulties not from antisemites but from co-religionists who have resisted Orthodox incursions into their own neighborhoods. The prevalent mode of attack in these implicitly expressed, if discriminatory campaigns, have been appeals by fellow Jews to local governments to prohibit the construction of eruvs in their backyards. These wires — hung from telephone poles in designated areas to transform, in halachic terms, public domains into private ones—are the single most important physical per-quisite for the growth of a contemporary Orthodox community. As such, they have become the flash points for intra-Jewish battles royale.

Far more important than allowing the carrying of talis bags on the Sab-bath—Rabbi Segal's followers, it will be recalled, accustomed themselves to this practice a hundred years ago on the Lower East Side—the eruv allows young parents to push baby carriages around their neighborhood on the Sabbath. Such a religiously approved accommodation inestimably enhances the quality of pious life on the holy day. Mothers and fathers are not cooped up at home with their toddlers but can easily stroll to services and pray together as a family, albeit on opposite sides of a mechitza. It also facilitates easy socializing and the sharing of meals among families who reside across the streets and down the blocks from each other. An eruv even makes so simple an act as carrying a house key in the streets permissible. It is not the weight of an object that makes any differences under the halacha. In prior generations, when most locales did not have an eruv set up, an ingenuous observant man might purchase a specially designed tie clasp and "wear" his key to shul or elsewhere. A woman could do likewise with her stylish and utilitarian key-brooch. Now, no contemporary suburban Orthodox syn-agogue or community intent on growing can really be without its eruv. Realtors know this, as do fledgling congregations, both of whom are sure to advertise the availability of a community eruv to all comers. "In a heated real estate market," a Sharon, Massachusetts, real estate agent has observed, "the eruv is a pocket-buster for some, adding as much as 10 percent to the price of a home. . . . particularly if the home is close to the synagogue." But to her customers, there is nothing greater than "the peace of mind it brings, knowing that religious laws can be followed with ease and surety." Once that signal marker is in place and a committed contingent begins to grow, the locale will soon thereafter sprout an increased number of shuls, all within walking distance of the homes of members. Unlike other suburban syna-gogue-goers, they will not ride to services on the Sabbath. In addition, these dense Orthodox enclaves will typically boast of a modern mikveh, as well as a slew of rabbinically approved kosher eateries, including the almost om-nipresent pizza and falafel shop, that ready kosher hangout for observant teenagers.[10]

However, with these incursions—which start with those wires whose pres-ence is often not even readily noticeable—come some immense collateral problems, at least in the minds and hearts of those who have engendered eventual "Jew vs. Jew" confrontations, as one Jewish journalist has aptly called these public struggles. The expressed fears are that the "immigration by the Orthodox" will "radically alter the diverse" character of the towns.

The newcomers, it is alleged, carry with them an "air of separateness," if not "superiority." They create "segregation," as it is alleged that they "don't allow their kids to play with kids who aren't Orthodox." They are prone to create unwanted "foot traffic in S.U.V. heaven by walking to synagogue and steering clear of everything from shopping to kiddie sports leagues." During the struggle over an eruv in Tenafly, New Jersey, which for more than five years roiled a "family feud between Orthodox and non-Orthodox Jews," one City Council member went so far as to evoke an eventual nightmare scenario in which someday the "Ultra-Orthodox" Jews might "stone cars that drive down the streets on the Sabbath." Here a cruel irony for one outspoken observant Jew who felt the weight of that attack was that while he could have "purchased a home and moved into a neighborhood perceived as an Orthodox neighborhood," it was precisely his family's search "for a more diverse community" that had brought them over the George Washington Bridge. Had he been interrogated, he would have made it clear that he had absolutely no interest in transforming an American suburb into a homogeneous and intolerant replica of Jerusalem's Meah Shearim, where rock-throwing incidents punctuate hateful confrontations between Israeli ultra-Orthodox and secular. Still, to other Jews in Tenafly, the tightly constructed and expanding enclave was not the type of "diverse community" within which they had been comfortable.[11]

However, it was the Orthodox Jews' "lesser stake in the public schools" that troubled other Jews the most. Jews who were committed to public education worried that when toddlers from devout families were ready for school, their parents in Tenafly, like Orthodox counterparts elsewhere, would studiously avoid sending them to the local public schools. These children were third-generation day-school pupils. Non-Orthodox Jews asserted that as the newcomers acquired homes and replaced householders who in prior years had sent their children to public school, the district's pupil population would decline. The next unhappy condition, as protesters perceived it, would witness educational officials, mandated to balancing statewide school enrollments, pro-actively bussing or bringing into the neighborhood minority students who resided in surrounding urban locales. According to those who initially feared the Orthodox demographic growth, the public schools would ultimately decline in educational quality. In other words, Jewish suburbanites who left cities in search of the right educational experience for their children would find themselves on the losing end of social-planning dynamics. Meanwhile, Orthodox newcomers would contentedly raise their children in their own, religious day schools. As one speaker warned at a tension-filled Tenafly town meeting, which was called to discuss the eruv and the community's fate, "Just take a look at Teaneck." Such construction precipitated the growth of a predominantly observant

Orthodox community. "Teaneck was beautiful . . . Teaneck had beautiful stores. Almost every store in Teaneck today is geared toward the Orthodox. There is racial imbalance in the school system in Teaneck because most of the Orthodox children go to yeshivas. . . . Who's left in the Teaneck school system but those children [who] cannot afford to go to a private school." To head off this feared eventuality, the petitioner called upon neighbors and officials to join the battle to prohibit an eruv in their backyards.[12]

In other communities, where eruvs already exist, the prophylactic against further expansion of the pious Orthodox presence restricted the number and size of synagogues by required zoning variances. Such was the well-publicized situation and struggle that ensued in Beechwood, Ohio, in the last years of the twentieth century. There, intra-Jewish strife captured city-wide attention. For the old-timers in the Jewish community—who constituted 83 percent of the local population—Beechwood was a second-stop suburb, as most of its residents had first moved out of inner-city Cleveland after World War II and settled in Cleveland Heights. A generation or so later, they moved again. One of the prime motivating factors in the pulling up of stakes once more was the decline of neighborhood schools, a circumstance that they lay prominently at the doorstep of the staunchly Orthodox who followed them to Cleveland Heights. Those who were affiliated with the Telshe Yeshiva and those who sent their children to the modern local day school both disdained public schools. These Orthodox expansionists also did not support raising school tax levies. In time, this Orthodox enclave in rapid formation, complete with its stores, schools, and other institutions, would carry the rather unflattering moniker of "Rue de Peyes." (Peyes is the Yiddish word for earlocks that distinguish very devout Jewish males from others.) For the disaffected, as Cleveland Heights's educational system and neighborhood declined and its Orthodox presence soared, Beechwood was a fine next step in family migrations. Eventually, Jews took over a community that once housed nary a Jew. In any event, by the mid-1990s, in their view, separatist Jews once again were following their footsteps.

As a true harbinger of their incipient neighborhood hegemony, these newcomers tendered proposals to the local zoning committee to permit the construction of a synagogue–school–mikveh "campus." Committed Orthodox Jews of several stripes, from Young Israelites, to Lubavitchers, to supporters of the all-girls' Yavne High School who differed on many theological and sociological nuances, joined hands in an initiative. (A discussion of Orthodoxy's own internecine disagreements will follow in the next chapter.) But such a plan required significant accommodations in zoning policies, a decision that the majority of Jews in town roundly opposed.

As combatants took sides, not only were there hard words exchanged about the school issue, but bad neighborhood blood also spurted out as protestors recalled alleged unkind remarks that Orthodox Jews had made about their neighbors' lack of fidelity to tradition. References were made on the street to nasty proclamations that the Agudists and other of their ilk were saying about non-Orthodox forms of Judaism back in their parochial home base of New York. At any rate, the Jewish longer-term residents of Beechwood who felt aggrieved were not about to surrender their community and neighborhoods to those whom they perceived as aggressively Orthodox.[13]

In the Beechwood case, where the issues were put to a plebiscite, the opposition to the Orthodox "campus" prevailed and subsequent court rulings backed up the voters. But, more often than not in eruv cases, advocates from the National Commission on Law and Public Affairs have won, with local assistance. In the Tenafly case, they achieved victory after a five-year struggle that first saw the town council ban on an eruv upheld by a federal judge only to have the United States Court of Appeals reverse the decision. The justices finally determined, as they have generally elsewhere, that the denial of an eruv constituted an abridgement of the litigants' constitutional right to freedom to practice religion. Subsequent to this dispute, abundant fence-mending remained to be done between still-rival Jewish factions. As the Tenafly battle wound down, it remained for Barbara Rooney, a member of the town's Christian minority, to reflect on the sadness of the whole "unfriendly" dispute. Stopped for a comment as she carried her laundry to her car, this householder told a newspaper reporter: "It's caused a lot of friction in this town . . . I'm glad it will be finished, one way or the other. The money spent has been spent in the worst way possible for both sides."[14]

Nonetheless, whenever these devout Orthodox Jews stepped back from their frays — mostly with satisfied smiles from their victories in the courts — they could not help but acknowledge that, in so many other venues, their fundamental way of life had come fully of age. In addition to the economics of the "post-industrial age" and the politics of tolerance and understanding of this era that have elevated their lot, technological advances have also aided them substantially. For example, a most basic device, the "Intermatic Sabbath Clock," an electric timer that "turns lights and appliances on and off without human intervention" has facilitated "lighting and cooking on holy days without violation of sacred laws." Requiring "no further attention; no resetting or adjustment of any kind during the holiday period," it first became available to that ready market of consumers in 1958. For only $9.95, the devout could have a device, equipped with 875 watts of power, that also had some "wonderful uses . . . on ordinary days."[15]

For many families, these timers did, however, bring an end in their wake to a time-honored Jewish–gentile relationship; the accommodating, if usually reliable, neighborhood Shabbes Goy. Once a householder became ac-

Figure 8.1. Advertisement announcing the invention of the "Intermatic Shabbath Clock." *Jewish Life* (April 1958), 2.

customed to the new mechanism, reported one observant husband and father, "the wonderful little time piece [became] our Declaration of Independence from the Shabbos Goy." That is, when its owner finally figured out how to correctly utilize the darned instrument. This same man reported on the following trial and error. "Awakened on a chilly Sabbath morn," he found, "the refrigerator and freezer defrosted, the electric stove cold, and the oil-burner silent and inactive." Apparently, the "clock had turned off more than just the lights." After a dark and cold Sabbath, an electrician was engaged to "untangle the various circuits" and reset the system. It behooved the family to remember every week to disengage the mechanism and "to return . . . lights to normal operations."[16]

It has remained for Orthodox rabbinic decisors, whose opinions families like these respected, to determine the Sabbath Clock's range of functions. There was general agreement that using such a device to turn the lights on and off was permissible. The view was that the invention was the electronic equivalent of the time-honored practice of telling a Shabbes Goy beforehand when to throw the switches that the halacha precludes a Jew from doing on holy days. Besides which, the simple action contributed to enhancing "respect of Sabbath." However, there were significant differences of opinion over whether using a "time clock . . . to reheat (as opposed to 'cook') food on Shabbat" was allowed. (Today, in the first years of the twenty-first century, that procedure is a "one-touch" operation for any owner of a Thermador Built-In Convection Oven. Its users' manual offers special "Setting the Sabbath Mode" instructions for those of "religious faith with 'no work' requirements for the Sabbath.")[17] Here too, those who favored the practice relied on the precedent of Jews instructing gentiles to perform culinary functions, with again the idea in place that "eating hot food on Shabbat" constituted another act of honoring the special nature of the Sabbath. On the other hand, the rabbis strongly prohibited the use of the timer to turn radios or televisions on or off on the holy day or to have those entertainment and news media playing from before the onset of the Sabbath. One ruling in 1959 said that even when "there are times of tension and crisis when one wishes to hear the news . . . listening to the radio is certainly not characterized by or consonant with sanctity in any way and is therefore unbecoming of the Sabbath." Years later, in 1996, a jaundiced rabbi, perturbed over the state of popular American culture, determined that "much of the material being transmitted today over radio and television is forbidden in the Jewish home any time, Shabbos or during the week."[18]

But even as, by the 1960s, the neighborhood Shabbes Goy was becoming a thing of the past, comparable functionaries would return, in future decades, in very different venues. In the last decades of the twentieth century, entrepreneurial kosher caterers began to take over many nonkosher hotels for observant guests willing and able to spend the Jewish holidays away from home. In prior generations — the tradition dates back to as early as second decade of the 1900s — those who possessed both the desire and the means to "go away for the seders" typically sojourned at their own kosher establishments that also were open with accommodations for the summer. Or tour operators made arrangements for some sort of kosher commissary to be available at non-Jewish resorts or vessels that welcomed the minority of pious voyagers. Although some of these old-time hotel outlets survived, more luxurious resorts from all over the world beckoned well-heeled observant Jews enticingly, with hoteliers literally handing over their keys to Jewish entrepreneurs. For some Jews — with distant unhappy family memories — it was a triumphant experience to be so welcome with all of their needs accommodated at fancy establishments that just a few generations earlier had barred their ancestors. A quick perusal of advertisements prior to the 2001 Passover season revealed no less than a score of destinations that promised and promoted Passover with all of the extras.[19]

A tour operator who took over a resort in Colorado Springs told prospective customers that "There were Matzohs in Them Thar Hills." His other glitzy advertised option was "An Escape to the Cape [Cod]." Another entrepreneur boasted that Barcelona, Spain, was the site of his seventeenth "European Pesach," and the venue provided guests with gourmet meals and French wines, complemented with "stimulating lectures." The food both there and at his alternate location, the French Riviera, it was promised, would be scrupulously supervised to insure the highest standards of kashruth.[20]

Sadly for Israeli tourism, that year was particularly successful for Diaspora locales but was difficult for hotels in the Jewish state. Israel was suffering through a period of fearful bombings during the Intifada, a conflagration that scared off many Americans seeking a quiet holiday. Responding to this perceived weak-kneed reaction, many Orthodox congregations and groups — more than any other American Jewish contingents — made it a point of honor and loyalty to support the Israeli economy through missions on Passover and other Jewish holidays. As one Orthodox editorial booster of this action put it: without "lay[ing] a guilt trip on anyone or suggest[ing] that Israel provides a Club Med atmosphere these days, it is rather to suggest that each of us reflect on our own level of commitment to the Jewish state."[21]

In other quarters, displays of Orthodox conspicuous travel consumption — particularly those that were unmitigated by solidarity for Israel — engendered other spiritual concerns. Questioners wondered out loud whether, in fact, "an entire generation of young Jews lives under the impression that going to a five star hotel for Pesach [Passover] is one of the Ten Commandments. For all many of them know, it may be listed as "Thou Shalt Go to Florida (or a similarly warm climate) for Pesach." An equally chagrined critic has chimed in that "it is possible that a whole generation is being raised that will include children who will have never seen Pesach prepara- tions. How sad for them?" To be totally accurate, for several generations, some well-off young girls and their mothers and grandmothers had been thus spared the drudgery of the pre-holiday cleanups that were here roman- ticized. Even before 1920s, complainants were already reminiscing that "in those days of long ago Pesach was a holiday that young and old" — especially women and girls — helped to prepare for even as they advised the Jewish public to "bring that Pesach back . . . prepare for it yourself." But not until the contemporary era have so many done so little to welcome in this holiday. On the other hand, other observers within that same community have be- nignly reported that the Passover migration is an understandable outgrowth of a change in work habits of mothers in the contemporary era. "The entire Pesach industry began to thrive when it became reality that in many house- holds both husband and wife would go out to work and the burden of preparing for Pesach which usually fell completely on the woman was be- coming just too much for her to deal with alone."[22]

It was a remarkably simple matter for them to have their religious needs met from the moment they left home. Kosher airline food — a revolution in its own right when that culinary option first appeared in the 1950s — was always available. A skilled kashruth overseers' blow torch was all that really was needed for the caterer to transform a previously treif hotel kitchen into one suitable for the hordes of observant guests about to descend upon them. The burning out of the unkosher foodstuffs from the ovens, grills, or stoves made these appliances good as new for kosher cooking. Where the new-era Shabbes Goy's services were required was in such roles as running or pressing the buttons in the high-speed elevators that the new high-rise hotels offered, or in assisting guests into their rooms or cabins that could be opened only with halachicly problematic electronic keys. But these all- service resorts and ships were able and anxious to help out. In fact, as of the beginning of the twenty-first century, having an understanding of some of the ins and outs of Sabbath and holiday prohibitions has become part of the on-the-job training of students at some of this country's foremost schools of hotel management. A student who worked an Orthodox holiday event might put that acquired skill on a future job application or resume.[23]

But then again, this was an era in which observant and affluent consumers represented an important niche market. Emulating on the largest of scales an entrepreneurial–rabbinical concordat that dated back to at least Rabbi Tobias Geffen's times, smart businesspeople made the requisite adjustments in the formulas and supervision of their foodstuffs to garner them coveted kosher certification. Such sugary delights as Oreo cookies and M&M can- dies were among the some ten thousand products that as of the 1990s

*Great in Vienna . . . Greater in New York*

**SCHREIBER'S**

Strictly כשר

**RESTAURANT - CATERING**

## HOTEL MILBURN
242 WEST 76th ST. (nr. B'way) N.Y.
Tel. TR 4-2399
3 Banquet Rooms for Weddings and Parties of 15 to 150 guests.
*Schreiber meals served on request by Pan-American Airways & KLM.*

Figure 8.2. Advertisement announcing the availability of kosher airline food on Pan-American Airways and KLM. *Jewish Life* (September/October 1950), 83.

carried the Orthodox Union's kashruth label. Even items that looked patently treif—such as "bacon bits" made from soybean—graced the tables of the pious. Cynics might wonder where and how these punctilious Jews acquired a taste for that particular nontraditional addition to a tossed salad. Perhaps that supermarket selection gained its popularity from its hosts' and hostesses' desires to provide gentile or unkosher Jewish friends or business associates with tastes to which they were accustomed. The tradition of culinary substitution to help aspiring observant Jews feel comfortable inviting others into their homes without the fear of committing the "sin" of appearing uncultured has its own long and distinguished history.

Pricy wines that a budding kosher connoisseur served might also impress dinner or holiday guests. Such contemporary imbibers who wanted to do more than just fulfill the mitzvah of Kiddush had come a long way from their youthful memories when a syrupy wine with a picture of a pious white-bearded Jew on its label was the standard brand. Now, classy-sounding, domestic and foreign-produced dry and semi-dry wines from wineries in California, France, Italy, Australia, New Zealand, and Israel were common fare. An uncaring consumer of the best vintages might well be unaware, from the Romance-language name on the label, that an expensive wine was kosher. For a winery, the cost-benefit of taking an extra step in preparing rabbinically sanctioned wines was a relatively simple manner. The halacha does not require a change in the means of agricultural and commercial activities, just a knowledgeable and observant Jew's supervision.[24]

Sometimes, business operators were inadvertent beneficiaries of the proclivities of the pious as their services intersected with their consumers' needs and interests. Such has been the happy fate of "Curves." When founded in 1992, it did not have observant Jewish women in mind as it promoted its "comfortable . . . supportive environment" for women to "encourage . . . other women . . . to reach . . . fitness goals . . . to improve . . . quality of life." But in time, some of its proprietors recognized that its "for women only" setup, complete in many places with frosted windows that kept onlookers away, fit the religious values of modesty and training wants of both very religiously devout clients and others who just did not like the idea of men gaping at them. Curves has sunk its roots even in Lakewood, New Jersey, home of the renowned yeshiva world community, not known for its secular recreational interests. There the gym has found a group of enthusiastic customers. One observer of this local scene has observed: "in communities where women have a baby every year or two, getting fit, staying fit during pregnancy and nursing is a top priority."[25]

If such a woman wants to work out in the privacy of her house, she also can do her "reps" to the beat of a specially recorded "Jewish Aerobics" tape. A committed-to-fitness, devout wife and mother has only to pop in the cassette or CD and follow a woman's voice-over instructions to the sounds of the best-known wedding and other religious tunes. If she and her husband want a quiet interlude at home after the children are asleep, they can listen to soft, soothing music that Orthodox recording artists have produced. These couples might close their eyes and hum along with the remixed Hasidic tunes that are their families' traditional heritage but were never presented until now in quite that way. Other Orthodox mothers and fathers who are children of the sixties might be especially attuned to the music of the late rabbi — former "beatnik" — folksinger Rabbi Shlomo Carlebach. The first prime-time performer of this sort is now more popular more than a decade after his passing in 1996 than he was during his mercurial lifetime. In fact, in recent years, his religious sounds — his lyrics often were taken from Psalms — have

been transposed into liturgical music. The "Carlebach-style" Kabbalat Shabbat service has become very popular in many Orthodox congregations, but
not in Lakewood or Hasidic synagogues where, during prayer time, the time-
honored European traditional melodies of the shtibls hold sway.[26]

If a devout husband and wife wish to study together during their free time,
they can easily resort to innumerable tapes of rabbinical lectures to help
them wade through the sea of Torah and Talmudical learning. Assisting
them in their learning are scholars associated with every conceivable Orthodox institution. Similarly, working men and women can take these portable
study aids on commuter trains to the city. These educational and entertainment options are big business for many fellow Orthodox entrepreneurs who
are well integrated within the wider amusement industry. For example,
amid the millions of I-Tunes ready to be downloaded are specialty items that
Jews of this niche market avidly procure. Harry Fischel's idea of almost a
century ago of using a slide machine to teach Torah tales has been retrospectively vindicated. Today the most modern of media inculcate the most
ancient of messages.[27]

Similarly, if a committed couple want a night out on the town, after dining
at the kosher bistro of their choosing, and if, for them, Broadway shows,
first-run movies, or the opera are not appropriate for their religious beliefs,
pursuit of a star-studded program may take them far beyond their neighborhood shul. Major city theaters and concert halls have interested operators
featuring successors to Carlebach, including Mordecai ben David, Avraham
Fried, and the Miami Boys Choir. In their own quests for Orthodox consumer dollars, entertainment promoters accommodate their customers' religious wishes, and if the crowd so desires, a temporary mechitza will be
installed in the venue. Though such gender separation is not required under the Code of Jewish Law — a public auditorium is not a sanctuary — in
many places contemporary community mores demand such partitioning.[28]

In these public venues, kerchief- or wig-wearing women may unself-
consciously tap their feet or dance in the aisles to the finger-snapping beat
of the black-suited, tzitzith-flying moves of the stage performers. Assuming
they are willing to pay the price, such fans may wear the most stylish of head
coverings, as the fashion industry and hairdressers too have taken note of
the profitability in outfitting fervent females. Such has been the experience
of Sandra Darling, a Catholic Bostonian who has become knowledgeable of
all the ins and outs of her customers' desires to be halachicly modest even as
they opt for "the French top, the layered look, and the feathered cut, among
others . . . all imported from France." While such "elegant and expensive"
wigs can cost as much as $5,000 to fulfill the letter of dictates on chastity,
they are not exactly within the tradition's purposes. A head covering of this
sort could be as sexually alluring as a woman's real hair.[29]

Figure 8.3. Advertisement for Mordecai ben David concert,
2003. Courtesy of Mark Weisz Design.

Every seven-and-a-half years, a sanctification of a secular site takes place when the Siyum ha-Shas occurs. This event commemorates the completion of a cycle that the Agudath Israel's Educational Committee began in 1923, under the initiative of Rabbi Meir Shapiro of Lublin. Over that period of time, those who are so devoted dedicate themselves to study a *Daf Yomi* — a page each day — of the six sections, the sixty-three tractates, and more than 2,500 pages of the Talmud's laws, legends, discussions, and debates. Today, not only Agudists but also thousands upon thousands of Jews across a wide religious spectrum take time from their busy schedules to study either in their local congregational groups or through cassettes and even through a "Dial-a-Daf" phone link.

It is said that in 1934, the year of the second commemoration held at the Lublin Yeshiva, the event attracted twenty thousand celebrants. But in the contemporary era, in America, the program has grown so significantly that in April 1990, the Daf Yomi Commission, dominated by Agudath Israel leaders, determined that only the main arena of Madison Square Garden in New York City was immense enough to hold the crowd of local participants. The Torah proceedings were also beamed, through closed circuit links, to other indoor stadiums across the country. While the throngs that turned out that night did not comment on the irony of holding the event in such a locale, reporters from Jewish newspapers and subsequently an intrigued sociologist made much of the fact that in traditional Jewish culture, dating back to Talmudic admonitions, stadiums were places for "scorners." Rabbi Moses Feinstein, then still the most renowned Orthodox decisor, said as much about contemporary ballparks even if this particular rabbinical call was lost on so many pious Jews of this country who love athletic pastimes and habitually attend ball games. But Feinstein was not referring to the "Garden" when the Siyum was the home event. Arena officials went out of their way to capture these lucrative proceedings and worked with the organizers to assure, for example, that all of the refreshment stands served just kosher foods, and the prime souvenir available for purchase was a "pocket-sized," small lettered "commemorative edition of the Talmud." To help participants follow the action, the page numbers of textual references were posted on the arena's electronic message board. The women in the crowd were segregated in the upstairs seats. But they too were on hand as — to borrow a line from a sociologist on-the-scene's observation — God, the King of Kings, was honored in a place where Budweiser "the King of Beers," is normally venerated.[30]

If and when pious Jews step out of their most traditional cultural stances and attend stadiums for their usually assigned purposes, they often find proprietors similarly prepared to accommodate their religious needs. Many ballparks offer hungry patrons rabbinically supervised kosher hotdog and knish stands so that these loyal fans can sit like all others who believe in the fortunes of the hometeam. No one says a word if those committed both to Jewish traditions and the club of their choice glance at that day's Daf Yomi installment between innings or at halftime. Some baseball ownerships have gone even further in catering to these customers; be they baseball-capped or black-hatted fans who desire to recite their evening prayers while the game continues. Since 1996, at Baltimore's Camden Yards, "Orthodox Jews congregate after the fifth inning in a small kitchen behind a kosher food stand"; it has become "a stadium ritual." Beginning with the 2003 World Series, the same religious practices have prevailed at Florida Marlins games. The Orthodox rabbi from Hollywood, Florida, who championed this activity is proud that the "location of the Glatt Kosher Hot Dog stand is an item of note with us." He has bragged that "at Camden Yards the kosher stand is way out beyond the left field bleachers. At Marlin games we are right behind home plate. What *kavod* [honor]." Such tolerant moves are not unique treatments honoring observant Jews. Ethnic foods of all sorts are available at most sports locations along with special-group Irish, Italian, Latino, African American, and Jewish "Days," all reflecting the prevailing spirit of cultural pluralism in this country.[31]

Perhaps, the only meaningful decision an observant male fan of a visiting team has to make before embarking on an excursion to a ball park is whether to wear a cap sporting the emblem of the opposing team and thus opening himself up to the slings and arrows of outraged fans in a hostile athletic environment or to wear his yarmulke and sit in the crowd in "blissful anonymity." In 2002, Abraham Genauer reported that he had addressed just this "dilemma" when he entertained the notion of publicly identifying himself as a Seattle Mariner fan at Yankee Stadium. Before setting off to the Bronx, he wondered which form of identification, the yarmulke — an "outward recognition of my faith, heritage or history" or the Pacific Northwest club's insignia — to "take pride in the fact that I was a Mariner fan before they were any good" — would bring out the intolerance of what he called "those beer-swilling, battery-throwing, fussing, cussing Yankee fans." His compromise decision was to sit among the "bleacher creatures," in the volatile right-field section of the stadium with his yarmulke for all to see, but near enough "to some Mariner fans to get an appreciation for" the "heckling" that "I was missing." Left unsaid was that this experience only highlighted how far not only observant Orthodox Jews — but all co-religionists who habitually wear yarmulkes — had come in their comfort in identifying themselves as a minority in this country. There was no specific moment in time that caused such men to lose their fear or discomfit in wearing what was once called "an indoor garment" outside. I would say that Jews in the 1960s were possible emboldened when they saw African Americans with distinctive head coverings begin to openly display pride in their heritage. As youngsters we wore ballcaps to school to mitigate any potential problem. In any event, Genauer, and all who act similarly, operate in a different world from a half-century earlier when, as one memoirist has recalled, "one never saw a kipah bobbing down Fifth Avenue."[32]

Recalling the predicaments that boys of her "social circle" faced, a relative of Genauer has described "the big test" that took place when a young man wearing a hat "entered a public place — a theater, a movie house, a library." As she tells it,

> Unless it was a restaurant, most of the young men of my acquaintance, even the rabbinical students, would go bareheaded for the short duration. In addition, there were all sorts of permutations and combinations — putting on one's *kipah* before saying a blessing over an ice cream soda and then removing it before eating, or waiting until the lights in the theatre dimmed before slipping it on.

Looking back on that past era, social commentator Blu Greenberg has allowed sympathetically that "it wasn't that these things were done stealthily or with guilt. It was all a bit of harmless maneuvering." However, she also notes that these ways of "feel[ing] at home . . . in a wider range of social, public settings," are "something their sons would be horrified at today."[33]

Thus, in so many ways, as observant late twentieth–early twenty-first century Orthodox Jews of varying stripes sat back in their Adirondack chairs at a five-star resort or on their kosher cruise yacht vacation, they could rest comfortably as a courted and respected minority in America. Some might contemplate their satisfied status while lounging on the hotel's veranda or on the ship's deck dressed in traditional Jewish garb, diverted by their iPods set for a Mordecai ben David recording or keeping on schedule with their daily Daf Yomi installment, anticipating a cantorial concert as the evening's activity. Others at this or at different luxury excursion venues, outfitted in modern American clothes — but with the men and many of the married women covering their heads — may be attuned to different sorts of music as they check the time for the next feature film showing in their resort's grand ballroom. But no matter the differences in cultural affinities, some of which might roil them in internecine disagreements — much more on such contretemps in the next chapter — all of the these Orthodox Jews share the sense that their and the next generations' futures are well assured. The more triumphalist within their midst would even argue that not only had they proven that it was possible to remain true to the halacha while moving forward within an accepting society, but in fact, that their formula is the only recipe for future Jewish survival in America. Some go so far as to predict that by the end of the twenty-first century, Orthodoxy's committed cohorts might well be the only Jews left in the United States.

One widely disseminated and discussed sociological study—pilloried by its critics for an alleged polemical edge—asked the Jewish public: "Will Your Grandchildren Be Jewish?" The study concluded that descendants would certainly be Jews if they identified with Orthodoxy, the more stringent the commitment the better. Basing their conclusions on their analysis of the 1990 National Jewish Population Survey, the researchers argued that that Orthodox Jews' low level of intermarriage in an age of rampant exogamy, its higher fecundity in an era in which Jews raised smaller and smaller families, and the critical extensiveness and intensity of their children's exposure to all-day Jewish education pointed to a bright new century for the most pious of America's Jews and problematic days and years ahead for all others. Ten years later, these zealous observers looked into the 2000 national Jewish census and again declared, among other findings, that "the longer children are in Orthodox Day school, the fewer parents are likely to face the question of 'Guess who's coming to Seder?' "[34]

Critics of this rosy scenario for the future of this century's Orthodox Jews and of dark days ahead for all other Jews responded that these tendentious tabulators failed to consider the potential for expanding drop-out rates within even the most committed of Orthodox communities. Deviances of all sorts augur to tell a very different demographic tale as the twenty-first century proceeds. To begin with, the economics of fecundity may have, in fact, a boomerang effect on continuity. One nightmare scenario for the deeply devout portrays scions from Hasidic and yeshiva world families with their very high birth rates—due to their strict adherence to halachic prohibitions against contraception—frustrated with the overcrowding and poverty with which they have had to contend, "pushe[d] to other places and sometimes other ways of life." Some who perforce "leave the protective cultural boundaries" of their previous environments, in search of a higher standard of living, may find religious refuge among their more acculturated, albeit still observant "kin." Though such tentative moves away from their narrow fold might not sit well with many within that community who honor separatism above all else, the Jews who would leave would remain still within the broader committed Orthodox spectrum. But others, not unlike those of previous generations who lapsed out of observance, may find spiritual so-lace in "very non-Orthodox" settings among Jews who have fashioned their own ways "to balance Jewish commitments with living in plural life worlds." The economics of decline might not mean immediate abandonment of Sabbath observance or kashruth or family purity laws. But with catalysts toward conformity to the secular in play, erstwhile devout Orthodox Jews could potentially become deviants.[35]

Beyond acute economic challenges, the often irresistible lures of Ameri-can culture may move some of these same deeply committed Orthodox Jews away from their groups' accepted mores and practices. Hasidic women of the 1990s were observed, for example, choosing, as young marrieds, to pursue careers "outside the community as secretaries, teachers, or clerks and in a variety of jobs in the fashion industry." Though many may have traveled from their home bases in busses separated from men with a curtain down the middle of their vehicle and were dressed most modestly while on the job, they did place themselves within earshot of "voices that are discordant from those in their own society." So resocialized toward the secular world, they may continue — as they have demonstrated already — to want to know more about the movies and television shows and the questionable values there portrayed that they have become attuned to through reading the *New York Times,* the tabloids, or glossy magazines. Similar or greater temptations have engulfed husbands or siblings who possess greater communally sanctioned freedom of movement. Now, here too, a Hasidic man who scampers off not so surreptitiously from Williamsburg or Boro Park to Atlantic City to feed his gambling habit — one social pathology that has been prominently identified — may be sure to observe the Sabbath before boarding his southbound bus. While on the boardwalk, he will skip the casinos' unkosher dining buffet options. Nonetheless, it is entirely possible, as communal leaders fear, that both females away-from-home on business and males engaged in such dicey extracurricular activities are situated on a slippery slope that eventually may lead them toward profound halachic transgressions.[36]

A major force keeping so many Hasidim from slipping away is the power that they have invested in their rebbes as spiritual and practical guides in all matters. In most sectarian contexts, this man at the top has always been the consummate bulwark in this country against all outside lures. When most empowered, under the dictates of "*Da'as Torah*" — the teaching that rebbes have divinely-given wisdom in all areas of human endeavor — they advise followers on every conceivable personal, business, and family matter. But with the battles that have ensued in recent years over succession within several courts, a potential exists for a breakdown in the élan of cultural confidence that has helped these groups resist the pulls of the American world. Presently, the most publicized split within a Hasidic sect is among the Lubavitchers. Their disputes center not so much over who should succeed Rabbi Menachem Mendel Schneersohn who died in 1994 but between those who only revere his memory and those "messianists" who believe that he lives on and anticipate his "second coming."[37]

Students and their families who "check out" today from the yeshiva world have also continued that long — if unhonored — tradition of leaving that fold. While the vitality of the separatist system in a Torah center like Lakewood does not rest so heavily on the persona of the particular rabbinical figure in charge — even as his wisdom is also accorded the status of Da'as

Torah — exhortations and sanctions carry only so much weight among those who take, at first, tentative steps sway from its tightly controlled realms and then find comfort zones within the once-alien culture.[38]

While many formerly devout husbands and wives often mutually agree to moves away from strict communal norms, be they of the Hasidic or yeshiva worlds, frequently conflicts ensue between loved ones. Though defenders of separatist forms of religious behavior have trumpeted that divorce rates are lower in their midst than within the irreligious world around them, still, unequal levels of acculturation and differing social values have led to an increased parting of marital ways. While such tensions need not lead to the abandonment of commitment to the halacha, these fissures may have an impact upon the future religious values of children from these split or single-parent homes who will not possess warming and enduring memories of their family units observing the mitzvoth together.[39]

Meanwhile, there are troubled youngsters from the yeshiva world and Hasidic families who have been already diagnosed as "at risk." In 1999, the *Jewish Observer,* the official organ of the Agudath Israel, openly acknowledged a "slide downward . . . among children in the Torah community on the fringe . . . and beyond." Harboring "no illusions" about "societal maladies" within their own midst while sure to aver that "in relative terms" — to other groups in America— "the phenomenon is unusual," it called upon their rabbinic leaders and "mental health professionals" to address the needs of those caught up in the snares of "emotional distress, substance abuse or comparably marginal behaviors," not to mention "academic failure" in the high-pressured environment of intense Torah education. Ads that offered assistance to those with "addiction problems" who only "wish[ed] that they could speak to a frum therapist on the phone without giving [their] name" or announcements that reached out to those suffering domestic abuse offering the services of "recognized professionals for counseling" or the shoulders of "some very special rabbis" to cry on only punctuated the growing presence of these troubling realities, so reminiscent of problems facing all American families. The continued affinity of those at risk for a pious lifestyle is certainly in question.[40]

Finally, some Orthodox Jews simply no longer feel the call of the faith's strict commitments. In 2007, a *New York Times* feature article looked at one ephemeral aggregation of such disaffected "freethinkers and misfits" who may "question aspects of their religion" yet "yearn to form a community of their own." These individuals find each other on Internet Web sites or in "under-the-radar" congregations, including one the reporter found called "Chulent," named for the traditional Sabbath stew that most "members" had enjoyed as youngsters. Among those intent in participating in a "mutant yet richly textured variation of the culture they grew up with" at its "informal weekly gatherings" on the top floor of the Millinery Center Synagogue in Manhattan are those hopeful of "dancing at two weddings," as one informant described the attempt of those who frequent Chulent's activities to "live with one foot in the Orthodox world and the other in the secular world." Within a new accepting environment, they pray that they can find a middle spiritual path together. Though these people retain intense feelings for Judaism, their lives of punctilious practice are for the most part behind them forever.

Concerned but not overly apprehensive, an articulate defender of such Hasidic and yeshiva-world deviants has commented on this situation, allowing that while the disaffected have "increased in recent years . . . [given] the blandishments and temptations of the outer world, which are ever more in your face. People want to sow their wild oats. Eventually some may come back. Others don't."[41] On the other hand, if there is but one constant in American Orthodoxy's history it is that the power of Americanization is an undeniable and constant opponent of traditional practice. Nonetheless, at the turn of the millennium, that minority of Jews who both identified with and practiced Orthodox teachings did so with ever intensifying commitment. Moreover, the deeply devoted Orthodox baby boomers of that moment — people who then were in their late forties to mid-fifties and presumably were in communal leadership positions while they raised the next generation of observant youngsters — were proving themselves daily to be more punctilious than their own parents. For example, when surveyed in 1990, more than eight out of ten of these middle-aged people were shown as using separate dishes in their homes and refraining from handling money on the Sabbath, sure signs of fidelity to these cardinal halachic principles. Their parents' generation scored considerably lower on these basic kashruth and Sabbath behavior scales. Looking back to the year 2000, it was clear that what Orthodox day school advocates had hoped for some fifty years earlier had come to mature fruition. Over that past half-century, so many children exposed to intensive all-day Jewish education assimilated its halachic values. Their own youngsters, as we will soon see, are more committed to following the nuances of Jewish law than even they have been.[42]

Adding to American Orthodoxy's contemporary sense that the future was theirs — if not theirs alone — were those newcomers to staunch commitments; the renowned *Baalei Teshuvah* of this era [Jews who return, as it were, to Orthodoxy]. These individuals either found their way into the fold or were attracted through major outreach efforts. Missions to Jews engaged in personal and familial quests have emanated both from Lubavitch Hasidic bases, with their conspicuous "mitzvah mobiles" that are often situated at the corners of urban thoroughfares, equipped with the most avant-garde audiovisual mechanisms, and from more subtle operations that move initiates more slowly and carefully toward observance with the ultimate goal of their arriving at pious Orthodox religious destinations.

In 1980, the Lincoln Square Synagogue of New York's Upper West Side initiated one of the most carefully constructed and successful efforts when it inaugurated a "Turn Friday Night into Shabbos" program for what it prayed would be "hundreds of curious residents who for the first time in years are going to usher in the Sabbath . . . in the same way their ancestors have ushered it in for centuries." Its advertising pitch to an anticipated largely youthful, single, and upwardly mobile clientele asked rhetorically: "How about sharing red wine for Kiddush instead of white wine for cocktails?" We may project that the red wine served that evening was of a pricey dry or semi-dry vintage. The program that enveloped the tasty food offerings promised not a formal service but merely a "real Shabbos meal . . . lots of singing, maybe some dancing" — of the Jewish and not the disco variety — "a lot of questions, a lot of answers and plenty of Shabbos spirit." In its own way, this intense and attractive religious experience, which began not at sundown Friday night but at a more convenient hour for young professionals, constituted a comeback for the late Friday night forums that had once been so popular within the American Orthodox world. But now, in a very different era, the driving force behind such activities was not rabbis or lay leaders forced to accommodate its congregational rank and file. Rather, these contemporary efforts expressed a confident and even aggressive Orthodoxy on the move extending itself beyond a committed core constituency.[43]

Those who have been receptive to outreach approaches have come aboard for a variety of reasons. In some cases, they have sought a sense of belonging to a community of shared commitments. In many instances, the devotees had previously experimented with, or had been caught up in, other non-normative movements either of a Christian or anti-establishment nature before turning to a demanding traditional form of Jewish life. Other times, it is a person's spiritual yearning of a different sort, as among those who have felt that despite their secular accomplishments there was a chasm in their lives that needed to be bridged. In pursuit of business or professional success, they had lost touch with what they ultimately believed life was all about. Then there are more prosaic chain migrations as siblings have led each other, serious daters or fiancés have influenced their partners, or youngsters have motivated their parents — or vice versa — to change their religious lifestyles.[44]

Many of the single baby-boomer women of the late 1980s who were attracted to Lincoln Square's "resocialization" processes reportedly were aspirants who had "found it difficult to construct lives that were completely fulfilling." While "many aspects of their lives were in order — their living situations were stable, they achieved some measure of professional success," they nonetheless felt a "hunger" to fill a missing "core to their lives" through "being rooted in some firm, stable and clearly defined way of being." Specifically, they frequently desired to be counted within a community that espoused and lived the value of an ongoing, enduring nuclear family life. Concomitantly and similarly, middle-aged single women who became devotees of Lubavitch Hasidism sought "an ordered sense of self on a personal level" even as they too were troubled by the absence in their lives of "comfortable, established patterns for forming nuclear families." Each movement's rabbis ultimately required different levels of change and commitment from initiates and pushed for personal transformations at different speeds. The more subtle Lincoln Square outreach professionals spoke warmly and enthusiastically about "women's roles in the home" but also "allowed for women's seeking secondary fulfillment in other spheres." The Hasidic rabbis, on the other hand, "focused exclusively on women's roles as wives and mothers." Still, in the end, each ministry found a way of reaching groups of Jewish women who were engaged in religious quests.[45]

But whatever the deep internal psychological or social drives of Baalei Teshuvah, they have brought a palpable intensity to committed Orthodox communities. While these newcomers have not outnumbered those who have drifted away to the more liberal movements or to secularism and total disaffection in this era, the Ba'al Teshuvah's (male) or Ba'alat Teshuvah's (female) new-found faith have sometimes inspired their shul-mates who were born into observant families to redouble their own religious allegiances. Other times, however, conspicuous zealousness has had its problematic repercussions. While newcomers are generally seen as a source of Orthodox pride, when they display or practice Judaism with exaggerated punctiliousness, they occasionally engender in their new communities "hostility for what is perceived as a 'holier than thou' attitude." These converts to Orthodoxy have also been seen as a "source of irritation to Conservative and Reform Jews" — starting with members of their family — who do not share or even comprehend these religious impulses and values. "Separation" from past lives can be "difficult and painful" when, for instance, men and women who have newly found the faith "decline food in others' homes and severely limit options for eating out."[46]

Finally, over the past thirty years or so, committed Orthodox families have counted the mixed blessings that result from their youngsters' post–high-school study sojourns in Israel. Although this educational phenomenon has been traced back to the late 1950s–early 1960s, as of the mid-1970s, it became increasingly a religious rite of passage for boys and girls to top off their secondary Jewish schooling through a capstone year or more of learning in an Israeli yeshiva. There, often in total-immersion Torah study programs, the more studious and impressionable develop not only a greater facility in handling traditional texts and an interest in continuing such study in the college years and beyond. But, with the enthusiastic encouragements of their Talmud instructors and spiritual mentors, these young adults have also opted to follow the rigors of ritual and custom assiduously. This newly found dedication ranges across a wide spectrum of behaviors — from the care with which they recite daily prayers, to making sure to say the appropriate blessings sanctifying every aspect of a daily routine, to abstaining from eating even kosher foods like a cold fresh salad in a nonkosher restaurant where the dishes are treif, to the emulation of more traditional Orthodox sartorial and tonsorial patterns than they had stateside along with a commitment to strict modesty in any interaction as singles with members of the opposite sex and even, in some cases, to aversions to secular cultural activities. Follow-up studies also seem to indicate that the levels of observance reached during the time spent in Israeli yeshivas generally have been maintained upon their return to the country of their birth, at least during the first year. These inspired young men and women also see themselves continuing their punctilious practices as a permanent lifestyle. They look forward to raising their children in devout surroundings, like the Tenaflys of the future, with day-school education as their highest family priority.[47]

As with every away-from-home cohort, there have been some who have used that opportunity to act in a completely opposite manner than intended. Out of the sight and earshot of their schools' teachers and administrators, they have hit the secular Israeli streets and have broken away from traditional family and religious mores. Observers of this scene have publicly exhorted parents of Orthodox youngsters who were already at risk at home to think twice before exposing those "who have slipped over the brink" to this overseas Israel experience. Fantasies that the year in the Holy Land will turn their youngsters back toward more normative behaviors are often far from fulfilled.[48]

Nonetheless, on balance, the year or more in Israel has been a positive intellectual and maturational experience for most students. Certainly it has produced a recruitment bounty for all schools of Orthodox higher education. For Yeshiva University's undergraduate schools, the program has strengthened the commitment to Torah study of those who, as high-school seniors, were already attracted to its dual curriculum mission that trumpets equal dedication to both religious and secular studies. With traditional Jewish studies now more important to them than ever before, they look forward to continuing such training and growth even as they pursue their B.A. degrees. Perhaps as important to its enrollment managers, such sentiments have led Israel-year classmates who previously had not contemplated a Yeshiva College or Stern College education and who were admitted to Princeton or Yale — or to a myriad of other American universities that respect these students' religious values — to opt for the Jewish school.

A dual-curriculum competitor, Touro College, established in 1970, with major branches in Manhattan, Queens, and Brooklyn, also enrolls students en masse from the year in Israel environments, including young men and women who had signed stateside with Yeshiva University but who are now attracted — under the sway of Israeli religious advisers — to Touro's far less integrated approach toward teaching the religious and the secular. Well-established yeshiva world institutions also benefit from the year(s) of maturation that its students gain from study in its brother schools in the Holy Land. And most notably in the case of Ner Israel Yeshiva in Baltimore, this separatist school picks up students who were previously enamored with the way Yeshiva College educates its undergraduates but who now have come to believe that secular study should be relegated to tertiary status, to evening college classes after they spend the lion's share of their time in the traditional house of study. An accommodating Johns Hopkins University that offers these courses toward a B.A. is simply continuing a tradition that dates seventy or more years to Brooklyn College and later to Queens College in New York and to Loyola College in Baltimore; these institutions have long attracted the yeshiva world's youthful core constituent. Along these same lines, in the metropolitan area, whether in Queens, New York, or Rockland County, a veritable cottage industry of small yeshivas have set up shop to offer comparable day-long, Torah-only learning for students who then matriculate at city or state colleges at night.[49]

For many of these students' parents back in the states, particular those of the more modern set, the sons' or daughters' year or two in Israel produce both admiration and anxiety. On the one hand, most parents are understandably proud of their children's growth in a traditional scholarship that often exceeds their own learning. They also may be impressed with their progeny's careful observance of the traditions, behavior patterns that might comfortably affect their own approach toward fulfilling the mitzvoth. However, all is not always well in these households, when returnees have *flipped* or *frummed out,* as two pop sociological terms characterize youngsters who have not only raised the religious bar high for themselves, but who are intolerant of the ways their elders have lived their religious lives. As one chagrined parent told a researcher: "We want them to learn more, but to a certain degree . . . we want them to come home the same way." But many do not. In a reversal of generational roles rarely seen in the history of Orthodoxy in America, it is growing children who may be raising their eyebrows at parental lack of punctiliousness.

The questioning youngsters who grew up in households where both religious and secular education was highly valued likewise may wonder out loud why a separatist yeshiva world orientation is not for their elders. Conflicted parents, who were also products of the day-school movement within which their families flourished religiously in turn, may ponder how their grown children have come both to disdain the way parents have behaved religiously and to criticize the intellectual and professional paths that synthesize Jewish and American patterns. Mothers and fathers who would be pleased if their sons and daughters, after the Israel year, opted for Yeshiva University's integrative educational mission or alternatively might be as proud — or prouder — if they lived a devout life at Yale and fought the good battle there for Orthodoxy within the Ivy League might reflect with sadness on how their child opted for Ner Israel by day and Hopkins at night and then brought that yeshiva's values and opposition to modernity back home. In many cases, the answer often is that the Israel-based instructors and mentors, whom their youngsters have come to revere, had preemptively warned them in no uncertain terms about the crisis of re-entry into the secular culture of America. These highly influential guides frequently have tendered explicit "survival" advice on how to navigate the challenge of remaining true to the clear, unadulterated Torah message they have offered in their cloistered environments while exposing themselves only to that which is entirely necessary in college training. Their message is that the secular–religious synthesis that their parents lived by is not the preferred religious path for a pious Jew.[50]

When they step back from what they see in their houses and among their children, chagrined parents may well understand that the intergenerational issues they face are much larger than their own situations. Rather, they reflect the greatest of social tensions within the tent of committed Orthodox Jews of the new millennium: a contemporary period of contretemps and confrontations among Orthodoxy's faithful followers.

# 9

# ORTHODOX VS. ORTHODOX

The tensions may be palpable within homes all over America as Israel-yeshiva returnees and their perplexed parents seek religious rapprochement. But the problems and dilemmas that underlie these disagreements over the details and nuances of how to live a pious life are larger and more pervasive than any family or community. While all devoted Orthodox Jews of this contemporary era have been accorded unparalleled social status and recognition within our country's tolerant society and many have earned economic comfort, for some, these days have been also times of defensiveness and even self-doubt. At the turn of the millennium, cohorts of committed Jews, dedicated to the fundamental rubrics of the halacha—they observed the Sabbath and kashruth and were mindful of the constraints of family purity laws—found the subtler aspects of their religious behaviors and ideas subjected to harsh criticism from other Orthodox Jews. Antagonists attacked their cultural and social affinities and intellectual proclivities and repeatedly questioned their allegiance to traditional faith. In the most strident critics' view, all paths for living with all due respect for Jewish law while embracing contemporary mores, customs, and trends rendered such Jews miscreants against the tradition.

Only intermittently have those pilloried fired back with responses that sometimes have been quite personal. They took note of the perceived hypocrisy of those who projected themselves as the guardians of unadulterated religious fidelity but who could be guilty of highly offensive immoral and unethical acts that made a mockery of what was called a Torah lifestyle. These transgressions might be committed in dealings with the government or even more grievously with exploited, victimized fellow Jews and non-Jews. Alternatively, those whose religious lifestyles were critiqued highlighted the possibilities of living harmoniously with America's values and with the highest regard for Judaism.

In the midst of Orthodox antagonisms, some of those on the offensive took occasional nasty swipes against the leaders of Jews living non-halachic lifestyles. The most noteworthy of these attacks took place before the High Holidays in 1985 when the Agudath ha-Rabbanim, revisiting its long-standing position, warned Jews "not to pray in Reform nor Conservative Temples . . . whose Clergy" — they would never refer to them as rabbis — "have long rebelled against numerous sacred laws of the Torah and misled thousands of innocent souls." But the greater contemporary battle lines that have roiled Orthodoxy in America have pitted those within their own tent who have so much in common, starting with their essential mutual commitment to the halacha.[1]

Throughout Orthodoxy's history in the United States, there have been tense disagreements among the committed about the depth of the challenges that modern Jewish movements and general cultural influences pose to their faith's continuity. But now, criticisms redoubled on a multitude of fronts, with voices speaking vociferously of the lack of "authenticity," or of the "compromised" or "compartmentalized" deportment or commitment or even "illegitimacy" of those who did not fervently share insular religious outlooks.[2]

Those under attack were typically seen as engaged in, as one sociologist put it, "a perpetual juggling act," as they navigated through some of the enduring complexities of living well within both the Orthodox Jewish and secular American worlds.[3] On the religious behavioral level, the accusation was made, to begin with, that when push came to shove, there were good Sabbath-observant Jews — like those Orthodox baby-boomer success stories whom we have met — who were just not punctilious enough in their approach to revered teachings and traditions. There were countless commandments beyond those relating to the Sabbath and kashruth that had to be consistently observed. There were also a myriad of social mores and daily practices that set Orthodox Jews apart from all others that needed to be minded. Those who were characterized as not *frum* enough — as that term returned vigorously to the popular vernacular — were denigrated as people leading "watered-down" religious existences.[4] These alleged miscreants had pushed toward the periphery those laws or standards that were either inconvenient or uncomfortable for them.

Naysayers particularly focused on personal priorities that smacked of inauthenticity. Men were upbraided for rushing through their daily prayers at home and for rarely attending the daily minyan as they sprinted to catch their commuter trains. They found little time for regular Torah study. If they had free hours, they and their wives comfortably wasted them in front of their television sets or at plays, ball games or movies—even if they avoided "R"- and "X"-rated films. These men dressed like all of those around them, save for their head covering. In business settings, they might have their heads uncovered, except when dining on their kosher meals—or on cold salads or fruit cups with plastic cutlery, eating options that were permissible within the tradition—which sensitive associates were sure to provide. Otherwise, wearing a knitted yarmulke as opposed to a black fedora suggested that they did not want to set themselves apart culturally from other Americans. None of these acts violated the halacha, but they bespoke an affinity for the American way of life.

In their living "with self-satisfaction that no conflict exists between their Jewishness and the secular world," said their disparaging critics, these so-called "mitzvah-culture" Jews upheld but "a minimum level of *mitzva* [*sic*] performance." Their behavior was acceptable only within "the most lenient interpretations of the *Shulchan Aruch*." The goal should be maximal not minimal, strict not lenient standards of Orthodox behavior. Those who observed the Sabbath and limited their "fare in non-kosher restaurants to cold tuna fish and salads," barely fulfilled their halachic obligations. The bottom line for one outspoken critic was that "this watered-down form of *mitzva*-culture Judaism is not our Sinai-Torah tradition. Our heritage cannot be promulgated by spending Sunday afternoons and Monday evenings glued to the football game-of-the-week on television."[5]

Even more jaundiced attention was focused on the areas where so-called compromisers cut some halachic corners. For example, the Code of Jewish Law unquestionably prescribes that all historical fast days should be observed. But while for most committed Orthodox Jews the Fast of the Ninth of Ab—which commemorates the destruction of the two Holy Temples and has been linked to other horrific events in Jewish history—carried much enduring cache, other signal days such as the Fast of Tevet—which reminds Jews of the beginning of the siege that led to the fall of Jerusalem in 586 BCE or the Fast of Esther, which precedes the joyously observed feast of Purim— were simply not honored.[6]

But behavioral transgressions that rankled critics most were those related to defining the parameters of modest and immodest conduct between men and women. Outright censure was heaped upon those otherwise pious Jews

who would not abandon such long-standing practices as swimming or dancing with members of the opposite sex. These Sabbath- and kashruth-obser-
vant Jews had grown up in a prior era where such activities — if evaluated at
all — were judged as good, clean fun. Now, however, what they once blithely
did at home or at parties, at the pool, or at beaches was fundamentally at
odds with their contemporaries' mores. Their rabbis, whose predecessors
had suffered these practices in silence tarred them and their actions as
immodest. Still, these once very common practices persisted enough to
have critics and scholars note them as prime examples of "compartmentalization"; the "separate[ing] out [of] the Jewish from non-Jewish aspects
of . . . lives," with secular pursuits trumping those that are holy.[7]

Could a case be made that such co-educational activities were acceptable
as part of a halachic lifestyle? While few of those who swam or dance ever
rose to defend their actions, in 1985, an Orthodox social commentator,
David Singer, tried to explain first to a friendly questioner — and then to a
reading audience — that what he and his wife did to commemorate their
twentieth wedding anniversary was not unwarranted compartmentalization.
It was rather an honorable case of "synthesis," proof that living well within
the Orthodox legal system as acculturated Americans could be accomplished. If anything, he was proud that what he and his wife had done, could
be done as observant Jews.

The Singers chose Club Med in the Dominican Republic — renowned or
notorious for its "swinging paradise" reputation — as their getaway destination. As a graduate of Yeshiva College some twenty-three years earlier, he was
part of a generation that not only believed that there was nothing "as appealing as modern Orthodoxy," but was comfortable with its social decisions
that had been made in a less contentious era. Remaining true to his religious values — while, as he put it, "the Orthodox community as a whole
goes marching off in a traditionalist direction (the widely noted 'move to
the right')," he proudly reported that while on vacation he took "care not to
violate kashruth laws, saying the afternoon prayers on a wind swept beach"
after spending an afternoon "soak[ing] up the sun, loll[ing]" on the same
beach and "maybe down[ing] a pina colada or two under the swaying
palms." To his way of thinking, minding the halacha through dining on
"fruit cups and vegetable platters" in "a 'non-Jewish' vacation environment
such as Club Med speak[s] more directly and eloquently to synthesis than
do the same observances put into practice in a 'Jewish vacation' setting."

But, what of the "gorgeous-looking girls in bikinis" and the club's "let-
loose philosophy" played out in front of him? This avowed monogamist was
equally proud that he had "once refused to appear on a radio program
because the host — a rabbi — was a known adulterer." So disposed, one
might project that Singer would also have looked askance at the practices of

singles who took part in what were then known as "tefillin-dates." These were liaisons where a man anticipating, or hopeful of, sleeping over at his girlfriend's apartment after an evening out and presumably engaging that night in sexual intercourse made sure to pack his phylacteries so that he would not miss saying his regular prayers the morning after. This was compartmentalization to an unconscionable extreme. The moralist within our Orthodox vacationer might say that premeditated concern over ritual observance before and after acts of moral impropriety were nothing more than a perversion of the tradition.

However, well beyond his own personal "conservative" predilections in such matters, there was the mighty weight of the Code of Jewish Law — with its strictures of which he was well aware — "pertaining to such things as personal modesty, proper attire, socializing between men and women, sexual arousal, etc." that were arrayed against his and his wife's decision. Was he not "clos[ing] his eyes . . . to what the Law requires" as he watched "scantily clad women" sashay by?

In his demurral, Singer contended, first, that he "nurse[d] no sense of guilt" about what he could have comfortably characterized as his "permissiveness . . . within the framework of the permissible." For him, had he possessed second thoughts about his lifestyle, such emotions would be a sure sign of unwarranted compartmentalization. Three years earlier he had gone on the record in averring that compartmentalization was the "Frankenstein of modern Orthodoxy." If anything, the "problematic element" in the Club Med scenario was not his activities, which he considered "fully appropriate." Rather, he was "frustrated" with the absence of recognized rabbinic authorities who would opt for an expansive reading of the Shulhan Aruch and might formally "legitimate his behavioral patterns." To his chagrin, "virtually to a man," those who made the religious decisions were "either unattuned to the modern experience or actively hostile to it," especially in cases like his where there were no explicit set parameters to the limits of the Singers' deportment.[8]

This apologia did not pass public muster even within the circles of the Rabbinical Council of America, within whose journal this provocative piece appeared.[9] That Singer knew he was fighting a "lonely," uphill battle was certain. Just three years earlier, no less of an accommodationist rabbi as Steven [Shlomo] Riskin of Lincoln Square Synagogue had written, within the same symposium, that "our values must emanate from our sacred Torah text and our every action — including the manner in which our women dress and the places in which we are permitted to swim — must be sanctioned by halachic authority." That meant that "social dancing in the Pink Elephant Lounge with a *kippah* on one's head" or "a swinging singles *Shavuot* in Aruba replete with *minyanim* and blintzes" had "no ultimate significance for traditional Jewish history." If Singer had his supporters, they gave silent assent to this perspective when they behaved in the same manner on their own vacations. But one did not have to countenance the Club Med vacationer's religious values to feel that a strident wind of intensifying gender separation, constraints that transcended rabbinical codes, was pervading the atmosphere within observant Orthodox communities.[10]

For example, voices critiqued synagogues whose partitions were deemed too low or visually permeable. A raised bar was erected to assure that women who were allegedly alluring in their part of the sanctuary would not distract men during the latter's devotions. As early as 1975, a Hasidic congregation in Brookline, Massachusetts, ever-ready to use technology to advance the cause of the faith, installed a 550 lb "thermopane mirror-coated one-way panel," initially designed for use in the Hancock Tower in downtown Boston, for its mechitza. Such a partition made it possible for women to see the ritual goings-on from their section, but men would not be able to see the women. Those who were concerned that men were looking at the females in this arena were also quick to object that when services were not in session, offending congregations contributed to unwarranted social scenes among singles and nonmarrieds. A generation or so earlier, Americanized Orthodoxy had purged itself of its mixed-seating congregations and had savored those rare victories when congregations installed mechitzas as it battled for constituents. Now, attitudes toward interior sanctuary architecture bespoke a rising wave of insularity and a narrowing of its tent.[11]

Within this judgmental spirit of separation, Riskin's congregation at the Lincoln Square Synagogue came most notably to be tarred with the decidedly unflattering moniker of "Wink and Stare Synagogue" because of its glass see-through partition with men on the interior and women on the exterior of concentric circles of seating. When founded in 1965, this congregation and its dynamic young rabbi were poster children for Yeshiva University in its battles with the Conservatives for control of communities. In winning a battle for Orthodoxy, a decision was made, in configuring its sanctuary, to construct a mechitza that would attract Jews who alternatively could have been very comfortable sitting with men and women together. Through its modern mechitza, Riskin and his followers offered a proactive response to the challenge of that era's Debate Night; a strategy that attracted many who wavered between affinities for Orthodoxy and Conservatism. The rabbi and lay leaders also recognized that their constituency would be drawn from among the religiously and socially unattached on the fashionable Upper West Side of Manhattan. Riskin encouraged programming directed at singles. These moves anticipated Lincoln Square Synagogue's future efforts, on a larger scale, to draw unaffiliated Jews to traditional practice through its soft-pedaled advocacy of Orthodoxy. But while these policies implicitly linked the congregation to some time-honored in-clusionary American Orthodox traditions, now these values raised challeng-ing eyebrows.[12]

Ultimately, the internecine Orthodox questioning of religious values tran-scended personal behavior and institutional practices. People who would not consider a Club Med vacation and who, for that matter, prayed in shuls that had the highest mechitzas, found that the ways in which they conducted their Jewish lives were subject to harsh scrutiny and challenge. Critics now interro-gated the very fundamentals of how devout Jews should deal with the outside world. The most basic of issues — the value of secular education, the limits of cooperation with Jews leading non-halachic lifestyles and their organizations and the question of what the "modern miracle of the State of Israel" should mean to Jews became points of great contestation.

Though most of those whose values came under siege did not respond in kind or with vitriol, occasionally some voices spoke of their antagonists as dwellers within stained-glass sanctuaries who were all too ready to cast stones and aspersions. While sure to never gainsay the importance of punctilious observance, those who countered their frum opponents spoke of the "im-balance caused by over emphasis on ritual aspects at the expense of socio-moral requirements demanded by the halacha." In that same spirit, those "practitioners of Orthodoxy" who "are at times strong in adherence to the letter of the law but weak in the province of noble behavior" were upbraided for creating a "feeling that Orthodoxy is a host of practices somewhat di-vorced from profound faith." Some critical jaundiced observers of the "Or-thodox right" were "distressed" when "the study of Torah . . . bec[a]me the very justification for forbidden behavior ranging from cheating on exams to presenting fraudulent transcripts" — most likely when they engaged in secu-lar studies — "to obtaining funds by questionable means." David Berger, a staunch advocate for unabridged "ethical behavior" coupled with Ortho-dox commitment, would be, some years later, on guard against what was for him the most egregious form of transgression possible among those "widely perceived as Orthodox." In 1998, Berger identified the "greatest danger to Orthodoxy" as emanating not from "the obvious 'deviationist' movements" — that is, Conservatism or Reform — but "from Lubavitch Messianists." For him, there was no less than idolatry within the most famous Hasidic group in America. A somewhat more circumspect commentator who spoke with "sorrow" about those who conducted "unsavory business practices, de-frauding the government," and so on, was quick to remind all who might be smug or self-satisfied that "the right wing has no monopoly of piety and the modern Orthodox no monopoly on interpersonal decency and honesty."[13]

At that moment, the sorrow expressed in that unambiguous ethical im-perative had everything to do with the utter embarrassment so many observant Jews, and for that matter, all Jews, felt in the 1970s–1980s about public scandals that erupted over the misuse of government funds. Certain trials witnessed Jews who wore yarmulkes and otherwise observed the Torah's ritual commands subjected to "perp walks" and other distasteful criminal appearances in front of media spotlights. Seemingly, white-collar, victimless crimes were becoming endemic within segments of that community. In one felony, stockbrokers were sent to jail for "manipulating prices in [a] company's stock and paying $133,000 in kickbacks to other brokers, using Orthodox yeshivas and other Jewish charities as conduits" for these illegal transfers. Several years later, the news got even worse, when officials of Brooklyn's B'nai Torah Institute were convicted for victimizing "needy children" in its federally funded program. The bill of indictment spoke of "unserved food, for serving food at unauthorized sites and to adults instead of children." The stories became worse still as it was revealed that a Brooklyn landlord who was president of a local yeshiva was cited for two hundred uncorrected violations in his property, including, reportedly, "rats and vermin, no heat or hot water, falling ceiling plaster [and] no building superintendent."[14]

For most of those who were outraged, the most deleterious developments involved nursing-home kingpins Rabbi Bernard Bergman and philanthropist Eugene Hollander. These two well-known Orthodox communal figures with ties to a myriad of institutions — in Bergman's case, leadership links to Mizrachi, Agudah and Yeshiva University — came to personify all that was ethically wrong within that community. Their nefarious activities victimized the completely helpless, from the aged to the physically and mentally challenged entrusted to their care. Specifically, Bergman was convicted of absconding with more than a million dollars in Medicaid funds, neglecting patients who never benefited from these government entitlements, bribing officials to keep inquiries at bay, and of "laundering" funds through named Orthodox synagogues and yeshivas.[15]

Consternation and condemnation were, however, far from universal within what again proved to be a deeply conflicted saintly constituency. Young activist rabbis Riskin and Avraham [Avi] Weiss quickly drafted a petition pillorying these miscreants. Students at Yeshiva University came up with their own statement calling for "no whitewashing, no condoning, no apologizing in behalf of the desecrators." An Orthodox Union's magazine editorial writers "openly profess[ed] our shame with those of our brethren whose behavior has brought them to the public eye." David Weingarten, a columnist for the *Jewish Press,* an organ that claimed, with much justification, to be the voice of Brooklyn, if not New York's, most devout Orthodox Jews, opined that "at a time when *glatt* [very strict] kosher is so popular ... how about some *glatt* kosher money? Why, my distinguished spiritual leaders, don't you emphasize that point with the same zeal and fervor that you emphasize the stomach religion." Torah Umesorah announced plans to redouble the ethical components in its curricula and extracurricular initiatives in yeshivas. In what promised to be the most far-reaching palliative response, a group called Yosher — a Jewish Ethics Committee — was formed. Seeing this communal humiliation as an opportunity to address and rectify an entire slew of long-standing ethical abuses, this ultimately ephemeral organization also hoped to "galvanize opposition to 'Las Vegas Nights' " — where gambling took place in synagogues as a fund-raising stratagem — damning such activities "as a desecration of places of worship." It likewise sought to publicize the problem of inflated kosher meat prices and issue halachic perspectives on the need for complete honesty in income tax preparation.[16]

But those who spoke out against nursing home operators saw their efforts run up against both walls of silence and even opprobrium from other Orthodox Jews. The Mizrachi organization that Bergman led was silent on his case, as was the Agudah, its usual ideological opponent on matters Zionistic. Riskin and Weiss had a hard time finding more established Orthodox leaders who would sign their petition. Meanwhile the *Jewish Press* editorialized that antisemitism was behind these investigations designed to "blacken the Jewish community," The non-Jewish writer for the *New York Times,* John Hess, who was constantly on the case and who helped break open the webs of conspiracy, would only reply that concerned, morally upright Jews were "the earliest and some of the most effective critics of the nursing home racketeers." In time, the civil courts would toss out a suit Bergman brought against Hess and two government officials, alleging the promulgation of "malicious, false and prejudicial" reports against the rabbi. Irate voices in the defendant's camp argued that even if Bergman and the others were guilty as charged, those Jews who aided the investigators were themselves guilty of the serious transgression of *mesirah*. In pre-modern times, there were halachic injunctions against Jews giving up their own kind to persecuting governments for fear that such revelations might result in reprisals against the Jewish people as a whole. An "ex-Bergman aide," a former administrator at his Towers Nursing Home, would cite this "Talmudic law" as grounds for her refusal to appear before a special grand jury. In staking out or banking on that claim, those who would condemn whistle-blowers were essentially saying that for all the freedoms and safety that America provided them, this country was still a hostile environment for Jews. They supported a dishonest Jew rather than the American legal system.[17]

Rising to the challenge of defending those who were effectively denounced as disloyal Jews for "pervert[ing] . . . the Jewish sense of shame . . . into an unprecedently shameless exercise in public breast-beating . . . as though silence were itself a sin, only to be atoned for by public repudiation of the sinner," Rabbi Irving "Yitz" Greenberg, an admirer of Yosher and a close colleague–mentor of Riskin and Weiss, offered his own rabbinic-based source to lodge an attack against those who enabled corruption to exist and thrive in ostensibly pious circles. Quoting the Talmud as having "once put it; 'It's not the mice who are the thieves, it is the holes that enable them to enter.' " For him, "the unwillingness to speak out, the looking the other way, the desire to hush up rather than to embarrass, the outright connivance or acceptance of corruption have created the atmosphere for the criminal behavior which has achieved such notoriety."[18]

Ironically, a quarter-century later, Greenberg's own behavior toward an infamous malefactor was roundly critiqued. In January 2001, on his way out of the White House, President Bill Clinton stopped to pardon 140 criminals and people under indictment, including fugitive commodities trader Marc Rich, who had fled the country seventeen years earlier to avoid prosecution on "fifty-one counts of tax evasion, racketeering and violating sanctions against trading with Iran." As public debate ensued over the propriety of Clinton's eleventh-hour acts of either magnanimity or, some said, of payback for support of his political campaigns, it was revealed that Greenberg, who was then chairman of the United States Holocaust Memorial Council, was among a group of prominent and red-faced Jewish leaders who had written to Clinton to pardon the unrepentant Rich. On Holocaust Council stationery, the rabbi had implored the president "to perform one of the most Godlike actions that anyone ever can do." When Greenberg's words got out, his own critics were sure to note that the Marc Rich Foundation was a multi-million dollar backer of philanthropist Michael Steinhardt's Birthright Israel program, an arm of Steinhardt's own charitable foundation which Greenberg also directed. This creative initiative was praised for bringing thousands of Jewish students to Israel on whirlwind trips as a proactive way of inculcating Jewish and Zionist identity in young people. But what of the questionable funding source? While even Greenberg's harshest critics did not allege "a quid pro quo," the appearances of impropriety here were seen as damning enough for the rabbi to resign or be fired from his Holocaust Council post. The rabbi weathered this storm of protest, but the controversy did cause the American Jewish community to reassess again its policies toward accepting monies and honoring benefactors who possessed less than sterling ethical resumes.[19]

In the midst of this era of contretemps among committed Orthodox Jews over what constituted acceptable behavior and allegiance to traditional faith, in 1990 the President of Yeshiva University, Dr. Norman Lamm, sought to re-explicate and thus re-energize those within his community who believed in "the 'synthesis' of Torah learning and Western culture that goes by the name of *Torah Umadda,* or the study of sacred Jewish texts along with the secular wisdom of the world."

Waxing autobiographical, Lamm explained that it was the pursuit of that harmonious worldview, along with his ambition for a career in the secular world — as an undergraduate he thought of becoming a chemist — that had brought him from Brooklyn's enclave of separatism, Torah Vodaath, to Yeshiva in 1945 at the onset of the Belkin–Soloveitchik epoch. He would have a "lifelong romance with this ideal," which was known to him as having emanated from the mind and spirit of Bernard Revel. But it was the chance to "sit at the feet" of Rabbi Joseph Soloveitchik that made the hegira from Williamsburg most worthwhile for this precocious young scholar. Some forty-five years later, in response to forces within his institution that, he asserted, wanted clear historical sources and concrete definitions for ideas that had long pervaded Yeshiva's halls, he wrote his book-length inquiry into that tradition's roots and offered strategies for its continued persistence if not revivification in a era of challenge to its teachings.[20]

Although the book did well within Lamm's own circles and certainly served as a capstone to Yeshiva University's Torah U Madda Project, his thesis and analysis re-raised the hackles of opponents of that Orthodox way of life. The *Jewish Observer*, Agudath Israel's monthly publication, led the chorus of critics as one of its contributors lambasted Lamm for undermining "the traditional vision of Torah learning in significant ways through the open-ended approbation he gives to secular studies and the value that he attributes to these studies."

While this writer readily "concede[d] that a proper understanding of both science and history can bring one to a deeper appreciation of *Hashem* [God]" and that "there are those who require some post high school [secular] education to earn a livelihood . . ." the modern yeshiva head's advocacy of "synthesis is to transform Torah and Madda into what appear as co-equal forms of knowledge." Lamm was accused of raising the study of the sciences and humanities to the level of the learning of the Talmud, making diligent immersion in such disciplines a fulfillment of the mitzvah of Torah study. Even worse, he and his school foisted this perspective upon "a young college student, who is simultaneously exposed to Torah and secular studies and left to work out their interrelation for himself." Quick to damn Lamm with faint praise, this critic suggested that he "is far too astute and his association with Yeshiva University far too long-standing for him not to recognize the very grave dangers inherent in an open approach to virtually every aspect of secular knowledge." Yet, in what was deemed a troubling and unfortunate book, he "consistently downplays the danger that lies in an exposure to heretical ideas or in an educational structure that conveys the message to students that Torah and non-Torah studies are fully compatible."[21]

Subsequently, at the winter of 1993 convention of the Agudath Israel, Rabbi Yaakov Perlow, the Novominsker Rebbe, a leading member of Agudath Israel's highest-ranking presidium, went even further in denouncing "the primary spokesman for the mixture known as Torah U Madda." Deigning not to mention his opponent by name and averring that the public rostrum was "neither the time nor the place to discuss the falsehood and the insidious implications of such a philosophy" — comprehensive refutation, he was pleased to say "has been done by others" — he called upon "the rabbis and laymen in the Modern Orthodox world" to dissociate themselves from Lamm and his school's heretical creed. He prayed that they might align themselves with the "pure *emes* [truth] of Torah, untampered with, undiluted, uncompromised by alien creeds." He called upon those whom he hoped wavered in their fidelity to Yeshiva's deeply nuanced message to break with "watered down versions of *Yahadus* [Judaism] and Torah" and to "seek not the values of humanistic liberalism nor the lifestyle of modernity."[22]

For Lamm and his supporters, the most troubling aspects of these polemics were not the tenor of the highly personalized attacks but the fact that his opponents' pervasive message of Torah-only study was being heard and assimilated into the religious outlook of many within his own core constituency. One front in this cultural struggle was in those Israeli schools that Yeshiva's students attended, where strident messages of separatism were propagated. Then there was the battle zone within the expanding day-school educational field where Agudists, and those of comparable sympathies, had an army of faithful followers dedicated to inculcating their separatist values among students. Driving these troops was a mature and focused Torah Umesorah organization that had come a long way from the soft-touch pedagogic approaches of its early decades. Though still committed to reaching all Jews, when its dedicated faculty, armed with its sense of mission, was given their opening, they aggressively inculcated their ideologies and practices among impressionable youngsters from an early age. One estimate offered in 2003 placed the proportion of such teachers working in American day schools at two-thirds of all educators. When charismatic, they pushed effectively to "redefine Orthodoxy in the modern world as uncompromisingly parochial."[23]

In this environment, one observer of the contemporary Jewish educational scene has remarked that "modern Orthodox schools have been hard pressed to maintain their fidelity to their founding principles." Youngsters did not have to wait for their years in Israel to bring back home ideas that questioned accepted family practices. They could start learning to be different from their mothers and fathers in elementary or secondary schools.[24]

To a large degree, those who lamented the types of perspectives that were offered to their children had only themselves to blame. Growing up as they did, in this era of American tolerance toward those who maintained traditional faith practices, Orthodox baby boomers had taken full advantage of worldly acceptance and of burgeoning career opportunities. They became

Sabbath-observant physicians, attorneys, business people, accountants, and so on. They secured niches in the professoriate. If their discipline was Jewish studies, they might find a spot within these burgeoning academic programs all over the country. For such aspirants, Jewish education — teaching in a day school or a yeshiva — was not rewarding intellectually, emotionally, and financially. In many quarters, day-school teaching was viewed as "not a job for a Jewish boy." While these Jewish boys and girls, who, in one commentator's view, grew up to be observant fathers and mothers and showed great "allegiance to the professions, to academic Judaica, or to communal leadership," they minimized their own personal dedication to "Torah study" and left "*avodat ha-Shem* [God's work]," like teaching youngsters to others far more parochial than they.[25]

In the late twentieth century, there were few signs suggesting a resolution of this so-called dilemma of pedagogic recruitment. So many students returned from their year(s) in Israel with religious commitments that departed noticeably from those of their parents — even if they were not newly avowed separatists. Still, they retained their elders' low opinion of Jewish education as a career for them to pursue. This younger generation might refuse to join its adults at a family beach gathering. (We can only wonder whether the 1980s "Club-Medders" vacationed there in celebration of their fortieth anniversary and whether their children joined them for fun in the sun, pina coladas, and cold salads on those plastic dishes.) Some might cause a rumpus in the car if they demanded that an excursion be halted immediately to permit them to recite their afternoon or evening prayers at the mandated times. Likewise, young women might fervently predict that they, unlike their mothers, will keep their heads covered when they are married. Both male and female young adults also might look forward to more conscientious personal growth in Torah study. But, just like their less punctilious parents, they did not seek careers in day-school education or the rabbinate.[26]

Perhaps as troubling for Lamm as his students' lack of predilection to go the extra yard to propagate what he had been calling "Centrist Orthodoxy" since the mid-1980s, was the reality that separatist parochial teachings and worldviews were insinuating themselves into his own institution.[27] Such incursions created in their wake invidious triangulations. Influential Talmud instructors emulated their school's ideological opponents, and talked the talk of separatism to their disciples. These role models imparted messages that some students chose — against the general flow of student-body career interests — as educators, to spread as gospel within Israeli yeshivas to youngsters who upon their return to Yeshiva University disdained the Torah U Madda alchemy. Rather, they aggressively pursued their learning of the Torah on campus and steered clear of embracing the study of Madda as an intellectual or religious endeavor. They took from the worlds of secular study only what they needed to succeed economically or professionally in America.

One particularly powerful and resonate flash point of a change in the mood at Yeshiva appeared in the debate over what Rabbi Joseph B. Soloveitchik *really* had believed; these discussions began after his death in 1993. By then, for close to a half century, this leader had been the ideological standard bearer and consummate role model for the possibilities of Torah U Madda. Now, upon his death, those who adhered to those teachings not only lost their touchstone eminence — although, in truth, his geriatric illnesses had taken him from the active scene several years earlier. But they were soon to hear, in the years that followed, that in his heart of hearts he actually harbored distinctly separatist values.

From almost the very moment of Soloveitchik's death, Lamm recognized that "revisionism" was afoot. In eulogizing his teacher, he had called upon his community to abstain from "misinterpreting the Rav's work in both the worlds." Soloveitchik was "not a *lamdan* [Torah-learned Jew] who happened to have had and used a smattering of philosophy; he was certainly not a philosopher who happened to be a *talmid hakham,* a Torah scholar." Rather, Lamm implored all to "accept" this "highly-complicated, profound and broad minded personality" and to "confront" those who "may well attempt to disguise and distort the Rav's uniqueness."[28]

Significantly, the incipient revisionism to which Lamm alluded did not emanate explicitly from the organized Agudist chorus. Its terse obituary merely noted that "many of [Soloveitchik's] works revealed a strong tension between the [Talmudic world of] Brisk of his youth and the [philosophical universe] of Berlin of his early adulthood" and that "exponents of Torah Umadda emphasized" how "these works offered an eloquent portrayal of a turbulent inner struggle." Rather, members of the esteemed rabbi's own family and a number of his most prominent disciples, who had been trained at Yeshiva — but who clearly attuned to what its long-term ideological opponents were saying — offered visions of Soloveitchik's worldview that placed him squarely in the Agudist camp.[29]

For starters, Rabbi Aaron Soloveichik, the Rav's younger brother, took this revisionist position in his funeral eulogy. There he asserted that while his sainted sibling, the consummate rosh yeshiva, also "delivered lectures in Jewish philosophy [and therein] from time to time he mentioned Plato, Aristotle, Descartes, Hobbes, Kant, and Hermann Cohen," the referencing of these secular sources was merely a stratagem "to reach many opaque people from different camps." The younger Soloveichik's message, as one commentator has deconstructed it, essentially was that his brother's resorting to secular sources was "apologetic . . . to lend an air of respectability to traditional Jewish teaching by presenting it through the prism of Jewish and general philosophy." Subsequently, in an effort to further delimit Joseph Soloveitchik's differences of opinion with those of the yeshiva world, his nephew, Rabbi Moses Meiselman, would state that he "remembered distinctly when the Rav told Rabbi Aharon Kotler, 'our goals are the same, we differ only on how to achieve that end.'" According to this relative's and disciple's reconstruction of events and attitudes, his revered teacher "in all his concerns, was exceedingly parochial." Meiselman argued that there was not a "single instance where the Rav was involved in any universal issues of the day," since "his efforts revolved around his parochial concerns for the well-being, both spiritual and physical of the Jewish people." Policy-wise, that meant that Soloveitchik never deigned to speak out on general international crises and rejected out of hand any mode of conversation — not only theological dialogue — with Christian leaders, deeming all such interaction as detrimental to Jewish survival. Perhaps most critically, Soloveitchik was envisioned as agreeing with Agudists on the all-important question of what the modern State of Israel should mean to Orthodox Jews who prayed daily for the messianic return to Zion. To hear this interpreter tell it, Soloveitchik, who notwithstanding his decades-long position and presence as a central figure in the Mizrachi camp, actually believed in the depths of his being that "the secular government in Israel does not fit into any halakhic categories, it is religiously irrelevant." In other words, the state does not represent on any eschatological level — as many of Mizrachi's Religious Zionists would faithfully aver — the beginning of the ultimate redemption. So positioned, his disciple argued that the late leader's "difference of opinion with other Torah giants was the degree of accommodation with the government of Israel. It existed on a pragmatic level only."[30]

Similarly disposed, Rabbi Hershel Schachter, arguably Soloveitchik's successor as Yeshiva's most respected Talmudic scholar, who learned his Torah at the feet of his master in that school's classrooms, projected his rebbe as more a follower than an innovator "concerning theoretical halachic principles and practical rulings," dedicated at his core to continuing the "exceptionally powerful tradition in the realm of *hashkafah* [traditional religious outlook] and faith" which was his Lithuanian family legacy. If Schachter reluctantly, but honestly, admitted that his teacher differed from his own revered ancestors in those critical areas of secular education and Religious Zionism, it was only the force of "changing circumstances" and not a deeply felt different worldview that engendered those opinions.[31]

These appreciations of Soloveitchik did not go unchallenged. Lamm, other Soloveitchik family members — including his devoted and learned sons-in-law Rabbis Aaron Lichtenstein and Isidore Twersky — and a coterie of equally influenced former students, scions of the modern yeshiva, all rose to assail these reinterpretations as "misunderstandings," "oversimplifica-tions," or, worse as "misrepresentations." For example, Twersky argued that Soloveitchik's teaching "drawing freely from Torah and *hokhmah* [secular wisdom] fascinates us for its compelling interpretive insights . . . its theologi-cal subtleties, philosophical perceptions and moral nuances." Lichtenstein has chimed in that his father-in-law's religious outlook was "neither an ex-tension nor an expansion of existing tradition, but a genuine innovation."[32]

But if this touchstone rabbinic scholar's ideas and his specific practical religious positions could be opened to alternate evaluation, some respon-sibility may be placed at his own feet. Soloveitchik himself was not unaware that his style of pedagogy and his mode of leadership might lead ultimately to such posthumous problems. Humbly, he had projected himself more as a mere *melamed* (religious teacher) than as a strictly constructed decision maker. The scholar has been quoted as having said that "I have many pupils, I have many disciples but I never impose my views on anyone."[33] As impor-tant, though the author of several, far-reaching essays — his classic, *The Lonely Man of Faith,* published in 1965, has influenced far more thinkers than just Orthodox believers and intellectuals — much of his teachings were not published in his lifetime. His "traditions" — note the plural — were more commonly recorded in the notes students took during his classes offered over several generations or derived from private conversations that individuals had with their mentor out of others' earshot or in the cassette recordings that his followers made of his public lectures. In the decade and a half since his passing, a cottage publication industry arose as so many have edited and prepared parts of their versions of Soloveitchik's torah for an eager reading public. Still, even as his words were now placed down on paper, they remained open to different interpretations and available to divergent religious rulings, with ideological antagonists able to hold onto Soloveitchik as their legal source and guide.[34]

Indeed, controversy over what Soloveitchik said, or did not say, permitted or ruled against, nuanced or articulated explicitly has become one of the flash points of the most far-reaching Orthodox confrontation of our times. He has become posthumously the touchstone source for all sides in the contemporary debate over the role feminism may play within Orthodoxy. Here, more than anywhere else, the question of whether, or to what degree, the halacha was "open" — to use a loaded term of the times — to admit American attitudes, social mores, and cultural values into committed life-styles and religious ritual has engendered vitriolic disagreements among those who shared so many of the most basic traditional Jewish values. For supporters of change, their point was that the tradition has always had the flexibility — as it should have now — to accommodate and simulate wider world ideas and currents as the faith moved forward. For opponents, the innovations that they were seeing around them were unconscionable, unprecedented deviations from Jewish law; nothing less than dangerous emulation of the ways of the gentile world, in this case, of "Women's Lib." It is to this contemporary contretemps par excellence, a controversy among committed Orthodox Jews that the Orthodox Union's magazine in 1998 characterized — a decade and a half into this polarizing struggle — as "perhaps the most explosive issue facing Orthodoxy," that we will now turn our attention.[35]

# 10

## OPEN AND CLOSED TO FEMINISM

By the early 1970s, a decade had passed since the publication of Betty Friedan's landmark work, *The Feminine Mystique,* which sounded a clarion call for women's liberation in America. Dissatisfied women and their male supporters began to question gender inequality on so many fronts — from the workplace to politics to sexism in how men and women conducted themselves in their livingrooms, kitchens and bedrooms. The most aggressive feminists pushed hard for changes in the power relationships between the sexes. Activists within Conservative and Reform Jewish circles took to heart the words of Jewish feminists, such as national movement leaders Friedan and Letty Pogrebin, who criticized what they perceived as sexism within their ancestral faith. Ezrat Nashim was identified, early on, as "perhaps the first group publicly committed to equality for women within Judaism." A prime cause, which came to fruition in subsequent years, was the admission of their sisters to the Jewish Theological Seminary's rabbinical school student body. The Reform movement had already ordained its first female rabbi, Sally Priesand in 1972, and the Reconstructionists had followed suit two years later when Sandy Eisenberg Sasso completed her rabbinical training. In 1974, the Jewish Feminist Organization was founded and committed itself to "nothing else than the full, direct and equal participation of women at all levels of Jewish life — communal religious, educational and political." Resonate to, if not influenced, by the tumult around them, groups of dedicated Orthodox women — with male backers, including most importantly, handfuls of outspoken Orthodox rabbis — began taking hard looks at how their religious community was treating its mothers, sisters, and daughters. Efforts were made to ascertain what openings were possible within what they perceived to be the limits of the halacha.[1]

Admission of women to the boards of directors of Orthodox congregations was an early struggle. Those who advocated for such change in synagogue governance did not note that what they wanted was linked to debates going back hundreds of years in American Jewish history to times when women were excluded even from membership in synagogue. For the new advocates, policies about lay leadership were not halachic issues. Those at the forefront of change also apparently did not know that there was at least one idiosyncratic precedent in the history of American Orthodoxy for their petitions. Some seventy years earlier, under the imprimatur of Rabbi Henry S. Morais, Congregation Mikveh Israel was far ahead of its time in admitting two women to its original twelve-person board of directors. That, and other avant-garde efforts, earned Morais the encomium — among his backers — as the "only Rabbi in Harlem who stands for principle."[2]

Efforts to create conditions, within an open, expansive halachic framework, whereby women could take an active part in the synagogue service produced far more controversy. Incipient innovations were initiated on some college campuses where generally new ideas have freer reign. Reportedly, at the Orthodox service at the University of Wisconsin's Hillel Foundation in the start of the 1970s, the "Orthodox graduate students" who ran that service — most likely males — decided that women may be "called to the Torah, but only when women read the Torah." That meant that "each Sabbath morning, at a certain point in the Torah reading, the male *gabbaim* [those who supervised the rituals] and Torah readers are replaced by women and women are called up." More typically, however, change advocates did not go this egalitarian route, but opted for separate women's activities, patterned after what men had traditionally done. The first of these women's tefillah [prayer] services took place on Simhat Torah in 1972, when Riskin permitted women to dance with the Scrolls and then read, as the men did in the main sanctuary, the concluding portions of Deuteronomy and the opening chapter of Genesis to each other. Subsequently, his Lincoln Square Synagogue hosted periodic — usually monthly Sabbath — services for women only. By 1978, Riskin's colleague Avi Weiss had welcomed a women's tefillah group into his Riverdale congregation, spiking a trend, among those so disposed, that would lead to, by 2005, the existence of no fewer than forty-seven sister groups in fifteen states — New York City was home to seventeen of them — and four foreign countries, including seven contingents in Israel. Another estimate, as of 1998, placed the number of active groups at sixty. Weiss's Hebrew Institute of Riverdale was also the first Orthodox congregation to permit women to carry the Torah around their section of the main sanctuary before and after the Scroll has been read from the reader's desk.[3]

Though many of the women's tefillah services differ in some details of their ritual, the basic halachic procedure that they employ is to create a religious experience where women are praying together as individuals but not as a minyan. The practice of women praying privately is permitted, if not encouraged under Jewish law, but public worship is reserved for a men-only quorum of ten. Women's tefillah devotees insist that "these groups are not minyans." These advocates of change also pointedly accuse their detractors of "persistently and erroneously" using that term to denigrate their actions. Practically, this procedure means that the public aspects of the service — such as the *Borchu,* the "call to prayer" — are omitted from the liturgy. However, women can read the Torah and serve as cantors, without the ruled-out public sections. They also can offer sermons and other Torah teachings to the assembled. Men are forbidden to observe these proceedings, except in the case of male family members of a Bat-Mitzvah girl's reading of her Torah portion. Then, in a "Sadie Hawkins-like" reversal of religious positioning, her father, grandfather, and siblings are permitted to listen in on her performance behind a men's mechitza.[4]

The women attracted to such tefillah services attached enormous emotional and spiritual power to these activities, opportunities which they, and their usually supportive families, perceived as resting comfortably within the realm of the halacha. More than a decade after the Women's Tefillah of Riverdale was founded, long-time members reflected on what the group meant to them and even to their spouses. One recalled how moved she was when she first observed "several women eloquently reading from the Torah (touching the Torah!?) [*sic*] and many more praying and listening, all somehow fortifying the unique spiritual energy engendered through davening together." Another devotee looked back at her own childhood where sequestered in the women's gallery she felt "inconsequential whether I was present at services or not [since] . . . there was little I could contribute or indeed that was expected of me." A third remembered how "struck" she was "how women's voices were always drowned out in the regular shul by the overpowering men's voices and here women were actually singing out with gusto." As a child, she had always thought, "why couldn't I sing '*Ein Kelo-heinu*' and '*Adon Olam*' " — the concluding hymns which male minors were allowed to lead. "I could sing better than some of the boys. [Now] here was an opportunity to finally stand at the *bimah* [altar]." Her only reservation before departing for her service was her concern over how well her husband was doing babysitting their infant son while she "was out davening."[5]

As these separate prayer activities came into vogue within congregations attuned to women's aspirations and sensitivities, other innovations became part of their synagogue scene. In many of these shuls, women and men both recite *kaddish* for their dear departed. Some like-minded synagogues allow — with their rabbis' assent — egalitarian megillah readings on Purim and the Three Pilgrimage Festivals. Bat-Mitzvah ceremonies, where girls offer a Torah talk to the entire congregation during or after the regular services, are countenanced in many other places, well beyond those where there is no demand for a women's tefillah reading at her own service. In his idiosyncratic Orthodox congregation, Weiss's Hebrew Institute of Riverdale allows mothers and fathers to ascend the bimah together — with each rising out of their respective sides of the mechitza — to offer a blessing of thanksgiving and separation on the occasion of their son's or daughter's religious coming of age. In the spirit of full disclosure, I should acknowledge that my family and I have been Weiss's congregants and supporters for now more than thirty years. With this affiliation, we have also witnessed the rabbi remove from the preliminary morning blessings offered publicly everyday, the offensive-to-many recitation that men have traditionally made thanking the Almighty "for not making me a woman." Women have always thanked God for "creating me according to his will."[6]

Outside of the confines of the synagogues, families dedicated to what they believe is the malleability of the halacha "have drawn upon Jewish tradition and their own creativity to create" other life-cycle celebrations. In the case of baby-naming ceremonies, these events may not necessarily replace the ways girls have always been welcomed into the covenant. A father may still name the child as part of his being called to the Torah. But, in addition, parents may adapt existing rituals for this special occasion of their own authorship. Time-honored blessings pronounced when happy events take place, the prayer of thanksgiving for women after birth, and the blessing appropriate after safe return from a dangerous situation have been integrated with biblical selections along with a few choice words of Torah, perhaps combined with an upbeat American aphorism, topped off with a sumptuous collation.[7]

In a no-less momentous Jewish life-cycle event, brides and grooms, their families, and the rabbis who have led them in the granting of speaking parts to women during wedding ceremonies have presented their additions as permissible tweaks to what the tradition has historically provided. Although here, too, formulations vary within a spectrum of activities, they may in-

Figure 10.1. Bat Mitzvah ceremony on Purim day at the
Hebrew Institute of Riverdale, March 1997. Courtesy of the
Becher family, Riverdale, New York.

clude a bride vocalizing her acceptance of the wedding ring from her be-
trothed, thus mutually consecrating the marriage "according to the Laws of
Moses and Israel." Elsewhere, subsequent to men — the rabbi, or a cantor, or
perhaps male family members or distinguished friends — reciting the seven
marriage blessings, women may be invited to render portions or versions of
the same holy statements in English. Notwithstanding these personally edifying additions to the Orthodox wedding, the crucial witnessing of the traditional marriage contract has remained reserved for Sabbath-observant men
to sign. While in some places a woman may be granted the high personal
privilege of reading the contract to the assembled, the legality of the *ketubah*
is derived from the men's names on the bottom line.[8]

But beyond gaining the franchise to sit at congregational board meetings,
having a chance to gather together with their sisters to pray and read the
Torah, and witnessing their life-cycle events honored, many committed contemporary women have striven to secure opportunities to study sacred texts
the same way and to the same extent as their fathers, brothers, and husbands.

Although by the 1980s, seventy years had passed since intensive, all-day
Jewish education had been judged as warranted and valuable within all

committed Orthodox circles worldwide, a distinct gender gap remained in almost all schools toward the teaching of Talmud to girls. From the founding of Beth Yaacov schools in interwar Poland through today's yeshiva world and Hasidic girls' yeshivas and advanced seminaries, school curricula, designed to intensify Jewish women's commitment to the old ways, disdained Talmud as an unnecessary, if not dangerous, discipline for their female charges. The most restrictive understanding of the tradition, derived from a Talmudic teaching, compares the exposure of females to Talmud study to a father's teaching "lewdness" to his daughter. Less harsh, but no less compelling was Maimonides' view that it was "preferable" not to instruct women in this subject. Biblical studies would be the most advanced subject offered to girls.[9]

In the early 1940s, when the first students in their co-educational day schools came of Talmud-study age, both rabbis Joseph Soloveitchik and Joseph Lookstein, at Maimonides in Brookline and Ramaz in New York City respectively, broke with this tradition and offered Talmud to their girls, creating precedents that were emulated in many — but far from all — postwar Orthodox day schools. Soloveitchik's assent became the touchstone for such developments as he subsequently rose to become a towering eminence among those Orthodox Jews who looked to him to set authoritative standards for religious behavior.[10]

Nonetheless, as the movement for increased female opportunities within Orthodoxy began, some calls for more advanced Talmudic training were heard from women — both from some who had attended these pathbreaking schools and others who had not. An oft-referenced and early turning point moment in this regard took place in 1972 when Soloveitchik delivered a formal Talmudic discourse at Yeshiva's Stern College for Women and thereby lent his uncommon imprimatur to the inauguration of concentrated Talmud study within its curriculum. During that same generation, a number of additional influential college-level and post-baccalaureate women's Talmud programs were established in the United States and Israel. Drisha in New York became the most notable of these initiatives. Since its founding in 1979, it has provided "advanced study of classical Jewish texts" to women — and occasionally to men too in separate classes — including a "scholars circle," where three years of full-time study leads students to "certification in Talmud and Jewish law." Meanwhile, Stern College, more than twenty-five years after Soloveitchik first smiled upon Talmud study for women, expanded its Talmud offerings to students who desired that optional course of training. In 2000, it established a graduate program in Talmudic studies. Stern also has linked itself to Israel-based institutions such as Midreshet Lindenbaum, Matan and Nishmat: women's schools that place a strong emphasis on developing Talmud-learning skills among its students.

They are constituent institutions in Stern's year(s)-long programs that bring cadres of committed students back to its New York campus.[11]

However, many of the schools on Stern's "Israel program" are not very dedicated to extensive Talmudic training for women. Other schools offer oral law courses as "optional," and in some places it is made clear that there is "no Gemara" in the curriculum.[12] Most of the alumnae who return to Stern do not register for courses in Talmud. They may study these Talmudic sources collaterally within Jewish history and Jewish law. A diversity of attitudes obtains among these young women for whom innovative and traditional educational opportunities are now abundant. And while the past thirty years have witnessed the production of the most Jewishly educated cadre of women in Judaism's history, many of those who want to study Talmud do not desire new leadership roles or new rituals. Baby-boomer women may have wanted to lead services and to read the Torah publicly because they were denied so many chances, as youths, to participate in Orthodox ritual life. The next generation of women, on the other hand, possessed of so many advantages to express themselves religiously, have gravitated toward behaving like the young men, opting for advanced study in the traditional *beth ha-medrash* (house of Torah study). One focus group — conducted in 2000 — of "younger Orthodox women" who saw themselves "as much more educated than their mother's generation of 'women in their fifties'" found some voicing the view that since they were "part of the club," with membership earned through their more extensive Jewish training, "high level text study is far more important . . . than expanding women's roles in public worship or giving women' access to Torah scrolls."[13]

Even when all numbers are counted, women's prayer groups have attracted only "a relatively small number of Orthodox women." One commentator, sympathetic to these groups' goals, has gone so far as to suggested that "their visibility has been enhanced astonishingly by those who oppose and demonize them."[14] Even in Rabbi Weiss's synagogue, where a preternatural atmosphere of tolerance for change prevails, more women have, over the years, ignored the congregation's sponsored Women's Tefillah than have attended it. Some women — like the men who have left the shul because, as one dissenter feared, "*tzores* [bad occurrences] have befallen the Jewish people because the women are kissing the *sefer torah* [Torah scrolls]" — have openly disdained these innovations.

Indeed, for other women of this same baby-boomer generation who have not been interested in prayer groups, it was precisely the differentiation of gender roles in public religious life that made Orthodoxy compelling. Among female newcomers to halachic practice at Lincoln Square Synagogue — the place where in the same congregational realm women's tefillahs began — initiates did not object to "lack of access to participation in the synagogue."

That did not mean that these religious "returnees" acquiesced to women taking back seats in secular endeavors. But as one woman who was attracted to this religious community explained: "I am glad to see sexual differentiations in the area of ritual. People come in two flavors, and it's nice to see this emphasized."[15]

However, within the younger generation of women whose "mothers'" pushed for a greater role within Orthodoxy, some have built on these ritual initiatives. For them, participation in a women's tefillah is so very important that they have elevated it to a daily obligation. Such were the proud and excited sentiments of those who announced, in 1997, the establishment at Columbia University of a "daily women's tefillah." While admittedly a "diverse" contingent that also included women who "are Reform, Conservative . . . unaffiliated, or unlabeled," with thus an inherent "potential . . . to divide our community," its leaders averred nonetheless that they were "very careful to follow the guidelines of halacha in every manner." For those who got involved, "women's tefillah . . . provided . . . the chance to lead davening, to read from the Torah, and to create beautiful melodies together." However, at almost that same moment, their sisters at Stern College showed themselves far less committed to ritual activism. There, "the level of participation in women's tefillah [was] minimal (77 percent had never attended such a group), and approximately 80 percent of those who [had] attended would either not attend in the future or were doubtful about attending." Moreover, "the overwhelming majority" of those who prayed in an Orthodox synagogue declared themselves to be "content with their role in services." Conversely, only 12 percent of those who tried women's tefillah perceived themselves as "more spiritually uplifted than in a traditional service."

Reportedly, "non-attendance, rejection or support" of ritual activism was "*not* a function of perceived halakhic permissibility but rather of other socio-cultural, political and spiritual interests and considerations." Perhaps many Stern undergraduates fear that being dubbed as "feminists" through association with these activities will tar their personal reputations within Yeshiva's larger, male-dominant Torah community within which they want to be always a part. One "interim interpretation" of this reticence — not only at Stern but elsewhere within Orthodoxy — suggests that "as a result of negative social pressure, the 'daughters' fear that their involvement in such groups would stigmatize them as 'Women's Libbers,' affecting possible *shiddukhim* [marriage possibilities] and employment opportunities." The "influence of religious studies teachers during their post high school year of study of Israel" have also caused them to be disinterested in their mothers' religious affinities. Their counterparts at Columbia and Barnard — where fewer are Israel-year alumnae — may not worry as much about marriage and employment opportunities, at least within Orthodox realms.[16]

Amid this complex mix of sentiments and interests among this well-trained and motivated younger generation, to date (fall 2007), only one woman has attempted to study for ordination and to advocate for acceptance as an Orthodox rabbi. In 1993, Haviva Ner-David, then known as Krasner-Davidson, began her idiosyncratic journey when she applied for formal training toward ordination at the Yeshiva Rabbi Isaac Elchanan. Having already assumed what she called "the empowering time-bound commandments required of men" — such as donning tefillin, praying three times a day, and wearing tzizith — she eventually aspired for formal rabbinical training and ultimately ordination. For her, "the title 'rabbi' means something. It carries with it connotations of authority, morality, commitment to Judaism and a certain mastery of texts . . . all things a woman who studies at Drisha would not get." As she saw it, "nothing is comparable to a rabbinical degree if you want to teach Torah and be involved in the halachic process." Ordination from Conservative Judaism did not move her, even as she admitted being "torn between the ideologies of the Orthodox and Conservative movement." She perceived Yeshiva's ordination as carrying the legitimization that she craved.[17]

Krasner-Davidson received no written response to her petition, a reaction that did not surprise her. She understood that "I am applying to a school that will not accept me." The school's Dean, Rabbi Zevulun Charlop, refused to publicly discuss the process that led to her tacit rejection. Still, he did contend that while his school was "sensitive to what's going on vis-à-vis women and what the needs are today," what Krasner-Davidson wanted "is halakhically untenable." He further asserted that "any Orthodox rabbi who ordains a woman is by definition not Orthodox." Angry but undaunted, she then proceeded to Israel where under the tutelage of Yeshiva alumnus Rabbi Aryeh Strikovsky, she began working assiduously toward her ordination. Thirteen years later, in 2006, concomitant with her earning her doctorate in Jewish Studies from Bar-Ilan University, she completed her rabbinical studies. However, her mentor stopped short of granting her "ordination," contrary to initial featured reports in the Israeli press. Rather, he signed a document that was "more of an official recognition of her studies and was not intended to be construed as an ordination." While Strikovsky made clear that Ner-David "covered exactly the tractates and the issues that men have to master in order to get an ordination," he also acknowledged that "in the Orthodox world and society it is not acceptable yet to ordain a woman."

Ner-David, reportedly, was unperturbed that Strikovsky was not "so bold as to actually give [me] the title 'rabbi.'" Reflecting on the road she had traveled and the distances that she had yet to traverse, she constructed what her teacher had done as an "acknowledgement" of "my readiness to go out in the world and act in the role of a rabbi and he left it up to my community to decide what title to give me." For the present, she was pleased that her egalitarian-minded community in Jerusalem "has decided that it is ready for a women rabbi."[18]

Notwithstanding the openness of Ner-David's friends and congregants to change, the employment record shows that almost all established Orthodox congregations in the United States are not as ready as these Jerusalemites are for females in pulpit positions, nor even in roles that are not as contentious as those of rabbis. For example, as of the summer of 2007, only two sister congregations, Weiss's idiosyncratic Hebrew Institute of Riverdale and Chicago's Congregation Anshe Sholom B'nai Israel, under Rabbi Asher Lopatin, have engaged female quasi-clergy. In 1997, Stern College alumna Sharona Margolin Halickman was appointed a "congregational intern" at the Riverdale synagogue and was soon promoted to the staff position as its *madricha ruchanit*—spiritual guide. In both posts, she basically performed the educational and pastoral duties that young rabbinic interns and fledgling newly ordained assistant rabbis normally fulfilled, with the clear proviso, to which she assented, that she would stop short of rendering any halachic decisions. She taught at the shul, helped with public programming, and counseled men and women who were in need. On occasion, she would deliver Torah talks from the pulpit, which in her and the rabbi's view constituted no abridgement of Jewish law. Margolin Halickman would remain at the synagogue for seven years before moving to Israel. In 2004, Drisha alumna Sara Hurwitz took over in her stead.[19]

Even more recently, Rachel Kohl Feingold assumed a comparable calling in Chicago. In July 2007, she became Anshe Sholom B'nai Israel's programming and ritual director. In that post, she, too, was assigned to duties generally incumbent upon an assistant or associate rabbi, including preaching and teaching from the pulpit on Sabbath and holidays; leading "explanatory services," which were minyans usually for those new to Orthodox practice; conducting children's services on the High Holidays; and performing "pastoral functions" while assisting in synagogue programming. At the time of the appointment, it was Rabbi Lopatin's "hope" that "in the future the shul gives her the title of '*rabbanit*,'" a designation even more rarified than madricha ruchanit, but stopping short of calling her a "rabbi." In this way, as one advocate of this title has strategized, a halachicly committed and well-trained woman "can have the connotation of the title 'rabbi,' yet still espouse the Orthodox philosophy that men's and women's roles remain distinct."[20]

However, many more congregations that are not doctrinally opposed to such positions remain reluctant to follow suit, perhaps born of lay leader unwillingness "to be perceived as the forerunners on an issue still considered somewhat controversial."[21] There was no enduring momentum at the Lincoln Square Synagogue for posts of this genre after its one and only congregational intern, Julie Stern Joseph — the first such designee, hired scant days before Margolin Halickman — concluded her two-and-a-half-years of service. Looking back on her experience some years later, Stern Joseph did not see her efforts as particularly pathbreaking. Preferring not to identify herself as a feminist, she saw her job in the most traditional of terms, as a skilled complement to her husband's position as assistant rabbi. She was pleased to have the "on the job training as a professionalized rebbetzin" — performing many of the social and pastoral functions that rabbis' wives had done for generations, but also having the chance to teach Torah lessons to men and women. This combination of skills, honed at the Lincoln Square Synagogue made her and her spouse a most attractive rabbinical couple for any future position they might occupy.[22]

But economic considerations also contribute substantially to the lack of large-scale efflorescence of female quasi-clergy opportunities. As one woman advocate who wishes to see more done has recognized: "synagogues, constantly balancing financial needs and constraints, may hesitate to commit the necessary funds to new initiatives not deemed integral and vital by synagogue leaders." She has frankly conceded that "there is not currently a clear career path for Orthodox women whose interests may be in this area." One male leader at Lincoln Square Synagogue has commented that his congregation's foray into this area with the hiring of two members of the Joseph family was that his shul effectively received two bright, scholarly religious functionaries — an unusual husband-and-wife team — for the price of one. In the light of this financial reality, Anshe Sholom B'nai Israel's hiring of Finegold was, to some degree, more remarkable than developments at the Riverdale synagogue. While Halickman and Hurwitz were engaged in addition to male assistant rabbis, in Chicago the female designee replaced a departing male colleague, "using money reserved for that position" for her.[23]

Presently, there also has been no discernible great groundswell of ambition expressed among most Stern graduates, alumnae of Drisha, and other such committed Jewish educational institutions to assume these new leadership roles that female rights advocated have envisioned for them. Again the economics of Jewish professional life has produced a type of gender equality of a different sort. Like their male counterparts who study for the rabbinate and then end up in secular careers, most of these bright young women who have studied long and well do likewise. As one older female activist has said about the career trajectories of her younger sisters: "A year or two at Drisha — and then they become investment bankers."[24]

By a similar token, as summer 2007, only four North American women have devoted the "two years (over 1,000 hours)" to intensive study with rabbinic authorities at the Nishmat Institute of Advanced Torah Study in Jerusalem to gain the credential as a "*yo'ezet halacha*" — female halachic adviser — to answer women's questions on family purity laws, fertility, and sexuality. As of that date, that school had graduated some forty advisers, most of whom work within Israel. Throughout the ages, rabbis' wives had quietly fulfilled some of those roles, assisting their husbands in these delicate personal areas. But now, these official designees come to this family issue armed with both Talmudic erudition and instruction in women's medicine. Still here too, a mixture of social and economic issues has retarded the efflorescence of this warranted service. One of the three *yoazot* who work in the metropolitan New York area has said with sadness: "There is such a need . . . but because of political, financial issues they have not been hired by other shuls. Because of privacy issues involved it can be hard to gauge the need and raise the finances." To her great dismay, "sometimes women come to me years after issues have arisen and only if they had known about us . . . we could have prevented or at least diminished heartache and frustration and sometimes (misdirected) anger at halacha." Time will tell how many congregations will eventually request such female authorities and whether enough women will be willing to set aside so much time and expend enormous energies to meet an undeniable need.[25]

More generally, women who have received advanced Talmudic training and desire careers in Jewish lines of endeavor have found their niches in the realm of education. If they are destined to become an "elite cadre of female scholars of Talmud and halacha, who will serve as leaders and role models for the Orthodox Jewish community," they are doing so mostly as teachers in day schools or as lecturers or scholars-in-residence to both men and women. Those were the careers to which Stern Joseph and Margolin Halickman gravitated. The former taught in day schools on Long Island and as of 2007 was seeking a doctorate in Jewish education. After settling in Israel, Margolin Halickman became the founder and director of an organization that she has reported operates "Torah study groups for residents of Jerusalem who would otherwise not have access to Torah study (senior citizens, moms with babies, etc.)" and has written a volume of weekly Torah thoughts. In another inadvertent aspect of gender equality, women who have acquired advanced Talmudic training are pursuing career paths comparable to many rabbinical students. These are men who upon gaining ordination prefer to teach rather than preach, and who find their calling too in Jewish education. Of course, as Orthodoxy is today configured, men can also move, if they choose, to rabbinic positions. Women cannot.[26]

The long-term opponents who were closed to innovations in the roles women were playing within Orthodoxy, saw all of these positions, except for women instructing women but not teaching them Talmudic texts, as the latest feminist perversion of tradition. The Ner-David case was deemed by them to be ultimately just the most abhorrent attack against the halacha and the Jewish family. In 1982, as women's tefillah groups began to gain popularity, the Agudath ha-Rabbanim unequivocally condemned these "minyanim," as they were quick to call these assemblages, and admonished those "rabbis" — the quotation marks were indicative of their opprobrium — who "have promoted such an undertaking" that "we will take the strictest measures to prevent such 'prayers' which are the product of pure ignorance and illiteracy." Without question, they declared that "a daughter of Israel may not participate in such ceremonies that are totally contrary to halacha." To all, they cried: "Do not make a comedy out of Torah."[27]

Having said this unequivocally, the resistant group's most influential decisor, Rabbi Moses Feinstein, did leave open, at least theoretically, the possibility that what he called "a women's minyan" could be countenanced halachicly. Beginning in a private answer tendered in 1975, and then in a series of published responsa, the first of which was printed in 1982, Feinstein ruled that "all women are permitted to perform even those commandments which the Torah did not obligate them [to do]." Those who do so "have fulfilled a mitzvah and [receive] a reward for the performance of these commandments." Practically that meant, according to that eminent sage, that a woman, for example, "would be permitted to wear tzizith, provided the garment be of a fashion different from the standard men's talis." There is a rabbinic prohibition against gender cross-dressing. Presumably, a women's tefillah group, whose procedures a widely respected rabbinic authority oversaw, could be accepted. For him, crucially, the overriding determinant of the permissibility of such practices was the intention and motivation of the woman in taking these acts upon herself. "Only if her soul desires to fulfill mitzvoth," Feinstein opined, unfettered "by grievance with God and His Torah" would the tradition judge her activities favorably. Otherwise, these innovations constituted "forbidden acts . . . violating the prohibition of heresy — since she thinks that the laws of the Torah are subject to change — [not only in thought, but] also in deed, which is [all the more serious]."

However, as Feinstein's bottom-line viewpoint became clearer — based on the notes that his grandson secretary, Rabbi Mordecai Tendler, recorded — the reality was that he believed that "de facto, it is hard to find an instance where this fault will not be present." Tendler would write that his "grandfather pragmatically feels that the possibility of a group of women, or for that matter, men, existing in one community which will fulfill the lengthy philosophical criteria" — of piety, of unquestioning fidelity to "God's Torah and Jewish custom" — to justify such activities is "extremely rare." Therefore, realistically speaking, he does not commend or actually condone the establishment of women's prayer groups."[28]

Still, some women who desired the revered rabbi's imprimatur clung to his initial hypothetical scenario, asserting that they were conducting themselves "for the sake of heaven." Such was the response of city councilwoman Susan Alter, a leader of the Flatbush Women's Davening Group, to a biting and deprecating published call for her and her members to "be rid of our toys and trinkets . . . quit pandering to our petty psychological chimeras . . . [and] unite, men and women . . . to fulfill *His will,* for *His* greater glory." Responding to her attacker who called for his "sisters" of the Flatbush group "to attend the synagogue when they pray," Alter asserted that "all of his 'sisters' do just that, three weeks out of every month. It is only once a month that they conduct their own halachic service," a "beautiful, once-a-month women's Shabbat prayer service" to which she invited his "wife, daughters, if he has any" to attend.[29]

Feinstein's leaving the door somewhat ajar on the question of females as a group reading the Scroll of Esther gave Alter and her compatriots both consolation and encouragement. As Tendler explained in 1985, Feinstein decided that since women are obliged to hear the Megillah on Purim, he saw no statutory prohibition to a public reading by women.[30]

That same year of 1985 found five leading *roshei yeshiva* at the Yeshiva Rabbi Isaac Elchanan unmoved with women's tefillah advocates' representations of their piety and commitment to the halacha. In a one-page responsum to president of the Rabbinical Council, which Hershel Schachter elaborated upon in a subsequent piece that year in a Yeshiva journal on halacha, these influential Talmudists explicitly accused those participating in women's "minyans" — again that appellation — of multiple transgressions. They were engaged in "licentiousness," and in breaking down appropriate religious gender differences. Partakers were unconscionably emulating the "ways of the gentiles," in this case with the women's liberation movement. Such services, deemed misrepresentations of the Torah's teachings, as well women's Megillah readings and their carrying of the Torah around their sections of the sanctuary, were major abridgements of the traditionally ascribed modest and private status of Jewish women. Through these words, these Yeshiva rabbis aligned themselves closely with the position of the Agudath ha-Rabannim and the Agudath Israel, organizations that on many other fronts opposed Yeshiva's mission and outlook.[31]

It was a cruel irony — "a sick joke" — that these five rabbis aligned themselves with those who regularly opposed everything that Yeshiva preached and taught. Such was the angry opinion of the Orthodox social commentator David Singer who, reflecting that same year on the dilemmas of being kosher at Club-Med, admitted to being "frustrated" with the absence of recognized rabbinic authorities who would opt for an expansive reading of the Shulchan Aruch. Four of them, Singer also reported, were trained at the institution that "now provides all of them with their livelihood." Essentially, for this disenchanted Yeshiva alumnus, the women's issue was but another indication that his alma mater was losing its way.[32]

These heated comments provoked a Yeshiva rabbinic alumnus to defend his teachers and to, in turn, upbraid Singer for his "lack of understanding of halacha." There was a world of difference between denying the value of secular education — as staunch Agudists might do — and to oppose emulated "*chuqat hagoyim* [following gentile ways] with regard to liturgical innovations," as these loyal Yeshiva rabbis, devoted to their school's and the faith's traditions had properly done.[33]

As battles like these within and without Yeshiva's constituencies continued, an even-tempered Rabbi J. David Bleich, whose sympathies clearly lay with his fellow roshei yeshiva, allowed that now "that the dust generated from the controversy has settled somewhat," it behooved all to step back and consider his "dispassionate argument." For him, no one should gainsay that "many women who participate in women's prayer groups are highly sincere and are prompted by the loftiest of motives." The problem, however, stood with "their rabbinic mentors [who] have misled them by reason of the latter's own lack of erudition." For Bleich, these other Orthodox rabbinical associates were not essentially evil. They simply were ill equipped to render religious judgments.[34]

Where did Rabbi Soloveitchik, Schachter's teacher and Bleich's faculty colleague, stand on this tumultuous question? Here too, as in other areas, disciples and spokespeople who claimed to have the Rav's inner ear offered different visions of where this central eminence at Yeshiva stood. One reported that Soloveitchik, early on, "after expressing his own negative opinion on the subject," passed the ultimate determination of the propriety of women's tefillah over to Feinstein. But, in general, those who quote their Rav project him as possessed of a decisive vision. However, they differ fundamentally over what Soloveitchik actually decreed. As always, claiming a unparalleled understanding of his uncle's torah emanating "not only from the perspective of a close disciple, but also from one who was privileged to be part of his family and household, and who was able to know him, speak to him, and learn from him as only a family member can," Moshe Meiselman has averred "clearly, for the record, that the Rav halakhically forbade, without equivocation, women's prayer groups, pseudo-*keriat ha-Torah* [Torah readings] and all forms of women's *hakafot* with *sifrei Torah* [carrying the Torah around the synagogue]." According to this telling, as Soloveitchik considered circumstances that called these innovations into practice, the motives of the women who committed themselves to these activities were of no consequence in ascertaining the permissibility of women's tefillot. It was black-letter law that such innovations were forbidden, and no questions to be asked about whether these people were religiously sincere in their actions. In Meiselman's heated rhetoric, "to associate the Rav with positions and events that he viewed as silly is to desecrate the memory of a Torah giant."[35]

Chiming in, possessed of comparable familial cachet and with the same theological and intellectual disposition, Soloveitchik's grandson Rabbi Mayer Twersky, who followed in his footsteps as a member of Yeshiva's Talmud faculty, argued that "the Rav's consistent opposition to women's tefilla groups was dictated by *halachic values* [emphasis his], not halachic details. " As he understood Soloveitchik, despite a women's tefillah group's "technical compliance with the particulars of *hilkhot tefilla* [laws of prayer]," they "distort the fundamental concept and experience of *tefilla.*" For his grandfather, "desiring and emphasizing active participation and leadership" were concepts "antithetical to authentic service of the heart, which expresses the sentiment of [calling out to the Almighty] 'from the depths,'" the essence of prayer.[36]

Twersky's projections of Soloveitchik's views came as no surprise to advocates of change who also claimed the Rav as their authority. Just two years earlier, writing in a similar, if arguably even more controversial vein, Twersky had projected his grandfather as actually tempered, rather than expansive, in his approach toward Talmud training for women. While not gainsaying the historical reality that Soloveitchik had initiated this discipline for girls at Maimonides and had delivered that landmark inaugural lecture at Stern College, Twersky nonetheless asserted that the Rav's activities did not "bespeak a modern instinct and reformist proclivities." A closer look at Soloveitchik's position, he maintained, revealed a rabbinic authority who wanted girls to learn the portions of the Talmud that were germane to their better performance of the commandments. At Maimonides, Twersky pointed out, the Talmud curriculum focused on the sections of the Oral Law that deal with holidays as well as the specific tractate that was concerned with the laws of kashruth. But that style of learning, he continued, did not constitute an open invitation to women to study all aspects of the Talmud, as men did.[37]

Also acting in character, those who disputed Meiselman's and Mayer Twersky's representation of Soloveitchik's thought and opposed the viewpoints of Schachter and his colleagues tendered a very different understanding of their rebbe's orientation. Based too, reportedly, on their own and colleagues discussions with the eminence, they depicted Soloveitchik, not unlike Feinstein, as accepting, at least in theory, that a women's tefillah could be countenanced under Jewish law. As another supporter of the Orthodox women's movement, Rabbi Simcha Krauss of Queens, New York, interpreted the Rav, "though problematic" it was "certainly not beyond the pale" of the halacha. In this view, what the women wanted did not deeply offend his core halachic values, as Mayer Twersky argued. Rather Soloveitchik's reservations were in the realm of religious outlook and public policy.[38]

Had the import of these women's activities been otherwise, said this side of the argument, and thus constituted a clear and present challenge to the tradition, Soloveitchik surely would have signed on with his five respected colleagues. As this version of the Rav's activities has it, he refused to succumb to repeated pressures to be part of a united front as resisters. According to his personal assistant, in 1985 Soloveitchik gave the latter unequivocal instructions "that if anyone should ever assert that he did . . . sign the responsum," he "should publicize the falsity of the claim." Also part of the story, says his erstwhile assistant, was Soloveitchik's ill health that precluded him from reviewing the "*pesak* [decision] and therefore [he] neither expressly accepted nor rejected its specific arguments."[39]

Still, Soloveitchik had major concerns about this religious phenomenon. As one supporter of change unabashedly listed them, the Rav did not like, for example, the clear deviations from accepted synagogue customs that women's tefillahs fostered. He was fearful of "brinksmanship." If rabbis acquiesced on this policy where there was some room for "flexibility," were they not opening the door "for a call for change in other areas . . . where there was little or perhaps no room for maneuvering"? He was uncertain whether these women were out for "greater spirituality . . . or consciously or not something else, perhaps public peer approbation, conspicuous religious performance, or a sense of equality with men." Sensing that these groups would not fully meet these females' expectations, he worried that they "would merely foster increasingly unfulfillable expectations, resulting in greater frustration and perhaps even a break with the halacha." He also looked down the road and wondered whether "rabbinic approval of these activities "might be interpreted as an implicit validation of the claims and principles of feminism, thus leading to *hillul Hashem* [a desecration of God's name]."[40]

Nonetheless, as this camp represents Soloveitchik's actions beginning in the 1970s, when specific communities or individuals approached him about the propriety of women's tefillah, the Rav acquiesced. As this history has been retold in almost legendary fashion, the first deputations to Soloveitchik came not from rabbis but from a group of women students from Brandeis University who were intent on forming such a group whatever his ruling was. Attempting to make the best out of a bad situation, to mitigate the damage that might accrue to Jewish law, Soloveitchik decided to give specific guidelines on how to proceed to those who were going to move ahead with their initiative. These protocols then became the basis for procedures that would be countenanced among those so moved for change within established congregations.[41]

Riskin reportedly received the same unbridgeable ruling from Soloveitchik — that public prayer elements had to be removed from all such activities — when he turned to his mentor for guidance and approbation before Simhat Torah in 1971. While Soloveitchik declared the entire women's tefilla endeavor both "tokenism" and not worthy of the "political price," still Riskin has said that "the Rav conveyed to him a sense that he had confidence in [his] judgment of . . . community needs." It was the particular Jewish societal context of committed people clamoring for change that carried the day toward grudging approval. Riskin also has allowed that subsequently he afforded Soloveitchik the opportunity to rescind his permission. As the story goes, "a few short years" after the women's group became a feature of his synagogue, the loyal student was informed that Soloveitchik was "displeased" with the goings-on. Riskin inquired whether he should "pull back on the whole thing." When he received an unequivocal response of "no" from his revered teacher, the services continued as before.[42]

As testimonies and intellectual brickbats were exchanged both from within Yeshiva's diverse circles and the larger devout Orthodox community about what the great rabbis said — and did not say, and to whom, when, and why — critics of feminism within Orthodoxy reviled the movement's most outspoken supporters. Bleich, as noted, asserted that women had been "misled" by their "rabbinic mentors . . . by virtue of the latter's lack of erudition." Meiselman pulled no punches in alleging that Soloveitchik "felt betrayed by those of his students who willingly took advantage of his name and failing health to create a movement that was opposed to his most basic philosophical and halakhic views." Agudist Rabbi Nisson Wolpin, editor of the *Jewish Observer,* joined a co-author, Levi Reisman, in characterizing those whom they denigrated as "initiat[ing] . . . clear breaks with the *Mesorah* [Orthodox tradition]" as "social activists, even if they are ordained" who have arrogated "weighty decisions [which] are the province of *Gedolei Hador* [leading Sages of the Generation]."[43]

Although many who advocated for prayer groups and other changes in women's roles were thus upbraided, rabbis Saul Berman and Avi Weiss were particular high-profile targets of attack. Berman's provocative pedigree included his authorship as early as 1973 of "The Status of Women in Halakhic Judaism." There, after identifying "the sources of discontent" — including "deprivation of opportunities for positive religious identification, disadvantaged position in areas of marital law and relegation to a service role" — he affirmed much of "the justice of the complaints" and made "some modest proposals for confronting the problems." In the course of his prescribing, he made clear to all who might belittle the weight of the complaints that it was "both dishonesty and dysfunctional to attempt through homoletics [*sic*] and scholasticism to transform problems into solutions and to reinterpret discrimination to be beneficial."

He remonstrated that "to suggest that women don't really *need* [emphasis his] positive symbolic mitzvoth because their souls are already more attuned to the Divine, would be an unbearable insult to men; unless it were understood, as indeed it is, that the suggestion is not really to be taken seriously but is intended solely to placate women." He also took a strong stand on another point of high communal tension that in time would pit Orthodox groups against one another, namely, that "it is time to stop talking about the reluctant husband-Agunah problem and to do something about resolving it." In one of the most egregious transgressions of this era, some men who were hypocritically dedicated to observance of the ritual commandments, but not Judaism's moral codes, were leaving much human damage in the wake of their refusals to grant writs of divorce to their former wives. For Berman, "apologists only serve to exacerbate the problem and to convince increasing numbers of women that the Rabbis are engaged in an all out battle to keep women subjugated."[44]

That article appeared just a year after Berman had already heightened his profile on women's issues when as chairman of Jewish Studies at Stern College; he welcomed his rebbe, Rabbi Soloveitchik, as the latter helped him open the school's Talmud curriculum. In 1984 Berman would leave his chairmanship at Stern to succeed Riskin at the avant-garde Lincoln Square —a post he would hold for six years—while he continued to teach and preach his messages to a coterie of students who enrolled in his classes. Outside shul and classrooms, he was a frequent featured guest speaker at major Orthodox feminist conclaves.[45]

Meanwhile Avi Weiss, Berman's friend and long-time colleague at Stern, where he too developed his own devoted cadre of female disciples, allowed in his own synagogue more experimentation and innovation than within any other Orthodox congregation in the United States. His rationales, as expressed fully in his *Women at Prayer* (first edition, 1990) —considered a "start-up" book for many women's prayer groups—were based on a very expansive understanding of Soloveitchik's do's and don'ts. As he related his own crucial conversation with the Rav on the question of whether women could carry Torahs through their section of the sanctuary, he admittedly heard, "with great clarity," the authority's response of: "Don't do it." However, according to Weiss, when he posed a follow-up question: "But Rebbe, are you saying it is *assur* [prohibited]," Soloveitchik replied: "I didn't say it's *assur*. It's *mutar* [permissible], but I want to protect you."

From this encounter, Weiss divined that Soloveitchik's opposition was not "a halakhic *pesak* [decision]," but a kindly reticence, "an expression of concern" to protect his erstwhile student. Thus, deeming his teacher's call as "certainly not halakhically binding," Weiss chose "respectfully" not to follow it.[46]

In a subsequent edition of *Women at Prayer*, Weiss went even further and allowed that "the Rav . . . always encouraged me and my colleagues in the rabbinate to *pasken* [make halachic decisions] for our respective communities on these matters, for he realized that it is for the individual Rav who has the responsibility to decide what is best for his community." Weiss also has claimed, based on his own conversations with Rabbi Mordecai Tendler, that such was the pragmatic position of Rabbi Moses Feinstein. "In any event," the Riverdale rabbi asserted, "public policy can be fluid and what was bad policy years ago might be beneficial, or to the contrary." In this respect, Weiss argued that with the experience of a generation of women's activities behind everyone, "some of the Rav's hesitations . . . based on the fact that these groups may be a first step in moving toward egalitarian practices of non-Orthodox movements have just not been realized." After twenty years of women's prayer groups, it was clear for Weiss, "that these practices are not a slippery slope" away from traditional practice.[47]

Beyond staking his claims to a correct reading of Soloveitchik's views that served as the underpinning for his Hebrew Institute of Riverdale activities, Weiss was, already by the mid-1990s, quite the institution builder in promoting feminist Orthodox activities. As of 1997, he had established — with Berman as a key colleague — MeORoT, a "Modern Orthodox Rabbinic Training Fellowship" and, subsequently, a distaff educational and leadership group called Torat Miriam. Both outlets were designed to sensitize, first men and then women disciples too, to the challenges of feminism among the welter of contemporary concerns that they deemed of vital communal importance.[48]

Weiss's assertions and activities on the women's issue earned him considerable criticism. One reviewer of *Women at Prayer* suggested that Weiss had "not fully considered the effects of bitter disputes that may arise in congregations where such groups may emerge." His advice was that "before seeking to establish such groups, all of the ramifications and aspects of minhag must be carefully considered and fully clarified by recognized authorities." It was not, thus, the local rabbi's decision as Weiss had asserted.[49]

But, as disconcerting as Weiss's advocacy of women's prayer groups was to his opponents, it was his unbounded openness toward, and willingness to cooperate with, rabbis of all religious stripes that brought down formal censure upon him. Conservative and Reform rabbis were always welcome to speak in his shul. He sustained friendly working relationships with all types of Jewish interdenominational boards of rabbis. His refusal to cancel his affiliation with the ultimately short-lived Fellowship of Traditional Orthodox Rabbis led, in 1991, to efforts to strip him of his membership in the Rabbinical Council of America. In many ways, the Fellowship was made up of rabbis who ministered in congregations that Orthodoxy's time had forgotten. Most of them had mixed seating or no mechitza, and their otherwise Orthodox practices and rituals were reminiscent of the bad old days of the movement even as they were avant-garde in their support of feminism within Orthodoxy. As the Rabbinical Council and the Orthodox Union moved incrementally to completely disenfranchise these congregations, those who were so marginalized bonded together hoping that their strength in numbers would preclude "the . . . recourse for such congregations . . . join[ing] Conservative organizations."

Weiss applauded the Fellowship's stances on women as well as its attitude toward working with all Jews "regardless of denominational affiliation." He felt "empathy with rabbis who were in . . . the difficult position of trying to bring a mixed-seating synagogue into full compliance with Orthodox law." However, for the Council, his affiliation smacked of "dual loyalty"; he was demanded to choose between the two. When the unintimidated rabbi refused to conform, Weiss was notified that he was no longer a member in good standing. Quick to jump to his defense, Weiss's congregation rushed to place full-page ads in Jewish newspapers, lauding his contribution to both their Riverdale community and to all Jews worldwide. There also was talk about lawsuits against the Council, charging that its move against Weiss constituted "abuse of . . . right of free association and an alleged improper denial of credentials." In the end, Weiss retained his Council membership.[50]

Notwithstanding these battles, Weiss did, however, get a partial personal pass in some of the same Orthodox quarters for his high-profile efforts in fulfilling the great mitzvah of *pidyon shevuim*, redeeming captives, especially in speaking out and fighting for the freedom of Soviet Jews. His congregation would make just that point in defending him in 1991. But even here, within the contentious realm of Orthodox Jewish politics kudos for his activism were not universal. There were vocal disagreements on how to perform that crucial commandment of saving other Jews that loomed large over the contemporary scene.

Rabbi Pinchas Teitz, the unofficial but highly influential and powerful chief rabbi of Elizabeth, New Jersey, was especially critical of Weiss and his associates, many of whom were the Orthodox members of the confrontational though nonviolent Student Struggle for Soviet Jewry, for their demonstrations against Soviet officials and institutions in America. For Teitz, public protests would only "convince the Russian government that Jews are the enemies of Russia." Instead, he advised Jews to send telegrams to Russian officials applauding their positions and calling upon them to do their utmost to improve the lives of Russian Jews. A more efficacious strategy was to "contact American officials and induce them to make Soviet-Jewish emigration an American problem."

As a distinguished leader of the Agudath ha-Rabbanim, Teitz acknowledged that there might be situations when taking to the streets was appropriate. Recalling his organization's actions during World War II, Teitz declared "when the Agudath ha-Rabbanim thought it was necessary during the Holocaust, we did. But now we don't because we see it's harmful." Weiss responded: "When we screamed the loudest, the doors . . . opened up. . . . Didn't we learn anything from the Holocaust? Appeasement is not the way."[51]

While his persistent, if nonviolent confrontational style raised the hackles of Orthodox political conservatives, the extremist Orthodox Rabbi Meir Kahane, founder of the Jewish Defense League in New York, belittled Weiss's strategies toward Soviet diplomats as weak-kneed. Kahane, who headed his own Kach party after his migration to Israel in 1971, also criticized Weiss for not being prepared to go to any extreme to preserve and protect the West Bank settler movement and the territorial integrity of Israel itself, a basic mandate to which they were commonly dedicated. Though Weiss would go so far as to defend Jewish gunmen, aligned with Gush Emunim who attacked three Arab village mayors who had supported terrorism against Jews, Weiss would in no way support Kahane's proposal, criticized worldwide as racist, to solve the Arab problem in Israel through their deportation.[52]

Standing as he does near Orthodoxy's accommodationist pole on women's rights and on cooperation with Jews of all persuasions in America while stationing himself at its resistant borders on Israeli politics, Weiss occupies an uncommon spot within Orthodoxy's contemporary ideological spectra. He has thus, for example, found himself sharing common cause with Agudists and some Yeshiva people who oppose any plans for Israel to give back land to the Palestinians, the same antagonists who oppose his views on women and do not have his staunch affinity for the teachings of Religious Zionism. At the same time, while he is in league with leading advocates of feminism within Orthodoxy and is an irrepressible Mizrachiite, his views differ from his colleagues in their sense of Israeli strategic needs and priorities. Berman, for example, was a charter member of *Shvil HaZahav* (Golden Path), an Orthodox Zionist advocacy group made up largely of Yeshiva rabbis who have actively supported land-for-peace plans in attempting to find an equitable solution to the ever present Israel–Palestinian crisis. For their efforts in this most critical Jewish foreign-policy realm, similarly opinioned people such as rabbis Shmuel Goldin of Congregation Ahavath Torah in Englewood, New Jersey, Marc Angel of Congregation Shearith Israel, Haskel Lookstein of Kehilath Jeshurun, and Adam Mintz, then of Lincoln Square Synagogue, among more than a score of colleagues, many of whom also have pro-Orthodox feminism profiles, have absorbed the strident criticism of others within and without Yeshiva's Talmud faculty. In 1998, Rabbi Moses Tendler, Mordecai's father and the late Rabbi Feinstein's son-in-law, went so far as to say it was a "desecration of God's name for an Orthodox rabbi to present a position that is contrary to God's law." For Tendler, it was "a fundamental axiom of Judaism: You cannot sacrifice a Jew today in order to save many Jews tomorrow." Wholeheartedly in his corner were Aaron Soloveichik and others associated with an organization called the International Rabbinic Coalition for Israel that more than seconded his condemnations in advertisements appearing in Jewish and general circulation newspapers. Aaron Soloveit-chik's nephew by marriage, Rabbi Aaron Lichtenstein, on the other hand, defended the Shvil HaZahav as, once again, crisscrossing battle lines were drawn in deeply dug Orthodox sands.[53]

However, well beyond Berman, Weiss, and all other spokespeople attacked for their positions on feminism and the other religious and political issues, one controversial couple, Rabbi Irving "Yitz" and Blu Greenberg share the unrivaled distinction of being the greatest objects of opprobrium from those antagonistic toward accommodationist stances. At the same time that they have been reviled, this maverick rabbi and his spouse, the "mother" of women's rights within Orthodoxy, also have been revered by their devoted followers. Possessed as they are with an uncanny ability to organize those committed to their causes and to articulate counterattacks to their opponents, the Greenbergs have always shown themselves at the ready to rebuff those who have attacked them and their visions.

By the time Rabbi Greenberg scolded his community during the Bergman affair for enabling corruption to exist in its midst, he was already establishing a reputation, on many fronts, as a confrontational critic within Orthodoxy. Referring to himself as an "impatient lover" of his movement, he chided it for "refus[ing] to come out of the East European ghetto" and as having "lost all connection with modern life." The professorial lectern at Yeshiva College, where he taught history after taking his doctorate in history at Harvard in 1959, was his initial rostrum for expressing his views. The Brooklyn-born Greenberg had achieved his baccalaureate degree at Brooklyn College six years earlier, while earning ordination in his home borough from the Beth Joseph Seminary. Quick to emerge as a "campus celebrity," he gathered around him a coterie of student intellectuals who would stick with him and his opinions for the next forty years. He would also incite the ire of other thoughtful students who would oppose his positions over the same long time period.[54]

According to Greenberg's recollections, his challenging ideas were first presented publicly — outside, that is, of his classroom — in 1966 when he sat for what he thought was a private interview with a student about Greenberg's "thinking on Modern Orthodox issues." Soon, however, his "unguarded" remarks were in the public domain as his ruminations appeared "improperly," without his review in the student newspaper.[55] Whatever was Greenberg's knowledge aforethought of the appearance of his ideas, his contention, to begin with, that there was a need for a "thorough reexamination of the Shulchan Orach [*sic*]" since "today, there are some experiences which halacha doesn't cover adequately and we are unwilling to apply many *halachot* [laws] that deal with contemporary problems," stirred much discussion within and without the school. His views that the *Poskim,* the revered Orthodox decisors, "aren't meeting their responsibilities in updating and fully applying our law codes" raised hackles in many quarters.

One area in particular where Greenberg believed these religious leaders were unresponsive was in the area of sexuality (perhaps a more apt term is gender relationships, to use a more contemporary term). Greenberg would say and the periodical would report that "today the Poskim . . . should promulgate a new value system and corresponding new halachot about sex," the "basis" of which "should be the concept that experiencing a woman as a *zelem elokim* [a creation in the image of the Almighty] is a mitzvah just as much as praying in Shul." On another set of critical issues, like those that swirled around the propriety of the Vietnam War that was then splitting America, Greenberg was dismayed that students did not delve into the Torah's teachings to determine proper, active Jewish responses to this crisis. He asserted that it was the mission of a forward-thinking traditional faith to "operate with the classic halachic framework that would be willing to relate symbolically and sympathetically to the modern experience and shape it with the categories of the halachah."

Perhaps as unsettling to many listeners and readers, Greenberg allowed that even as "Orthodoxy refuses to show sympathy to those who respond authentically to the fact that Orthodoxy has lost all connection with modern life, Conservative and Reform have taken the risk . . . and dealt seriously with the problem." Greenberg did not concur with these liberal movements solutions to present-day dilemma, but he was uncommonly appreciative of their efforts.[56]

As Greenberg tells it, with a firestorm growing over his remarks within Yeshiva's circles, pressures were placed on Rabbi Joseph Soloveitchik to condemn him. However, the Rav, who according to Greenberg "had a limited but special relationship" with this faculty member, told him "that no matter what they do, I will never denounce you publicly." Greenberg recalled that Soloveitchik "recognized and was pleased with his strong influence on my thinking . . . though many of my controversial views grew out of pushing his insights farther than he was willing to go, at least, publicly." Forty years later, Greenberg would still regret that he then lacked the courage to ask Soloveitchik "to speak out and make clear how much these controversial views are rooted in yours."[57]

Greenberg's faculty colleague Aaron Lichtenstein was, however, more than ready to debate Greenberg's views — though he was also not prepared to condemn him. In his view, Greenberg, for the sake of "shaking up the kids" at the school, had taken strident stances and had thus acted irresponsibly and inexactly in criticizing the "Torah Halachic" approach. "Anyone who undertakes to discuss an issue publicly," Lichtenstein let his colleague know, "assumes a double obligation — of inquiry and expression . . . to come as close as possible to the truth and to be as accurate as possible in communicating" it. For example, on the questioning of Greenberg's professed respect for non-Orthodox Jews, Lichtenstein wondered out loud whether his "ecumenism" applied to the vast majority of Reform and Conservative Jews who did not observe or at least countenance the performance of traditional mitzvoth.[58]

In the Agudist world, the critiques were less restrained. Rabbi Shelomoh Danziger characterized Greenberg's attitudes as "pseudo-Orthodoxy" and denigrated him as an apostle of "modernism couched in Orthodox forms," a far cry from the "classical Orthodoxy in modern times" that this interlocutor espoused. Though Greenberg responded pointedly to this attacker, Danziger's treatise also possessed an unsettling personal dimension. His attacker was a neighborhood rabbi in Riverdale where Greenberg, just a year earlier, in 1965, assumed the pulpit at the Riverdale Jewish Center. Greenberg allowed that he had "had the privilege of being a congregant" of Danziger and "appreciated his learning [and] cogent reasoning" even if here "he has not read my own words with . . . sensitivity or accuracy." On this personal point, Danziger revealed his own gentlemanly side when he praised Greenberg's high moral qualities and "his humility, which mark all his personal dealings." Still, he asserted that "we do not want men of Dr. Greenberg's stature to become alienated from the mainstream of Orthodox tradition. *We want him with us, not against us*" [emphasis his].[59]

While these criticisms perturbed him, Greenberg was not deterred. The principles expressed here incipiently would consistently inform his thoughts and activities in succeeding decades. Orthodoxy had to be open within broad halachic boundaries to contemporary mores and concerns, starting with gender issues. The Rav's teachings affirmed Greenberg's positions and proposals. The world's crises, be they at home or abroad, had to be Orthodoxy's. Tolerance of divergent Jewish religious viewpoints was a virtue, if not a desideratum, to maintain unity within this American religious minority group. However, as of the early 1970s, neither Yeshiva nor Greenberg's Riverdale synagogue would be the institutional locus for his ever-maturing ideas. Looking back, he reflected that a combination of growing inhospitality at Yeshiva toward divergent points of view, its lack of enthusiasm for his growing interest in teaching about the philosophical and theological implications of the Holocaust, coupled with his low teaching salary prompted him to accept a professorial post at the City College of New York. There he headed up its new Jewish Studies Department. He also left the Riverdale Jewish Center in 1972 because of a discernible lack of enthusiasm among lay leadership for a proposed Center for Jewish Survival that "could deal with the needed response to the *Shoah* [Holocaust] and Israel and with the growing challenge of freedom and choice." This plan foundered, according to the rabbi, over opposition in the ranks to "the participation of non-Orthodox" Jews in the think tank.

Instead, after a bit stint at City College, where he was again unable to establish his Center, Greenberg created a bully pulpit for the promulgation of his beliefs at the National Jewish Center for Leadership and Learning (CLAL). There, in an unfettered environment, where he could calmly and confidently describe himself "as among the first postmodern Orthodox," he brought together what he considered the best and brightest young rabbis and students from all Jewish movements, to contemplate strategies for Judaism's survival under the contemporary challenges of freedom while they taught Jewish studies and his orientations to a wide and appreciative Jewish audiences. Committed as he was to "Jewish ecumenism," he gained the appellation, in many quarters, as the "Orthodox Jewish Spokesman to non-Orthodox Jewry."[60]

But increasingly his ideas and comments outraged the larger Orthodox community. Although seemingly every position he took touched sensitive nerves, three dimensions of his world outlook, in particular, troubled his critics. His deeply felt personal questioning of God's inactivity during the Holocaust led him to believe that the extermination of six million Jews had destroyed the traditional covenant between the Almighty and Israel. In its wake, he argued, Jews had chosen to affirm a new "voluntary covenant" with God. Now men and women were obliged to be active participants "to reduce evil and suffering . . . bringing out to the fullest the individuality, the equality, and the value of every human being." To his opponents' ears, his crying out over the Shoah was irreconcilable with their allegiance to the eternal binding Abrahamic covenant between God and his chosen people.[61]

Greenberg absorbed additional biting censures when he looked ahead again at the future of his faith community and wondered out loud whether there would be one Jewish people in the twenty-first century. As early as 1984, he warned that "unless action for unity through Jewish learning and law is started soon, Jews will be engaged in a religious civil war." He offered CLAL as a serene safe-zone between battling denominations. Fifteen years later, he said sadly that "the language of argument has turned to the language of delegitimization. This is not the language of family members fighting. This is the language of divorce." He consistently placed responsibility for disunity at the doorsteps of Orthodox leaders. As he saw it, they tragically did not share his view that notwithstanding deep theological disagreements over the divine authorship of the Torah and the authority of the halacha, all Jews were theologically one by virtue of "the covenant of fate of the Jewish people." They myopically refused to dialogue with non-Orthodox rabbis who "are serious scholars and serious religious leaders deserving great respect" who have "made me a better Orthodox Jew." To this set of beliefs, the jaundiced response was that "the issue . . . is not non-Orthodox Jews' or rabbis' character, intellectual acuity, *chesed* [good works] or strength. The issue is their — and our — respective claims to truth. Greenberg's theological pluralism compromises Orthodox Judaism's exclusive claim."[62]

Perhaps, however, Greenberg's most egregious transgression, as far as his opponents were concerned, was his affirmation not only of the value of ongoing ecumenical dialogue with Christians, but his suggestion, in conversing with them, that the original Christians of the first century of the Common Era were "good, faithful Jews" who, in coming to put their faith in Jesus, ended up believing in a "failed" rather than a "false" messiah. This conceptualization of the persona and message of Christianity's central historical and theological figure caused those whom he angered to argue that he had "cross[ed] the line not merely into other forms and fashions of Judaism, but into Christianity itself."[63]

In attempting to marginalize Greenberg as outside the pale of Orthodox thought, those who opposed his philosophies asserted — at least with reference to intra Jewish and Christian ecumenical dialogue — that he broke with the Rav's core beliefs. Had not Soloveitchik, they averred, during the 1950s era of Conservative–Orthodox battles for control of American Jewish communities, come down hard in setting down strict, inflexible rules for Jewish engagements? Likewise, they contended that starting in the 1960s, when Catholic–Jewish discussions were first in vogue in the wake of Vatican II, the Rav unequivocally opposed theological exchanges. However, Greenberg asserted quite to the contrary, first, on the question of Jewish ecumenism. that just as Soloveitchik permitted his followers to work with antireligious Zionists during these times of "historical urgency," so now with American Jewry facing a crisis of spiritual survival, the Rav's teachings can be applied to cooperation and joint efforts with Conservatives, Reformers, and Reconstructionists without surrendering the integrity of Orthodoxy. With reference to interfaith communication, Greenberg recalled that when he and colleague Rabbi David Hartman "informed the Rav in private conversations that they would engage . . . in theological dialogue, he did not express any opposition." Unconvinced by his answers, as of the mid-1980, many colleagues from the Rabbinical Council called for Greenberg's expulsion.[64]

Through these conflicts, Greenberg advocated for feminism within Orthodoxy. In 1985, he combined his belief in the efficacy of a malleable Orthodox halachic process, with his affinity for finding good in what other Jews were doing, and announced that he "respected" the Conservative Movement's "decision not to wait any longer" to permit the ordination of women. For him, "women in the rabbinate will make a major contribution to the enrichment of Jewish life and this step is a moral upgrade of the status of women." But to do so correctly, he argued, "the decision should have been coupled with a commitment to strengthen observance standards so as to reassure traditionalists that admitting women to the rabbinate is not another 'dilution,' but rather a strengthening of Judaism." His preferred scenario would have witnessed an "offer . . . made by women rabbis to refrain from serving as witnesses on halachic personal status documents for a decade — on condition that an intensive Conservative-Orthodox dialogue to work through the issue be pursued."[65]

Irving Greenberg's statements and actions in this arena echoed and reinforced those of his equally outspoken spouse, Blu. Though not a founder of any of the early local women's prayer groups — in Riverdale, she was merely a frequent worshipper at the Hebrew Institute's Women's Tefillah — she emerged in the early 1980s as the most renowned spokeswomen for the Orthodox feminist cause. Eventually she would be awarded the figurative title of "mother" of feminism within Orthodoxy. Part of the prominence of this self-described "mild-mannered yeshiva girl" who found "happiness among the feminists," derived from her writing a comprehensive manifesto articulating the varied dilemmas and concerns of her similarly committed sisters. Her autobiographical exposition focusing on her conflicted loyalties resonated strongly with many of her readers who found themselves in the same existential predicaments.

Growing up in a "strongly traditional" Orthodox family in Seattle, Blu Greenberg felt totally at home with its designated lifestyles. Unlike some of the women who would years later join women's prayer groups because they had felt excluded from ritual action, she remembered not being at all jealous of the boys who had the obligation of public performance at their Bar Mitzvahs. If she took additional note of male responsibilities, she recognized that daily prayer was their burden but not her religious regimen. As a young married woman, she was gratified that she had a supportive husband who encouraged her to expand her secular horizons even as she gave little thought to what she might be missing in the religious realm. She certainly did not envy his trudging off to shul on a cold Sabbath morning, while she could "linger an hour longer in a nice warm bed and play with the kids." As far as barriers were concerned, she did not view the mechitza as a "denigration of women."

But then, like so many other women, she had her consciousness raised through reading *The Feminine Mystique*. However, while Friedan's calls for gender equality engulfed her, Greenberg would travel a long intellectual and social road before she would be ready to apply any provocative principles to Orthodox Judaism. Steps along the way included delivering an opening address at the First National Jewish Women's Conference in 1973. In mixing with her sisters, she discovered that there were other women who aspired to find a place for themselves as observant female Jews within what she described as the "orthodoxy" of feminism, a cause that was to many "a religion—sacrosanct, untouchable, inviolable." From that experience, she also saw a need to create a cohort of like-minded folks to engender the requisite "support, the testing of ideas, the cross-fertilization." Until then, she admitted, "except for conversations with [her] husband, the process had been . . . a very private one." Finally, she learned "to relax" and "not to be so rigid when it came to women's experimentation with new responsibilities." She really resonated to what she saw at "a women's minyan" where she heard female voices at prayer and saw her counterparts read from the Torah much as men had always done.

The book that eventually emerged from her mind, heart, and soul reflected the next eight years of exploration of what the tradition allowed women to do within the realms of Orthodox ritual and practice. She concluded, for example, that there was much open room for "redefining women's status in communal prayer." Negative language that had always been applied to women in the prayers or toward their core mitzvahs of family purity had to be eliminated. And a solution had to be found to the tragic predicament of the agunah. The key for her on all fundamental issues was for the rabbis to have the "will" to find a "way" to progress with all due deference to the Codes.[66]

Blu Greenberg would be from then on widely associated in the public eye with that "will-way" epigram, most notably and controversially when she answered affirmatively, some ten years later, in 1993 to her own rhetorical question: "Is now the time for Orthodox women rabbis?"

Writing at precisely the same time and in the same journal, where Krasner-Davidson announced her matriculation intentions, Blu Greenberg asserted that she believed "the ordination of Orthodox women is close at hand." For her, the growth of Talmud and halachic learning among females, the expansion of educational opportunities for them, and momentum from "the presence of respected women rabbis in the liberal denominations" had all converged to create "a powerful agent for change."

Explaining her understanding of what the rabbinic role was, she exclaimed that "a close look at the convention of ordination . . . reveals that it is not a conferral of holy status nor a magical laying on of hands to transmit authority. Nor does the process uniquely empower a rabbi to perform special sacramental functions." Her analysis of the conceivable halachic objections to such a move proved that a "selective choice of precedents" was in place to retard acceptable progress. As she saw it, the idea that a woman in the pulpit would wound the "honor of the community" surely had to be rethought in light of contemporary values and mores. However, she allowed that, at present, Jewish law prohibited a woman from serving as a witness in a Jewish court of law. That would preclude a woman rabbi from designating herself as a signatory on a marriage contract. Greenberg could live with such a restriction, at least for the time being. But she also asserted, sounding notes resonate of her husband's torah, that "halacha is not static. It contains internal mechanisms of repair; it holds sparks of dynamism and creativity; it's and always has been responsive to special interest groups (if women can be called such) and cases of special pleading." While ostensibly patient, Blu Greenberg remained on the offensive as she concluded that once the ordination of women, that major step in assuring full gender equality within Orthodoxy, is achieved, "from there, we shall see where to go next."[67]

Greenberg's views and strategies rankled critics who challenged not only her Talmudic erudition and methodologies, but questioned her fidelity to Judaism. In one of the more heated confrontations of this era, female Agudist Sori Tropper exclaimed that while "Mrs. Blu Greenberg calls herself an unorthodox Orthodox Jew . . . without touching upon the validity of her arguments, she cannot even consider herself an 'unorthodox Orthodox Jew.'" For Tropper, the feminist's "assertion that it is merely because a group of male-oriented rabbis decreed women's status to be inferior that it is so—smacks of heresy." Greenberg's "implication," Tropper continued, "that cowardice is behind the lack of rabbinic will to flex their halachic muscle to ameliorate women's role denies the Torah view of women." While this self-described "mother of six" from the "Flatbush section of Brooklyn" credited "Mrs. Greenberg" for "not scoffing at the incredible grandeur that is involved in raising a family"—Blu Greenberg was the mother of five— Tropper nonetheless spoke out strongly for her sense of Orthodox family values which she believed Greenberg's movement undermined. In arguing for completely distinctive roles for both sexes, Tropper asserted, with reference to women studying as long and as hard as men do, "I think HaShem created an equally absorbing task for women, not something that they can pick up and leave at will, but rather something that absorbs them totally."[68]

Such retorts were of little moment to Blu and Yitz Greenberg. Of much greater import was their desire to build around them a community of like-minded men and women who believed as passionately as they did in the women's issue as well as their other Orthodoxy–modernity crusades. The Agudists had their cohorts who bore their messages with intense enthusiasm. Yeshiva had its established, if more ephemeral, ranks of followers. Yitz Greenberg, on the other hand, for all the bounties of independence, was often a singular voice, lacking a consistent tangible constituency. Blu, who back in 1973 first experienced the creative power of sisterhood, recalled that beginning in the 1980s, she, as did many other sister activists, had dreamed of convening masses of Orthodox feminists and their male supporters to work as one to advance the cause.

These focused fantasizes were actualized in February 1997 when the First

International Conference on Feminism and Orthodoxy met in New York, with Blu Greenberg as its chairwoman. Though this was surely not its intention, just a few weeks before the gathering's opening, the Vaad Ha-Rabbanim of Queens not only provided the conference with abundant publicity but energized delegates by prohibiting women's prayer groups within Queens. An invitation tendered to girls at a local day school to attend a classmate's Bat Mitzvah, where she would be reading from the Torah, precipitated the ruling. In rendering their negative decision, the rabbis invoked the by-then long-standing views on this issue of rabbis Joseph Soloveitchik and Moses Feinstein or at least their understandings of the Rav's and Rabbi Feinsten's positions. The organizers of the conference, and most of its attendees, did not agree. For one activist, it was the same old story of the predisposed "jump[ing] to conclusions about women's motivation . . . without ever asking the women how they felt or why they were pushing for these changes." Here too, in response to canards, the Rav's name and memory was invoked to bless the proceedings. Yitz Greenberg, reportedly, "cited the writings of the late Rabbi Joseph Soloveitchik . . . to show that increased women's participation is consistent with Jewish law."

Settling down to their workshops and plenaries, the participants celebrated the spread of their maturing ideas and activities and hatched plans for future innovations within Orthodoxy. It was a variegated group that countenanced their obligations toward the Jewish laws governing female behavior in many different ways. One attendee would quip that in the sessions there were "women who wore pants, women who cover their hair and women who wear pants and cover their hair." But in all seriousness, these sartorial and tonsorial decisions reflected varying individual Orthodox women's understanding of religious desiderata. For example, while for some delegates the rabbinic prohibition against gender cross-dressing meant that women could not wear pants, other conference attendees loosely constructed this regulation and allowed themselves to wear slacks cut and styled specifically for women. Nonetheless, there was general agreement in the rooms that women tefillah groups were there to stay, that advances can occur, and had been made in the extent of female participation in daily and family rituals. Pride was expressed at the noticeable advances in growth of Torah scholarship by women. Most attendees applauded Blu Greenberg's assertion that these improvements would in the near future, lead to women attaining Orthodox ordination. There was much sympathy around for her published rejoinder to the Vaad as she said that "it would have been nice for [it] to have treated women with dignity, not like a few little girls to be put in a box."[69]

There was, however, far from full consensus on what could, and should, be done about the pressing problem of the agunah. No unacceptable situa-

Figure 10.2. Scene from the First International Conference
on Feminism and Orthodoxy, 1997. Courtesy of the Jewish
Orthodox Feminist Alliance.

tion spoke more explicitly of what delegates perceived as the double standards in Jewish law as divorce protocols, particularly in the most egregious
cases where recalcitrant husbands literally extorted money from their estranged spouses before agreeing to provide them with a get.

In recent years some progress had been made of a prophylactic nature, to
head off future tragic situations. In 1993, the Rabbinical Council of America
officially recognized that in "some unfortunate instances . . . husbands or
wives, for reasons of spite or venality, refuse to cooperate . . . [in] the
termination of their marriages with a get." A woman, too, can be a recalcitrant in such ugly proceedings and not accept the writ, albeit with less
dire religious consequences. Coming to grips with this reality, the council
adopted "a prenuptial agreement . . . so as to guarantee that the get will not
be used as a negotiating tool in divorce proceedings." Perhaps largely because the author of this innovation was Rabbi Mordecai Willig of Yeshiva's
rabbinical faculty, a man with no affinity for feminism within Orthodoxy, the
agreement gained wide but not universal acceptance. But activists wanted
more than just the promulgation and enforcement of this approach through
"the mediums of Shabbat sermons, synagogue bulletins and other forums,"
none of which did anything for those already afflicted.[70]

To end their pain, those outraged first called upon rabbis to punish
recalcitrant husbands who were regular shul goers through public excoria-

tions and denial of synagogue honors. To their minds, they were miscreants far worse than the Sabbath desecrators. Beyond that form of attack and far more controversially, Agunah International advocated for an annulment formula under a beth-din to free those chained under the existing system of Jewish law. Rabbi Emanuel Rackman was the prime rabbinical force behind the piece of halachic legislation. The elderly leader who, for the entire prior half-century, had been identified by friend and critic alike as one of this country's arch-Orthodox accommodators — he certainly was a hero and role model to younger colleagues like Greenberg and Weiss — legitimized his lenient "halachic practices and procedures" as within the spirit of Rabbi Feinstein's policies on annulments. His daughter in-law Honey Rackman, an outspoken Agunah International official, also unquestionably encouraged the rabbi's effort. Essentially, Rackman and the four other rabbis who signed on to this policy — including Rabbi Irwin Haut, the husband of Rivka Haut, a noted Orthodox feminist author and another major Agunah leader — used, among other modern determinants, "a psychoanalytic concept of human behavior" to ascertain "seeds of deviant behavior . . . at the outset of a marriage," to render such nuptials retroactively invalid.[71]

When the resistant council of sages of the Agudath ha-Rabbanim received wind of this development, acting in character it issued a "cry and protest" against "arrogant 'Orthodox rabbis' " — with those words in quotation marks — whose "spurious 'halachic' reasoning . . . rooted in falsehood and misrepresentation . . . will lead G-d forbid to the proliferation of *mamzeirus* [bastardry] in the Jewish community." But more than just these rabbis, delegates to the feminist Orthodox conference, both then and subsequent to the gathering, voiced reservations to Rackman's ideas and institution. To those like Riskin or Krauss or Goldin, the "actions of this beth-din will not provide solutions but make matters worse."[72]

Still, even as delegates and their supporters walked away from their conference not completely united over how open the halacha could be to address all female concerns, Greenberg and her sisters had armed themselves with an organizational mechanism to advance their struggle and to rebut their constant opponents. The Jewish Orthodox Feminist Alliance started, say its organizers, "around a member's kitchen table" — evoking a domestic image — and took their concerns well out of its constituents' homes in the hope "of continually moving forward while remaining connected to our past." In its first decade of activities, the Alliance sponsored six international and six regional conferences, developed a "gender-sensitive curriculum" for teaching Bible in day schools, and commissioned halachic monographs delving into the sources as Orthodox Jews always do in determining courses of future action, including "listing of dissenting opinions and possibilities for alternative practices."[73]

Championing the cause of the agunah, the Alliance sought to rouse the

Orthodox community from its complacency. In 2006, the Alliance believed that it had scored a major coup when that organization was among those most instrumental in developing an international conference in Jerusalem under the auspices of Israel's Sephardic chief rabbi to find ways and means of ending the misery of those chained, be they in Israel or in the Diaspora. This conclave augured to bring together not only the Alliance's activists but also more conservative Orthodox groups including the Council of Young Israel Rabbis, men who traditionally were closed to most of the women's innovations. However, the initiative foundered when Rabbi Shlomo Amar cancelled the event literally days before its opening. Although Amar did not articulate his reason for backing out, reports had it that "ultra-Orthodox" elements, starting with Rabbi Yosef Shalom Elyashiv pressured him to do so. His colleague apparently argued that any conceivable change would "weaken the Jewish family." The gathering, it was said, "would give the appearance that rabbis are responding to feminist pressure." This decision caused one chagrined American Orthodox rabbi to worry that, in fact, the cancellation of the conference would only "strengthen feminist tendencies because now the perception is that rabbis are not willing to deal with the issue." The Alliance published a petition containing more than three thousand names fittingly during the week of the Fast of Esther — that ancient, heroic Jewish woman activist — calling for "Action for Rabbis and the Orthodox Community," as it endeavored to keep this issue before the public eye.[74]

Almost concomitant with the Alliance raising its first cudgels, in 1996, Edah, an organization with comparable sympathies and constituencies, initiated an intrinsically related effort. Under the chairmanship of Rabbi Saul Berman and asserting that it had "the courage to be modern and Orthodox," this group set out to promote, with all due respect for "Torah, halacha and *kedushah* [holiness], . . . open intellectual inquiry in both secular and religious realms; engagement with the social, political and technological realities of the modern world" and "the religious significance of the State of Israel; and the unity of *Klal Israel* [the Jewish people]." Through that mission statement, these advocates took on — even more than did the Alliance — those who had long tarred their segment of the Orthodox community for its efforts to live in two worlds. They, likewise, critiqued Yeshiva for not standing tall against those — within and without its school — who would delegitimize Torah U Madda. Claiming themselves too as the appropriate bearers of Rabbi Joseph Soloveitchik's legacy, they understood him as encouraging his true disciples — "not clones but people who knew the difference between the text and the living community" — to "have their own [views]" on the "political and social matters" of the day so long as they accepted his "authority on halacha" as "binding." Thus empowered, they were intent on "swing[ing] the community back to the classic Modern Orthodox position," to prove that their understanding was not "a compromised" — or compartmentalized Orthodoxy—that the "Torah is not intended for us to live outside the world."[75]

So disposed, it identified the Orthodox day school as a prime proving ground for the viability and necessity of its ideas. While sure to acknowledge the "powerful passion and piety" of those who chose the Jewish pedagogic calling, its leaders and members lamented time and again that the messages of "the value of general education as a path to God, Zionism, ethics, combating racism and the love of all Jews" were not being imparted to school children. The problem, in Edah's view, was that long-standing one. The best and the brightest "modern and Orthodox" young people had not chosen this rarely honored and poorly paid profession. To reverse that deleterious trend, Berman called for creation of a new "tribe of Levy"—spiritual descendants of those who ministered in the ancient Temple—"educators who would have a high status in the community as servants of God and the Jewish people." That idea translated itself, by 2000, into an incipient "Jewish Teachers Corps program to recruit and train young college graduates for two-year day school teaching assignments, on the model of Teach for America." It was hoped that those who would step up into the perceived void would be charged to imbue students with "a commitment to Jewish heritage, a love of fellow Jews, and receptivity to the world."[76]

Given its agenda and the people driving it, Edah likewise backed all of the Alliance's high profile issues, from the agunah problem "to halachic responses to the changing role of women in the Orthodox world." But there proved to be limits to its commitment to egalitarianism within Orthodoxy. Indeed, 2001–2002 proved to be a time of testing for its pronounced desire to be "an inclusive and multivocal community," when a minority pushed for a form of egalitarianism within Orthodoxy that even the most tolerant part of Edah's majority could not accept.[77]

The problem within its own ranks began when the *Edah Journal,* its scholarly publication, in its avowed spirit of openness to diverse ideas and opinions, printed an article that asserted, based on Talmudic sources, that it was permissible for women to come out of their section of the sanctuary and be called to the Torah in a mixed-gender service. The open-to-all-opinions journal also published a piece that disputed such a claim. Rabbi Mendel Shapiro's treatise in favor of the changes—what he would subsequently call an effort to "create a halachic steamroller" to obliterate all formal prohibitions against women receiving that signal synagogue honor—served as the textual rationale for the emergence of handfuls of egalitarian minyans in Israel, Australia, and the United States. Though never acknowledged as an antecedent, what took place during those services was more than vaguely reminiscent of the ad hoc moves that students at the University of Wisconsin had taken without authorization of any kind some thirty years earlier.[78]

Though proud that his organization was open to "reasoned discourse on issues of enormous importance," and notwithstanding voices both within the Feminist Alliance and Edah to which he was attuned that supported this innovation, Berman remained unconvinced that the study had "created a good enough foundation for varying an 1,800 year-old practice." Pulpit rabbis Mintz and Lookstein and even Weiss—all with strong pro-feminist Orthodoxy pedigrees—agreed. For them, while affirming open discussion, absent of a recognized authority that could approve such a "radical" change, established congregations and their leaders were not ready for such a move. But Rabbi David Silber, Dean of Drisha, also a member of the Alliance's and Edah's rabbinical "inner-circle" demurred. For him, "If a voice came down from heaven" stating that egalitarian minyans were prohibited, he "might [reconsider]." But for now, this most avant-garde thinker and teacher supported such a gathering within his educational institution, as did comparable groups elsewhere in New York, including Riverdale, and in Teaneck, Boston, and on several college campuses.[79]

These intramural disagreements within the Edah mission were of absolutely no moment to its strident critics. Rabbi Moshe Tendler, speaking for the opposition, articulated a refrain to which people like Berman and the Greenbergs were long inured. When asked for his reaction to Edah having drawn reportedly fifteen hundred delegates to its inaugural 1999 conference, this Yeshiva rosh yeshiva denounced Berman, his Stern College colleague, and the other organizers, as lacking "integrity." For him, "they are outside the pale of Judaism, they are ignorant of halacha and most of their leadership lack scholarship."[80]

In January 2006, after a decade of activity, citing unspecified financial reasons having much to do, it is said, with the burdens of ongoing fundraising, Edah formally closed its operations. Proud of its efforts to re-energize Religious Zionism, of its advocacy for women, and its affirmation of the value of secular studies among yeshiva students, and claiming victory in "creating a new benchmark for Modern Orthodoxy" through creation of "some very powerful instruments to transmit its values," Berman and his associates, looked to a variety of local and national organizations with which they were linked to redouble their efforts to implement Edah's "think-tank function." An alternate, uncharitable view of Edah's demise saw it as a triumph for its separatist opponents. According to this dark vision, "the pendulum of leadership and a sense of empowerment has swung to"—or had remained still with—closed, oppositional forces that "control the rabbinate and increasingly the nature of how to define Jewish education."[81]

But while some observers argued that Edah's "passing from the scene" diminished the vitality of voices that augured to "offer a broader spectrum of definitions of what constitutes Orthodoxy," Berman placed his faith for the future within a new Orthodox rabbinical school. In 2000 he helped his long-term friend and colleague Avi Weiss found Yeshiva Chovevei Torah on the Upper West Side of Manhattan. From the school's founding, Berman would lecture to its students and advise Weiss. With the close of Edah, he came on board full time as its director of continuing rabbinic education. Asserting that this school was the place where "Open Orthodoxy Begins," Yeshiva Chovevei Torah articulated as its core values many of the teachings that the Greenbergs and those sympathetic to them had been talking about for, by then, two generations, along with the ideas that Weiss had espoused in a provocative 1997 piece entitled "Open Orthodoxy: A Modern Orthodox Rabbi's Creed."[82]

As a Torah U Madda institution, Yeshiva Chovevei Torah dedicated itself to "inspiring a passionate commitment to the study of Torah . . . and the scrupulous observance of halacha . . . integrating it into all learning, religious practice and worldly pursuits." Under such a mission, it would "encourage intellectual openness, questioning and critical thinking as essential components of . . . service to God." Pluralistic in its approach to all Jews, the school "affirmed the shared covenantal bond" that united them, "promot[ed] *Ahavat Yisrael* [love of all Jews]" while "actively pursuing positive and respectful interaction of all Jewish movements." Attuned to expanding female roles within Orthodoxy, Chovevei embraced "the need to enhance and expand the role of women in *talmud Torah* [the study of Torah], the halachic process, religious life and communal leadership within the bounds of halacha." Ever the Religious Zionist institution, it "recognize[ed] *Eretz Yisrael* [The Land of Israel] as our homeland and affirm[ed] the religious and historical significance of the State of Israel for all Jews in Israel and the Diaspora." On the most basic human level, the school likewise "affirmed the shared *tzelem Elokhim* [image of God] of all people and our responsibility to improve the world." Finally, a pledge was made to "liv[e] our personal, family and public lives guided by the highest ethical and moral standards, reflective of *yosher* [doing what is right] and *kiddush shem Shamayim* [sanctifying God's name]."[83]

All of these teachings — resonant of the many issues that had embroiled their community during this Orthodox vs. Orthodox era — constituted an unambiguous counterattack against the forces that had long excoriated its founders, friends, and mentors. Implicit, but no less significant, Yeshiva Chovevei Torah also challenged the state of affairs at the Yeshiva Rabbi Isaac Elchanan, the school that had trained both Berman and Weiss. Berman would once remark, evoking the legacy of Rabbi Joseph Soloveitchik, that when his rebbe was at the school "there was little thought that anything could compete with that." But, simply put, in his view, times had changed with the decline of Soloveitchik's presence that began in the decade before his death. Projecting itself, without saying so much, as a successor institution to the best that was the Yeshiva that he knew, Weiss initially recruited heavily within the beth ha-medrash where he had once studied even as he welcomed devout students who had received their undergraduate training elsewhere.[84]

Though Weiss and Berman were consistently circumspect in their criticism of Yeshiva for not standing strongly enough against forces within and without their alma mater that undermined its Torah U Madda philosophy — Weiss claimed and lauded Norman Lamm as his "rebbe" — Yeshiva Chovevei Torah's outspoken board chairman was not.[85] At a dinner in June 2004 commemorating the yeshiva's ordination of its first nine rabbis and in a subsequent interview, businessman Howard Jonas excoriated Yeshiva. Resorting to the purplest of prose, Jonas opined that "a lot of right-wing rabbis hijacked the institution. You couldn't put a sheet of paper between most right-wing yeshivas in Brooklyn and RIETS [Yeshiva University's rabbinical school, Rabbi Isaac Elchanan Theological Seminary]." Lamenting the demise of what he called the "last great days" of that school when it "still cared about the world," he characterized it as "gutless and spineless." Although Weiss, Berman, and Chovevei students distanced themselves from this heated rhetoric, a discernible degree of additional damage was done as the two schools offered themselves as vanguards of modernity within Orthodoxy. Though the long-standing Yeshiva — with its many more students and much larger operation — would project itself as *the* flagship institution for their movement, from the Chovevei point of view "there was room for both." As one of its earliest graduates would observe, notwithstanding "a healthy competition . . . both institutions are necessary and have different focuses." For him, "YU serves the community that is the right half of Modern Orthodoxy and Chovevei Torah serves the left half."[86]

Given this era of internecine Orthodox confrontations, whatever criticisms of Chovevei and Open Orthodoxy have emanated from Yeshiva's circles only pale in comparison to those heaped on it from Agudists and those of comparable sentiments. By February 2007, the school had gained enough traction in spreading its message and personnel across this country that it was time for the Monsey, New York, weekly *Yated Ne'eman* — an organ that was formerly allied with an Agudist political party in Israel — to launch an "exposé on [this] threat to Halachic Judaism." In its view, since Yeshiva and the Rabbinical Council of America were not waging enough of an ideological battle against those who "hijacked the title 'Orthodox' to describe its affiliation," it behooved this newspaper to alert the truly devout to a movement that "is a greater threat to Orthodoxy than Reform and Conservative due to their constant refrain that they are 'Orthodox,' while they espouse positions that are decidedly unorthodox and even anti-Orthodox." Among Chovevei Torah's most "egregious . . . transgressions" were its affinities for "pluralism, interfaith relationships and Bible criticism, God-spare us." Chovevei faculty members who "purport to call themselves students of Joseph B. Soloveitchik" were called out to prove that their conduct "would have been sanctioned by Rav Soloveitchik." In this newspaper's opinion, "no amount of 'good,' no amount of '*kiruv*' [bringing the affiliated back toward tradition], 'combating assimilation,' or any other justification can rationalize this clear *ziyuf* " — forgery of Orthodoxy — practiced at Chovevei.[87]

# EPILOGUE: THE TENTATIVE ORTHODOX OF THE TWENTY-FIRST CENTURY

For most of American Jewish history, Orthodox Jews who were not committed to the demands of the halacha outnumbered their deeply devoted brethren. They were drawn to this most traditional expression of Judaism and stayed within its confines out of a belief in the authenticity of Orthodoxy or because of the warmth that emanated from shuls and religious practices that reminded them of the best of ancestral traditions. Or perhaps they were not comfortable in Conservative or Reform surroundings. Over many generations, these men and women filled out Orthodoxy's wide tent as American Jewry's most popular religious movement. In the early post–World War II period, the majority of those who then began to be called "nonobservant Orthodox Jews," left that fold. If they were religiously inclined, they and their children identified with more modern forms of Judaism. Others who became disinterested with Jewish life simply dissociated.

Yet as the old century ended and the new millennium began, tentative Orthodox Jews persisted, especially in communities away from their movement's central venues, even if their existence often went unnoticed among Orthodoxy's committed rank and file. In 1986, a former student of mine,

Rabbi Shmuel Singer, sought to raise national Orthodox consciousness when he wrote a piece for *Tradition,* the scholarly publication of the Rabbinical Council of America. There, reflecting on what Orthodox life was like in the smaller-city communities like Youngstown, Ohio [estimated Jewish population of 5,000], where he had served and the "parallel experiences of colleagues in similar positions," Singer lamented that "religious observance and knowledge" among members of Orthodox synagogues "are in a sorry predicament." It was his unhappy lot to minister to "non-practicing Jews" who "almost always view . . . faith in sociological terms."

Where he, and his counterparts, were Orthodoxy's standard bearers, it was "rare to find a shomer Shabbat family, aside from the Orthodox synagogue clergy and the faculty of the day school, assuming that such an institution existed." Significantly, when he spoke of Sabbath observers, he was referring to public displays of piety. What these folks may have been doing behind closed doors was another matter entirely. On the kashruth front, the "minority who claim to follow the rules . . . usually do not mean that they do so when 'eating out.' " For them, "a kosher kitchen at home" was the extent of their commitment. Looking ahead, for this pessimistic observer, "as the older generation, whether European or American disappears from the scene, the number of individuals for whom *shemirat Shabbat* and kashruth have any meaning continues to decline." Lucky for him, by the time he put his pen to paper, he had secured a position in Providence, Rhode Island which had all the perquisites to make pious Orthodoxy thrive. Most notably, it was blessed with a yeshiva that attracts committed youngsters not only from the New England area, but from other parts of the United States as well.[1]

Though intrigued by Singer's piece, I was motivated to learn more about such communities only subsequent to my publication of an article entitled "Twentieth-Century American Orthodoxy's Era of Non-Observance, 1900–1960," in the *Torah U-Madda Journal,* a Yeshiva University academic publication, avidly and critically read by its core constituency. In that study, I asserted themes that are now familiar to readers of this book. During at least the first fifty years of the twentieth century, "if and when an American Jew attended synagogue, he or she most likely prayed and socialized in an Orthodox synagogue." But that showing up in shul did not necessarily mean that outside of its sacred space, they lived according to the halacha. I also contended that the Orthodox congregations "that serviced these masses were themselves not especially punctilious in their adherence to the demands and requirements of Jewish law as prescribed in the Shulhan Arukh."[2]

Soon after my "nonobservance" article was published, I received an appreciable amount of very uncomplimentary e-mails of two different sorts. Some of my naysayers contended that I was wrong about the religious values of Jews who traditionally attended Orthodox synagogues. Other critics admitted that I was correct in the picture that I had painted, but wondered why I was so moved to recall Orthodoxy's bad old days. Two of the more reasoned and even-tempered interlocutors sent letters to the editor; missives that were published in a subsequent issue of the journal. One recalled and lauded his ancestors' efforts in building "a community vitally interested in Torah learning" and observance of the commandments and was dismayed that my work did not "do justice to the memory of those staunch and persistent Jews." The other writer deemed my article "basically accurate" but he was intent on writing warmly about what religious life had been like in the Brooklyn of his youth during the 1940s–1950s. Interestingly enough, in regaling the journal's readers about the "Orthodox community . . . of Borough Park," he acknowledged that while it consisted "overwhelmingly of people who did not go to work on Shabbat . . . most carried keys or handkerchiefs and answered the phone." That honest recollection only alerted me to the spectrum of religious behavior that then existed among this country's Orthodox affiliates, even within that borough renown for its committed communities.

My rejoinder was that I was keenly aware of the devoted Orthodox efforts and lifestyles of the past and I would continue to tell their story. But my point was that "for the first sixty years or more of the past century, nonobservance within the American Orthodox community was a given and accepted fact of life." It was this other side that "other historians of Orthodoxy have overlooked" that I was determined to recall, warts and all, neither for tribute nor for disparagement. I concluded my reply with the understanding that "what this research . . . reveals is how variegated this community was and continues to be, [making] each of its segments . . . worthy of serious study."[3]

Nonetheless, it was with some uneasiness that I accepted an invitation to speak about my arguments, some months later, at a national conference of the Rabbinical Council of America. Though I was confident with my findings, who likes to think about the possibility of being attacked publicly? To make the situation potentially even more uncomfortable, one of the leading Orthodox rabbis from Chicago who just happened, ironically, to be the older brother of the rabbi of the congregation that I grew up in, was my co-panelist. However, ever the gentleman, and knowledgeable of our "familial" linkages, he was respectful of my presentation. I, in turn, appreciated his study of sources for examining early twentieth-century rabbinic responsa in America. What surprised me, however, was the reaction of the members of the audience at our mid-morning session. Rather than attack my piece of history, during the question-and-answer period, and in informal discussions in the corridor that followed, several young rabbis made it clear that the people I had talked about still populated, if not predominated, within their congregations far removed from New York. For them, the typical minimally committed congregant of their times was the Jew who drove his or her car to Sabbath services, much like their ancestors whom I had mentioned in my talk had done, and parked their vehicles around the corner from the sanctuary.

Indeed, while all of the research is not done on what is an ongoing social phenomenon, my subsequent investigations and personal observations have only confirmed the continuing presence of tentative American Orthodox Jews. They live on today and are not merely a circumscribed graying constituency destined for extinction. Rather, the more I looked particularly, but not exclusively, at communities away from New York, the more I found middle-aged people and their children too who affiliate with Orthodox synagogues but are not committed to devout religious lives, at least not in their entirety.

For example, in 2004, as part of its celebration of 150 years of service to its community, Beth Sholom Beth Israel, the Orthodox synagogue in Charleston, South Carolina, commissioned me to study its history. In examining its most contemporary era, I found that while the shul, over the past thirty years, has watched its membership rolls drop appreciably, with the local Conservative congregation being the prime beneficiary, still the main downtown, historic, synagogue venue continued to welcome "close to six hundred" worshippers during the primetime moments in the Jewish year, "the first day of Rosh ha-Shanah and Yom Kippur right before yizkor." Many of those then in the pews, by the way, also held membership in the competing Conservative congregation. One family in town belongs to all three of Charleston's Jewish houses of worship, including K.K. Beth Elohim, where Reform Judaism started in America back in the nineteenth century. When they are drawn to the Orthodox synagogue, they come often out of a strong sense of filiopietism. That is the holy place where their families attended and fought over for past generations. However, to arrive at that sanctuary on the Sabbath and Jewish holidays, 90 percent of members drive their cars. In keeping with another long-maintained American Orthodox tradition, they park their vehicles out of sight of the shul's front door.

Charleston's Orthodoxy does have its frum families—beginning with the 10 percent who walk to shul on holy days. Their youngsters populate the fine community day school. However, this smaller Jewish community— there are some six thousand souls in the city and environs—has never developed a critical mass of families committed to secondary yeshiva education. All too often, children from observant families leave town as teenagers and never really return. As a case in point, the Orthodox rabbi and rebbitzen who then shepherded that community were blessed with seven children. As adults, their children are making significant contributions to their local Jewish communities, but not in their birth place. Though their beautiful hometown offers a synagogue, a modern mikveh, an eruv, and even Pita King, a kosher eatery that is closed on the Sabbath, in the end, Charleston is just not as attractive as the big cities, where Orthodox Jews can find all their amenities.[4]

As I was finishing *Orthodoxy in Charleston,* a conference presentation at Creighton University brought me to Omaha, Nebraska, where I found an Orthodox congregation and community with similar dynamics and problems. My first indication of struggles in this town was a "Shabbat Service Schedule" flyer that was handed to me when I attended Beth Israel Synagogue on Saturday morning. Besides listing the pages for many of the prayers and the approximate times for their recitation, an asterisk was placed next to "Borchu," that public call to prayer, and other such central elements, with a corresponding note at the bottom of the document that read "only said with a minyan." Apparently that synagogue did not always have a quorum for worship, even on the Sabbath.[5]

Returning three years later to that smaller Midwestern community—its Jewish population, like Charleston's, was approximately six thousand—I found its upbeat, optimistic rabbi asserting that the congregation draws "120 [worshippers] on a big shabbes and 70 regularly" even as he readily acknowledged that only "twenty to thirty" families out of a congregational body of two hundred were Sabbath-observers. A significant portion of his regular attendees drive to synagogue, particularly those who remained in the downtown section of Omaha after Beth Israel and most Jews had relocated some years earlier. Like Charleston, too, many of those who belong to his synagogue also maintain affiliation with the neighboring Conservative congregation. Apparently in this community, Jews gravitate to and from different synagogues, based on their interest in a particular program or exciting rabbi. So when folks drift into his shul, the rabbi makes every effort to sustain their attention short of engaging in "poaching," which by mutual consent among Omaha's rabbis is prohibited. In fact, these colleagues have a rule that no family can join another congregation if they have an outstanding membership balance elsewhere.

But while Rabbi Jonathan Gross makes every honest effort to build his flock and, as his synagogue flyer states, "welcomes all persons of the Jewish faith . . . and accepts the diversity of practice and thought among its members," he too worries about the brain drain among his most committed congregants. Omaha has its mikveh, a dairy kosher restaurant—a modest bagel store—kosher foods in its supermarkets, and a day school that has existed for four decades. However, while the rabbi is proud that the institution had, as of 2007, attracted its largest cohort "in a long while," only forty children attend its kindergarten-through-sixth grade classes. To encourage more families to opt for a dual curriculum school through easing the burden of tuition payments, Beth Israel, somewhat uniquely, offers congregational families a 50 percent scholarship break per child. Nonetheless, Omaha's minority of observant families — again like Charleston's — tend to send their teenage youngsters to out-of-town schools in cities such as Chicago, Cleveland, or Memphis, and "only some return."

Still, Rabbi Gross told me "for the record" that he "became a rabbi to be a rabbi in Omaha." Looking down the road, after he signed a five-year renewal contract in 2007, for him, the major gauge of whether he is successful in his calling will be his ability to "see a generation of kids" stay in town through high school — through the extension of the day school — by "making this a place that youngsters will want to return." At present, the building of an eruv is the critical step in reaching for his dream. As he explained the situation in that same summer when he recommitted to his synagogue; "The main reason we don't yet have an eruv is because until recently we did not have the critical mass of young families that would warrant the expense. It doesn't pay to build an eruv so that a few people can carry their keys to shul. Now we have all of these little children, an eruv is an imperative and please God we will have one very soon."[6]

The problems this young rabbi faces pale, however, in magnitude to those that a much older colleague situated in Portland, Maine, was confronting in 2004 when my lecturing travels brought me to his small community. The Jewish population was approximately 3,900. I was in town during the days preceding Tisha Ba'Av, under the sponsorship of both the local Jewish federation and the rabbi's hundred-year-old congregation. There I witnessed the rabbi struggle to have a minyan the evening of the Fast when the Book of Lamentations is read. He succeeded that night, but not the next morning when eight of us prayed without a quorum. My greatest personal concern that day was whether anyone would have the patience to listen to me for my 6 PM talk after a long day without food or water. The rabbi reassured me, albeit with much sadness, that there would be a turnout since local people like to hear outside speakers. He also told me not to worry about their attention spans since probably only he, his rebbetzin, and I would be the only ones in the sanctuary fasting on that day of Jewish mourning.

Surveying the general communal scene, it seemed that there was little potential for the growth of Orthodox life. Though kosher meat was available for home dining, the only public kosher establishment was the dining room of the local old-age home, to which the rabbi treated me when he and his devoted wife were not feeding me at their house. Indeed, I received the sense that they both lived very lonely existences, especially on the Sabbath when they were perhaps the only observant couple in town. As far as attracting back the grandchildren or great-grandchildren of those who had built this once immigrant congregation, those who affiliated with synagogue life were more than comfortable in Portland's far more vibrant Reform temple. It had plenty of room in its sanctuary for them as well as Jewish newcomers to the city and environs.

A winter 2007 trip to Dallas, Texas exposed me to happier conditions and prospects outside of New York. This substantial community with its Jewish population of roughly 37,000 possesses all the requisite accoutrements for comfortable Orthodox existences — the eruv, mikvehs, kosher eateries, a number of yeshivas and days schools of varying ideological stripes that run from kindergarten through secondary school, including a modern one oc-cupying a magnificent campus. After their childhoods there, their year in Israel and university training, a solid core of young adults returns and builds families and careers in their hometown. Observant migrants from the cold northern rust-belt states also augment the numbers. There are similarly blessed communities — like those in Miami or Atlanta or Boca Raton, Mem-phis or Houston to name just five in Dallas's region — throughout the United States. Still, a visit to the vibrant synagogue that Rabbi Ari Perl, another former student of mine, ministers to also reminded me that in shuls like his there are significant numbers of tentative Orthodox Jews to go along with his majority observant day-school and yeshiva crowd. But the good news for this rabbi is that the "newly initiated" to his form of accepting Orthodoxy who "have previously been affiliated with (and maybe even frequented) Tradi-tional, Conservative and Reform synagogues (maybe even Chabad [Luba-vitch])" make up that impressionable cohort. These Jews are not baalei teshuvah in the classic sense of the term. They may not yet subscribe to all of the teachings and regulations that the halacha prescribes. In some cases they may never do so. Nonetheless, they are moving, as the dynamic rabbi sees it, in the proper direction. The trick for this leader — a model early twenty-first-century accommodationist — is "to create a . . . service that is comfortable and satisfying for the veterans of Orthodoxy while being welcoming, accessi-ble and meaningful to the newly initiated."[7]

Finally, in searching for heterodoxy within contemporary Orthodoxy, in-quire of any Hillel director at a college in the United States about the religious values of many day-school products generally from observant homes who upon arrival at school affiliate with the Jewish college student association. On campus, these affiliates "flip out" from their family religious practices in a very different way from their fellow secondary school alumni who end up at Jewish universities or separatist yeshivas. They partake of their Hillel's kosher meals on the Sabbath and enjoy the camaraderie after at-tending the Orthodox service, one of several options at Hillel' pluralistic center for Jewish life on campus. That synagogue choice reflects their re-sidual affinity for the most traditional of Jewish rituals. However, after the prayers and the communal meal, much like their spiritual ancestors who, back in the downtown enclaves, went out to the Yiddish theater, Friday nights, these students are off to the movies or clubs — compartmentalizing — with their Jewish and gentile dorm mates.

During the week, they do not appear at the Hillel House for all of their meals. Their kosher regimen is not that strict. Besides which, to sign on to the complete meal plan that those accommodating universities accord them would effectively limit their range of associations to the few frum kids on campus. However, they also disdain blatantly treif food — no pork or shell-fish for them. But, they are more than comfortable sending out for non-kosher cheese pizza, especially when they "pull an all-nighter," studying or partying with classmates of all religious persuasions.

But even as the story of these tentative Orthodox Jews is still unfolding, when Orthodox leaders have contemplated this religious challenge, a four-way Orthodox tug of war has ensued among groups eager to lead trans-gressors back toward the tradition. On this very different front, it is but another Orthodox vs. Orthodox encounter, albeit of a far more civil nature, as Lubavitch Hasids, yeshiva-world activists, Religious Zionists from within and without Yeshiva University and Chovevei Torah rabbis compete — each with their own degree of intensity — for the allegiances and souls of the uncommitted.

I initially became attuned to this competition when in 2003–2004, I watched Charleston's Orthodox synagogue search for a successor to its Yeshiva-trained rabbi who began stepping down in 2001 after thirty years of service. It would take the shul three years to find a successor. Always on the ready were Lubavitch operatives; three rabbinic couples tendered applica-tions during the protracted deliberations. They go where their movement directs them, whether to college campuses or to congregations like Charles-ton's or, for that matter, Omaha, where a long-time emissary works primarily among a Beth Israel minority of committed Jews or even to lonely Portland, Maine. Meanwhile, Yeshiva, the retiring rabbi's alma mater, found it quite difficult to locate candidates ready to apply for this outpost job even as it was pitched as a "historical synagogue . . . located in a great city with a wonderful quality of life rating" who would find "warmly engaging, accepting and embracing fellow Jews." The director of rabbinical placement at Yeshiva candidly admitted to me that he was having a hard time convincing young rabbis to assume the challenge of ministering to communities "made of Orthodox-affiliated, non-observant members with a 10 to 20 percent base of shomer shabbat members." If they are called to "avodat ha-kodesh" — holy work among Jews — and not a secular career after ordination, Yeshiva's young rabbis prefer teaching in metropolitan area day schools. Or they put their names forward for pulpit posts within the same New York or other major Orthodox areas.

Ultimately, a Yeshiva graduate stepped forward, a candidate who had an idiosyncratic dual allegiance. In addition to his Yeshiva rabbinic pedigree, he was also Avi Weiss's associate in Riverdale during the years that witnessed the opening of Chovevei Torah. (More full-disclosure, I am this rabbi's congregant too.) However, after an enjoyable tryout weekend in Charleston, he withdrew his candidacy. The list of some forty-one functions that his predecessor performed week after week and which would be incumbent upon him — from reading the Torah, to monitoring the mikveh, to teaching Judaism classes in the local college — put him off to a great extent. He was also far from enamored with his potential congregants' constant fussing and feuding, not about him and his qualifications, but over a generation-long question of where the synagogue should be located as the congregation moved forward in the twentieth-first century.

But an equally young twenty-six-year-old rabbi, Ari Sytner, who was then beginning his first pulpit career in Des Moines, Iowa, was not deterred. After his tryout Sabbath experience, he would write back to the Charleston folks expressing his admiration for this "beautiful" southern city with its "great people (great weather) and an incredible balance between the history of its past and the modernity of its future." For him, not incidentally, the post in Charleston offered a chance to move up from his present position among some 2,800 Jews, where apart from his family and a cadre of transient Orthodox educators in the Des Moines Kollel, there were but "two or three shomer Shabbat families." In due course, he was elected their spiritual leader and was still on that job as of the fall 2007.[8]

How this young rabbi and his family got his erstwhile Midwestern post alerted me to a growing phenomenon within the yeshiva world community. That he had on his resume, under work experience, that "kollel connection," a two-year tenure as a member of a community outreach Torah operation in Iowa seemed, at first glance, inconceivable. In its classic form, whether historically in Eastern Europe or in its transplanted incarnation in America, a kollel is a post-graduate Torah institution that grants stipends to rabbis to continue their studies, full time, unfettered with outside occupational obligations, with the goal of producing an elite of Torah scholars. Long identified with Rabbi Aaron Kotler, the largest of these schools has been located since its inception in the early post–World War II years in Lakewood, New Jersey. As of the 1980s, it boasted of some five hundred cloistered students, along with their wives and children. What was such a separatist construct doing in this hardly Orthodox Hawkeye town?

In the last quarter century, kollels have expanded their geographical previews on a large scale, certainly reflecting the growing confidence and expansiveness of separatist Orthodoxy on this continent. As of 2006, there were some seventy such operations in North America. First, they were established in "out-of-town" communities where a goodly number of devout Jews already resided. In such cities as Miami, Los Angeles, Toronto, and Chicago, a kollel's presence has promoted punctiliousness in observance among the already committed. The influence of the scholar rabbis on the scene is often dramatic. Significantly, when they take time off from their own studies — a very subtle break with past protocols — they often teach in, and influence, the religious outlooks of the local day schools, fulfilling in their wake the dreams of its leaders to change "committed Jews into Torah Jews."[9]

For his part, Charleston's new rabbi was part of the next, more adventurous, stage of American kollel activity. Approximating, when they were not competing against, Lubavitch emissaries, efforts were made, beginning in the late 1980s, to target cities and communities where they would reach out to all Jews "whether you're Reform, Conservative, Orthodox unaffiliated or somewhere in between." In some cases, those ready for the challenge would take their books and their enthusiasm for outreach far "out of town." Often, initiatives were sponsored from an Agudist home office back in New York with its operatives armed with its specific religious orientation. Indeed, in the wake of what these separatists were doing, more "modern kollels" — a seeming oxymoron — with their own Mizrachi Religious Zionist orientations have also entered the field.[10] In Des Moines, the program was the brain child of an independent Miami-based rabbi who ran a kollel in Florida and was able to convince an affluent congregant, a businessman from Des Moines, that good work could be done for Judaism in Iowa. With funding assured, the incipient kollel recruited and financially supported a group of driven young teachers, like this young rabbi, who started to make their impact both within Des Moines's indigenous marginally Orthodox synagogue — until the late 1990s it had no mechitza — and within the Jewish population generally. When the long-time rabbi of Des Moines's Beth El Jacob synagogue semi-retired — he would continue to read the Torah every week for the congregation, sparing his successor one onerous burden — a pulpit opportunity availed itself for the future Charleston rabbi. Interestingly enough, although the young leader was grateful to that Miami rabbi who started him on his rabbinic career, he did not necessarily share his mentor's separatist stance. Both in the midwest and more recently in Charleston, he has evinced profound sympathy to the approach toward religious life that Yeshiva University projects, even if he did not train there.[11]

Starting in early 2005, his new synagogue became a focus of concerted attention as Yeshiva too became a locus for contemporary American Orthodox outreach efforts. Under a new president, Richard M. Joel — not a rabbi but a Jewish communal leader who previously had headed up Hillel — the school established a Center for the Jewish Future. With much fanfare, it picked up the calling of ministering to "out-of-town" communities with their tentative Orthodox majorities. The Charleston synagogue was selected for what was trumpeted as a "new, innovative Commuting Kollel program." Students would be sent down to Beth Sholom Beth Israel twice monthly "to educate and inspire the greater Jewish community in Charleston." Here Yeshiva was reconnecting with its long history of community service, dating back to the early Belkin years. Its "Torah Tours" where undergraduates and rabbis-in-training fanned out across the country on holiday missions, were long a staple of school religious activism. Concomitantly, and perhaps spurring on Yeshiva in this area, Weiss's Chovevei Torah emphasized that its graduates would take on the challenge of reaching Jews, through its "Open Orthodoxy" creed, wherever they resided on the North American continent. In Weiss's view, Yeshiva, his alma mater, had not focused its attention sufficiently on those co-religionists who were often only hearing the voices of Lubavitch and the kollels. In any event, as the first decade of the twenty-first century proceeded, Chabad, kollels of all sorts, Yeshiva, and Chovevei Torah were all out on the hustings courting those Orthodox Jews — and all others — who were not committed to halachic lifestyles.[12]

Nonetheless, amid all of this competition for those Jews who are receptive to these soft-touch approaches, there are Jews on the edges of Orthodoxy's contemporary tent who remain comfortable with their religious lifestyles. They do not want to change. Back in the 1980s, a sociologist colleague and friend identified these folks when he wrote about a "common type who populates many modern Orthodox synagogues" who "likes to come late to synagogue and talks more than he prays once he arrives." He — and I would say, just as well, she — enjoys "play[ing] Frisbee on Sabbath afternoon (within the eruv, of course)" and she "is not likely to use a mikveh." Such a Jew, comfortable with his choices, does "not fall into . . . [the] category of nonobservant Orthodox because he sends his children to a yeshivah, has a strictly kosher home, will not eat meat on the outside, and will generally adhere to the Sabbath laws like not watching television or driving a car, though he may cheat a little on the side."[13]

I personally observed the persistence of this sort of Orthodox behavior several Passovers ago. The vantage point venue was an Arizona resort that was effectively turned over for a holiday in the sun to devotees of strictly kosher meals and buffet tables, tended around the clock as far as the eye could see and the stomach could digest. Hundreds of well-heeled customers turned out for the Seders and attendance was more than respectable — even with latecomers — for the three-times-a-day services that were conducted with complete fealty to the Code of Jewish Law. Additionally, a distinguished lineup of guest speakers — from Yeshiva University and elsewhere — presented during the holy days classes on Torah topics and lectures on issues of contemporary concern. But significantly, only a minority of the deeply committed regularly sat through these most appropriate holiday activities. Far more sun-worshipped at the pool areas, where in mixed company, men and women got along agreeably, with some putting their toes in the refreshing waters and others wading right in. The swimmers clearly contravened holy day strictures. Others volleyed on the tennis courts or putted on the well-kept miniature golf greens. These sports enthusiasts were in violation less of the letter of the law than its traditional spirit of repose. During the intermediate days, where restrictions on normal activities are largely lifted, in addition to the horse backpaths and the dune-buggy trails that some explored and the beautifully manicured golf links that attracted its duffers, it was "everyone in" for many more people at the hotel's several pools.

For families who indulged, these poolside activities were a multigenerational pleasure with once baby-boomer adults, now salt-and-pepper-haired grandparents, teaching their grandchildren the same swimstrokes, under watchful male and female eyes, that they had learned in co-ed classes two generations earlier. Watching this phenomenon play out alerted me again to the complexities involved in delineating a spectrum of Orthodox practice. It reminded me of the goal that I enthusiastically assumed in writing this book.

# NOTES

1. For a compilation of some sources on deviants from halachic strictures in pre-modern times — including those who did not keep the Sabbath — see Adam S. Ferziger, *Exclusion and Hierarchy: Orthodoxy, Nonobservance and the Emergence of Modern Jewish Identity* (Philadelphia: University of Pennsylvania Press, 2005), 193–205.

2. For a learned discussion of the chronology for the term *Orthodoxy* as applied to eighteenth–nineteenth century Europe which has relevance to our discussion of challenges to traditional Jewish ideology and behavior in America, see Jacob Katz, "Orthodoxy in Historical Perspective," *Studies in Contemporary Jewry* 2 (1986): 3–17.

3. This reference to natural spring as a substitute is reflective of the early history of New York — one of the nation's two largest Jewish communities in the eighteenth century. It most probably also applies to smaller towns and villages for a longer time period. See, on this issue, Hyman B. Grinstein, *The Rise of the Jewish Community of New York, 1654–1860* (Philadelphia: Jewish Publication Society, 1945), 297.

## 1. ALL ALONE AND OUT OF CONTROL

1. The most recent research on Levy argues that he was not one of the refugees from Brazil "fleeing imminent persecution" who arrived in New Amsterdam in September, 1654 but that he came primarily as a fortune seeker with two other Jews, probably in August of that year. Moreover, unlike his poor co-religionists, with his company passport Levy possessed from the outset the right to stay. See on this question, Leo Hershkowitz, "By Chance or Choice: Jews in New Amsterdam 1654," *The American Jewish Archives Journal* (2005): 1–13. See also Leo Hershkowitz, "Asser Levy and the Inventories of Early New York Jews," *American Jewish History* [hereinafter *AJH*] (Autumn 1990): 25. For texts of Stuyvesant's complaint against the refugee Jews and the response of the Dutch West

India Company, see Jacob Rader Marcus, ed., *The Jew in the American World: A Source Book* (Detroit: Wayne State University Press, 1996), 29–30, 32–33. On the question of Levy serving in the colonial defense force and Stuyvesant's negative attitude, see Malcolm H. Stern, "Asser Levy: A New Look at Our Jewish Founding Father," *American Jewish Archives* [hereinafter *AJA*] (April 1974): 68, and James Horace Williams, "An Atlantic Perspective on the Jewish Struggle for Rights and Opportunities in Brazil, New Netherlands and New York," in *The Jews and the Expansion of Europe to the West, 1450–1800*, ed. Paolo Bernardini and Norman Fiering (New York: Berghahn Books, 2001), 380.

2. On Jewish service in the Dutch militia in Brazil and their lack of such rights yet back in Holland, see Williams, 375, 377, 380.

3. On the rights of burgher status in Holland, see Arend H. Huussen, "The Legal Position of the Jews in the Dutch Republic, 1590–1796," in *Dutch Jewry: Its History and Secular Culture (1500–2000)* (Leiden: Brill, 2002), 25–42. On Levy's lawsuit over an alleged antisemitic remark, see Stern, 70.

4. On the acquisition by these first Jews of a cemetery area, see David de Sola Pool, *Portraits Etched in Stone* (New York: Columbia University Press, 1952), 7–12, 25. For the origins and then the return of the first Torah scroll in New Amsterdam, see I. S. Emmanuel, "New Light on Early American Jewry," *AJA* (January 1955): 18–19. On the tolerance shown to a Sabbath observer in New Amsterdam courts, see Samuel Oppenheim, "Early History of the Jews in New York," *Publications of the American Jewish Historical Society* [hereinafter *PAJHS*] (1909): 23. Hershkowitz argues, based on an examination of colonial tax rolls for 1663 that Levy was by then the only known Jew in town. See his "Asser Levy," 31. But clearly from this same source, Mrs. Miriam Levy, his wife, was also resident in the colony. On Miriam Levy, see Hershkowitz, "Original Inventories of Early New York Jews (1682–1763)," *AJA* (September 2002): 248.

5. For a consideration of the sources of the economic problems that beset New Amsterdam which may have influenced decisions to outmigrate, see Eli Faber, "Prologue to American Jewish History: The Jews of America from 1654 to 1820," in *From Haven to Home: 350 Years of Jewish Life in America,* ed. Michael W. Grunberger (Washington, D.C.: George Braziller, Inc. and the Library of Congress, 2004), 24–25.

6. On Levy's occupation and level of affluence, see Hershkowitz, "Original Inventories," 252.

7. On Asser Levy's Vilna origins, his peregrinations from Europe, and his gaining the right not to slaughter hogs, see Hershkowitz, "Asser Levy," 25–29. Marcus contends that the aforementioned "parcel of old books" was "undoubtedly well-thumbed dog-eared Hebrew liturgies," but there is no hard evidence to support that contention. See Jacob Rader Marcus, *The Colonial American Jew, 1492–1776,* vol. 2 (Detroit: Wayne State University Press, 1970), 955.

8. On Levy's shop and kitchen items that suggest to Hershkowitz that he kept kosher, see Hershkowitz, "Asser Levy," 29–30. See the same source, p. 32, for the names of the family's gentile friends.

9. Jonathan D. Sarna suggests that Levy "resolutely observed the principal rituals . . . including the Sabbath and the Jewish dietary laws." See Jonathan D. Sarna, *American Judaism: A History* (New Haven: Yale University Press, 2004), 9. The sources do not permit

that definitive statement about Levy's religious lifestyle. So many aspects concerning keeping the Sabbath and kashruth beg documentation.

10. On the relationship between an organized Jewish community and former crypto-Jews who re-entered the community, see Miriam Bodian, *Hebrews of the Portuguese Nation: Conversos and Community in Early Modern Amsterdam* (Bloomington: Indiana University Press, 1997), 112–14, 119–25, and Yosef Kaplan, "The Jews in the Republic until about 1750: Religious Social and Cultural Life," in *The History of the Jews in the Netherlands*, ed. J. C. H. Blom, R. G. Fuks-Manfeld, and I. Schoffer (Oxford: Littman Library of Jewish Civilization, 2002), 123–24,152–55.

11. Isaac S. and Suzanne A. Emmanuel, *History of the Jews in the Netherlands Antilles* (Cincinnati, Ohio: American Jewish Archives, 1970), 45–52. See also Yosef Hayim Yerushalmi, "Between Amsterdam and New Amsterdam: The Place of Curacao in Early Modern Jewish History," *AJH* (December 1982): 184–91.

12. On the Levy–Pieterson relationship, see Hershkowitz, "Asser Levy," 25–26. For the use of Pieterson as symbolic of Jews who easily drifted away in the earliest years of Jewish settlement in North America, see Sarna, 9.

13. On British policies that prohibited public prayer see Oppenheim, 33, Marcus, *The Colonial American Jew*, 401–402.

14. Todd M. Endelman, *The Jews of Georgian England, 1714–1830* (Philadelphia: Jewish Publication Society, 1979), 16–20.

15. Hershkowitz attempts to unravel the mystery of when the first public services were held. He considers the notation on Miller's map that was drawn from memory "somewhat questionable." See his "The Mill Street Synagogue Reconsidered," *American Jewish Historical Quarterly* [hereinafter *AJHQ*] (June 1964): 404–410.

16. On the founding of synagogue in these cities, see Ellen Smith and Jonathan D. Sarna, "Introduction: The Jews of Rhode Island," in *The Jews of Rhode Island*, ed. George M. Goodwin and Ellen Smith (Waltham, Mass.: Brandeis University Press, 2004), 2.; Saul Jacob Rubin, *Third to None: The Saga of Savannah Jewry, 1733–1983* (n.p., 1983), 1–3; Theodore Rosengarten and Dale Rosengarten, eds., *A Portion of the People: Three Hundred Years of Southern Jewish Life* (Columbia: University of South Carolina Press, 2002), xvi, 3, 11, and Edwin Wolf 2nd and Maxwell Whiteman, *The History of the Jews of Philadelphia from Colonial Times to the Age of Jackson* (Philadelphia: Jewish Publication Society, 1956), 41–42, 53, 60–61, 114–15. Some of these sources are noted in Faber, 26–28. See Jacob Rader Marcus, "The Handsome Young Priest in the Black Gown: The Personal World of Gershom Mendes Seixas," *Hebrew Union College Annual* (1969–1970): 400–67, and Thomas Kessner, "Gershom Mendes Seixas: His Religious 'Calling,' Outlook and Competence," *AJHQ* (June 1969): 444–71 for biographical sketches of Seixas.

17. David Brener, *The Jews of Lancaster, Pennsylvania: A Story with Two Beginnings* (Lancaster, Pa.: Congregation Shaarai Shomayim and the Lancaster Historical Society, 1979), 6–7; Joshua Trachtenberg, *Consider the Years: The Story of the Jewish Community of Easton, 1752–1942* (Easton, Pa.: Centennial Committee of Temple Brith Sholom, 1944), 27, 79, 129.

18. On Aaron Lopez's observance of the Sabbath, see Morris A. Gutstein, *The Story of the Jews of Newport: Two and A Half Centuries of Judaism* (New York: Bloch, 1936), 132, and

Stanley F. Chyet, *Lopez of Newport: Colonial American Merchant Prince* (Detroit: Wayne State University Press, 1970), 158; noted in Sarna, *American Judaism,* 23. On Phillip's background and religiosity and his family's values, see Wolf and Whiteman, 62–63, 198–200, and "Minute Book of the Congregation Shearith Israel," *PAJHS* (1913): 107.

19. See Trachtenberg, 75, for the Hart family problems. For information on Manuel Josephson, see Wolf and Whiteman, 42, 82, 99, 128, 133, 140.

20. On this incident, see Wolf and Whiteman, 73 noted in Sarna, *American Judaism,* 24.

21. For a comprehensive study of the phenomenon of the "Shabbes Goy" through much of Jewish history, see Jacob Katz, *The Shabbes Goy: A Study in Halakhic Flexibility,* Yoel Lerner, trans. (Philadelphia: Jewish Publication Society, 1989). On the McClure–Simon relationship, see Marcus, *The Colonial American Jew,* 956, noted in Sarna, *American Judaism,* 22–23.

22. See Marcus, *The Colonial American Jew,* 986 for information on Sheftall. See Brener, 3 for information on Jacobs. See Trachtenberg, 27 for Hart as a slaughterer. See also Jacob Rader Marcus, *American Jewry-Documents Eighteenth Century* (Cincinnati, Ohio: Hebrew Union College Press, 1959), 3–4 for the Gomez's activities.

23. For information on Gratz's entrepreneurial kosher activities, see Wolf and Whiteman, 41–42, 48, and Marcus, *American Jewry-Documents,* 93, 104.

24. For Josephson's petition, see Marcus, *American Jewry-Documents,* 135–36.

25. "Minute Book of the Congregation Shearith Israel," 4, 35–36, 72, 84–85, 106.

26. On Seixas's problems with his board, see Jacob Rader Marcus, *United States Jewry, 1776–1985,* vol. 1 (Detroit: Wayne State University Press, 1989), 280–81. On monitoring efforts of education and slaughtering, see "Minute Book of the Congregation Shearith Israel," 72, 112–13, 162–63.

27. Marcus, *United States Jewry,* vol. 1, 260–61.

28. "Minute Book of the Congregation Shearith Israel," 124, 164.

29. For texts of the New York, Philadelphia, Savannah, and Charleston regulations, see "Minute Book of the Congregation Shearith Israel," 74–75; Marcus, *American Jewry-Documents,* 94, 179, and Barnett A. Elzas, *The Jews of South Carolina from the Earliest Times to the Present Day* (Philadelphia: J.B. Lippincott, 1905), 153. If there was an early constitution and regulations at the Newport synagogue, these records are no longer extant.

30. Marcus, *American Jewry-Documents,* 181.

31. Marcus, *The Jew in the American World,* 142–43.

32. See Jacob Rader Marcus, *The Jew in the Medieval World: A Source Book* (Cincinnati, Ohio: Hebrew Union College Press, 1990), 72–73. On the religious values of the Lancaster fur trader, see Marcus, *The Colonial American Jew,* 997.

33. Marcus, *American Jewry-Documents,* 137–38.

34. On the Franks family saga, including Abigail's admonition to one of her children about kosher observance, see Leo Hershkowitz and Isidor S. Meyer, ed., *The Lee Max Friedman Collection of American Jewish Colonial Correspondence: Letters of the Franks Family (1733–1748)* (Waltham, Mass.: American Jewish Historical Society, 1968), 8. See also "Minute Book of the Congregation Shearith Israel," 5–6.

35. On Franks's connectedness to Jewish tradition and family life, see Wolf and

Whiteman, 33, 42, 259, 389–90. See also, Marcus, *United States Jewry*, vol. 1, 44 for a discussion of Margaret Frank's religious values.

36. Hyman B. Grinstein, *The Rise of the Jewish Community of New York*, 335–36.

37. Marcus, *United States Jewry*, vol. 1, 256–57; Wolf and Whiteman, 127. On Nathans's prior position of synagogue leadership, see Marcus, *American Jewry-Documents*, 139.

38. On the decisions rendered by Shearith Israel and Josephson's leadership role, see "Minute Book of the Congregation Shearith Israel," 86, 143, and David and Tamar de Sola Pool, *An Old Faith in the New World: Portrait of Shearith Israel, 1654–1954* (New York: Columbia University Press, 1955), 187–88. On the rationale for this hard-line approach, including the idea of not letting down the bars, see Marcus, *American Jewry-Documents*, 188. On the problem of the absence of established rabbinical courts and the intermarriage question, see Sidney M. Fish, "The Problem of Intermarriage in Early America," *Gratz College Annual of Jewish Studies* (1975): 85–86.

39. Marcus, *American Jewry-Documents*, 188–89; Wolf and Whiteman, 99, 127.

40. Sabato Morais, "Mickve Israel Congregation of Philadelphia," *PAJHS* (1892): 18. See Wolf and Whiteman, 416, for an observation about the neglect of the commandment against shaving among these Jews.

41. Wolf and Whiteman, 128–29; Fish, 91–94.

42. Marcus, *American Jewry-Documents*, 138–41; Wolf and Whiteman, 128–29; Fish, 91–94.

43. Wolf and Whiteman, 235–36, 240–41, 452.

44. Edward Davis, *The History of Rodeph Shalom Congregation, 1802–1926* (Philadelphia: Edward Stern and Co., 1926), 28–29, 32–33, 35. See also, Wolf and Whiteman, 240–41. On the connection between Dropsie's affluence and his special treatment, see Leon Jick, *The Americanization of the Synagogue, 1820–1870* (Hanover, N.H.: University Press of New England, 1992), 47. See also Lance Sussman, *Isaac Leeser and the Making of American Judaism* (Detroit: Wayne State University Press, 1995), 220–21, 247 for the Leeser–Dropsie relationship.

45. Davis, 47.

46. On gender membership rules and nonattendance of women at synagogues in the European past, see Karla Goldman, *Beyond the Synagogue Gallery: Finding a Place for Women in Judaism* (Cambridge, Mass.: Harvard University Press, 2000), 4–6, 55–56.

47. Goldman, 41–42, 51–54.

48. Ibid., 41–42, 44, 46–48.

49. Joseph C. Blau and Salo Wittmayer Baron, *The Jews of the United States, 1790–1820: A Documentary History* (New York: Columbia University Press, 1963), 541–42.

50. Blau and Baron, 542; see also on this incident, Sarna, *American Judaism*, 55–56.

51. Blau and Baron, 543. See also on its restrictive policies and the founding of B'nai Jeshurun, Jick, 48.

52. On Cohen's description of his town, see Sarna, *American Judaism*, 46. On Hart's well-known strict religious values, see Jacob de la Motta, *On the Private and Religious Character of the Late Mr. Nathan Hart* (Charleston, S.C., 1840), 12–15. See also Elzas, 153 for congregational regulations. Elzas characterized the Beth Elohim community as "ortho-

dox in its ritual and observance." See 155. On Charleston Jewry's owning of slaves, see Deborah Dash Moore, "Freedom's Fruits: The Americanization of an Old-Time Religion," in Rosengarten and Rosengarten, 11.

53. Additional considerations — such as concerns over their political status in America, growing intolerance in Charleston, and worry about evangelical missionary successes among unsynagogued Jews — also motivated their petition. See on these other factors, Moore, 11–14, Robert Liberles, "Conflict over Reforms: The Case of Congregation Beth Elohim, Charleston, South Carolina," in *The American Synagogue; A Sanctuary Transformed*, ed. Jack Wertheimer (New York: Cambridge University Press, 1988), 274–96; James William Hagy, *This Happy Land: The Jews of Colonial and Antebellum Charleston* (Tuscaloosa: University of Alabama Press, 1993), 131–41.

54. For the names of the intermarrieds, see Hagy, 162. See Gary Phillip Zola, *Isaac Harby of Charleston, 1788–1828: Jewish Reformer and Intellectual* (Tuscaloosa: University of Alabama Press, 1994), 12–13, and Zola to the author, e-mail communication, September 2, 2006. See also, Zola, 119 for a dismissive characterization of the petitioners "as not recognized as Jews by the congregation" by an Orthodox Jew, Jacob Mordecai. See also Blau and Baron, 554 for statements from the 1824 petition.

55. Blau and Baron, 554–60.

56. Reznikoff and Engelman, 125. The author of that nasty comment was Nathan Levin, a trustee of Shearith Israel of Charleston, recalling those angry times in the *Occident*.

57. Allan Tarshish, The Charleston Organ Case," *AJHQ* (June 1965): 411–49.

58. Liberles, 274–96.

## 2. AMERICAN CHALLENGES AND JEWISH CHALLENGERS

1. For a discussion of the rural–urban migration of Central European Jews, see Hasia Diner, *A Time for Gathering: The Second Migration, 1820–1880* (Baltimore: Johns Hopkins University Press, 1992), 10, 13, 25–26. On the movement of Jews within the Russian territories, see Ezra Mendelsohn, *Class Struggle in the Pale: The Formative Years of the Jewish Workers Movement in Tsarist Russia* (Cambridge: Cambridge University Press, 1970), 4–5.

2. Diner, 151–56. See also Rudolf Glanz, *Studies in Judaica Americana* (New York: KTAV Publishing House), 19–21. On tsarist legislation, see Mendelsohn, 2–3.

3. On the process of migration, see Pamela S. Nadell, "The Journey to America by Steam" (Ph.D. diss., Ohio State University, 1982).

4. Guido Kisch, "A Voyage to America Ninety Years Ago: The Diary of a Bohemian Jew on His Voyage from Hamburg to New York, 1847," *PAJHS* (1939): 65–78.

5. Glanz, 40–41. See also p. 42 for other sources of religious needs accommodated on board.

6. Hyman L. Meites, *History of the Jews of Chicago* (Chicago: Jewish Historical Society of Illinois, 1924), 40.

7. On struggles between old-timers and newcomers that split communities, see Leon Jick, *The Americanization of the Synagogue, 1820–1870* (Hanover, N.H.: University Press of

New England, 1992), 24–26, 48–49, and Hyman B. Grinstein, *The Rise of the Jewish Community of New York, 1654–1860*, 40–44.

8. *Jewish Messenger* 13, no. 7 (February 14, 1863): 60 noted in Moshe D. Sherman, "Bernard Illowy and Nineteenth Century American Orthodoxy" (Ph.D. diss., Yeshiva University, 1991), 37–38.

9. Abraham Sussmann, *Beit Abraham* (Konigsberg, 1853), 1, noted in Sherman, 33.

10. *The Occident* 10, no. 8 (November, 1852): 374, noted in Sherman, 36.

11. *The Asmonean* 14, no. 2 (September 12, 1856): 172, noted in Sherman, 35. See also Jeremiah J. Berman, *Shehita: A Study in the Cultural and Social Life of the Jewish People* (New York: Bloch, 1941), 291.

12. See Berman, 291–94. See also the discussion in Sherman, 38.

13. Sherman, 29–30, 47–51.

14. Sherman, 30–31. Sherman notes that Adler's response appeared in *The Occident* 7, no. 10 (January 1850): 523–24.

15. For a brief biographical sketch of Leeser, see Sherman, *Orthodox Judaism in America: A Biographical Dictionary and Source Book* (Westport, Conn.: Greenwood Press, 1996), 127–29. For a comprehensive biography of Leeser, see Lance Sussman, *Isaac Leeser and the Making of American Judaism* (Detroit: Wayne State University Press, 1995). On Leeser's 1867 admonishment, see Berman, "The Trend in Jewish Religious Observance in Mid-Nineteenth-Century America," *PAJHS* (1944): 46.

16. For a brief biographical sketch of Rice, see Sherman, *Orthodox Judaism*, 173–74. For a full-length biography of Rice, see I. Harold Sharfman, *The First Rabbi: Origins of Conflict between Orthodox and Reform: Jewish Polemic Warfare in Pre-Civil War America: A Biographical History* (Malibu, Calif.: Pangloss, 1988).

17. For a brief biographical sketch of Illowy, see Sherman, *Orthodox Judaism in America*, 101–103. See Sherman's dissertation on Illowy for a full treatment of this important nineteenth-century rabbi in America.

18. Glanz, 51–52.

19. For an account of Lilienthal's problems in the period when he was an Orthodox rabbi, see Jick, 118–20.

20. On the American Protestant tradition of treatment of clergy, see Sidney E. Mead, "The Rise of the Evangelical Conception of the Ministry in America (1607–1859)," in *The Ministry in Historical Perspective,* H. Reinhold Niebuhr and Daniel D. Williams, eds. (New York: Cambridge University Press, 1956), 217, noted in Sarna, *American Judaism*, 91. See chapter 1 of this study for early American Jewish congregational relationships.

21. Sherman, "Bernard Illowy," 39–45.

22. On Jewish population statistics pre-1861, see Jacob Rader Marcus, *United States Jewry, 1776–1985*, vol. 2 (Detroit: Wayne State University Press, 1991), 21, 328–30. See also Glanz, "The Spread of Jewish Communities through America before the Civil War," *YIVO Annual* 15 (1974): 7–45 and idem. "Where the Jewish Press Was Distributed in Pre-Civil War America," *Western States Jewish Historical Society Quarterly* 5 (1972): 1–14. This article speaks to the question of the some 1,200 localities that had some Jews, noted in Sarna, 69, and Diner, 57–58.

23. Lee Shai Weissbach, "The Jewish Communities of the United States on the Eve of

Mass Migration: Some Comments on Geography and Bibliography," *AJH* (September 1988): 83–87.

24. This description is derived from an excerpt from Mayer Klein's memoir published in Meites, 40, and from Isaac Mayer Wise's classic observation of the types of peddlers he encountered in mid-century. See Isaac Mayer Wise, *Reminiscences* (Cincinnati: Leo Wise, 1901), 38. For examples of peddlers being the first Jews in various cities coast to coast, see S. Joshua Kohn, *The Jewish Community of Utica, New York, 1847–1948* (New York: American Jewish Historical Society, 1959), 9–10; Louis J. Swichkow and Lloyd P. Gartner, *The History of the Jews of Milwaukee* (Philadelphia: Jewish Publication Society, 1963), 8–10; Louis Wirth, *The Ghetto* (Chicago: University of Chicago Press, 1928), 155–56; Max Vorspan and Gartner, *History of the Jews of Los Angeles* (Philadelphia: Jewish Publication Society, 1970), 5–7.

25. David Brener, *The Jews of Lancaster, Pennsylvania: A Story with Two Beginnings* (Lancaster, Pa.: Congregation Shaarai Shomayim and the Lancaster Historical Society, 1979), 41; Glanz, *Studies in Judaica Americana*, 113.

26. Marcus, *Memoirs of American Jews, 1775–1865*, vol. 3 (Philadelphia: Jewish Publication Society, 1956), 229; Glanz, *Studies in Judaica Americana*, 113; Abram Vossen Goodman, "A Jewish Peddler's Diary, 1842–1843," *AJA* (June 1951): 96–98. On the question of the reliability of the writers' accounts, see Selma Stern Taeubler, "The Motivation of German Jewish Migration," *Essays in American Jewish History* (New York: KTAV Publishing House, 1975), 247–48.

27. Wolf and Whiteman, *The History of the Jews of Philadelphia from Colonial Times to the Age of Jackson*, 355.

28. On peddling in America being almost exclusively a male occupation, as opposed to Europe where women historically also took part, see Diner, "Entering the Mainstream of Modern Jewish History: Peddlers and the American Jewish South," *Jewish Roots in Southern Soil: A New History*, Marcie Cohen Ferris and Mark I. Greenberg, eds. (Waltham, Mass.: Brandeis University Press, 2006), 86–108.

29. I. J. Benjamin, *Three Years in America, 1859–1862*, Charles Reznikoff, trans. vol. 1 (Philadelphia: Jewish Publication Society, 1956), 235–36.

30. Meites, 40.

31. Goodman, 98, 99, 107. Kohn's statement about his religious problem can be characterized as the "classic" statement on the subject since literally every historian who has attempted to highlight this issue of identity has relied on this diary as representative of the thousands of immigrant merchants who were so perturbed. See, for example, Lee Max Friedman, "The Problems of Nineteenth Century American Jewish Peddlers," *PAJHS* 44 (1954): 1–7; Sarna, 70; Diner, 67; Marcus, *Memoirs*, 1–2; Jick, 34–36.

32. Goodman, 97.

33. Diner, 67–69.

34. For a suggestion of this possible scenario of welcoming the peddler and marriages, see Diner, "Entering," 98.

35. Marcus, *The American Jewish Woman: A Documentary History* (New York: KTAV Publishing House, 1981), 190–93.

36. Berman, "The Trend," 39–41.

37. Ibid., 35–38.

38. Ibid., 33.

39. Benjamin, *Three Years*, vol. 1, 79–80, 235–36; vol. 2, 95.

40. Jick, 30, 41–42; Diner, 21–24.

41. *Constitution and By Laws of the United Hebrew Congregation of Saint Louis* (1841), 2 (American Jewish Archives collection).

42. *History of Congregation Adath Israel Louisville Kentucky* (Louisville: n.p., 1906), 16.

43. David Philipson, *The Oldest Jewish Congregation in the West* (Cincinnati, 1894), 21–22; James G. Heller, *As Yesterday When It Is Past: A History of the Isaac M. Wise Temple-K.K. B'nai Yeshurun of Cincinnati* (Cincinnati: Isaac M. Wise Temple, 1942), 25, 27.

44. Meites, 43, 47.

45. Swichow and Gartner, 34–35.

46. Benjamin, vol. 1, 199, 201.

47. For information on Jonas's religious activities, but not his specific level of observance, see Philipson, 9, 13, and Marcus, *United States Jewry*, vol. 2, 225.

48. Meites, 44.

49. Irving Cutler, *The Jews of Chicago: From Shtetl to Suburb* (Urbana: University of Illinois Press, 1996), 11.

50. *Constitution and By-Laws of the United Hebrew Congregation*, 2. For other examples of congregational toleration of members but not officials' observances, see Jick, 151–52 and Trachtenberg, *Consider the Years: The Story of the Jewish Community of Easton, 1752–1942*, 144, 158.

51. Clearly Jick's pathbreaking conceptualization about the "Americanization of the Synagogue" in mid–nineteenth-century America informs this analysis. See for example, about the mindset of changemakers, Jick, 81, 91, 136, 177–78.

52. On the disinterest that children of mid–nineteenth-century Jewish immigrants showed toward not only the synagogues of their parents but also to the Jewish "Ys," see Jeffrey S. Gurock, *Judaism's Encounter with American Sports* (Bloomington: Indiana University Press, 2005), 36–42.

53. Trachtenberg, 154–57. For a retrospective critique of nonobservance among Orthodox synagogue goers of this period, see Lewis Dembitz's statement noted in the *American Hebrew* (June 20, 1898), 172.

54. Meites, 63.

55. Heller, *As Yesterday When It Is Past*, 86–87, 91, 94–95.

56. Philipson, 48–49, 51, 63.

57. Jick, 151–52; Jane Priwer, *The United Hebrew Congregation, St.Louis, Mo. 1837–1963: The Oldest Jewish Congregation West of the Mississippi* (St. Louis: United Hebrew Congregation, 1963), 11.

58. Israel Goldstein, *A Century of Judaism in New York: B'nai Jeshurun, 1825–1925* (New York: Congregation B'nai Jeshurun, 1930), 63, 85, 147, 159. See also, Sarna, 95.

59. Grinstein, *The Rise of the Jewish Community of New York*, 354–55.

60. This description is based on a letter to *Die Deborah* published April 4, 1856, noted in Glanz, 66. On the threat of burning down the synagogue, see *History of Congregation Adath Israel*, 16.

61. On the establishment of this community and the problem of pork, see Elizabeth Shaikun Weinberg, "Hoosier Israelites on the Ohio — A History of Madison's Indiana Jews," *Indiana Jewish History* (July 1991): 6–7, 10–11, 21–24, 26–28.

62. This information on Felsenthal, Adas Israel, and the controversies over transformation of the synagogue ritual are derived primarily from Felsenthal's account of the meetings that were held; this was noted initially in an anonymous article submitted to the American Jewish Historical Society in the late 1990s entitled "The Zealous Mr. X: German Language, American Rhetoric and the Debate on Religious Reform in a Nineteenth-Century Small Town."

63. Meites, 46, 54–55, 65, 69; Cutler, 15–16.

64. Philipson, 50.

65. Isaac M. Fein, *The Making of an American Jewish Community: The History of Baltimore Jewry from 1773 to 1920* (Philadelphia: Jewish Publications Society, 1971), 54–56, 114–17.

66. For a discussion of how American Jewish attitudes differed from European ones in resorting to secular courts, see Robert Liberles, "Conflict over Reforms: The Case of Congregation Beth Elohim, Charleston, South Carolina," in *The American Synagogue,* ed. Jack Wertheimer, 290–92.

67. Nancy J. Ordway, "A History of Chizuk Amuno Congregation: An American Synagogue" (Ph.D. diss., Peggy Mayerhoff Pearlstone School of Graduate Studies, Hebrew University of Jerusalem, 1997), 12–15.

68. Marsha Rozenblit, "Choosing a Synagogue: The Social Composition of Two German Congregations in Nineteenth-Century Baltimore," in Jack Wertheimer, ed., *The American Synagogue,* 343–55.

69. Fein, 117; David and Tamar de Sola Pool, *An Old Faith in the New World: Portrait of Shearith Israel, 1654–1954,* 99–101.

70. Swichkow and Gartner, 40–41, 50.

71. Sharfman, 71; Fein, 55–56.

72. Fein, 60.

73. Fein, 84; Sharfman, 280–81, 294.

74. Sussman, 13, 66–69, 153–54.

75. Lloyd P. Gartner, "Temples of Liberty Unpolluted: American Jews and the Public Schools, 1840–1875," in a *Bi-Centennial Festschrift for Jacob Rader Marcus,* ed. Bertram W. Korn (New York: KTAV, 1976), 172, noted in Sarna, 80. On the mission of Maimonides College, see Moshe Davis, *The Emergence of Conservative Judaism: The Historical School in Nineteenth-Century America* (Philadelphia: Jewish Publication Society, 1965), 379, and Bertram Wallace Korn, "The First American Jewish Theological Seminary: Maimonides College, 1867–1873," in Korn, *Eventual Years and Experiences: Studies in Nineteenth-Century American Jewish History* (Cincinnati: American Jewish Archives, 1954), 154.

76. Sussman, 61–62; Sarna, 78.

77. On the issue of decorum and the desire of Americanized Jews of that era to be stylish, see Sarna, 79–80.

78. Sussman, 194–96.

79. Sussman, 125, 169, 196–99.

80. Sussman, 201.

81. Sherman, *Orthodox Judaism*, 101–103.

82. Sussman, 197–200.


### 3. RELIGIOUS DILEMMAS OF A *TREIF* LAND

1. Yekutiel Yehudah Greenwald, *Ritual Slaughters and Ritual Slaughter in Rabbinic Literature* (New York: Feldheim, 1955), 12; Kimmy Caplan, *Orthodoxy in the New World: Immigrant Rabbis and Preaching in America (1881–1924)* [Hebrew] (Jerusalem: Zalman Shazar Center for Jewish History, 2002), 83.

2. Aaron Rakefet-Rothkoff, *The Silver Era: Rabbi Eliezer Silver and His Generation* (Jerusalem and New York: Yeshiva University Press/Feldheim Publishers, 1981), 18–19; Lloyd P. Gartner, "Jewish Migrants en Route from Europe to North America: Traditions and Realities," *Jewish History* (Fall 1986): 57. See also on the hypothetical immigrant whom Kagan thought might make it religiously in America, a family memoir tale suggesting that one particular immigrant was judged by the rabbi as able to withstand the lures of the free country, noted in Samuel C. Heilman, *Defenders of the Faith: Inside Ultra-Orthodox Jewry* (New York: Schocken Books, 1992), 243.

3. For statistics year by year and country by country on migration from East Central and Eastern Europe to America, see Moses Rischin, *The Promised City: New York Jews, 1870–1914* (Cambridge, Mass.: Harvard University Press, 1962), 270. On the question of return Jewish migration to Europe, see Jonathan D. Sarna, "The Myth of No Return: Jewish Return Migration to Eastern Europe, 1881–1914," *AJH* (December 1981): 256–67.

4. On the question of pogroms as opposed to the other factors noted in stimulating migration to America, see Simon Kuznets, " Immigration of Russian Jews to the United States: Background and Structure," *Perspectives in American History* (1975): 86–88, and more recently, Tobias Brinkmann, "Jewish Mass Migration between Empire and Nation State," *Prezeglad Polonijny* (2005): 99–116. See also Gerald Sorin, *A Time for Building: The Third Migration, 1880–1920* (Baltimore: Johns Hopkins University Press, 1992), 35.

5. Isaac Levitats, *The Jewish Community in Russia, 1772–1844* (New York: Columbia University Press, 1943 ), 21.

6. Salo W. Baron, *The Russian Jew under Tsars and Soviets* (New York: Macmillan, 1964), 18, 32–34. See also Levitats, 69.

7. Levitats, 32; Baron, 34.

8. Michael Stanislawski, *Tsar Nicholas I and the Jews: The Transformation of Jewish Society in Russia, 1825–1855* (Philadelphia: Jewish Publication Society, 1983), 12–21.

9. On the flight of those who wished to avoid conscription under Nicholas to Germany and to the United States, see Hasia Diner, *A Time for Gathering: The Second Migration, 1820–1880*, 83. On the founding of Beth Hamidrash, see Judah David Eisenstein, "The History of the First Russian-American Jewish Congregation," *PAJHS* (1901): 63–74. See also Jeffrey S. Gurock, *Orthodoxy in Charleston: Brith Sholom Beth Israel and American Jewish History* (Charleston: College of Charleston Library, 2004), 1–7 for a discussion of the rise of this congregation with an East European constituency.

10. Kuznets, 84, 86–87, 91–92, 121; Baron, 39–41.

11. Kuznets, 74–79, 121.

12. Baron, 41, 66; Gartner, "Jewish Migration," 52. See also Baron, *Steeled by Adversity: Essays in American Jewish Life and Thought* (Philadelphia: Jewish Publication Society, 1971), 276.

13. Baron, *Russian Jews*, 47–49, 50; Kuznets, 87.

14. Joseph Kissman, "The Immigration of Rumanian Jews up to 1914," *YIVO Annual of Jewish Social Science* (1947/48): 160–79.

15. Raphael Mahler, "The Economic Background of Jewish Emigration from Galicia to the United States," *YIVO Annual of Jewish Social Science* (1952): 255–67. See also Robert Perlman, *Bridging Two Worlds: Hungarian Jewish Americans, 1848–1914* (Amherst: University of Massachusetts Press, 1991), 32, 110–13.

16. Pamela S. Nadell, "The Journey to America by Steam: The Jews of Eastern Europe in Transition," *AJH* (December, 1981): 269–84. See also Kissman, 169–76.

17. Caplan, 215–17.

18. Ibid., 216–17.

19. Ibid., 85.

20. Ibid., 89–90.

21. On Michael's reported sentiments, see Akiva Ben Ezra, "Rabbi Pinchas Michael Zt"L" [Hebrew], in *Antopol: Sefer Yizkor* (Tel Aviv, 1972), 49, noted in Sarna, *American Judaism*, 155.

22. Michael Stanislawski, *For Whom Do I Toil? Judah Leib Gordon and the Crisis of Russian Jewry* (New York: Oxford University Press, 1988), 5–7, 25–27.

23. On the decline of ritual observance among enlightened Jews of this time period in Eastern Europe, see ChaeRan Y. Freeze, *Jewish Marriage and Divorce in Imperial Russia* (Waltham, Mass.: Brandeis University Press, 2002), 196–98; Baron, 126–31, 137–40, 144–46.

24. Elias Tcherikower, ed., *The Early Jewish Labor Movement in the United States*, Aaron Antonovsky, trans. and ed. (New York: YIVO 1961), 254, 266.

25. David Blaustein, *Memoirs of David Blaustein*, Miriam Blaustein, ed. (New York: McBride, Nast and Co., 1913), 190–99; Maurice Fishberg, *The Jews: A Study of Race and Environment* (New York: Scribners, 1911), 538–39; Caplan, "Rabbi Isaac Margolis: From Eastern Europe to America," [Hebrew] *Zion* (1992–1993): 225. Blaustein, "The Inherent Cultural Forces on the Lower East Side," *Report of the Year's Work, University Settlement Society* (1901): 20, all noted in Annie M. Polland, "The Sacredness of the Family: New York's Immigrant Jews and Their Religion, 1890–1930" (Ph.D. diss., Columbia University, 2004), 91.

26. Abraham Cahan, *Bleter fun mein leben*, vol. 5 (New York: Forward Association, 1931), 144–46. Such libertine activity on the Sabbath and other violations of Orthodox practice were readily observable in the libertine and idiosyncratic city of Odessa from which many radicals emerged. Lemberg is more typical of Russian Jewish cities. See on this point, Arthur A. Goren, "Preaching American Jewish History: A Review Essay," *AJH* (Summer 1990): 546.

27. Caplan, 225.

28. Aaron Rothkoff, "The American Sojourns of Ridbaz: Religious Problems within the Immigrant Community," *AJHQ* (June 1968): 560–61.

29. Julius Greenstone, "Religious Activity," in *The Russian Jews in the United States,* ed. Charles Bernheimer (Philadelphia: John C. Winston, 1905), 158.

30. Joshua Hoffman, "The Institution of the *Mikvah* in America," in *Total Immersion: A Mikvah Anthology* (Northvale, N.J.: Jason Aronson, 1997), 78, 83. See also Asher C. Oser, "The Promotion of *Mikvah* Ritual, 1900–1920," unpublished seminar paper, University of Connecticut, 2007.

31. On the percentages of Jews who had to work on the Sabbath, see Polland, 95.

32. Ephraim Lisitzky, *In the Grip of Cross Currents,* quoted in excerpt form in *How We Lived: A Documentary History of Immigrant Jews in America, 1880–1930,* ed. Irving Howe and Kenneth Libo (New York: Richard Marek, 1979), 96.

33. Ray Stannard Baker, *The Spiritual Unrest* (New York: Frederick A. Stokes Co., 1910), 117–18; Rischin, 146–47.

34. Ewa Morawska, *Insecure Prosperity: Small-Town Jews in Industrial America, 1890–1940* (Princeton, N.J.: Princeton University Press, 1996), 154–56.

35. Hal Rothman, "Same Horse, New Wagon: Tradition and Assimilation among the Jews of Wichita, 1865–1930," *Great Plains Quarterly* (Spring 1995): 98, discussed in Lee Shai Weissbach, *Jewish Life in Small Town America* (New Haven, Conn.: Yale University Press, 2005), 281. See also David J. Goldberg, "In Dixie Land, I Take My Stand: A Study of Small City Jewry in Five Southeastern States" (Undergraduate thesis, Columbia College, 1974), 13, discussed in Weissbach, 281. On the Benton Harbor experience, see Weissbach, 280.

36. Gurock, *Orthodoxy in Charleston,* 24–25.

37. On this family phenomenon in an immigrant community in a small town outside of New York, see Morawska, 156–57.

38. Polland, 106, 130, 138.

39. On the phenomenon of early Saturday morning services for workers about to go to their labors, see Herbert S. Goldstein, ed., *Forty Years of Struggle for a Principle: The Biography of Harry Fischel* (New York: Bloch Publishing Co., 1928), 17–19, cited in Sarna, *American Judaism,* 163. See also, Polland, 107.

40. Mowarska, 155.

41. Hutchins Hapgood, *The Spirit of the Ghetto: Studies of the Immigrant Quarter of New York* (New York: Funk and Wagnalls, 1902), 125–26. See also Polland, 138.

42. On the purchase of tickets before the Sabbath, see Irving Bunim, "A Father's Appreciation of Young Israel," *Jewish Forum* (December 1926): 540–41.

43. Andrew R. Heinze, *Adapting to Abundance: Jewish Immigrants, Mass Consumption and the Search for American Identity* (New York: Columbia University Press, 1990), 65–66.

44. Polland, 236; Heinze, 65–67.

45. On the history of the so-called "great synagogues" of the Lower East Side during this time period, see Gerard R. Wolfe and Jo Renee Fine, *The Synagogue of New York's Lower East Side* (New York: Washington Mews Press, 1978), 41–102. On the social history and American proclivities of one of the major downtown New York synagogues, see Gurock, "A Stage in the Emergence of the Americanized Synagogue among East European Jews,

1890–1910," *Journal of American Ethnic History* (Spring 1990): 7–25. On the history of Chicago-based early "Russian" synagogues, see Irving Cutler, *The Jews of Chicago*, 74. See also Gurock, *Orthodoxy in Charleston*, 10, for its East European synagogue's involvement in the nationwide "hazan craze" of the 1890s.

46. For the most complete account of the entire landsmanshaft phenomenon, see Daniel Soyer, *Jewish Immigrant Associations and American Identity in New York* (Cambridge, Mass.: Harvard University Press, 1997).

47. On the piety that obtained on the High Holidays, including Cahan's observations, see Howe and Libo, 104, 117.

48. Hollace Ava Weiner, "Whistling *Dixie* while Humming *Ha-Tikvah:* Acculturation and Activism among the Orthodox in Fort Worth," *AJH* (June 2005): 219, 236.

49. On the problem of those "temporary halls of worship," see *American Hebrew* (January 15, 1901), 431. See Fishberg, 539, for a report on the Yiddish theaters that were open on Rosh Ha-Shanah and the fans who attended these performances.

50. Polland, 72, 75, 77.

51. Polland, 55–56.

52. Tony Michels, *A Fire in Their Hearts: Yiddish Socialists in New York* (Cambridge, Mass.: Harvard University Press, 2005), 216.

53. Hoffman, 79.

54. Goldstein, ed., 2, 5, 7, 12.

55. Hapgood, 19; Sarna, trans. and ed., *People Walk on Their Heads: Moses Weinberger's Jews and Judaism in New York* (New York: Holmes and Meier Publishers, 1981), 116.


## 4. STRATEGIES OF NEW YORK'S ORTHODOX ACTIVISTS

1. Jonathan D. Sarna, trans. and ed., *People Walk on Their Heads*, 55.

2. Lloyd P. Gartner, "Temples of Liberty Unpolluted: American Jews and Public Schools, 1840–1875," in Bertram W. Korn, ed, *A Bicentennial Festschrift for Jacob Rader Marcus*, 157–90; Hutchins Hapgood, *The Spirit of the Ghetto: Studies of the Immigrant Quarter of New York*, 27–28.

3. Hapgood, 27.

4. Gartner, "Temples," 166, 171, 172.

5. Jeffrey S. Gurock, *The Men and Women of Yeshiva: Higher Education, Orthodoxy and American Judaism* (New York: Columbia University Press, 1988), 11.

6. Broadside of the Association of the American Orthodox Hebrew Congregations, April 1888, published in appendix 3 of Abraham J. Karp, "New York Chooses a Chief Rabbi," *PAJHS* (March 1955): 191. On the interrelatedness of the founders of Etz Chaim with the leadership of the Association, see Gurock, *The Men and Women of Yeshiva*, 12–13.

7. Karp, 191.

8. For a study that notes the sustained communal interest in kosher meat and the activism of women to drive down the costs of even scrupulously observed kosher meats, see Paula E. Hyman, "Immigrant Women and Consumer Protest: The New York City Kosher Meat Boycott of 1902," *AJH* (September 1980): 91–105.

9. Karp, 191.

10. Ibid., 131–33, 139–44. On Joseph's debts in Russia, see Karp, 149.

11. Gilbert Klaperman, *The Story of Yeshiva University: The First Jewish University in America* (London: Macmillan, 1969), 26, 28; See also Annie Polland, "The Sacredness of the Family: New York's Immigrant Jews and Their Religion, 1880–1930" (Ph.D. dissertation, Columbia University, 2004), 191; Karp, 163.

12. On Rabbi Joseph's preaching both Sabbath morning and afternoon, see Karp, 168.

13. Karp, 162–65; Hyman, 99, 101.

14. On Vidrowitz's and Segal's background and scholarly productivity, see Judah David Eisenstein *Otzar Zikhronothai: Anthology and Memoir* [Hebrew] (New York: J.D. Eisenstein, 1929), 77, 118, 180.

15. The only soft figures on early enrollment patterns come from 1905 when Eisenstein estimated that 150–175 students attended Etz Chaim. See on this question, Gurock, *The Men and Women of Yeshiva*, 15, 259 n. 12.

16. Gartner, "From New York to Miedzyrecz: Immigrant Letters of Judah David Eisenstein, 1878–1886," *AJHQ* (March 1963): 242–43.

17. On the Kaplan family's educational decisions with reference to Mordecai, see Gurock and Jacob J. Schacter, *A Modern Heretic and a Traditional Community: Mordecai M. Kaplan, Orthodoxy and American Judaism* (New York: Columbia University Press, 1997), 13–15.

18. Gartner, "From New York," 236.

19. On the place of secular education at the Volozhin Yeshiva, see Jacob J. Schacter, "Haskalah, Secular Studies and the Close of the Yeshiva in Volozhin in 1892," *Torah U Mada Journal* (1990): 91–92.

20. Gurock, "How 'Frum' was Rabbi Jacob Joseph's Court? Americanization within the Lower East Side's Orthodox Elite, 1886–1902," *Jewish History* (1994): 258–59.

21. On the founding of the Andron's school, see Alexander Dushkin, *Jewish Education in New York City* (New York: Bureau of Jewish Education, 1918), 75–77; Ruchama Shain, *All for the Boss* (New York: Feldheim, 1984), 47–48. See also *Jewish Forum* (October 1920): 450.

22. For a full discussion of the evolution of all-day Jewish education for girls in its varying forms, both in Europe and the United States, see below, chapter 6.

23. *Sefer ha-Yovel shel Agudath ha-Rabbanim ha-Ortodoksim de-Arsot ha-Brit ve-Canada* (New York: n.p., 1928), 13–21, 24.

24. On the constitution of the Union of Orthodox Rabbis, see Aaron Rakeffet-Rothkoff, *The Silver Era: Rabbi Eliezer Silver and His Generation* (Jerusalem and New York: Yeshiva University Press/Feldheim Publishers, 1981), 320–21.

25. On the founding of the Yeshiva Rabbi Isaac Elchanan and its early curriculum, see Gurock, *The Men and Women of Yeshiva*, 18–21. See also, Rakeffet-Rothkoff, 317–19 for the union's connectedness to the early advanced yeshiva.

26. Rakeffet-Rothkoff, 319.

27. Dushkin, 66–68.

28. Ibid., 68–70.

29. Rakeffet-Rothkoff, 317–20.

30. On the idea of evening schools and classes for girls, see the report on the 1903 and 1904 rabbis' annual meetings in the *American Jewish Year Book* 5664 (1903–1904): 160 and 5665 (1904–1905): 282.

31. Davis, 237–38; Bernard Drachman, *The Unfailing Light: Memoirs of an American Rabbi* (New York: Rabbinical Council of America, 1948), 177–82; Cyrus Adler, "Semi-Centennial Address," in *The Jewish Theological Seminary of America: Semi-Centennial Volume* (New York: Jewish Theological Seminary, 1939), 5–7; Henry Pereira Mendes, "The Beginnings of the Seminary," ibid., 35–42.

32. On the significance of the Pittsburgh Platform, see Sefton D. Temkin, "The Pittsburgh Platform: A Centenary Assessment," *Journal of Reform Judaism* (Fall 1985): 1–12.

33. John J. Appel, "The Treyfa Banquet," *Commentary* (February 1966): 75–78. On Wise's original agenda to build a rabbinical school for all movements in America, see Alan Silverstein, *Alternatives to Assimilation: The Response of Reform Judaism to American Culture, 1840–1930* (Hanover, N.H.: University Press of New England, 1994), 61–62.

34. On the definition of this coalition between Conservatives and American Orthodox in the Seminary's founding, see Gurock, "Resisters and Accommodators: Varieties of Orthodox Rabbis in America, 1886–1983," *AJA* (November 1983): 100–102.

35. Robert E. Fierstien, *A Different Spirit: The Jewish Theological Seminary of America, 1886–1902* (New York: Jewish Theological Seminary, 1990), 81–84.

36. Drachman, 132–53, 167, 177; Gurock, "From Exception to Role Model: Bernard Drachman and the Evolution of Jewish Religious Life in America, 1880–1920," *AJH* (June 1987), 456–84; Davis, 335.

37. Drachman, 197–200, 206.

38. Fierstein, 80–81; Davis, 335.

39. On the founding of the Orthodox Union, see *American Hebrew* (January 4, 1901), 231.

40. *Hebrew Standard* (October 18, 1901), 4; *American Hebrew* (January 18, 1901), 284; (February 8, 1901), 379; (April 5, 1901), 596; Drachman, 225ff.

41. Gurock, "Consensus Building and Conflict over Creating the Young People's Synagogue on the Lower East Side," in *The Americanization of the Jews,* Norman J. Cohen and Robert Seltzer, eds. (New York: New York University Press, 1995), 234, 236–37.

42. See *Hebrew Standard* (October 24, 1902), 4; June 12, 1903, 10; *American Hebrew* (February 7, 1902), 400 for examples of turn of the century Orthodox Union lobbying and advocacy efforts.

43. Gurock, "Consensus," 242–43.

44. *American Hebrew* (May 30, 1902), 37–38. The educational philosopher who was most influential on Jewish pedagogic thinking of that era was John Dewey. See on these ideas that resonated in the plans of Drachman and others, John Dewey, *Democracy and Education* (New York: Macmillan, 1963), 53, 241–49. See also Ronald Kronish, "The Influence of John Dewey on Jewish Education," *Conservative Judaism* (Winter 1976): 49–52.

45. *American Hebrew* (August 19, 1904), 348; Zvi Scharfstein, ed., *Sefer ha-yovel shel Agudat ha-Morim ha-Ivrim* (New York: Modern Linotype, 1944), 156; Hapgood, 53, 55–58.

46. *Yiddishes Tageblat* (March 27, 1905), 4. This new educational mission is discussed in greater detail in Gurock, *When Harlem Was Jewish, 1870–1930* (New York: Columbia University Press, 1979), 100–101.

47. *Yiddishes Tageblat* (May 11, 1905), 4; (May 15, 1905), 4 discussed in Gurock, *When Harlem Was Jewish*, 102.

48. Elias A. Cohen to Louis Marshall, March 31, 1908 (Marshall Papers–American Jewish Archives), discussed in Gurock, *When Harlem Was Jewish*, 103. On Marshall's support for the Jewish Theological Seminary, notwithstanding his personal Reform affinities, see Morton Rosenstock, *Louis Marshall: Defender of Jewish Rights* (Detroit: Wayne State University Press, 1965), 32, 50.

49. Jacob H. Schiff to the board of directors of the Uptown Talmud Torah Association, February 16, 1910 (Marshall Papers–American Jewish Archives), discussed in Gurock, *When Harlem Was Jewish*, 104. On Schiff's interest in the Seminary and his fears of atheism and radicalism among the children of immigrants, see Naomi W. Cohen, *Jacob H. Schiff: A Study in American Jewish Leadership* (Hanover, N.H: University Press of New England, 1999), 96–102.

50. See Arthur Goren's authoritative study of the Kehillah, *New York Jews and the Quest for Community: The Kehillah Experiment, 1908–1922* (New York: Columbia University Press, 1970), particularly chapters two and three for a discussion of the evolution of the organization's mission.

51. For examinations of the Kehillah's approaches to criminality and education, see Goren's chapters 5 through 8.

52. *American Hebrew* (January 4, 1910), 235; *Hebrew Standard* (March 5, 1909), 8; Goren, 54. See also, the minutes of the executive committee of the Kehillah, April 7, 1909, and April 10, 1910, in the Judah Magnes Papers [Hebrew University], noted in Gurock, "Resisters," 170. On Fischel's affinity for Schiff, see Goldstein, ed. *Forty Years of Struggle for a Principle: The Biography of Harry Fischel* (New York: Bloch Publishing Co., 1928), iii.

53. Gurock, *When Harlem Was Jewish*, 103.

54. Ibid., 108–109. See also, *Morgen Zhurnal* (February, 23, 1914), 1; (February 24, 1914), 2.

55. Harry Fischel to Jacob H. Schiff, February 27, 1914 (Schiff Papers, American Jewish Archives), noted in Gurock, *When Harlem Was Jewish*, 109.

56. Gurock, "Jacob A. Riis: Christian Friend or Missionary Foe? Two Jewish Views," *AJH* (September 1981): 29–47.

57. Idem., "The Americanization Continuum and Jewish Responses to Christian Influences on the Lower East Side, 1900–1910," *Christian Missionaries and Jewish Apostates*, Todd Endelman, ed. (New York: Holmes and Meier, 1987), 255–71.

58. Idem., "Why Albert Lucas Did Not Serve the New York Kehillah," *Proceedings of the American Academy for Jewish Research* (1984): 55–72.

59. *Ha-Ivri* (September 17, 1897), 12; (October 15, 1897), 10, cited in Klaperman, 40.

60. *Yiddishe Welt* (July 3, 1902), 4, cited in Klaperman, 42.

61. Judah David Eisenstein, "The Establishment of the New Seminary," [Hebrew] in *New Yorker Yiddishe Zeitung* (1886) republished in Eisenstein's *Otzar,* 210.

62. *American Hebrew* (November 24, 1889), 86; quoted in Fierstien, 126.

63. For evidence of affluent downtowners who supported the chief rabbi initiative and the Yeshiva as well as the Seminary, see Gurock and Schacter, 22. See also this source, 23–25 for the Kaplan family's decision and the thinking of other comparable families in sending their sons to the Seminary.

64. *Sefer ha-Yovel shel Agudath ha-Rabbanim*, 18.

65. On the Agudath ha-Rabbanim's nonrecognition of American Orthodox rabbis as respected colleagues, see Gurock, "Resisters," 111–12.

66. Aaron Rothkoff, "The American Sojourns of Ridbaz: Religious Problems within the Immigrant Community," *AJHQ* (June 1968): 560.

67. Gurock and Schacter, 41–42, 47–48.

68. Ibid., 183–84.

69. Rothkoff, 561–62.

70. On the excoriation statement, see *American Hebrew* (June 17, 1904), 130; (July 1, 1904), 174, 180.

71. Gurock and Schacter, 48.

72. Goren, 50.

73. See David Ellenson, *Rabbi Esriel Hildesheimer and the Creation of a Modern Jewish Orthodoxy* (Tuscaloosa: University of Alabama Press, 1990), 12–20 for a discussion of the fundamental ideological differences that separated Hildesheimer from Sofer, and 138–42 for a consideration of the curriculum at Hildesheimer's schools. For a brief biography of Klein's early life and education, see *Sefer ha-Yovel*, 140.

74. *American Hebrew* (January 4, 1901), 235.

75. For a listing of the founders of the rabbi's organization, see Rakeffet-Rothkoff, 320.

76. Polland, 93–98.

77. On Drachman's relationship with Klein at Ohab Zedek, see Drachman, 277–90; Gurock, *When Harlem Was Jewish*, 119; First Hungarian-American Congregation Ohab Zedek, *Golden Jubilee Journal* (New York: Ohab Zedek Congregation, 1923), passim. On Klein's Kehillah connections, see the Minutes of the Executive Committee of the Kehillah, April 17, 1909 in the Judah Magnes Papers [Hebrew University], noted in Gurock, "Resisters," 121, 170.

78. See *American Jewish Year Book* (1903–1904), 79, for a brief biographical sketch of Margolies. See Gurock and Schacter, 49, for a discussion of how Ramaz came to serve at Kehilath Jeshurun, 93.

79. Gurock and Schacter, 49–50, 53.

80. Polland, 93.

81. Gurock, *When Harlem Was Jewish*, 102, 135; "Resisters," 112.

82. The saga of Klein and Margolies's involvement with the Kehillah, their formal resignation, and continued affinity for American ways discussed in the foregoing paragraphs is noted and analyzed in great detail in Gurock, "Resisters," 118–23.

83. *American Jewish Year Book* (1903–1904), 74; Naomi W. Cohen, *Not Free to Desist: The American Jewish Committee, 1906–1966* (Philadelphia: Jewish Publication Society, 1972), 563; Alex Goldman, "Bernard L. Levinthal: Nestor of the American Orthodox Rabbi-

nate," in *Giants of Faith: Great American Rabbis* (New York, 1964), 160–76; *Sefer Kavod Chachomim* (Philadelphia, 1935), 75 and passim. One of the long-standing, if not documented, traditions about Levinthal was that throughout his career, he tightly ruled his community and played major roles in determining the type of American Orthodox or Conservative rabbi who could find pulpits there.

84. For more on the founding of the yeshiva and its earliest students, see Gurock, *The Men and Women of Yeshiva*, 20–21 and Klaperman, 88.

85. For an analysis of the rabbis' organizational constitution, see below, 118–122.

86. For a discussion of the multiple reasons why students left the yeshiva during this era of turmoil, see Gurock, *The Men and Women of Yeshiva*, 4–28. See also Ephraim Lisitzky, *In the Grip of Crosscurrents* (New York: Bloch; Yeshiva University Press/Feldheim, 1950), 90–94.

87. Gurock, *The Men and Women of Yeshiva*, 24–26, 29–30, 33–35. See also Klaperman, 88, for Klein, Margolies, and Levinthal's multiple roles at the early yeshiva.

88. See A. S. Sachs, *Worlds That Passed* (Philadelphia: Ayer, 1928), 251 for comments on the impact of the Jewish Enlightenment upon yeshiva students. On Reines's ideas and the yeshiva he created, see Gedalyahu Alon, "The Lithuanian Yeshiva," Sid Z. Leiman, trans. in *The Jewish Experience*, ed. Judah Goldin (New York: Bantam Books, 1970), 454; Hayyyim Z. Reines, "Isaac Jacob Reines," in *Jewish Leaders, 1750–1940*, ed. Leo Jung (New York: Bloch, 1928), 279–89; and see also William B. Helmreich, *The World of the Yeshiva: An Intimate Portrait of Orthodox Jewry* (New York: Free Press, 1982), 13.

89. See Gurock, "Resisters," 166, for a discussion of the Agudath ha-Rabbanim's affinity for Mizrachi ideas.

90. Aaron Rothkoff, *Bernard Revel: Builder of American Jewish Orthodoxy* (Philadelphia: Jewish Publication Society), 27–39.

91. Ibid., 38–39.

92. Gurock, *The Men and Women of Yeshiva*, 48–53; Ira Robinson, "Cyrus Adler, Bernard Revel and the Prehistory of Organized Jewish scholarship in America," *AJH* (June 1980): 497–505.

93. Gurock, "An Orthodox Conspiracy Theory: The Travis Family, Bernard Revel and the Jewish Theological Seminary," *Modern Judaism* (October 1999): 241–54.

94. Mordecai M. Kaplan, "Affiliation with the Synagogue," *The Jewish Communal Register of New York City, 1917–1918* (New York: Kehillah [Jewish Community] of New York City, 1918), 117–22.

95. Dushkin, 154–56.

96. Gurock, *Judaism's Encounter with American Sports*, 91.

97. Ibid., 59–63, 65–66. See Gurock and Schacter, 95–97 for a discussion of Kaplan's early concessions on Orthodox ritual at the synagogue.

98. See Gurock and Schachter, A Modern Heretic, 91–92 for a discussion of how witnessing youngsters playing ball in the streets on the Sabbath motivated Kaplan and his supporters to move forward with their Jewish Center plans. For a comprehensive biography of Kaplan and his career, see Mel Scult, *Judaism Faces the Twentieth Century: A Biography of Mordecai M. Kaplan* (Detroit: Wayne State University Press, 1993). See also Schacter, "A Rich Man's Club? The Founding of the Jewish Center," *Hazon Nahum: Stud-*

*ies in Jewish Law, Thought and History Presented to Dr. Norman Lamm on the Occasion of His Seventieth Birthday*, Yaakov Elman and Jeffrey S. Gurock, eds. (New York: Michael Scharf Publications Trust of Yeshiva University Press, 1997), 693, 716.

### 5. CRISIS AND COMPROMISE

1. Ronald Sanders, *Shores of Refuge: A Hundred Years of Jewish Emigration* (New York: Henry Holt, 1988), 383, 386, 394; Henry L. Feingold, *A Time for Searching: Entering the Mainstream* (Baltimore: Johns Hopkins University Press, 1992), 29.

2. "Landlocked in America," *American Hebrew* (September 26, 1924): 521.

3. For the necrologies of these rabbis, see *Sefer ha-Yovel shel Agudath ha-Rabbanim ha-Ortodoksim de-Arsot ha-Brit ve-Canada* (New York: n.p., 1928), 137–47.

4. Henry Pereira Mendes, "Orthodox Judaism (The Present)," *Jewish Forum* (January 1920): 35; Samuel Koenig, "The Socioeconomic Structure of an American Jewish Community," in *Jews in a Gentile World: The Problem of Anti-Semitism*, Isacque Graeber and Stuart Henderson Brit, eds. (New York: Macmillan, 1942), 227, 229; Gerald Sorin, *The Nurturing Neighborhood: The Brownsville Boys Club and Jewish Community in Urban America, 1940–1990* (New York: New York University Press, 1990), 15–16.

5. Langer, "The Jewish Community of Easttown, 1931–32," unpublished abstract of thesis written at the Graduate School for Jewish Social Work, New York, 1932, American Jewish Historical Society.

6. Beth S. Wenger, *New York Jews and the Great Depression* (New Haven, Conn.: Yale University Press), 173–75, 178–79. See also the unpublished memoirs of Victor B. Geller in the possession of the author.

7. Nathan Goldberg, "Religious and Social Attitudes of Jewish Youth in the U.S.A.," *Jewish Review* (1943): 146–49; Samuel P. Abelow, *History of Brooklyn Jewry* (Brooklyn: Scheba Publishing Co., 1937), 334; Sorin, 15–16.

8. Jenna Weissman Joselit " 'A Set Table': Jewish Domestic Culture in the New World, 1880–1950," in Jenna Weissman Joselit and Susan L. Braunstein, eds., *Getting Comfortable in New York: The American Jewish Home, 1880–1950* (New York: Jewish Museum, 1990), 39–40, 57–58.

9. Jenna Weissman Joselit, *The Wonders of America: Reinventing Jewish Culture, 1880–1945* (New York: Henry Holt, 1994), 172.

10. Deborah Dash Moore, *GI Jews: How World War II Changed a Generation* (Cambridge, Mass.: Harvard University Press, 2004), 54–57, 281.

11. Gottfried Neuburger, "An Orthodox G.I. Fights a War," *Commentary* (March 1949): 265–72.

12. Joselit, *Wonders of America*, 174, 176, 216.

13. For a complete discussion of the lack of religiosity of interwar Ys and JCCs, see Jeffrey S. Gurock, *Judaism's Encounter with American Sports*, 95–100.

14. On informal neighborhood relationships helping Jewish identification in interwar New York, see Moore, *At Home in America: Second Generation New York Jews* (New York: Columbia University Press, 1981), especially 19–60. On interethnic tensions, see Ronald

P. Bayor, *Neighbors in Conflict: The Irish, Germans, Jews and Italians of New York City, 1929–1941* (Baltimore: Johns Hopkins University Press, 1978), especially 150–63.

15. *Orthodox Union* (June 1936), 1.

16. Wiiliam B. Helmreich, *The Enduring Community: The Jews of Newark and Metrowest* (New Brunswick: Transaction Publishers,1999), 247.

17. On the history of Young Israel, see National Council of Young Israel Organizations, *Annual Convention 5694/1934* and "Constitution of Council of Young Israel and Young Israel Synagogue Organizations," circa 1935, both documents on file at the American Jewish Historical Society.

18. Louis Bernstein, *Challenge and Mission: The Emergence of the English-Speaking Orthodox Rabbinate* (New York: Shengold Publishers, 1982), 35–36. See unpublished Proceedings of the Seventh Annual Convention of the Rabbinical Council of America, June 30–31, 1942, document on file at the offices of the Rabbinical Council of America. I am grateful to Rabbi Ari Perl for having uncovered this source. See also *Orthodox Union* (February 1945): 11.

19. David I. Macht, "The Jewish Dietary Laws," in *The Jewish Library*, second series, ed. Leo Jung (New York: Bloch Publishing, 1930), 205, 214–15. See also Jung's "Introduction," viii–ix.

20. Jenna Weissman Joselit, *New York's Jewish Jews: The Orthodox Community in the Interwar Years* (Bloomington: Indiana University Press, 1990), 109–12.

21. Ibid., 115–19.

22. Ibid., 118–21.

23. Joselit, "A Set Table," 11.

24. Jonathan D. Sarna, "The Debate over Mixed Seating in the American Synagogue," in *The American Synagogue: A Sanctuary Transformed*, ed. Jack Wertheimer, 378–79.

25. Moore, *At Home in America*, 30–36, 39; Marshall Sklare, *Conservative Judaism: An American Religious Movement* (Glencoe: University of Illinois Press, 1955), p. 103.

26. Jack Wertheimer, "The Conservative Synagogue" in *The American Synagogue*, 119–20.

27. Arthur L. Reinhart, *The Voice of the Jewish Laity; A Survey of Jewish Layman's Attitudes and Practices* (Cincinnati: National Federation of Temple Brotherhoods, 1928), 11–13. See also on the ethnicity of these members of temples, Commission on Research, Union of American Hebrew Congregations, *Reform Judaism in the Large Cities* (New York: Union of American Hebrew Congregations, 1931), 9–10.

28. Jeffrey S. Gurock, *From Fluidity to Rigidity: The Religious Worlds of Conservative and Orthodox Jews in Twentieth Century America* (Ann Arbor: University of Michigan, 1998), 25–27.

29. Jacob J. Weinstein, *Solomon Goldman: A Rabbi's Rabbi* (New York: KTAV Publishing House, 1973), 13–16. See also Rakeffet-Rothkoff, 112–14.

30. The details about the forum are derived from an Orthodox Union article that Fasman wrote about his soon-to-be-published guide. However, the guide seems to have never been published. See Oscar Z. Fasman, "The Friday Night Forum," *Orthodox Union* (February 1944): 4–7.

31. Isadore Goodman, "Trends in Orthodoxy," *Orthodox Union* (June 1942): 8–9.

32. Jeffrey S. Gurock, "The Late Friday Night Orthodox Service: An Exercise in Religious Accommodation," *Jewish Social Studies* (Spring/Summer 2006): 140–41.

33. David de Sola Pool, "Judaism and the Synagogue," in *The American Jew: A Composite Portrait*, ed. Oscar Janowsky (New York: Harper and Bros., 1942), 50–54.

34. Mendell Lewittes, "Principle and Practice in American Orthodoxy," *Orthodox Union* (October 1944): 7.

35. For a biographical study of Epstein, see Mark K. Bauman, "Rabbi Harry H. Epstein and the Adaptation of Second-Generation Jews in Atlanta," *AJA* (Fall/Winter, 1990): 133–46. See also Gurock, "From Fluidity to Rigidity," 52–53, note 85 for a discussion of Epstein and his synagogue's membership and role in the Orthodox Union. On the Southeastern Conference resolution, see Mark H. Elovitz, *A Century of Jewish Life in Dixie: The Birmingham Experience* (Tuscaloosa: University of Alabama Press, 1974), 91, 93–95, 99, 163–64.

36. Sarna, *American Judaism*, 242.

37. Saul Adelson, "Chicago's Hebrew Theological College," *Jewish Life* (December 1947): 43–48; Eliezer Berkowitz, "A Contemporary Rabbinical School for Orthodox Jewry," *Tradition* (Fall 1979): 56–64; Oscar Z. Fasman, "After Fifty Years, an Optimist," *AJH* (December 1979): 162.

38. See Rothkoff, *Bernard Revel: Builder of American Jewish Orthodoxy*, 166–67, for Revel's excoriation of an unidentified miscreant.

39. For a source on the projected needs of these congregations, see Rothkoff, *Bernard Revel*, 169.

40. "Report on the Reorganization of the Placement Committee," *Proceedings of the Rabbinical Assembly* 3 (1929): 123–24.

41. For an account of the merger plans, see Rothkoff, *Bernard Revel*, 94–114.

42. Jeffrey S. Gurock, "Yeshiva Students at the Jewish Theological Seminary," in *Tradition Renewed: A History of the Jewish Theological Seminary*, vol. 1, Jack Wertheimer, ed. (New York: Jewish Theological Seminary, 1997), 492–98.

43. For a source on the incipient mission of the Synagogue Council of America, see *Central Conference of American Rabbis Yearbook* 37 (1927): 98–100.

44. *Orthodox Union* (August 1935): 1, 7.

45. *Orthodox Union* (May 1935): 1; (April 1935): 14.

46. For a brief biography of Pardes, see Sherman, *Orthodox Judaism in America*, 160–61; Samuel A. Pardes, "Ha-hiluf ve-hatemurah," *Ha-Pardes* (October 1930): 5–6.

47. The positive responsum on depilatories was authored by Rabbi Samuel Landau, sometime between 1793–1811 and appears in Ezekiel Landau, *Noda B'Yehuda, Yoreh De'ah* #81, 2nd ed. (New York: M.P. Press, 1956).

48. See *Ha-Pardes* (May 1932), 25–26 for Rabbi Pardes's responsum and 32 for the Schick ad. See also Fasman, "Historical Reminiscence: After Fifty Years, An Optimist," *AJH* (December 1979): 161, for his accounting of his role in this arrangement.

49. For an example of the monthly Gem ad, see *The Jewish Forum* (March 1938): 46.

50. Nathan M. Kaganoff, "An Orthodox Rabbinate in the South: Tobias Geffen, 1870–1970," *AJH* (September 1983): 67–68. See also Joel Ziff, ed., *Lev Tuviah: On the*

*Life and Work of Rabbi Tobias Geffen* (Newton, Mass.: Rabbi Tobias Geffen Memorial Fund, 1988), 14–15.

51. Kaganoff, 66–69.

52. On Epstein's career moves, his self-definition, and his policy toward services, see Gurock, *From Fluidity to Rigidity*, 22–25, 50–51. See also Pamela S. Nadell, *Conservative Judaism: A Biographical Dictionary and Source Book* (Westport, Conn.: Greenwood Press, 1988), 80–81.

53. On the question of desertion among immigrant Jews of this era, see Ari Lloyd Fridkis, "Desertion in the American Jewish Immigrant Family: The Work of the National Desertion Bureau in Cooperation with the Industrial Removal Office," *AJH* (December 1981): 285–99.

54. Louis Epstein, *Hatsa'ah le-ma'an takanot agunot* (New York, n.p., 1930), 39.

55. For a discussion of the nature of Epstein's approach and sources on the Agudath ha-Rabbanim's excoriation of Epstein, see Sarna, *American Judaism*, 240. See also Agudath ha-Rabbanim d'Arzot ha-Brith ve-Canada, *Le-Dor Aharon* (New York: Moinister Press, 1937), title page.

56. Rakeffet-Rothkoff, 107.

57. Rothkoff, *Bernard Revel*, 171.

58. See Rakeffet-Rothkoff, 43–95 for a detailed account of Silver's European training and American rabbinical career.

59. Ibid., 99–105, 169–180.

60. The Youngstown response, dated circa 1930, is from a manuscript collection of responses to Rabbi Silver's questionnaire given to, and in possession of, the author, by the late Rabbi David Silver.

61. Rothkoff, *Bernard Revel*, 169.

62. Bernstein, 91–121.

63. Gurock, *The Men and Women of Yeshiva*, 128–29.

64. For a biographical sketch of Margolis, see Sherman, 144–47.

65. On Margolis's conflicts with other rabbis over kashruth, see Harold P. Gastwirth, *Fraud, Holiness and Corruption* (Port Washington, N.Y.: Kennikat Press, 1974), 92–93. 119–122, and passim. See also Joshua Hoffman, "The American Rabbinic Career of Rabbi Gabriel Z. Margolis," (M.A. thesis, Bernard Revel Graduate School of Yeshiva University, 1992). For the Knesset ha-Rabbonim's specific declaration on the question of kosher supervision, see *Sefer Knesset ha-Rabbonim ha-Ortodoksim be-America*, vol. I (New York: Assembly of Hebrew Orthodox Rabbis of America, Inc., 1921), 2, 9 for texts of its draft resolutions.

66. For a comprehensive examination of the range of Orthodox reactions to Prohibition and the battles between the two competing groups of rabbis, see Hannah Sprecher, " 'Let *Them* Drink and Forget *Our* Poverty': Orthodox Rabbis React to Prohibition," *AJA* (Fall/Winter 1991): 135–79.

67. On the problems observant young men faced in the 1920s even at "Jewish" schools such as CCNY and NYU and the practical, religious, and ideological solution Yeshiva College offered as articulated by Revel, see Gurock, *The Men and Women of Yeshiva*, 82–89.

68. For Margolis's attitude toward Revel's initiatives, see *Charuzei Margoliot,* vol. II (New York: Levi and Associates, 1918), 394, and *Sefer Knesset ha-Rabbonim be-America,* vol. II (New York: Assembly of Hebrew Orthodox Rabbis of America, Inc., 1924), 44–45. See also Hoffman's discussion of these attitudes in his "The American Rabbinic Career."

69. On the concomitance of the Zionist meeting and the rabbis' planning gathering, see Gurock, "American Orthodox Organizations in Support of Zionism, 1880–1930," in *Zionism and Religion,* Shmuel Almog, Jehuda Reinharz, and Anita Shapira.eds. (Hanover, N.H.: University Press of New England, 1998), 221.

70. Ibid., 222–23, 231–32, n.13.

71. *Sefer ha-Yovel,* 21–22, 81–82. See also *American Jewish Year Book* 5664 (1903–1904):124; 5665(1904–1905): 240, 282.

72. On the founding and structure of the Agudath Israel, see Gershon Chaim Bacon, "Agudat Israel in Poland, 1916–1935: An Orthodox Jewish Response to the Challenge of Modernity" (Ph.D. diss., Columbia University, 1979), 41–43. See also Isaac Lewin, *Unto the Mountains: Essays* (New York: Hebrew Publishing Co., 1975), 71–74. On the founding and agenda of the U.S. affiliate, see *Sefer ha-Yovel,* 76–77.

73. *Sefer ha-Yovel,* 110.

74. Hoffman, 5, 9.

75. *Sefer Knesset ha-Rabbonim,* vol. 2, 11–21, 22–25, discussed in Gurock, "American Orthodox Organizations," 228–29.

76. Gurock, "American Orthodox Organizations," 229–230.

## 6. BROOKLYN'S COMMITTED COMMUNITIES

1. On patterns of religious disinterest in Brownsville, Gerald Sorin, *The Nurturing Neighborhood: The Brownsville Boys Club and Jewish Community in Urban America,* 1940–1990 (New York: New York University Press, 1990), 16–17. On strict observance within Williamsburg, see George Kranzler, *Williamsburg: A Jewish Community in Transition* (New York: Feldheim, 1961), 17, 18, 214–15.

2. For a statistical comparison of Torah Vodaath-style education in Brooklyn, which includes the yeshivas of Chaim Berlin of Brownsville, Ohel Moshe of Bensonhurst, and Toras Chaim of East New York with similar Manhattan schools, see Jacob I. Hartstein, "Jewish Community Elementary Parochial Schools" (unpublished typescript., ca. 1934, Yeshiva University Archives), table 1, 14, and Alvin I. Schiff, *The Jewish Day School in America* (New York: JEC Press), 39, 69, discussed in Jeffrey S. Gurock, "Jewish Commitment and Continuity in Interwar Brooklyn," in *Jews of Brooklyn,* Ilana Abramovitch and Sean Galvin, eds. (Hanover, N.H. and London: University Press of New England, 2000), 240, n.8.

3. On Mendlowitz's background, see Alexander Gross and Joseph Kaminetsky, "Shraga Feivel Mendlowitz," in *Men of the Spirit,* ed. Leo Jung (New York; Feldheim, 1964), 557–63. See also, for discussions of Mendlowitz's agenda by his followers, Yonoson Rosenblum, *Reb Shraga Feivel: The Life and Times of Rabbi Shraga Feivel Mendlowitz, the Architect of Torah in America* (New York: Mesorah Publications, 2001), 78, 90.

4. William B. Helmreich, *The World of the Yeshiva*, 27–29.

5. Meir Kimmel, "The History of Yeshivat Rabbi Chaim Berlin," *Sheviley ha-Hinuch* (Fall 1948): 51–54; Alter Landesman, *Brownsville: The Birth, Development and Passing of a Jewish Community in New York* (New York: Bloch, 1969), 234–35; Helmreich, 33–34.

6. Joseph Friedenson, "The Mother of Generations," in *The Torah World: A Treasury of Biographical Sketchesi*, ed. Nisson Wolpin (Brooklyn, N.Y.: Mesorah Publications), 162–74; Judith Grunfeld, "The Story of Beth Jacob," in *Jubilee Book Agudas Israel Organization* (London: n.p., 1942), 36–39; Zevi H. Harris, "Trends in Jewish Education for Girls in New York City" (Ph.D. diss., Yeshiva University, 1956), 94, 134–37.

7. Helmreich, 25–26, 30, 32–33

8. Gurock, *The Men and Women of Yeshiva*, 111; Helmreich, 26; Rosenblum, 90.

9. Gurock, *The Men and Women of Yeshiva*, 111.

10. Helmreich, 26, 29, 36–37.

11. Rothkoff, *Bernard Revel*, 155–56.

12. Gurock, *The Men and Women of Yeshiva*, 112.

13. For these statements of interest in Revel's college, see the student files of that institution utilized in Gurock, *The Men and Women of Yeshiva*, 114–15.

14. Ibid., 115–16.

15. Kranzler, 142.

16. Max Kufeld, "The Hebrew Institute of Boro Park," *Jewish Education* (April 1924): 268–69.

17. Moses I. Shulman, "The Yeshivah Etz Hayim-Hebrew Institute of Boro Park," *Jewish Education* (Fall 1948): 47; Noah Nardi, "A Survey of Jewish Day Schools in America," *Jewish Education* (September 1944): 22–23; idem., "The Growth of Jewish Day Schools in America," *Jewish Education* (November 1948): 24–25; Lloyd P. Gartner private communication to Jeffrey S. Gurock, September 3, 1998, noted in Gurock, "Jewish Commitment," 240, n.21.

18. On the Zionist expectations of the parents involved with these day schools, see Nardi, "The Growth of Jewish Day Schools in America," 25.

19. On recollections of Torah Vodaath's earliest Zionist incarnation, see Harold C. Wilkenfeld interview with University of Maryland Oral History program, November 29, 1973, referenced in Gurock, "Jewish Continuity," 234.

20. Gross and Kaminetsky, 553.

21. On the relatedness of Mizrachi and Young Israel ideas and activities, see Kranzler, 163, 169, and Jenna Weissman Joselit, *New York's Jewish Jews*, 17–18. See also Gurock, *The Men and Women of Yeshiva*, 118.

22. On the general disinterest students at that time had in attending Hebrew Schools, see Azriel L. Eisenberg, "A Study of 4473 Pupils Who Left Hebrew School in 1932–1933," *Jewish Education* (April–June 1935): 93. For a memoir of a student who cared about her training, see interview with Sylvia Cutler Ettenburg, July 12, 1989, Ratner Center, Jewish Theological Seminary of America.

23. Nathan H. Winter, *Jewish Education in a Pluralist Society: Samson Benderly and Jewish Education in the United States* (New York: New York University Press, 1966), 112–18; 131–37; Isidor Margolis, *Jewish Teacher Training Schools in the United States* (New York: National

Council for Torah Education, 1964), 88–91, 242–53; Wilkenfeld, 1, 37. On Hebrew in the New York City public schools, see Judah Lapson, "A Decade of Hebrew in the High Schools of New York," *Jewish Education* (April 1941): 34–45.

24. For a discussion of Torah Vodaath and other strong Talmud students at Revel's school, see Gurock, *The Men and Women of Yeshiva*, 114–15. On Torah Vodaath and Yeshiva competing with each other for students, see Helmreich, 27.

25. Gurock, *The Men and Women of Yeshiva*, 106–107, 118.

26. For information on the backgrounds of Brooklyn-born and based students who aspired to attend the Seminary—including those who were denied admission—see "Reports of the Committee on Admissions," contained in Faculty Minutes, 1928–38 (Library of the Jewish Theological Seminary), discussed in Gurock, "Yeshiva Students at the Jewish Theological Seminary," in *Tradition Renewed*, ed. Jack Wertheimer, 492–98.

27. Jerome R. Mintz, *Hasidic People: A Place in the New World* (Cambridge, Mass.: Harvard University Press, 1992), 21–26, 53–56.

28. Kranzler, 213–15.

## 7. A MORE FAITHFUL FOLLOWING

1. The absence of certifiable statistics on Orthodox Union membership, both the numbers of worshippers and the count of synagogues make determining the reliability of that 1937 contention of hegemony very difficult. See *Orthodox Union* (July 1937): 2 for their estimates. For an enumeration of the numbers that the Orthodox Union offered over time—including an estimate that in 1935, it had some 2,303 congregations affiliated—and a discussion of their reliability, see Marc Lee Raphael, *Profiles in American Judaism: The Reform, Conservative, Orthodox, and Reconstructionist Traditions in Historical Perspective* (San Francisco: Harper and Row, 1984), 138, 223. On these problems of observance noted by Orthodox leaders in the 1940s, see Bert Lewkowitz, "The Future of Judaism as a Layman Visions It," *Jewish Forum* (December 1940): 177; *Orthodox Union* (April 1943): 5, (February 1945): 11, (October 1944): 7.

2. Alvin I. Schiff, *The Jewish Day School in America* (New York: JEC Press, 1966), 49, 69.

3. Jeffrey S. Gurock, "The Ramaz Version of American Orthodoxy," in *Ramaz: School, Community, Scholarship and Orthodoxy*, ed. Jeffrey S. Gurock (Hoboken, N.J.: KTAV, 1989), 49–53.

4. Seth Farber, *An American Orthodox Dreamer: Rabbi Joseph B. Soloveitchik and Boston's Maimonides School* (Hanover, N.H.: University Press of New England, 2004), 50–53, 81–84.

5. Leo Jung, "A Plea to Organized Orthodoxy," *Jewish Forum* (February 1959): 6.

6. On the general nature of suburban living and attitudes, see Herbert J. Gans, *The Levittowners: Ways of Life and Politics in a New Suburban Community* (New York: Pantheon Books, 1967) and Kenneth T. Jackson, *The Crabgrass Frontier: The Suburbanization of the United States* (New York: Oxford University Press, 1985). On changed Jewish attitudes, see Herbert J. Gans, "Park Forest: Birth of a Jewish Community," *Commentary* (April 1951): 331 and Herbert Gersh, "The New Suburbanites of the 1950s," *Commentary* (March 1954): 220–21.

7. For a description of a suburban Conservative rabbi saying and doing what needed to be done to attract a constituency, see Morris Freedman, "New Jewish Community in Formation: A Conservative Center Catering to Present-Day Needs," *Commentary* (January 1955): 43–45. See also Shuly Rubin Schwartz, "Camp Ramah: The Early Years, 1947–1952," *Conservative Judaism* (Fall 1987): 12–25, and Michael Brown, "It's Off to Camp We Go: Ramah, LTF and the Seminary," in *Tradition Renewed,* ed. Jack Wertheimer, 829–30.

8. Jack Wertheimer, "The Conservative Synagogue," in the *American Synagogue: A Sanctuary Transformed,* ed. Jack Wertheimer, 123–26. See also Marshall Sklare, *Conservative Judaism: An American Religious Movement,* 199–212, and "Responsum on the Sabbath," Rabbinical Assembly, *Proceedings* 14 (1950): 112–18.

9. Victor B. Geller, *Orthodoxy Awakens: The Belkin Years and Yeshiva University* (Jerusalem and New York: Urim Press, 2003), 112–13.

10. On the guilt and embarrassment Sabbath-drivers to Orthodox synagogues felt during the 1950s, see Julius M. Hurst, "Sabbath Driving," *Jewish Life* (September–October 1952): 36–37. For more on Orthodox debate strategies, see Gurock, *The Men and Women of Yeshiva,* 147–48.

11. See Geller, p. 115, for an example of an Orthodox victory despite the voting system.

12. On the nationwide struggles for control of congregation, see Jonathan D. Sarna, "The Debate over Mixed Seating," in *The American Synagogue,* ed. Jack Wertheimer, 379–86.

13. On the debate in Charleston, see Gurock, *Orthodoxy in Charleston,* 33.

14. For an example of Conservative position taking, see Rabbi Solomon Goldfarb's letter to Congregation Brith Sholom, noted in Gurock, *Orthodoxy in Charleston,* 34.

15. Sarna, "The Debate," 381–85. On the Mt. Clemens case, see Baruch Litvin, *The Sanctity of the Synagogue: The Case for Mechitza* (New York: KTAV, 1987).

16. For statistics on the growth of the United Synagogue, see Wertheimer, "The Conservative Synagogue," in *The American Synagogue,* ed. Jack Wertheimer, 123. See Sklare, p. 254, for the sense of Conservative primacy. On Conservatism's growth both in northeastern and midwestern areas, see Morris Axelrod, Floyd J. Fowler, and Arnold Gurin, *A Community Survey for Long Range Planning* (Boston: Combined Jewish Philanthropies of Greater Boston, 1967), 119; Sidney Goldstein and Calvin Goldscheider, *Jewish Americans: Three Generations in a Jewish Community* (Englewood Cliffs, N.J.: Prentice Hall, 1968), 177.

17. Jung, 6; Samuel Yalow, "A Righteous Minority and the Individual," *Jewish Forum* (June 1959): 93–94; *Report of the President Submitted to the Sixtieth Anniversary National Biennial Convention of the Union of Orthodox Jewish Congregations of America,* November 13, 1956, 8–10.

18. On the different ways students and others referred to this rabbi, see Charles S. Liebman, "Orthodoxy in American Jewish Life," *American Jewish Year Book* (1965): 53; Joseph B. Soloveitchik, "Tribute to Rabbi Joseph H. Lookstein," in *Rabbi Joseph H. Lookstein Memorial Volume* (New York: KTAV, 1980), vii–viii; Louis Bernstein, *Challenge and Mission: The Emergence of the English Speaking Orthodox Rabbinate* (New York: Shengold Publishers, 1982), 34–63.

19. For examples of popular and scholarly literature defining Orthodoxy's position on mixed seating read by rabbis in the field, see Morris Max, "Mixed Pews," *Jewish Life* (October 1949): 16–23; Fabian Schoenfeld, "Review of *The Sanctity of the Synagogue,*" *Tradition* (Spring 1960): 340–41; Norman Lamm, "Separate Pews in the Synagogue: A Social and Psychological Approach," *Tradition* (Spring 1959): 161–64.

20. Mark K. Bauman, *Harry H. Epstein and the Rabbinate as Conduit for Change* (Rutherford, N.J.: Farleigh Dickinson University Press, 1994), 54; Liebman, 56.

21. Liebman, 34.

22. Gershon Jacobson, "Inside Jewish Suburbia, U.S.A.," *Jewish Forum* (December 1961): 32.

23. Bert Lescot, "Orthodoxy in Suburbia," *Jewish Forum* (February 1958): 21. Geller, 34.

24. Ralph Pelcovitz, "Who Is the Orthodox Jew," *Jewish Life* (November–December, 1964): 16. See also Liebman, 35–37.

25. Bernard Lazerwitz and Michael Harrison, "American Jewish Denominations: A Social and Religious Profile," *American Sociological Review* (August 1979): 659–61; Egon Mayer and Chaim I. Waxman, "Modern Jewish Orthodoxy in America: Toward the Year 2000," *Tradition* (Spring 1977): 99, 101. See also Liebman, 31.

26. Sklare, *America's Jews* (New York: Random House, 1971), 40.

27. George Kranzler, *Williamsburg: A Jewish Community in Transition* (New York: Feldheim, 1961), 111, 217–19; Mayer, *From Suburb to Shtetl: The Jews of Boro Park* (Philadelphia: Temple University Press, 1979), 24–34; Israel Tabak, "The Need for Jewish Missionaries," *Jewish Life* (June 1947): 34–35; Joseph Kaminetsky, "Boro Park," *Jewish Life* (October 1953): 18–23.

28. Michael Kaufman, "Far Rockaway — Torah Suburb by the Sea," *Jewish Life* (August 1960): 20.

29. William B. Helmreich, "Old Wine in New Bottles: Advanced Yeshivot in the United States," *AJH* (December 1979): 243.

30. Haym Soloveitchik, "Rupture and Reconstruction: The Transformation of Contemporary Orthodoxy," *Tradition* (Summer 1994): 89–90, 93.

31. Soloveitchik, 90; Schiff, 54–55, 98–100.

32. Israel I. Chipkin, "Jewish Education in the United States at the Mid-Century," *Religious Education* (September–October 1953): 335; Noah Nardi, "The Growth of Jewish Day Schools in America," *Jewish Education* (Fall 1948): 31–32; Joseph Kaminetsky, "Parents Too Grow through the Day School," *Jewish Life* (March–April 1952): 26; Judah Pilch, ed., *A History of Jewish Education in America* (New York: American Association for Jewish Education, 1969), 140–41. On parents' apprehensions about the problems of "undesirables" in the public schools, see Schiff, 79.

33. Kaminetsky, "Parents Too Grow," 25–28.

34. Kaminetsky, "The Jewish Day School-Action and Reaction," *Jewish Life* (September–October 1952): 28.

35. Louis Nulman, *The Parent and the Jewish Day School* (Scranton, Pa.: Parent Study Press, 1956), 13–14, 45, 53–54, 82–83, 91; Nosson Scherman, "After the Dismissal Bell," *The Jewish Observer* (February 1964): 11.

36. Irving Pinsky, "The Graduates of Rabbi Jacob Joseph School: A Follow Up Study," *Jewish Education* (Spring 1962): 180–81. See also Pinsky, "A Follow Up Study of the Graduates of One of the Oldest Existing American Jewish Day Schools: The Rabbi Jacob Joseph School" (Ed.D. diss., Yeshiva University, 1961), 112.

37. Harold U. Ribalow, "My Child Goes to Jewish Parochial School," *Commentary* (January 1960): 64–67.

38. George Pollak, "The Jewish Day School Graduate," *Jewish Spectator* (February 1962): 11–14. See also for more specific data, George Pollak, "The Graduates of Jewish Day Schools: A Follow-Up Study" (Ph.D. diss., Western Reserve University, 1961), 22, 47.

39. Eric Willner, "A Comparative Study of Home Background Factors of All-Day School and Afternoon Hebrew School Students," *Jewish Education* (March 1970): 30–33.

40. Alvin I. Schiff, "Jewish Day Schools in the United States," *Encyclopedia Judaica Year Book* (1973): 137.

41. Helmreich, *The World of the Yeshiva*, 39–44, 48–49. For hagiographic histories of the migration of these yeshivas and their leader rabbis to America, see Chaim Dov Keller, "He Brought Telshe to Cleveland," in *The Torah World: A Treasury of Biographical Sketches*, ed. Nisson Wolpin (New York: Art Scroll, 1982), 262–70; Saul Kagan, "From Kletzk to Lakewood," in ibid., 184–205; Eliyahu Meir Klugman, "Rosh Yeshivah in Mir-Poland, Mir-Shanghai and Mir-Jerusalem," in ibid., 245–61; Chaim Shapiro, "The Last of His Kind," in ibid., 239–44.

42. Helmreich, *The World of the Yeshiva*, 301–303, 303–308.

43. Jerome R. Mintz, *Hasidic People: A Place in the New World*, 27–31, 44.

44. Ibid., 51–52, 57–59.

45. For the most complete analysis of the social history of the implementation of the Hirsch philosophy in Germany, see Mordechai Breuer, *Modernity within Tradition: The Social History of Orthodox Jewry in Imperial Germany* (New York: Columbia University Press, 1992). On the Breuer community's relationship with the yeshiva world in America, see Liebman, 72.

46. Rothkoff, *Bernard Revel: Builder of American Jewish Orthodoxy*, 213; Helmreich, *The World of the Yeshiva*, 39.

47. Efraim Zuroff, *The Response of Orthodox Jewry in the United States to the Holocaust: The Activities of the Vaad ha-Hatzala Rescue Committee, 1939–1945* (New York: Michael Scharf Publication Trust of Yeshiva University Press, 2000), 134, 262; Helmreich, *The World of the Yeshiva*, 41.

48. Doniel Zvi Kramer, *The Day Schools and Torah Umesorah* (New York: Yeshiva University Press, 1984), 10–11, 68–69, 93–95. See also Rakeffet-Rothkoff, 290 and Liebman, 72–73 on the language question.

49. Will Herberg, *Protestant-Catholic-Jew: An Essay in American Religious Sociology* (New York: Doubleday, 1953), 19–20, 211, 257. See also Soloveitchik, 78 and Helmreich, *The World of the Yeshiva*, 304–305.

50. Moshe Sherer, "Political Action: Orthodoxy's New Road," *Jewish Observer* (November 1966): 7–9.

51. Celia S. Heller, *On the Edge of Destruction: Jews of Poland between the Two World Wars* (Detroit: Wayne State University Press, 1977), 173–81.

52. Mintz, *Hasidic People,* 189–90, 391. See also Mintz, "Ethnic Activism: The Hasidic Example," in *Dimensions of Orthodox Judaism,* ed. Reuven P. Bulka (New York: KTAV, 1983), 232.

53. On the evolution of Agudath Israel policies toward Zionism and the rise of Israel, see Yaacov Rosenheim, *Agudist World Position* (New York, 1941) and Agudas Israel World Organization, *The Jewish People and Palestine* (London, 1947). See also Rakeffet-Rothkoff, 157–62.

54. Rakeffet-Rothkoff, 140–42, 175–83.

55. Soloveitchik's statement was translated from his interview with the *Jewish Day* on November 19, 1954, quoted in Bernstein, 59. See also Bernstein, 141–56, which discusses the disputes within and without the Rabbinical Council over the ban and the options that presented themselves for response. See also Geller, 261.

56. Liebman, 85; Helmreich, *The World,* 231–32.

## 8. COMFORTABLE AND COURTED

1. Chaim I. Waxman, "Sabbath as Dialectic: The Meaning and Role," *Judaism* (Winter 1982): 44; Egon Mayer and Waxman, "Modern Jewish Orthodoxy in America toward the Year 2000," *Tradition* (Spring 1977): 107.

2. On the founding of the Commission, see *American Jewish Year Book* (1966): 129. Information on its independent stance comes from e-mail from Marvin Schick to Gurock, May 21, 2007. See also Schick, ed., *Governmental Aid to Parochial Schools — How Far?* (New York: National Jewish Commission on Law and Public Affairs, 1968), 7.

3. Jeffrey S. Gurock, *Judaism's Encounter with American Sports,* 5, 159.

4. On Lieberman's candidacy and the respect accorded his Orthodoxy in the public American mind, see, for example, Charles Krauthammer, "Demystifying Judaism," *Time* (August 21, 2000), 38 and Richard Lecayo, "Walking the Line," *Time* (August 21, 2000), 32–34.

5. Marianne Sanua, "Stages in the Development of Jewish Life at Princeton University," *AJH* (June 1987): 391–92.

6. Dan A. Oren, *Joining the Club: A History of Jews at Yale* (New Haven, Conn.: Yale University Press, 1985), 230–47.

7. Anna Arkin-Gallagher, " 'Yale Five' Lose Appeal in Court," *Yale Herald* (January 12, 2001), online edition; Phyllis Schlafly, "Yale Preaches Tolerance, Practices Intolerance," http://www.academia.org/campus—reports/1998/september—1998—3 .html (accessed June 8, 2007). See also on this coalition, Don Feder, "The Kosher Majority: Orthodox Jews As Political Conservatives," *National Review* (April 10, 1987).

8. Jonathan S. Tobin, "Are the 'Yale Four' representing U.S. Orthodox Jewry?" *Jewish News Weekly of Northern California* (October 24, 1997), on-line edition.

9. Schick, "Yale Five," *Jewish Week* (July, 1998) reprinted in http:// mschick.blogspot.com/1999/02/yale-five.html (accessed June 8, 2007).

10. On the importance of the eruv in the growth of an Orthodox presence in one community, see Sarah Schweitzer, "Observant Jews Pay a Price for Religious Location,"

*The Boston Globe* (July 10, 2005), online edition; Jennifer Kingson Bloom, "Enclosing a Neighborhood with a Symbolic String," *New York Times* (February 5, 1995), B13; Ethan Wilensky, "Ritual Fence Set for Jews in Manhattan Is Extended," *New York Times* (June 16, 2007), B2.

11. Tyler Maroney, "No Boundaries," *Legal Affairs* (September–October 2003), online edition; "Cover Story: Jew vs. Jew," http://www.pbs.org/wnet/religionandethics/week423/cover.html (accessed July 6, 2007); Matthew Purdy, "A Wire-Thin Line Sharply Divides a Suburb's Jews," *New York Times* (March 25, 2001), 1, 35.

12. Tenafly Eruv Assoc., 155 F. Su2nd at 153, quoted from Zachary Heiden, "Fences and Neighbors," *Law and Literature* (Summer 2005): 248. For other sources on racial fears, see Purdy, 35.

13. For a complete account of the Beechwood incident, see Samuel G. Freedman, *Jew vs. Jew: The Struggle for the Soul of American Jewry* (New York: Simon and Schuster, 2000), 284–338.

14. Nathan Lewin, "Protecting Jewish Observance in Secular Courts," *Tradition* (Spring, 2004): 96–99; Tina Kelley, "Town Votes for Marker Used by Jews," *New York Times* (January 25, 2006), B5.

15. *Jewish Life* (April 1958): 2.

16. Sholom Staiman, "The Shabbos-Goy and the Shabbos-Clock," *Jewish Life* (April 1958): 53–55.

17. "Thermador Care and Use Manual: Built-In Convection Ovens" (circa 2006), 25.

18. L. I. Halpern, *Shabbat and the Modern Kitchen.* English edition by Dovid Oratz (Jerusalem: Gefen, 1986), 72–73; Hyman Tuchman, "Review of Recent Halakhic Periodical Literature," *Tradition* (Fall 1960): 80–81; Yehoshua Y. Neuwirth, *Shemirath Shabbath: A Guide to the Practical Observance of the Sabbath* (Jerusalem/New York: Feldheim, 1997), 713; Dovid Ribiat, *The 39 Melochos*, vol. 1 (Jerusalem/New York: Feldheim, 1999), 82.

19. See Joselit, *Wonders of America*, 223 for early examples of kosher hotels for Passover. See also *Jewish Life* (January–February 1953): 60 and *Jewish Observer* (April 1966): 27 for example of 1950s–1960s travel accommodations for kosher eaters. I am grateful to my student Yosef Lindell for pointing out these sources.

20. *Jewish Week* (March 2, 2001), 67; (March 10, 2001), 52–58.

21. Gary Rosenblatt, "Between the Lines: Lovers of Zion from a Distance," *Jewish Week* (January 19, 2001), 7. See also Joshua Mitnick, "Tourists Returning to Israel," *Jewish Week* (September 17, 2004), 34 for a summary of the trends in tourism due to the Intifada.

22. For early twentieth-century complaints about Passover away from home, see Joselit, *Wonders of America*, 223. On the discussion regarding contemporary Orthodox conspicuous consumption, see http://www.cross-currents.com/archives/2005/04/19/the-exodus-from exodus/ (accessed June 8, 2007). See also http://www.shmais.com/pages.cfm?page=gordondetail&ID=53 (accessed June 8, 2007).

23. The precise date when kosher airline foods became available has yet to be determined. However, as early as 1950 ads for that convenience appeared in *Jewish Life*, a publication of the Orthodox Union, directed to just that type of consumer. See the earliest ad, *Jewish Life* (September/October, 1950): 83.

24. For a comprehensive study of Orthodox consumerism among those living in North American suburbs, which notes producers' accommodations of food and drink interests see see Etan Diamond, *And I Will Dwell in Their Midst: Orthodox Jews in Suburbia* (Chapel Hill: University of North Carolina Press, 2000), 112–25.

25. On the history and mission of Curves, see http://curves.com. On its popularity in Lakewood, see Gurock, *Judaism's Encounter with American Sports,* 185.

26. For an example of such tapes, see "Jewish Aerobics/Instructions by Ella Adler/ Neshomo Orchestra," noted in Gurock, *Judaism's Encounter with American Sports,* 184. On Carlebach's mercurial career and his posthumous legacy, see Yaacov Ariel, "Hasidism in the Age of Aquarius: The House of Love and Prayer in San Francisco, 1967–1977," *Religion and American Culture* (Summer 2003): 139–65; Adam Dicter, "Facing a Mixed Legacy," *Jewish Week* (September 8, 2004), online edition; Ted Merwin, "Rock Star Rabbi," *Jewish Week* (January 26, 2007), online edition.

27. On the multiplicity of educational tapes composed by a wide variety of Orthodox scholars, see Diamond, 127.

28. For an advertisement announcing a concert at the Metropolitan Opera House, starring Mordecai Ben David and Avraham Fried, see *Jewish Observer* (January 2001): 47.

29. David Abel, "Cutting to the Matter of Modesty with Style," *Boston Globe* (December 4, 2005), online edition.

30. Samuel C. Heilman, "The Ninth *Siyum Ha-Shas:* A Case-Study in Orthodox Contra-Acculturation," in Robert M. Seltzer and Norman J. Cohen, *The Americanization of the Jews,* 311–38. See also *Jewish Week* (April 20, 1990), 15; (May 4, 1990), 3, 41. For Feinstein's decision with regard to modern stadiums which contains the Talmudic precedents, see Moses Feinstein, *Igrot Moshe: Yoreh De'ah* vol. 4 (Jerusalem: Moriyah, 1996), 168–69.

31. Jeffrey S. Gurock, "Baseball, the High Holidays and American Jewish Status and Survival," in *What Is Jewish about America's 'Favorite Pastime'? Essays and Sermons on Jews, Judaism and Baseball,* ed. Marc Lee Raphael and Judith Z. Abrams (Williamsburg, Va.: College of William and Mary, 2006), 30–31.

32. Abraham Genauer, "Yankee Stadium's a Two-Hat Sort of Place," *Forward* (May 24, 2002), 19, discussed in Gurock, *Judaism's Encounter,* 157–58.

33. Blu Greenberg, *On Women and Judaism: A View from Tradition* (Philadelphia: Jewish Publication Society, 1981), 23–24.

34. "The Future of American Jewry: Will Your Grandchild Be Jewish?" *Washington Jewish Week* (May 22, 1997), 14. See also http://www.simpletoremember.com/vitals/ WillYourGrandchildrenBeJews.htm (accessed June 11, 2007).

35. Samuel C. Heilman, "Looking In: Is Future Really Rosy for Haredim?" *Jewish Week* (February 20, 1998), 26.

36. On these varied explorations by gender into the secular world, see Jerome R. Mintz, *Hasidic People: A Place in the New World,* 183–84.

37. On the issue of Daas Torah, see Lawrence Kaplan, "Rabbi Isaac Hutner's 'Daat Torah Perspective on the Holocaust': A Critical Analysis," *Tradition* (Fall 1980): 245–47. On the question of Lubavitch Messianism, see David Berger, *The Rebbe, The Messiah and the Scandal of Orthodox Indifference* (London: Littman Library of Jewish Civilization, 2005).

38. On the phenomenon of "deviance in the yeshiva," including students interested in secular dating patterns, their interest in the media, and school responses, dating from the 1980s, see Helmreich, *The World of the Yeshiva*, 192–214.

39. On the growth and etiology of divorce among Hasidic families and the context of acculturation, see Mintz, 234–35.

40. Eliyahu Meir Klugman, "Children on the Fringe . . . and Beyond," *Jewish Observer* (November 1999), inside cover; Norman N. Blumenthal, "The TOVA Program — Adding to the Full Vessel," *Jewish Observer* (November 1999): 39. See also, for examples of referral ads, ibid. (February 2001): 30, 36, 40. See also on psychological problems and addiction and religious therapists, Mintz, 219–30.

41. Jennifer Bleyer, "City of Refuge," *New York Times* (March 18, 2007), section 14, 1, 8.

42. These comparative data between Orthodox baby boomers and their Conservative counterparts are discussed in greater detail in Gurock, *From Fluidity to Rigidity*, 1–2.

43. For a discussion of the Lincoln Square activity, see Gurock, "The Late Friday Night Orthodox Service: An Exercise in Religious Accommodation," *Jewish Social Studies* (Spring/Summer, 2006): 149–50.

44. M. Herbert Danzger, *Returning to Tradition: The Contemporary Revival of Orthodox Judaism* (New Haven, Conn.: Yale University Press 1989), 222–50.

45. Lynn Davidman, *Tradition in a Rootless World: Women Turn to Orthodox Judaism* (Berkeley: University of California Press, 1981), 92–93, 108–109, 193–94.

46. Danzger, 272; Davidman, 202.

47. On the history, sociology and psychology of the year in Israel experience, see Shalom Berger, "A Year of Study in an Israeli Yeshiva Program: Before and After" (Ed.D. diss., Azrieli Graduate School of Jewish Education, Yeshiva University, 1997), 138, 147–48, 213, 216, and Daniel B. Jacobson, "Psychological and Religious Change of Orthodox Jewish Boys during a Post–High School Year of Study in an Israeli Yeshiva" (Ph.D. diss., Rutgers University, 2004), 22, 30–32, 39, 48. See also on the origins of these programs, Heilman, *Sliding to the Right: The Contest for the Future of American Jewish Orthodoxy* (Berkeley: University of California Press, 2006), 113–15.

48. Yeshara Gold, "Can 'Doing Their Year' in Israel Do Them In?" *Jewish Observer* (November 1999): 48.

49. Phone interview with John Fisher, Yeshiva University's Director of Enrollment Management, January 2, 2008. See also Helmreich, *The World of the Yeshiva*, 227–28 for a discussion of the Ner Israel–Loyola connection of the early 1980s.

50. Dodi F. Tobin, "Parent–Child Relationships in the Context of a Year of Study in a Post–High School Yeshiva Program in Israel" (unpublished study, ATID Fellows, 1999–2000), 17, 24, 27–30. See also on the range of emotions that parents have expressed about their youngsters' increased punctiliousness and concomitantly the children's criticism of elders' lifestyles, www.edah.org's chat room called "The Changing Haskafot of our Children," where a discussion ensued on the phenomenon of "flipping." This source was first noted by Heilman, *Sliding to the Right*, 336–37.

## 9. ORTHODOX VS. ORTHODOX

1. On this controversy, see "A Call to 'Every Jew' — and Some Responses," *Jewish Observer* (January 1985): 37–39.

2. For the use of these terms to describe the nature of criticism, see Walter S. Wurzberger, "Introduction to a Symposium: The State of Orthodoxy" [hereinafter "Symposium"], *Tradition* (Spring 1982): 3–6.

3. The characterization "perpetual juggling act" is David Singer's interpretation of Samuel C. Heilman's understanding of "compartmentalization" that appeared in Heilman's article "Constructing Orthodoxy," *Society* (May/June 1978): 32–40.

4. To be sure, the term *frum*, of Yiddish derivation, meaning pious or devout, has a long linguistic history. We noted its use certainly in the nineteenth-century East European context. For a full discussion of its etymology, see Heilman, *Sliding to the Right*, 2, 313. I am suggesting here that the term became very popular for identifying that sort of punctilious observance in the 1980s. Interestingly, as one marker, I would note that in an eighty-page symposium on "The State of Orthodoxy," published in *Tradition* in 1982, only one of some twenty-one writers used that term to describe what they often referenced as "right-wing" Orthodox behavior.

5. Aaron Twerski, "In Flight from Confrontation," *Jewish Observer* (February–March 1977): 7–8.

6. For a full discussion of the lack of commitment to these commandments as a marker of this sort of compartmentalized behavior, see Samuel C. Heilman and Steven M. Cohen, *Cosmopolitans and Parochials: Modern Orthodox Jews in America* (Chicago: University of Chicago Press, 1989), 46–48 .

7. For a working definition of "compartmentalization," see David Singer, "Is Club Med Kosher? Reflections on Synthesis and Compartmentalization," *Tradition* (Fall 1985): 27–36.

8. For this writer's articulation of his religious values — in favor of "synthesis" but opposed to compartmentalization — and his and his wife's experiences at Club Med, see Singer in "Symposium": 69–72 and is "Is Club Med Kosher?" For the phenomenon of "tefillin dates" and criticism thereof, see Heilman and Cohen, 175.

9. For a criticism within the publication itself, see Shalom Carmy, "Rejoinder: Synthesis and the Unification of Human Existence," *Tradition* (Fall 1985): 37–51.

10. Shlomo Riskin, "Symposium," 63.

11. For a discussion of the halachic and social implications of a mechitza's height, see the postings in the www.edah.org chat room on the issue of "Mechitza," from 2001. For another, earlier, recognition of this criticism over the height of mechitzas, see Moshe Gorelik, Symposium," 30. On the Brookline thermopane mechitza, see Ann Lapidus-Lerner, " 'Who Hast Not Made Me a Man': The Movement for Equal Rights for Women in American Jewry," *American Jewish Year Book* (1977): 14.

12. On the history and sociology of Lincoln Square Synagogue, with special reference to singles in the community and Riskin's early push for a mechitza, see Davidman, *Tradition in a Rootless World: Women Turn to Orthodox Judaism*, 62–63. See also, for contemporary canards about the synagogue's singles-attractive sociology, "Shull [*sic*] Reviews: How

Conducive Is Your Shull for Staring over the Mechitza," http://frumsatire.wordpress .com/2007/01/20 (accessed June 20, 2007).

13. Bernard A. Poupko, "Symposium," 51; Reuven P. Bulka, "Symposium," 18; David Berger, "Symposium," 11; Hillel Goldberg, "Symposium," 27–28. See also on Lubavitch messianism, Berger, "The Sea Change in American Orthodox Judaism: A Symposium," *Tradition* (Summer 1998): 29–30.

14. Perry Davis, "Corruption in Jewish Life: Some of Us Have Feet of Clay," *Present Tense* (Winter 1978): 20–22.

15. John Hess, "Bergman Pleads Guilty to a Fraud in Medicaid and Bribing Blumenthal," *New York Times* (March 12, 1976), 69; idem., "Records of Day Schools Sought in Medicaid Fraud," ibid. (February 21, 1976), 24.

16. Davis, 22–23; "Editorial," *Jewish Life* (Spring 1976): 6. See also Davis, "Yosher," *Present Tense* (Winter 1978): 24.

17. Hess wrote literally scores of articles about Bergman and his activities, beyond the ones indicated in note 14 of this chapter. See, for additional examples, Hess, "Opinions of Bergman as Diverse as His Background," *New York Times* (January 21, 1975), 20. On the lawsuit initiated against the reporter, see "Bergman sues Stein, an Official and a Reporter," *New York Times* (January 11, 1975), 1, 43. On the use of the "mesirah" defense, see Marcia Chambers, "Ex-Bergman Aide Declines to Talk," *New York Times* (April 30, 1975), 56. See also Davis, 23.

18. Bernard Weinberger, "Wanted: A Sense of Shame," *Jewish Observer* (May 1976): 12; Irving Greenberg, "Painful and Honest," *Present Tense* (Summer 1978): 2.

19. Peter Ephross, "Defending Greenberg," online edition (April 13, 2001). See also Julie Weiner, "Rich's Pardon Sparks Controversy about Ethics of Giving," *Jewish News Weekly of North California* (February 1, 2001), online edition. These articles derived from the Jewish Telegraphic Agency appeared in Jewish newspapers nationally.

20. Norman Lamm, *Torah UMadda: The Encounter of Religious Learning and Worldly Knowledge in the Jewish Tradition* (Northvale, N.J.: Jason Aronson, 1990), ix–xiii, 1–19.

21. Yonason Rosenblum, " 'Torah Umadda': A Critique of Rabbi Dr. Norman Lamm's Book and Its Approach to Torah Study and the Pursuit of Secular Knowledge," *Jewish Observer* (March 1992): 27–40. For criticism of Lamm, see also Chaim Dov Keller, "Love of Chiddush, For Better and For Worse: What's Wrong with Being Modern?" *Jewish Observer* (March 1994): 13–14.

22. Yaakov Perlow, "The Clash between Modernity and Eternity," *Jewish Observer* (January 1994): 13–14. See also a response to Perlow's remarks by a supporter of Lamm's position and the Novominsker Rebbe's rejoinder, "Question Interpretation of Balance between Torah UMada," ibid. (April 1994): 13.

23. Heilman, *Sliding to the Right*, 111. On Torah Umesorah's influence on the contemporary yeshiva environment, see Alvin I. Schiff, "The Centrist Torah Educator Faces Critical Ideological and Cultural Challenges," *Tradition* (Winter 1981): 287. On that organization still attempting to reach less observant Jews, see Joshua Fishman, "Through the Prism of Personality," *Jewish Observer* (March 1986): 13–14.

24. Jack Wertheimer, "Jewish Education in the United States: Recent Trends and Issues," *American Jewish Year Book* (1999): 59. See also Schiff, "The Centrist," 285.

25. On the dilemmas of teacher recruitment in day schools, see Joseph Grunblatt,

"Symposium," 33; Hillel Goldberg, "Symposium," 27; and Emanuel Rackman, "Symposium," 60. See also Wertheimer, "Jewish Education," 59 and Schiff, "The Centrist," 280, 285.

26. On these specific points of conflict within families, see Dodi F. Tobin, "Parent–Child Relationships in the Context of a Year of Study in a Post–High School Yeshiva Program in Israel" (unpublished study, ATID Fellows, 1999–2000), 28. For the religious behavioral as opposed to career choice and plans of Israel yeshiva year students, see Shalom Berger, "A Year of Study in an Israeli Yeshiva Program: Before and After" (Ed.D. diss., Azrieli Graduate School of Jewish Education, Yeshiva University, 1997), 213.

27. For an articulation and defense of "Centrism," see Lamm, *Do Not Let the Center Collapse: Address . . . to the Yeshiva University Alumni in Jerusalem, July 8, 1986* (pamphlet published by Yeshiva University, 1986).

28. Lamm, "Eulogy for the Rav," *Tradition* (1996): 6–20, noted in Lawrence Kaplan, "Revisionism and the Rav: The Struggle for the Soul of Modern Orthodoxy," *Judaism* (Summer 1999): 291.

29. "Rabbi Joseph B. Soloveitchik," *Jewish Observer* (May 1993): 43.

30. Kaplan, "Revisionism," 292, 298–300, 303–304.

31. Hersthel Schachter, *Nefesh ha-Rav* (Jerusalem: Reshit Press, 1994), 21, 23–24 derived from Kaplan, "Revisionism," 293–96.

32. Yitzhak Twersky, "The Rov," *Tradition* (1996): 13–44; Aharon Lichtenstein, "The Rav at Jubilee: An Appreciation," *Tradition* (1996): 48, derived from Kaplan, "Revisionism," 292–94.

33. For Rabbi Joseph Soloveitchik's reported self-assessment, see *Jewish Week* (April 16, 1993), 42.

34. As of August 2007, a preliminary, cursory examination of the growing, voluminous Soloveitchik posthumous library held at the Gottesman Library of Yeshiva University, his home institution, reveals some twenty-five volumes, in Hebrew and English, that include transcripts of his lectures, analyses of his thought, biographical sketches, and even study guides on how to understand his writings. This survey does not include the special memorial issues of Orthodox periodicals that discuss his writings and republications of his previously appearing works and a full-length documentary movie on his life that appeared in 2007.

35. *Jewish Action* (Fall 1998): 35, noted in Sarna, *American Judaism*, 344.

## 10. OPEN AND CLOSED TO FEMINISM

1. Lapidus-Lerner, " 'Who Hast Not Made Me a Man': The Movement for Equal Rights for Women in Judaism," 3–7, 11. See also Jonathan D. Sarna, *American Judaism*, 341; and Beth S. Wenger, "The Politics of Women's Ordination: Jewish Law, Institutional Power and the Debate over Women in the Rabbinate," in *Tradition Renewed*, ed. Jack Wertheimer, 515.

2. On the issue of board membership in the 1970s, see Lapidus-Lerner, 11; See also on Morais, Jeffrey S. Gurock, *When Harlem Was Jewish*, 118.

3. On the University of Wisconsin experiment, see Lapidus-Lerner, 7. A number of dates have been offered for the beginnings of the Simhat Torah women's activity at Lincoln Square. Lapidus-Lerner, 14 puts the date at 1974. A subsequent study bases its date of 1972 on interviews with women who assert that they were there at that moment. See Ailene Cohen-Nusbacher, "Efforts at Change in a Traditional Denomination: The Case of Orthodox Women's Prayer Groups," *Nashim* (Spring 1999): 112. See also http://www.edah.org for a listing of contemporary women's tefillahs, circa 2005.

4. For a full explication of this viewpoint of what Jewish law permits in this area, see Avraham Weiss, *Women at Prayer: A Halakhic Analysis of Women's Prayer Groups* (Hoboken, N.J.: KTAV Publishing House, 1990).

5. "The Women's Tefillah of Riverdale, Tenth Anniversary Celebration, Saturday Night, March 17, 1990," 6, 13 (typescript document in author's possession).

6. Sylvia Barack Fishman, *Changing Minds: Feminism in Contemporary Orthodox Jewish Life* (New York: William Petschek National Jewish Family Center of the American Jewish Committee, 2000), 40–45.

7. Joseph Siev, "The Orthodox Also Innovate," *Sh'ma* (January 25, 1985): 45.

8. Fishman, 42.

9. For a discussion of Beth Yaacov's educational system in Poland, see chapter 6. On the textual prohibitions regarding teaching Talmud to females, see the Tractate *Sotah* 3:4 and Maimonides, *Mishneh Torah, Laws of Talmud Torah* 1:13, noted in Seth Farber, *An American Orthodox Dreamer: Rabbi Joseph B. Soloveitchik and Boston's Maimonides School*, 81, 170. On non-Talmud styles of female education in the United States, see Israel Rubin, *Satmar: Island in the City* (Chicago: Quadrangle Books, 1972), 153–54 and Heilman, *Sliding to the Right*, 328–29.

10. On the emulation and nonemulation of Soloveitchik's policies, see Farber, 83.

11. For Drisha's self-defined mission, see, www.drisha.org; On Soloveitchik's landmark discourse and its linkage to later developments in Talmud education at Stern, see Menachem Butler, "The Stern Talmud Program — Four Years Later," *Commentator* (March 18, 2004), online edition.

12. A "Guide to Israeli Schools" available online through the Orthodox Caucus, an organization that as of 2006 was hosted by the Center for the Jewish Future of Yeshiva University, offers a survey of curricula, as well as other information about some twenty-five women's schools that American college students attend. (There are more than just these that "feed" Stern College.) Of the twenty-three schools that reported data, eight declared that they "emphasized" Talmudic training. Five asserted that Gemara was not taught and the others described themselves as in the optional group, among other terms used to explain their offerings.

13. As of the fall 2007 semester, approximately forty–fifty students were registered in specific Talmud courses out of a student body of well over one thousand. As indicated, many more study Talmudic texts within Jewish history and Jewish Law courses. See Registrar's data for the fall 2007 semester provided to the author by the Department of Jewish Studies, Stern College for Women, August 23, 2007. On the diversity of opinions among young women and differences with their mothers, see Fishman, 58–59.

14. Ibid., 39.

15. Davidman, *Tradition in a Rootless World: Women Turn to Orthodox Judaism*, 1991), 127–281. Remarkably this book, which seemingly focuses on all aspects of these "returnees'" relationship with Lincoln Square Synagogue, does not indicate any interest among these women in women's tefillah, nor does it discuss other congregational women's attitudes toward these newcomers' apparent disinterest.

16. Sidney Langer, "Women's Prayer Groups: A Case Study in Feminism and Modern Orthodoxy," *Ten Da'at* (Spring 1998): 43–48. See also Aryeh A. Frimer and Dov I. Frimer, "Women's Prayer Services — Theory and Practice, *Tradition* (1998): 108–109, 117; and Cohen-Nusbacher, 103.

17. Haviva Krasner-Davidson, "Why I'm Applying to Yeshiva," *Moment* (December 1993): 54–55.

18. Netty C. Gross, "Breaking Down the Rabbinate Walls," *The Jerusalem Report* (February 20, 1997), 36; Peggy Cidor, "For the Sake of Righteous Women," *Jerusalem Post* (May 5, 2006), 9. See also "In Response," *Jerusalem Post* (May 12, 2006), 16.

19. E. J. Kessler, "Women Interns to Invade Shuls, Reckons Riverdale's Rabbi Weiss," *Forward* (December 26, 1997), 1; On the Riverdale shul's limitations of the madricha's role, see www.hir.org/mdricha—ruchanit. See also, phone interview with Sara Hurwitz, August 20, 2007.

20. E-mail communication with Rabbi Asher Lopatin, August 23, 2007. On the derivation of the title *rabbanit*, see Sara Hurwitz, "Rabbanit Reclaimed," *JOFA Journal* (Winter 2006): 10–11.

21. Shayna B. Finman, "Congregational Interns: What Does the Future Hold?" *JOFA Journal* (Winter 2006): 17.

22. Phone interview with Julie Stern Joseph, August 18, 2007; phone interview with Rabbi Adam Mintz, August 16, 2007.

23. Finman, 17. This piece counts, as of winter 2006, seven congregational interns in four synagogues, all in the New York area, with the Riverdale congregation having appointed four of the seven. Again, these numbers are tentative as the tableau of this ever-developing field continues. In regard to the situation at Lincoln Square, see phone interview with Richard Kestenbaum, September 5, 2007. On the economics of the selection in Chicago, see e-mail communications with Rabbi Asher Lopatin, August 23–24. As of this writing, August 2007, there is also talk of the imminent appointment of a woman to a similar post at New York's Shearith Israel, occupying a position that was previously held by an assistant rabbi who was elevated to the congregation's senior rabbi job.

24. On female career choices after years of intensive Talmudic training, see Fishman, 24.

25. On the program that produces these experts see www.yoatzot.com. See also "Yoazot Program," *JOFA Journal* (Winter 2006): 13, and Michele Chabin, "The New 'Poseks': Orthodox Women," *Jewish Week* (October 8, 1999), 1, 35. For the opinion of one of the yoazot, Bracha Rutner e-mail communication, August 14, 2007.

26. On the mission of producing this elite of women, see www.yu.edu/GPATS. On women's career choices as teachers and lecturers, see Abigail Klein Leichman, "Leaders Lift Spirit in Orthodox Women's Section, *Women'sEnews* (July 26, 2007), online edition. See also "Moods of Mourning Series Explores Tisha B'Av Themes," *Washington Jewish*

*Week* (July 26, 2007), online edition. Margolin's career horizons as of 2007 were explored in an e-mail communication, August 23, 2007.

27. See *The Jewish Press* (December 10, 1982), 10 for this condemnation of women's services.

28. For translations of different excerpts from Feinstein's responsa, see Frimer and Frimer 32–35.

29. On this exchange of opinions, see Yaacov Amitai, "Sanctity and Self-Expression: Do Women Really Need a Minyan of Their Own?" *Jewish Observer* (February 1985): 23–25 and "Women's Minyan: Amitai Withholds the Truth," ibid. (May 1985): 35.

30. Frimer and Frimer, 35.

31. For a critical analysis of the decision, see Frimer and Frimer, 15–32; see also Michael Chernick's polemical answer, "In Support of Women's Prayer Groups," *Sh'ma* (May 17, 1985): 105–108; For Schachter's treatise, see Rabbi Zvi Schachter, "Go Thy Way Forth by the Footsteps of the Flock," [Hebrew] *Beit Yitzhak* (5745–1985): 118–34.

32. David Singer, "A Failure of Halachic Objectivity," *Sh'ma* (May 17, 1985): 108–110.

33. Kenneth Auman, "Orthodoxy Requires Sage Discussion," *Sh'ma* (October 18, 1985): 145–46.

34. J. David Bleich, "Religious Experience? tefillah be-tzibbur?" *Sh'ma* (October 18, 1985): 146–47.

35. Moshe Meiselman, "The Rav, Feminism and Public Policy: An Insider's Overview," *Tradition* (1998): 5, 20.

36. Mayer Twersky, "Halakhic Values and Halakhic Decisions: Rav Soloveitchik's *Pesak* Regarding Women's Prayer Groups," *Tradition* (Spring 1988): 15–16.

37. Twersky, "A Glimpse of the Rav," *Tradition* (Summer 1996): 98–99.

38. Simcha Krauss, "The Rav: On Zionism, Universalism and Feminism," *Tradition* (Summer 2000): 37.

39. Ibid., 105, n.247.

40. Ibid., 41–46.

41. Ibid., 202.

42. Ibid., 206–207.

43. Bleich, 146–47; Meiselman, 5; Nisson Wolpin and Levi Reisman, "Orthodoxy and Feminism: How Promising a Shidduch," *Jewish Observer* (April 1997): 11.

44. Saul J. Berman, "The Status of Women in Halakhic Judaism," *Tradition* (Fall 1973): 5–9.

45. For a biographical sketch of Berman's career, see edah.org/febbios.htm.

46. Weiss, *Women at Prayer,* 112n. See also Fishman, 26, for a comment on the importance of Weiss's book for women's prayer groups.

47. Weiss, "Introduction to the Expanded Edition," *Women at Prayer: A Halakhic Analysis of Women's Prayer Groups: Expanded Edition* (Hoboken: KTAV Publishing House, 2001), xviii.

48. E. J. Kessler, "Where Women Lead the Community in Study: Program Strives to Carve Out a Professional Role for Women in Orthodox Synagogues," *Forward* (November 7, 1997), 9.

49. Gedalia Dov Schwartz, "Book Review: Women at Prayer," *Tradition* (Spring 1992): 97–99.

50. Jonathan Mark, "Orthodox Rabbis Discipline Eight," *Jewish Week* (June 7–13, 1991), 4, 41. See also "What Can an Orthodox Synagogue Be?" text of advertisement in support of Weiss placed in the *Jewish Standard* (June 21, 1991); document provided by Hillel Jaffe, member of the executive board, Hebrew Institute of Riverdale.

51. Stuart Altshuler, *From Exodus to Freedom: A History of the Soviet Jewry Movement* (Lanham: Rowman and Littlefield, 2005), 77–79.

52. Transcript of radio interview by Rabbi Mark Golub with Rabbi Meir Kahane and Rabbi Avi Weiss, October 20, 1985. Tape in the possession of Jewish Education in Media.

53. Jane Calem Rosen, "Halachic Edict Denouncing Accords Divides Orthodox," Jewish Telegraphic Press Release, published in *Jewish News Weekly of Northern California* (October 6, 1995), online edition. See also edah.org/febbios.htm for Berman's charter membership in that organization. On the membership of that organization, see "Rabbis Say Wye, Torah Can Coexist," *Forward* (November 27, 1998): 5. On opposition within and without Yeshiva, see Larry Yudelson, "Orthodox Groups Issues Ruling on Land and the Palestinians" (Jewish Telegraphic Agency Press Release, June 20, 1998), 3.

54. Singer, "Debating Modern Orthodoxy at Yeshiva: The Greenberg–Lichtenstein Exchange of 1966," *Jewish History* (2006): 113–14.

55. For Greenberg's understanding of the origins of the interview, see Irving Greenberg, "Yeshiva in the 60s," in *My Yeshiva College: 75 Years of Memories*, Menachem Butler and Zev Nagel, eds. (New York: Yashar Books, 2006), 184.

56. For a discussion of these views, quoted from the school newspaper, see Singer, "Debating Modern Orthodoxy," 115–17.

57. Greenberg, "Yeshiva in the 60s," 184–85.

58. Singer, "Debating Modern Orthodoxy," 119–120.

59. For the Greenberg–Danziger exchange, see Shelomoh Danziger, "Modern Orthodoxy or Orthodox Modernism," *Jewish Observer* (October 1966): 3–9, and Greenberg's letter to the editor and Danziger's author's reply, *Jewish Observer* (December 1966): 13–20, first noted in Singer, "Debating Modern Orthodoxy," 122–23.

60. Greenberg, "Yeshiva in the 60's," 186–87; Nathalie Gittelson, "American Jews Rediscover Orthodoxy," *New York Times* (September 30, 1984), A 41. See also Hillel Goldberg, "An Orthodox Jewish Spokesman to Non-Orthodox Jewry: Is the Message Authentic," *Jewish Action* (Fall 1990): 82.

61. On Greenberg's Holocaust-related statements and ideas, see Micah Odenheimer, "Renewal of the Covenant," *The Jerusalem Report* (June 7, 1999), 4; idem., "Irving Greenberg and a Jewish Dialectic of Hope," *Judaism* (Spring 2000): 189–204; Kessler, "Radical Greenberg Shatters View of Covenant," *Forward* (August 14, 1998), 1. For specific comments by Greenberg on this subject, see his *The Jewish Way: Living the Holidays* (New York: Summit Books, 1988), 32 and *Living in the Image of God: Jewish Teachings to Perfect the World* (Northvale, N.J.: Jason Aronson, 1998), 37, 55.

62. On Greenberg's views on unity, see Kenneth A. Briggs, "American Jews Split Along Orthodox and Reform Lines," *New York Times* (August 19, 1984), A 20; Debra Cohen Nussbaum, "At Time of Bitter Divisiveness: Are the Jewish People Splitting" (Jewish

Telegraphic Agency Press Release, September 26, 1997), 1; Sandee Brawarsky, "The World According to Yitz: Leading Modern Orthodox Rabbi Irving Greenberg on God, Pluralism, A Divided Jewish Community and Building Bridges," *The Jewish Week* (January 15, 1999), 36; Greenberg, "On the Relationship of Jews and Christians and of Jews and Jews," *Jewish Action* (Winter 1990–91): 26. On opposition to this stance, see Goldberg, "Rejoinder," *Jewish Action* (Winter 1990–91): 33.

63. For an attack on Greenberg's position on dialogue with Christians and on his understanding of Jesus, see Goldberg, "An Orthodox Spokesman," 82–84 and "Rejoinder," 29–31.

64. For Greenberg's defense of his position on Jewish ecumenism, evoking Rabbi Soloveitchik's views on Zionism as backing, see Greenberg, "On the Relationship," 2, 26. For a source on Greenberg reporting on a private conversation with Hartman and Soloveitchik, see Lawrence Kaplan, "Revisionism and the Rav: The Struggle for the Soul of Modern Orthodoxy," 305; on the Rabbinical Council's displeasure with Greenberg, see Kessler, "Radical Greenberg," 1.

65. Irving Greenberg, "Will There Be One Jewish People in the Year 2000? II: The Denominational Politics of Separation," *Jewish Press (Omaha)* (July 21, 1985), 5.

66. Blu Greenberg, *On Women in Judaism*, 21–25, 27, 30–33, 47, 92–97, 120, 135.

67. Blu Greenberg, "Is Now the Time for Orthodox Women Rabbis?" *Moment* (December 1993): 52–54.

68. Sori Tropper, "Some Unorthodox Reflections on Feminism and Torah — A Portrait in Blu," *Jewish Observer* (Summer 1984): 21–22.

69. For reports about and statements from the conference, see E. J. Kessler, "Why Blu Greenberg Waxes Optimistic on Orthodoxy, Feminism and the Future," *Forward* (February 7, 1997), 1; Toby Axelrod, "Staking a Claim to Tradition: Orthodox Women at Their First Conference on Feminism Seek Greater Religious Involvement; Despite New Rabbinic Sanctions," *Jewish Week* (February 21, 1997), 1. For the voice of opposition that sympathetically describes the process and authority invoked by the Vaad, see Wolpin and Reisman, 81.

70. For a text of the resolution adopted in 1993 and reaffirmed in 1994, see www .oc.web/ resolutions of the rabbinical council.

71. Axelrod, "Staking a Claim," 1. See also, "Torah Sages Issue Cry of Pain and Protest Against Agunah Tribunal," *Jewish Observer* (December 1998): 40. See also www .agunahinternational.org for a description of its activities and a listing of its leaders.

72. For the resistant view, see its published document in *Jewish Observer* (December 1998): 40. For the reaction of so-called moderates within the Orthodox rabbinate against Rackman et al., see Kessler, "Orthodoxy's Feminist Challenge," *Forward* (February 27, 1998), 7; Eric Greenberg, "Divorce Court Battle Heats Up: Modern Orthodox moderates among 30 Rabbis to Denounce Controversial New Bet Din Started by Rabbis Rackman and Morgenstern," *Jewish Week* (June 5, 1998), 8.

73. For the Alliance's goals, missions and programs, see its Web site, www.jofa .org.

74. On the Conference planned and its cancellation, see Blu Greenberg, "Let Injustice Prevail," *Jewish Week* (November 10, 2006), online edition; "Editorial: Agunah Pressure," *Jewish Week* (November 10, 2006), online edition; Elliot Resnick, "Rabbi Yosef

Blau on the Cancelled Conference," *Jewish Press* (November 6, 2006), online edition. For the text of the petition and the list of names, see "Does Anyone Hear? Does Anyone Care?" *Jewish Week* (March 2, 2007), 22–27.

75. On the founding of Edah and its seeing its activities as within the spirit of Rabbi Soloveitchik's teachings, see E. J. Kessler, "As Berman Waxes, Orthodoxy Gets the Jitters," *Forward* (January 15, 1999), 1; Yigal Schleifer, "Trying to Fix What's Broken," *Jerusalem Report* (March 15, 1999), 15; E. J. Kessler, "Edah Conference Claims Legacy of Rav Soloveitchik," *Forward* (February 19, 1999), 3; Debra Nussbaum Cohen, "Between Torah and Democracy: Edah Conference Asserts Modern Orthodox Jews Should Bridge Fundamentalism and Tolerance," *Jewish Week* (February 21, 2003), 8.

76. E. J. Kessler, "Taking Back the Schools," *Forward* (May 26, 2000), 9. On these educational initiaves, see www.edah.org/pastevent.cfm.

77. Schleifer, 15.

78. "Modern Orthodox Journal Publishes Article in Support of Women's Role on Bimah," *Forward* (July 20, 2001), 4. See also "Women: The Changing Face of Orthodox Judaism," *Lilith* (January 31, 2003), 9. For the halachic arguments made to support this position, see Mendel Shapiro, "Qeri'at ha-Torah by Women: A Halakhic Analysis," *Edah Journal* (Sivan/5761, Summer 2001). For the opposing position, see in the same online edition, Yehuda Herzl Henkin, "Qeri'at ha-Torah by Women: Where We Stand Today."

79. Alana Newhouse, "Respected Israeli Rabbi Backs Torah Honors for Women," *Forward* (November 29, 2002), 7. See also on congregations that follow that new trend, Ami Eden, "Gender Taboos Fall at New Orthodox Prayer Services," *Forward* (September 20, 2002), 1, and Irene Sege, " 'A Radical Position': Orthodox Judaism Meets Feminism at Minyan Tehillah," *Boston Globe* (April 25, 2005), C1.

80. Tamar M. Sternthal, "Orthodox Centrists Stake Turf: While Many Move Right, Confab Draws 1,500," *Jewish Advocate* (March 4, 1999), 1.

81. Adam Dickter, "Modern Orthodox Think Tank to Fold," *Jewish Week* (June 30, 2006), 1.

82. "Weiss, Berman Open Seminary," *Forward* (December 24, 1999), 14; Jonathan Mark, "Modern Orthodox Rabbinical School Planned: Rabbis Weiss and Berman Set to Open Manhattan Yeshiva in Fall of 2000," *Jewish Week* (December 24, 1999), 9. See also Weiss, "Open Orthodoxy: A Modern Orthodox Rabbi's Creed," *Judaism* (Fall 1997): 409–22.

83. For the text of the school's core values, see *Drachei Chovevei Torah* (Spring–Summer 2007), 2.

84. On Berman's evocation of Soloveitchik in connection with the new yeshiva, see Mark, 9. On Weiss's recruitment efforts at Yeshiva, see Johanna Ginzberg, "Open Orthodox Yeshiva to Ordain First Class of Rabbis," *MetroWest Jewish News* (June 17, 2004), 10. See also Daniel J. Walkin, "New Rabbinical School Sees Itself as More Liberal," *New York Times* (April 19, 2004), B1.

85. On Weiss claiming and lauding Lamm as his "rebbe," see Mark, 9.

86. On Jonas and his views, see Ginzberg, 10; Rosenblatt, "Rabbinical School on the Map," *Jewish Week* (April 2, 2004), 3; Julie Wiener, "Keeping Up with the Jonases," *Jewish Week* (June 4, 2004), 1. See also Nacha Cattan, "Upstart Rabbinical School Set to Fight for Pulpit Jobs," *Forward* (June 13, 2003), 1.

87. Yisroel Lichter, "Yeshivat Chovevei Torah: Is It Orthodox? An Exposé on a Threat to Halachic Judaism," *Yated Ne'eman* (February 21, 2007), 53–66.

## EPILOGUE

1. Shmuel Singer, "Orthodox Judaism and the Smaller American Community," *Tradition* (Spring 1986): 59–63.

2. Jeffrey S. Gurock, "Twentieth-Century American Orthodoxy's Era of Non-Observance, 1900–1960," *The Torah U-Madda Journal* 9 (2000): 87.

3. "Our Readers Respond: American Orthodoxy, 1900–1960," *The Torah U-Madda Journal* 10 (2001): 182–87.

4. Gurock, *Orthodoxy in Charleston: Brith Sholom Beth Israel and American Jewish History*, 73–74, 81–83.

5. "Shabbat Service Schedule," congregational flyer, circa 2004, from Beth Israel Synagogue, Omaha, Nebraska; document in the possession of the author.

6. Interview with Rabbi Jonathan Gross, July 31, 2007; tape in possession of the author. E-mail communication with Rabbi Jonathan Gross, August 1, 2007.

7. For a guide to synagogue practice directed primarily for these "newly initiated," see Congregation Shaare Tefilla, *Rosh Hashana Trip Tick: A High Holiday Tefilla Companion* (Dallas: Shaare Tefilla, 2006). Rabbi Ari Perl explained his philosophy toward members of this synagogues, in e-mail communications dated August 26–27, 2007. For the philosophy toward members of this synagogue's rabbi, see e-mail communications with Rabbi Ari Perl, August 26–27, 2007.

8. Gurock, *Orthodoxy in Charleston*, 90–91.

9. On the growth of kollels in North America and their contemporary activities, see Adam S. Ferziger, *The Emergence of the Community Kollel: A New Model for Addressing Assimilation* (Ramat Aviv: Rappaport Center for Assimilation Research and Strengthening Jewish Vitality — Bar Ilan University, 2006), 13, 27–38.

10. For contemporary kollel outreach efforts and the ideological differences that separate them, see Ferziger, *The Emergence*, 44–50.

11. On the origins of the Des Moines community kollel, Rabbi Ari Sytner provided e-mail communication on August 27, 2007.

12. On the founding of the new Yeshiva center, see "Yeshiva University Establishes the Center for the Jewish Future," *YU Today* (December 2005), 1, 5. On the Charleston relationship, see "The Center for the Jewish Future Begins Commuting Kollel Program in Charleston, S.C.," Yeshiva University online press release, January 5, 2006.

13. William B. Helmreich, "Trends within Contemporary Orthodoxy," *Judaism* (Fall 1981): 381–82.

# INDEX

Page numbers in *italics* refer to illustrations.

# JEFFREY S. GUROCK

is Libby M. Klaperman Professor of Jewish History at Yeshiva University. He is the author or editor of fourteen books, most recently *Judaism's Encounter with American Sports* (Indiana University Press, 2005). He is former Associate Editor of *American Jewish History* and a former chair, Academic Council, American Jewish Historical Society.